ERRATA

Dedication Page: John Goodland should be spelled John Goodlad.

Page 190:   Thomas Kunn should be spelled Thomas Kuhn.

Macmillan Publishing Co., Inc. acknowledges that Professor Eisner is not responsible for these errors.

THE EDUCATIONAL IMAGINATION

The Educational Imagination

On the Design and Evaluation of School Programs

ELLIOT W. EISNER

Stanford University

Macmillan Publishing Co., Inc.
New York

Collier Macmillan Publishers
London

Macmillan Publishing Co., Inc.
866 Third Avenue, New York, New York 10022

Collier Macmillan Canada, Ltd.

Library of Congress Cataloging in Publication Data

Eisner, Elliot W
  The educational imagination.

  Includes bibliographies and index.
  1. Curriculum planning. 2. Curriculum evaluation.
I. Title.
LB1570.E4254   375′.001   77–24104
ISBN 0–02–332130–X

Printing: 1 2 3 4 5 6 7 8   Year: 8 9 0 1 2 3 4

This book is dedicated to five teachers who made a difference . . .

PHIL JACKSON, for a sense of the passionate

FRANK CHASE, for a sense of the compassionate

BEN BLOOM, for a sense of the rational

JOE SCHWAB, for a sense of the classical

JOHN GOODLAND, for a sense of the practical

Preface

All written works, but especially books that attempt to open some new ground, have an autobiographical character. This book is no exception. In it I have attempted to draw on a background in the visual arts that has, as long as I can remember, been an important part of my life. From my earliest recollections as a child in Chicago, art was always important to me and has continued to be a major interest. It is from this interest and professional involvement in art and art education that I have drawn many of the assumptions on which this book is based. The uses of art for dealing with the problems of designing and evaluating educational programs has not been a characteristic of educational inquiry, particularly in the United States. The traditions that we have drawn from are neither aesthetic nor artistic; they are scientific and technological. Our aspirations have been to develop systematic, scientifically based ways to conduct instruction and to plan school programs. That tradition, a strong one, is at least seventy-five years old.

Yet as attractive as that tradition has been to educational researchers working in universities scientific assumptions and procedures do not exhaust the forms of knowledge and methods of inquiry that humans use to give shape to the world. This book aims at illuminating the leads to a complementary approach to those that have for so long been salient in the design and evaluation of educational programs.

To distinguish between science and art is not to put them into competition but to recognize the distinctive ways in which they operate. If art and science were identical one of the two terms would be redundant. The distinction is important, if for no other reason than to show the extent to which each has been and can be used in educational inquiry.

The early training that I received as a graduate student in education virtually ignored the art of teaching, not to mention the possibility of using artistic assumptions to think about the study of education. The exclusive mode for research was a scientific one, although between the lines one could get a sense of the artistry with which my teachers conceptualized and analyzed educational problems, with which they interpreted data, and perhaps most of all with which they taught. Although they pursued educational problems in a form that gave their deepest bow to science, their teaching, their intuition, the way they organized their courses, the sense they made of the educational world did not really jibe well with what they were saying. Yet, graduate students must be professionally socialized if they are to wear the garlands at the end of a Ph.D. program. And so I, too, like so many of my fellow students, led two lives. We adapted to one mode of life and thought within the university and led quite another outside of it.

As I have continued to work in the field of education since my graduate days at the University of Chicago, these two lives have begun to merge. Increasingly I have begun to see the ways in which artistic forms of understanding and action can be used not just in art education but in all of teaching and curriculum development. Although I have had occasional glimpses of that realization since I completed my graduate work—it shows up in paragraphs and in various articles I have published—it is only within the last six years that this realization has been a conscious, systematic, and critical one. It is only during the last four years that I have tried to figure out what the arts might have to do with the problem of designing educational programs and in particular how they might help us evaluate what goes on in schools.

The significance of the absence of aesthetic theory in the education of students of education is, I believe, more important than most people realize. Scientific epistemologies are given attention in courses in the philosophy of education through analysis of Dewey's work and that of the neopositivists and in courses in research methods where the canons of social science research procedures are taught to aspiring doctoral candidates looking for a design they can use in their dissertations; however, aesthetic theory is nowhere to be found. As a result of this absence, such theory does not become a part of the conversation; it never enters the scene as a way of looking at things and talking about them. Most of us who have been professionally socialized in schools of education or in psychology departments come to accept a quite limited set of assumptions about what must be done to conduct meaningful educational research and to acquire knowledge or understanding. Precisely because alternative epistemologies are so seldom considered, a critical understanding of the methods we have been taught cannot be easily achieved. And to talk about art in the contexts of inquiry and education is to appear softheaded and romantic, not worthy of the standards of scholarship.

The major task of this book—to adumbrate some of the uses of artistic forms of understanding and reflection in the design and evaluation of educational programs—is an unfinished one. My effort has been more concerned with opening up attractive vantage points than in arriving at a destination. To do this I have approached the problem of designing educational programs in a manner congenial to the way in which many artists work, namely, to try to perceive and conceptualize the whole first and then, gradually, to work on problems of differentiation. The reason for this way of working, compared to the construction of an edifice brick by brick, is that the artist finds it useful to carry on a dialectic between whole and part in order to create some sense of organic quality in a work. One must—I must, at least—have some sense of the whole in order to know where things belong and how they function.

I am not making a claim here for a comprehensive theory of curriculum or evaluation. One never knows whether one has a whole; I am trying, rather, to describe a way of working in order for the reader to have a sense of how I developed the ideas in this book.

Another characteristic of my work is that it is unabashedly normative. For that I make no apologies. Education is a normative enterprise, and I believe that much too much social science attempts to be value neutral in order to increase scientific objectivity. This aspiration, of course, is hopeless. Scientific work in any field is never value neutral. Social scientists select the problems they will inquire into; in this selection, values are at work. Social scientists choose the methods they will use; in this choice, values are expressed. Social scientists interpret the data they secure; here, too, values are employed. Social scientists assign significance to their findings; to do this requires one to make value judgments. Indeed, the selection of scientifically treatable questions is itself an expression of the high value placed on science as a way of dealing with problems of social significance. To claim that science is value saturated is not to complain but rather to give scientific inquiry its due. Its negation is what is worth complaining about.

Because educational practice aims at the realization of certain values, the educational significance of educational inquiry must be appraised in relation to the virtues the enterprise seeks to attain. Indeed, if educational inquiry has any distinctive claim to make, it is in the application of educational criteria to the products of such inquiry. In short, the value of what we do in education must be determined by its relevance and utility to educational problems and educational aims. Because those problems and aims are normative, the significance of such inquiry can be appraised only in relation to the values they help realize.

Several other themes pervade this book. One of them is the need to consider problems in context. I do not believe that prescriptions for educational practice or the findings of educational research can be applied to educational situations in a straightforward manner. Such prescriptions as might exist in "well-documented" research conclusions always need to be placed in the perspective of the context in which they are to be used. To complicate matters further, the shape of that context, the configurations that it displays, shift over time. One therefore must be in a position to recognize both the characteristics of the context and the ways in which that context alters the appropriateness of the presciptions or findings. The meanings of prescriptions and findings, I am arguing, are contextual and dynamic.

In this feature, too, educational activity, whether teaching, evaluating, or curriculum planning, is much like the artistic activity a painter engages in as he or she copes with emerging visual configurations on a canvas. Each stroke alters the pattern, each new color changes the whole. This dynamic seeks ultimately a happy resolution: the realization of artistic virtue through the creation of an organic entity that "works." As the artist articulates new problems, new decisions must be made; when old decisions become routine (a part of the artist's stock response), new questions must be formulated so that new solutions can be sought. The joy of the ride, even more than the arrival, is the motive force behind the artist's work.

Is the work of educational scholars so different? I think not. The live organism is moved by the joys of inquiry, the discovery of new terrain, the fresh perspective, the unique resolution. Such satisfactions make inquiry itself an aesthetic undertaking.

I would argue that the joys secured from such activity are not the sole preserve of educational scholars and research scientists but are also experienced by children in their quest for competence, exploration, and discovery. All too often, alas, these satisfactions are found outside, rather than inside, schools.

To respond to the changing pattern of the context requires, as I have argued in this book, the ability to appreciate what is occurring. One cannot make educational judgments about what he cannot see or experience. Thus, another major theme of this book is in the conceptualization of what I refer to as educational connoisseurship. Educational connoisseurship is the art of appreciating what is educationally significant. It is a means through which the shape of the context and the configurations within it can be recognized so that intelligent decisions about that context can be made.

This term, *connoisseurship,* is also relevant in the arts, and I have consciously chosen to use it as a way of emphasizing the artistic aspects of educational thought and action. In choosing to use this term and its complement, *educational criticism,* I realize that I risk creating culture shock within the field of education. Terms out of the arts, particularly French terms, are not familiar ones in educational circles. Yet, culture shock, as the anthropologists have told us, can be useful. It enables us to become acutely aware of what we might otherwise fail to see. By pointing out the need for educational connoisseurship, I hope to persuade readers of the contingent nature of educational planning and of the hopelessness of seeking the kind of breakthroughs that are represented by the discovery of nuclear fission and the invention of radar and (even) the microwave oven. In education, we deal with a far more complicated set of problems.

In saying that educational criticism is one side of the educational connoisseurship coin I mean that not only can the "perceptive" side of educational decision making be regarded as an artistic activity, but the expressive side can be, as well. We have, of course, been taught to use a language in education that attempts to emulate the language used by our colleagues in the natural sciences, on the one hand, and that of those working in the industrial-military areas, on the other. Our language, we have been told, should be precise, operational, unambiguous, and technical: *entry and exit behaviors, reinforcement contingencies, retroactive inhibition, target populations, mathemagenic behavior,* and the like; these have been a part of our language, a language criticized by many literate people as incomprehensible jargon. Although I have encountered, as you have encountered, such jargon in professional publications, my claim here is not that technical language has no place in educational discourse, but rather that there are other expressive modes that also have a place. Surely there needs to be a place for metaphor, poetic statement, the nonoperational comment or insight, the descriptive assertion that one cannot measure. Why should we limit ourselves to one mode of discourse? Where is it inscribed that scientific propositions and logical analysis are the only legitimate ways to express what educators have experienced? One aspiration of mine is to contribute to the legitimation of artistic forms for describing, interpreting, and evaluating what goes on in classrooms and schools. To pursue this aim, my students and I, over the last few years, have been engaged in a variety of activities in the schools. First, we have attempted to develop useful curriculum materials, materials that would enable teachers to provide educationally significant programs in the visual arts even if the background that they possessed in art was limited. This experience, in particular, made it plain that the so-called principles and procedures that have been outlined in books and articles on curriculum development are seldom adequate for enabling curriculum planners to do what needs to be done to successfully develop curriculum materials. It quickly became apparent that some ideas—the characteristics of the subject matter, for example—tend to be used to a much greater degree than psychological theories dealing with child development. It also became apparent that the conceptual neatness that pervades much of the written material concerning curriculum development seldom approximates the reality that curriculum developers face as they try to figure out how to deal with the organization of planned activities, the use of specific materials to facilitate the teacher's work, and the particular aims that might be related to specific activities or projects within the program. The belief that one must always start with aims or objectives and then deductively proceed to evaluation simply did not fit the reality that we experienced in our curriculum development work at Stanford. Rather than to try to make the development process fit the models that were being published in books and articles, we attempted to use our practical judgment and in the context of deliberation to make this judgment effective in the classroom. What we learned was that curriculum development is both a practical and an artistic undertaking; it requires prudence, wisdom, and practical insight into the realities of elementary and secondary school classrooms; it also requires a sense of taste, design, and fitness. The parts must all hang together. They need to make sense; they have to be aesthetic.

The second arena in which we have worked is in our effort to test the ideas dealing with educational connoisseurship and educational criticism in classrooms in and around Stanford University. Conceptual notions, even those with a strong appeal by themselves, can be enriched and modified by the way they work (or fail to work) in the classrooms they are intended to serve. In the last three years I have received an enormous amount of help from graduate students who have taken to the notions of educational connoisseurship and educational criticism and have spent hours in classrooms trying their hand at the writing of criticism, at the making of films, and at the creation of videotapes. We have used such materials to try to educate ourselves to the vicissitudes and strengths of educational criticism.

One of the most striking features of this work has been the quality of the writing that doctoral students have been able to do. The written work of doctoral students, even students in residence in the School of Education at Stanford University, leaves much to be desired. Professors are quite aware that most written work of graduate students is not particularly interesting; too much of it is turgid and pretentious. The work that I have received from graduate students writing educational criticism has, surprisingly, reflected a level of sensitivity and insight that, in some cases, I have found remarkable. Initially I was puzzled about why the quality of the writing had changed so dramatically. I believe now that it can be explained by two factors. First, the writing emanates from the direct experience the students have at functioning as educational connoisseurs in classrooms. They have been counseled to attend to the pervasive qualities of classrooms, to the meaning of the hidden cues that teachers and students convey, to the little things that give the game away. Their experience in these classrooms has enabled them to secure a content for expression that is seldom available when graduate students in education are asked to write theoretical papers on educational problems. There being little to say; little is said.

Second, many graduate students were given academic permission to write expressively, to employ analogy and metaphor, to utilize whatever poetic sensibilities they might possess to deal with the problem of rendering their experience in classrooms into a form that would enable the reader to participate vicariously in their experience. The samples of such criticisms in this book are, in my opinion, not completely adequate examples of what educational criticism can be. For one, they tend to be thin in the areas of interpretation and evaluation. They stand, however, as examples of our first forays into educational criticism as a mode of educational evaluation. My hope is that the samples are sufficiently attractive to readers that they will recognize the potential that educational connoisseurship and educational criticism might have within the field.

Although educational criticism has a family resemblance to the case study in sociology and to fieldwork in anthropology, there are some important differences that the word *criticism* is intended to convey. One of the most significant of these differences is in the conscious intention to create an expressive language in criticism that artistically renders the character of the expressive forms perceived in classroom situations. Said another way: the critical disclosure of classroom life should create a living image of that life so that the reader will have a kind of visceral understanding of what the place or material described is like. Criticism itself is in art form.

A word should be said here about who this book is intended for. I have attempted not to prepare the standard textbook that provides a resumé of the state of the field, but rather a book that identifies what I consider to be important issues in the field of curriculum and in education. I have tried to prepare a book that will give readers a sense of the excitement and controversy that these issues generate. I have done this because I believe that it is critically important for students to experience this excitement and controversy, to become a part of it, and then to try to contribute to its temporary resolution.

This book does not provide a prescription for planning curriculum or evaluating educational programs. What it does provide are desiderata, ideas to work with, considerations to reflect on. Perhaps it is best suited for graduate students, although I happen to believe that the demarcation between graduate and undergraduate students is not easy to draw and that ideas, if they are sound, will benefit each group.

There are a number of people to whom I am indebted. First, I would like to express my gratitude to my graduate students who have worked more as colleagues than as students in developing some of the ideas used in this book. I particularly want to thank Gail McCutcheon and Tom Barone, who worked with me as teaching assistants in a course on educational criticism that I offered for the first time at Stanford in 1976. Their work is included in this book. I also want to thank Elizabeth Vallance, who contributed to my own thinking through her dissertation on aesthetic criticism and curriculum description. Robin Alexander, Bob Donmoyer, John Feilders, Frances Frey, Jim Henderson, Keith Jones, Ruth Richels, Robbie Schlosser, and Ann Sherman also made very important contributions to our work in the last two-year period. Without their criticism and participation, many of my ideas would fall far short of where they are at this moment.

A special debt of gratitude to Professor Alan Peshkin of the University of Illinois, Urbana, is acknowledged with great pleasure. Professor Peshkin has provided invaluable counsel over warm campfires in the cool of Colorado evenings. His prudence and criticism have provided the kind of caution that I needed during moments of overenthusiasm. I have learned a great deal not only from his counsel, but also his work.

My secretary, Mrs. Connie Barrell, has been of immeasurable assistance not only in preparing the manuscript, but also in caring for a myriad of details that would have otherwise clogged my mind and severely impeded the progress of my work.

Finally, I want to express my debt to my wife, Ellie, whose practical wisdom regarding the realities of schooling has been invaluable as a counteraction to the kind of naivete that the comforts of university life tend to engender. She has, on more occasions than I can remember, provided examples and illuminated issues that a professor of education should have had at his fingertips in the first place.

To all of these people and to others who have gone unnamed I express my deep appreciation.

Elliot W. Eisner

Contents

THE EDUCATIONAL IMAGINATION

1

The Curriculum Field Today: Where We Are, Where We Were, and Where We Are Going

ah yes,

> *We shall not cease from exploration*
> *And the end of all our exploring*
> *Will be to arrive where we started*
> *And know the place for the first time.*
> *Through the unknown, remembered gate*
> *When the last of earth left to discover*
> *Is that which was the beginning;*
> *At the source of the longest river*
> *The voice of the hidden waterfall*
> *And the children in the apple tree*
> *Not known because not looked for*
> *But heard, half-heard, in the stillness*
> *Between the waves of the sea.*
>
> T. S. ELIOT, *Little Gidding*

WHERE WE ARE

Even if we wanted to, we who work in the field of curriculum could not isolate ourselves from the problems of educational practice. What happens in the schools is a part of the subject matter we study. It provides incentives and direction to our work and it forms the field from which are drawn both our aspirations and our irritations as professional students of education.

In an examination of the current scene in American schooling, a number of features impose themselves on our consciousness. Perhaps first among these is the widespread interest in the back-to-basics movement. Throughout the country people are expressing their longstanding belief that it is the

1

school's responsibility to teach children to read, to write, and to cipher. This belief in the importance of "basic education" is reinforced by the publication of test results that tell the public that the schools are failing at their major task. SAT scores, we are told, have declined shockingly. National panels are appointed to study the causes. *Time* magazine, *Newsweek,* and the local press all use test results as sources of good copy, and they, too, bolstered by such information, raise questions about the directions and priorities that guide the public schools.

Test scores are so important in California that local newspapers, such as the *San Francisco Examiner,* publish the reading and math scores in rank order for all schools in the San Francisco Unified School District. In Palo Alto, California, test scores are published by school and by grade in a green book that is available to anyone in the community. In San Jose, California, a recall election of the school board was held, largely because of a decline of test scores in reading, language arts, and mathematics.

If the fact that these examples emanate from California leads you to believe that California is exceptional, banish the thought. The same phenomena are occurring in other parts of the country, as well.

The concern with measured performance in the so-called basic skill areas of the curriculum applies not only to secondary and junior high schools but also to elementary schools and to early childhood education (ECE) programs. In California the regulations that govern the monies made available to school districts for the development of imaginative ECE programs stipulate that pre- and posttesting in reading must be administered each year, with the exception of kindergarten, where only posttesting is required. Furthermore, although the initial legislation encouraged school districts to establish their own goals, program format, and priorities, state monitors who visit ECE programs use an observation schedule that for the most part focuses on instruction in reading and the language arts. Schools receiving ECE funds can do what they want to do, as long as they also do what the State Department of Education regards as important.

The reason I have chosen to start my discussion of the curriculum field with some observations on the impact of the testing movement is that I believe tests have a profound influence on the ways in which schools function. This influence is particularly strong with respect to the kind of educational programs they offer. One may wax eloquent about the life of the mind and the grand purposes of education, but must face up to the fact that school programs are shaped by other factors, as well. Communities led to believe that the quality of education is represented by the reading and math scores students receive come to demand that those areas of curriculum be given highest priority. When this happens, teachers begin to define their own priorities in terms of test performance. Indeed, I do not believe it an exaggeration to say that test scores function as one of the most powerful controls on the character of educational practice.

Consider, for example, the recent talk about "minimum standards." Throughout the country people wanting a high school diploma to mean something are demanding that minimum standards be established for high school graduation. In California, the Hart bill, S.B. 3408, will, as of 1980, require such standards. What about grade-level standards? Should there not also be grade-level standards so that promotion from one grade to the next will mean something? Obviously if there are grade-level standards some students will be unable to meet them, for if all students are able to meet the standards, surely the standards are too low. Those who do not meet the standards should repeat the grade.

If this narrative sounds strangely familiar, it's because you have heard it before. It may have been a part of the philosophy of educational practice you experienced when you were a child. It was a characteristic practice during the early part of the century. It is an attractive conception to many people because it is deceptively simple. Education is conceived of as a product that schools deliver into the performance systems of children. If the school does not have standards for student performance, it should have. Once such standards are determined, one teaches and tests to determine whether they have been met. If the standards are met, the student is promoted. If they are not met, the student is retained. At the end of the period of schooling, the effective school will graduate virtually all students, because they will have met the standards laid down.

To operationalize this conception of educational practice it is important to have definite goals and definite tasks. Performances, or competencies, should be demonstrable to the teacher, and children should have such performances checked on a card or contract that they carry. In 1920 Carlton W. Washburn described the principles of such a plan that was then used in the Winnetka Public schools:

The most important of these principles is that the goals of a grade's work in a subject must be absolutely definite, must be known to pupils as well as the teachers, and must be attainable by the slowest, normal, diligent pupil. The big goals of the grade must be subdivided so that a child's progress is obvious to himself. Goals must be in terms of concrete facts to be known, habits to be acquired, or skills to be developed. This is in contrast to the usual outline or course of study in which nothing is set forth by pages to be covered or general aims to be achieved.

In the second place, the plan requires the establishment of tests which are complete and diagnostic. These tests must show whether or not a pupil has attained all of the goals and must show his specific weaknesses. For under the individual system each pupil must achieve 100 per cent efficiency in the work he undertakes. Eighty per cent on a test does not mean passing; it means that there is 20 per cent of the work yet to be done before the pupil goes on. The results of the test must indicate exactly what the pupil has yet to accomplish.[1]

If we read such prose in light of our knowledge about individual differences and about the importance of context in educational planning, we might conclude that in the past fifty years we have come a long way from such a simplistic view. But just listen to what a former associate U.S. commissioner of education has to say about the importance of establishing standards in order to meet the requirements of educational accountability:

In its most basic aspect, the concept of educational accountability is a process designed to insure that any individual can determine for himself if the schools are producing the results promised. The most public aspect of accountability would be independent accomplishment audits that report educational results in factual, understandable, and meaningful terms. These independent accomplishment audits might be undertaken by groups drawn from universities, private enterprise, and state departments of education employed by local school authorities in a manner similar to the process now employed to secure and utilize fiscal audits. Such audits would serve our educational managers by telling them which educational processes are productive and which are nonproductive and by suggesting alternatives which are likely to be better.

Like most processes which involve a balancing of input and output, educational accountability can be implemented successfully only if educational objectives are clearly stated before instruction starts. One mechanism for insuring clarity in objectives is the performance contract.

An educational performance contract, as its name implies, would prescribe anticipated learning outcomes in terms of student performance. Unlike contracts which simply describe the work or service to be provided by one party and the payments to be made by the other, the educational performance contract would specify the qualities and attributes of the end product of the service or work performed. In other words, it would establish the quantity and quality of student learning anticipated rather than focussing solely upon the quality and quantity of effort expended by those providing the work or service.

Performance contracts make greater initial demands on both the purchaser and supplier, but they mitigate most postdelivery haggling because basically simple performance tests can be used to determine whether or not the product performs as promised.

If an air conditioning contractor promises that his installation will reduce interior temperatures 20 degrees below outside temperatures, it takes only an accurate thermometer to determine if the promise has been met. Similarly, if an educational manager promises that all children attending his school will be able to read 200 words per minute with 90 percent comprehension on their twelfth birthday as measured by a special test, simply giving the test to all children on their twelfth birthday will readily reveal if the promise has been fulfilled.[2]

The publication from which I am quoting, one issued by the Educational Testing Service,[3] is not fifty years old, but nine years old. One cannot help asking why this old wine, which has long since turned, should be fed not only to the lay public, who might not know better, but also to professionals attending a national invitational conference on testing problems. I believe that there are some plausible answers to this. But for the moment I would like to return to the impact of testing on the curriculum that is provided by the schools.

The impact of testing on the curriculum takes two forms. First is the impact on what is considered important in school programs. Schools whose quality is judged in terms of the test performance of their pupils tend to emphasize what the tests test. This means that the fields not tested are considered less imporant than those that are, at least operationally. At the kindergarten level, the playhouse is being replaced by the bookshelf; reading is tested and play is not, hence play is considered intellectually unimportant in school. At the primary grade level, social studies are becoming a vanishing species, and the arts are rapidly becoming thought of as areas that extraschool agencies such as community centers should care for. In California, for example, the number of art consultants in school districts dropped from 435 in 1970 to 128 in 1974,[4] and those who remain, probably fewer than fifty, provide, as a major portion of their professional responsibility, services in areas for which they have not been prepared.

The second way in which testing influences the curriculum is through the priorities that students feel compelled to set for themselves. Consider, for example, the influence of the Scholastic Aptitude Test (SAT). Students believe, whether true or not, that more work in mathematics will lead to high scores on the mathematics section of the SAT. To get such scores, some relinquish the opportunity to enroll in courses that genuinely suit their interests and aptitudes and enroll instead in courses that have little intrinsic meaning to them.

The students, like school administrators and teachers, are not ignorant. Important consequences flow from the choices they make, and therefore they yield to the criteria that have maximum payoff within the educational system. Students recognize that they must pay their dues if options in the future are not to be closed to them.

Now where in all of this are the curricularists? Where are the people who have made the focus of their professional attention the character and quality of school programs? I do not believe that those of us who work in the curriculum field have had much impact on the conduct of school practice. We do not at present have much of a political base. We have not been among the groups in education to receive much of the federal funding. We do not enjoy the status of either educational psychology or educational sociology as a field of scholarly inquiry. We have been concerned in much of our work with what schools ought to be and with the complex problems of practice. But we have created no tests that can measure "educational output." Our field has been largely devoted to conceptual problems and to the preparation of practitioners, and, as in other fields, we have had our share of strengths and weaknesses in each.

Those of us who are university professors often find ourselves in the interstices between the position of our colleagues in education whose reference group is "pure" scholars working in the mother discipline and the position of educational practitioners working in the schools. We often find it uncomfortable to refer to ourselves as scholars, but find the term *curriculum worker* awkward and out of date.

We find our graduate students entering a declining market and we hear from our colleagues that our field is moribund. Even we, from time to time, seem to take perverse pleasure in pronouncing ourselves on the verge of death.[5] But somehow the problems with which we are concerned will not go away. These problems continue to breathe life into our beings, and we find ourselves talking, arguing, and writing about questions of genuine educational importance.

WHERE WE WERE

Why are we in such a position? Why do the schools, so often, pursue simplistic, mechanical solutions to complex educational problems? Part of the answer, at least, rests with the assumptions of those who have shaped the thinking of the curriculum field and who have contributed so much to the way in which school administrators and teachers have been trained.

These assumptions have been rooted in the aspiration to develop a scientifically based technology of educational practice, something akin to agriculture, engineering, or medicine. When the field of education was developing, around the turn of the century, it was dominated intellectually by two men—Edward L. Thorndike and John Dewey—who both looked to science as the most reliable means for guiding educational practice. Thorndike's work was particularly influential not only in the development of educational psychology as the key theoretical field of education, but also in the professional socialization of tens of thousands of teachers and school administrators through the incorporation of his ideas and assumptions into textbooks.

The general aspiration that Thorndike held for schooling was the creation of a science of educational practice. Through experimentation it would be possible, he believed, to discover the laws of learning so that teachers could rely not on intuition, chance, artistry, or talent but rather on tested principles and procedures for managing the student's learning. Thorndike provided educational psychologists with a control-oriented conception of educational research that would eventually lead to a highly predictive educational science.

In 1910 when the first issue of the *Journal of Educational Psychology* appeared, the lead article titled "The Contribution of Psychology to Education" was written by Edward L. Thorndike. In this piece he states without ambiguity his conception of the role of psychology in the development of a science of education.

A complete science of psychology would tell every fact about everyone's intellect and character and behavior, would tell the cause of every change in human nature, would tell the result which every educational force—every act of every person that changed any other or the agent himself—would have. It would aid us to use human beings for the world's welfare with the same surety of the result that we now have when we use falling bodies or chemical elements. In proportion as we get such a science we shall become masters of our own souls as we now are masters of heat and light. Progress toward such a science is being made.

Thorndike wrote regarding the work needed to be done.

The first line of work concerns the discovery and improvement of means of measurement of intellectual functions. (The study of means of measuring moral functions such as prudence, readiness to sacrifice an immediate for a later good, sympathy, and the like, has only barely begun.) Beginning with easy cases such as the discrimination of sensory differences, psychology has progressed to measuring memory and accuracy of movement, fatigue, improvement with practice, power of observing small details, the quantity, rapidity and usefulness of associations, and even to measuring so complex a function as general intelligence and so subtle a one as suggestibility.[6]

For Thorndike evidence of progress was in hand and the future looked bright.

Dewey, too, regarded the optimal model for inquiry to be the scientific model. Although in his 1929 publication *The Sources of a Science of Education*[7] he pointed out that science could not provide prescriptions for practice because practical problems were always more complex than scientific conclusions could adequately encompass, the tone of his writing and the general thrust of his views were of means and ends, both linear and rational in spirit. It wasn't until he was 74 years old that we find his attention fully devoted to the arts and to the exercise of intelligence in that realm of human activity. Even then, in *Art As Experience*,[8] the flavor is one of the theoretician rather than of someone passionate about his subject or intimately informed about its state.

I mention the influence of Thorndike and Dewey because these men, I believe, set the intellectual tone and direction for inquiry into education that, in turn, shaped the assumptions and practices of the curriculum field. Thorndike and Dewey differed in their view of the means and ends of education but they shared a belief in the potential of scientific inquiries as a means of informing and guiding educational practice. In this respect they helped establish and legitimize a tradition that others were to follow. For example, Franklin Bobbitt's early published work also focused on the problem of creating scientifically efficient schools, and his early written work in curriculum shared the same set of assumptions. He saw curriculum planning as a species of social engineering. The problems were essentially to *discover* the appropriate ends through a type of needs assessment, to formulate those ends in specific terms, to order them over time in increasing levels of difficulty, and to help children learn at each level what is laid out.

Bobbitt writes: "In this analysis, one will first divide his field into a few rather large units, and then break them up into smaller ones. This process of division will continue until he [the curriculum worker] has formed the quite specific activities that are to be performed." [9]

The students of curriculum who followed the tradition initiated by Thorndike and Dewey did not make any major revisions in the basic theoretical assumptions that were to be used in the design and evaluation of curriculum. W. W. Charters, for example, continued the tradition in his efforts to identify the goals and content of the curriculum by the scientific analysis of the tasks that were typically performed by adults.[10] For Charters, as for Bobbitt, educational programs were to prepare the student for a competent life as an adult, and this required knowledge of the particular activities of which that life consists. Through activity analysis, as he called it, complex skills could be divided into component parts and then organized into a curriculum. The belief was one that grew out of the professional world-view that Thorndike advocated: Learning was regarded as the accretion of specific units or connections; gradually, as in the building of a house, the parts were put together to constitute a complex unit of behavior. These units of behavior eventually formed the architecture of human action. The major problem for Bobbitt and Charters was to identify what skills were useful for a productive adult life, to break those complex skills into simpler ones, and to organize them into a curriculum so that they could be efficiently learned. The implicit image is that of an assembly line that eventually produces a finished product in which all of the component parts work together.

By 1932 the curriculum field saw the publication of *The Technique of Curriculum Making* by Henry Harap.[11] This work, too, like Bobbitt's, has a technological flavor. Harap viewed the technique of curriculum making as a linear systematic activity. One first defines the aims of education and then the term *objective*. From these one identifies the major activities of life, consults subject matter specialists, analyzes the activities of children, determines the child's social needs, and eventually formulates those activities that are instrumental to the achievement of the objectives one has formulated at the outset.

What is clear from Harap's work, as well as that of his predecessors in the curriculum field, is the desire to create a systematic technology of curriculum development. In 1932, when his book appeared, Harap was able to write, "The process of systematic curriculum making is still in its infancy —it is hardly ten years old." [12] What I think we see in the work of these early curricularists is the desire to continue in the scientific tradition advanced by men as prestigious as Thorndike and Dewey. I do not believe that they anticipated that the tradition they embraced and used in their work would set such an important precedent not only for those in the field of curriculum, but for those in psychology, as well. Indeed, B. F. Skinner himself has said that he regards his work as a footnote to what Thorndike started.[13]

One cannot give an account of where the curriculum field has been without attention to the work of Ralph Tyler. Tyler's *Basic Principles of Curriculum and Instruction*[14] was first published in 1949 and since that time has undergone over thirty printings. One would be hard pressed to identify a more influential piece of writing in the field. In 128 brief pages, Tyler lays out the basic questions he believes must be answered by anyone interested in creating a curriculum for any subject matter field or level of schooling. Tyler's work follows the lead first laid down by Thorndike and Dewey and articulated for the field of curriculum by Bobbitt and Harap. From Thorndike, Tyler's curriculum rationale draws on the need for observable behavior as evidence of learning. He also shares both Thorndike's and Judd's faith in the educational utility of the social sciences, particularly in psychology as a source through which curriculum decisions can be "screened."

From Dewey's work Tyler extracts a belief in the importance of experience as the basic condition influencing what children learn. Tyler's curriculum work also shares a family resemblance to that of his predecessors in the curriculum field, notably Bobbitt and Harap. Bobbitt's emphasis on the importance of objectives is echoed in Tyler's observation that objectives are the single most important consideration in curriculum planning because, in Tyler's words, "they are the most critical criterion for guiding all the other activities of the curriculum maker."[15] Tyler's attention to the various data sources for objectives we find described twenty years earlier by Harap; the style is different, but the intent is essentially the same.

What Tyler has given the field of curriculum through his monograph is a powerful, although in my view oversimplified, conception of what considerations curriculum planning entails. Once learned, Tyler's four questions are hard to forget. These questions are:

1. What educational purposes should the school seek to attain?
2. What educational experiences can be provided that are likely to attain these purposes?
3. How can these educational experiences be effectively organized?
4. How can we determine whether these purposes are being attained?

Once having learned about the need for objectives and the form they should take, one is hard pressed to neglect them, at least in theory. The Tyler monograph on curriculum is a model of a rational, systematic approach to curriculum planning. Although it embraces no particular view of education, the technical procedures it prescribes are bound to have consequences for what individuals trained to use this rationale will come to consider professionally adequate decision making in curriculum. Ends, for example, are always to precede means, objectives come before activities; not a hint is given in the monograph that in complex organizations ends can be constructed out of action, that only a textbook rendering of educational planning would provide such a pristine view of rational thinking. Nothing is said in the monograph about the student's role in curriculum planning or about the idea that different views of education conceive of curriculum planning in different ways. Although Tyler emphatically says that the monograph deals with the principles rather than with specific steps in curriculum building, the tone of the work, like the tone of so much work that preceded it in the field, is a no-nonsense, straightforward, systematic conception of what in practice is a complex, fluid, halting, adventitious task.

Tyler's work on curriculum planning was and is influential not only because of the straightforward character of his writing—particularly his monograph on curriculum—but also because of the people in the field of education who had the opportunity to work with him. Robert Anderson, Benjamin Bloom, Lee Cronbach, John Goodlad, Ole Sand, and others constituted a generation of influential educators who devoted much, if not all, of their attention to curriculum matters. Like Tyler, these men can be characterized as basically scientific in their assumptions, systematic in their procedures, and means-ends oriented in their view of educational planning.

WHERE WE ARE GOING

The position that Tyler advocated regarding curriculum planning is in many ways a far more liberal and far less mechanistic position than the views espoused by those who made their curriculum mark during the 1960s. From the 1960s to the present, this nation has seen the emergence of individuals, who are trained not in the curriculum field but rather in psychology, developing both curriculum materials and ideas about curriculum planning that have had considerable impact in the field of education. I refer to such people as Carl Bereiter, Robert Gagne, Robert Glaser, Robert Mager, James Popham, and Patrick Suppes. For each of these individuals, the essential characteristic of curriculum and instruction is that it be a planned, sequential series of steps that lead to ends that are known in advance and that are realized with a maximum of pedagogical efficiency. Mager's monograph on instructional objectives[16] is a classic example of how educational aims can be converted into observable forms of behavior. Mager's monograph succeeds in reducing educational aspirations into test items, even when they lose what might be educationally significant in the translation.

Popham follows this tradition; the thrust of his work is technical.[17] It focuses on how one should form objectives—and if one cannot or does not want to create them, one can purchase them from the Instructional Objective Exchange that Popham has established in Los Angeles. For Glaser, one of the central problems of teaching and curriculum planning is that of finding or creating the correct sequence of tasks for a student;[18] again, systematics that yield predictable forms of student behavior is the desired end in view.

Perhaps the ultimate position that this line of thinking has led to is found in Bereiter's argument that schools are misguided in their attempts to educate students.[19] The role of the school, according to Bereiter, is to train children in the basic skills and to provide child-care services that make no attempt to educate the young. What schools should do is provide training; they should not attempt to influence the values or visions that students hold. That, according to Bereiter, is for the family. Lest you think I overstate his position, I quote him here:

> The argument of this paper is that schools should drop their educational function in order to do a better job of child care and training, and that furthermore child care and training should be separately carried out by different people according to different styles. Let me try to clarify my use of the terms *education, child care* and *training* . . . Child care is distinguished from education by its relative neutrality. It consists of providing resources, services, activities, love, and attention for children, but no attempt to influence the course of their development . . . . Training is also directive in its intent. However, its objective is not to produce a certain kind of child, but merely to produce a certain kind of performance in the child. What the child does with his acquired skill, how it is integrated into his personality, is a concern that lies beyond training. It is an educational concern. Therefore, to say that schools should abandon education but continue training children is to say that schools should narrow their teaching efforts to a simple concern with getting children to perform adequately in reading, writing, and arithmetic.[20]

I do not believe it necessary here to demonstrate the hopelessness of a value-free training program for the young. The problems with Bereiter's views in this regard are abundantly clear. What is perhaps not so clear are the consequences that views such as these have not only for the field of curriculum, but for education and educational research in the United States.

Consider the influence these views have had on educational research. To do research has come to mean to do scientific inquiry, and to do such scientific inquiry in education has meant to do inquiry in which variables are identified, measured, and analyzed statistically. The desired image of the educational researcher is that of a scientist who as far as possible emulates his colleagues in the natural sciences. To engage in other forms of inquiry, to do historical or critical analysis of existing educational or social problems, to engage in philosophic inquiry, is not to do research. To pursue such activities is to write, as they say, "think pieces," a phrase that is curiously pejorative. To count is somehow better, perhaps, because counting or measuring yields numbers that can be carried to the third or fourth decimal place and hence provide the illusion of precision. The belief that educational research is a form of inquiry whose conclusions can be couched only in numbers is so pervasive that, of the 47 articles published in the *American Educational Research Journal* during 1974–1975, only one was nonstatistical, a piece by Kenneth Strike on "The Expressive Potential of Behaviorist Language." [21]

The consequences of the scientific view for education as a field and for curriculum as a part of that field emerge not only within the conception and conduct of educational research, but also within the methods that people believe appropriate for educational evaluation. Because evaluation methods are largely the offspring of the educational research community as it is presently defined, this is not surprising. But surprising or not, I believe that these practices have had deleterious consequences for the curricula that are provided to children in American schools. One of these consequences is to reduce the term *evaluation* to *measurement*. Although each term is entirely independent—that is, one can evaluate without measuring and one can measure without evaluating (one can, of course, do both)—the belief that one must measure in order to evaluate is widespread. When this occurs, the fields that are most amenable to measurement are measured and those that are difficult to measure are neglected. What is measured then is emphasized in school programs because measurement becomes the procedure through which educational quality is determined.

For the curriculum of the school this means that evaluation practices, determined largely with respect to what can be measured, influence to a very large degree the kinds of programs that will be offered to the young. Educational practices based on a scientific model too often become not a tool for improving the quality of teaching and learning but rather an impediment to such ends. Students and teachers alike gear up to take tests, even though none of them believes those tests to be intrinsically important or that the tests really assess much of what has been learned and taught in schools.

The consequences of scientifically based approaches to educational evaluation extend beyond the issue of what subject matters should be emphasized. In many schools they influence how curricula will be organized and how teaching will occur. If one conceives of the curriculum as a kind of assembly line that produces at predictable intervals a certain complex of behaviors, then it appears reasonable to specify those behaviors and to set up the mechanism through which they can be measured. This involves breaking up complex forms of learning into smaller units of behavior or performance and then using a monitoring system to determine if these microperformances have been achieved. When combined with a reward structure to care for problems of student motivation and a set of minimum standards to ensure the public of good-quality education, we have a complete system—at least in theory—for the management and control of school programs. What happens is what Lewis Mumford described in the 1930s. [22] The technology we design to expand our freedom and flexibility becomes our constraint. The teacher who does not conceive of the educational process as a type of assembly line that processes the child in fields that are amenable to measurement has no alternative but to adapt to the demands placed on him or her by the school or school district, or to leave teaching, or to attempt to beat the system by providing the illusion of compliance.

The consequences I have described thus far have focused on the way in which evaluation is conceived: how scientific assumptions influence curricular priorities and how they affect the organization of curriculum and teaching. But the influence does not stop there.

As the current recapitulation of the efficiency movement grows, it widens the growing breach between teachers and administrators. If the school is to be judged in terms of measured student performance, then it also seems reasonable to evaluate teachers by their measured performance. The Stull bill in California is the natural offspring of an engineering view of the educational process. Now, if teachers are going to be judged by their performance, then the standards for teacher performance need to be specified and they need to be the same for all teachers. Furthermore, they need to be objectively applied. Teacher organizations make certain that administrators will not be cavalier in their evaluation of teachers, that they will use objective evidence in their assessments, and that there will be no room for vindictive administrators who want to take out their frustrations on teachers.

What occurs is that both administrators and teachers accept the assumptions implicit in this model of education and increasingly view themselves as managers on the one hand and as workers on the other. The workers protect themselves from managerial exploitation through unionization, and the administrators affirm their identity by creating organizations that bar teachers from membership. Each group hires negotiators to work out contractual arrangements under which relationships between labor and management are explicitly defined in thick, written documents. In the meantime, hundreds of thousands of dollars and years of man-hours are spent working out agreements between parties that increasingly see themselves as adversaries.

What is truly sad is that those of us in the field of education—teachers, administrators, professors of education—have so seldom tried to help the public understand the complexities of education as a process. Why have we been so willing to accept assumptions about teaching, curriculum, and evaluation that have at least questionable validity? Why is it that we have so seldom pointed out the practical naïveté of promises to make schools more effective by setting up minimum standards and by measuring, as the former associate U.S. commissioner of education said, the equivalent of educational air-conditioning?

Perhaps one reason for our apparent inability to function as educational leaders is that we have been professionally socialized to accept simplistic assumptions about acceptable methods of educational inquiry, methods that leave no room for nonscientific forms of understanding. For those of us who are professors, it is relatively easy to be seduced by the status system within the field of education in the United States, a status system that regards conceptual and practical work in education as unscholarly and of low status. In our professional culture a pound of insight is not worth an ounce of data. Too many of us are too willing to hop aboard the train, regardless of whether we believe it is going somewhere. Professional success has demanded it.

For school administrators, the tendency to acquiesce to demands for the scientific management of schooling is, I believe, explained adequately by Callahan's vulnerability thesis.[23] School administrators were vulnerable to public pressure in 1915, and they are vulnerable today. To keep one's job in a complex system, one must do what will look good, what is considered up to date, and what will be regarded as acceptable. The maintenance model of educational administration that I believe most school administrators embrace has as its first principle personal survival in the job. For this, the most useful tool is a wet finger in the wind.

One might hope that schools of education that prepare school administrators would provide the kind of professional education that would enable them to think critically about the virtues toward which education aims. One might hope that such people would be encouraged to think deeply about the aims of education and to provide leadership and educational services to the community on whose support the schools depend. Unfortunately, as schools become more industrialized, the training programs for administrators focus more and more on the development of skills of labor negotiation and on courses offered in business schools, departments of economics, and the like. Such courses might have utility for some aspects of educational administration, but they are essentially technical studies. Embedded within technique are implicit visions of what is important, and these visions are seldom appraised by criteria emanating from a conception of education itself.

For teachers, the buy-in to the technical/business orientation to schooling is, I believe, another form of self-preservation. Although there are some teachers who find professional security in an approach to educational practice that does not expect professional ingenuity, most teachers, particularly at the elementary level, regard that accountability movement a gross oversimplification of their work. Yet, I believe, we have to face the fact that in their professional education teachers are not given the kind of conceptual tools that would enable them to become sophisticated students of one of the most complex and intellectually challenging fields of study in existence: education. Although teachers may often feel that a set of prescriptions or demands is wrongheaded, they frequently find it difficult to say just what the problem is. They, too, acquiesce, like almost everyone else, to demands and expectations about which they have deep reservations.

All in all, when one looks back on the consequences the behavioristic, positivistic, scientific tradition has had on education in general and the curriculum field in particular, the following seem to me to be important.

First, the dominance of a scientific epistomology in education has all but excluded any other view of the way in which inquiry in education can legitimately be pursued. Scientific assumptions have not only set theoretical constraints on the field by prescribing the acceptable criteria for knowledge about educational problems, they have also defined the parameters within which those problems can be posed. Problems that do not lend themselves to measurement or to scientific solutions have been considered intellectually ill-conceived.

Second, the kind of science that has dominated educational research has, in my opinion, been preoccupied with control. The goal of the educational scientist was not only to be able to understand and predict, but also to control the phenomena into which he or she inquired. The offshoot of this view has been to regard educational practice, including curriculum development, as a technology that uses knowledge provided by the social sciences as the primary basis for its management and control. The models to be emulated are medicine, agriculture, and engineering. What has been sought is a set of procedures derived from social science research that will prescribe methods that curriculum developers and teachers can follow. In the field of curriculum this has found its apotheosis in the aspiration to create teacherproof curriculum materials. In teaching it has manifested itself in the belief in the diagnostic-prescriptive model. In school evaluation it has showed up in an input-output model of productivity. Seldom have the basic assumptions underlying such beliefs been subject to the kind of critical scrutiny they deserve.

Third, a consequence of these assumptions has been the preoccupation with standardized outcomes. The testing movement that has grown out of the field of educational psychology depends on assumptions that required a uniform set of test items and a uniform set of methods of test administration to measure educational achievement. Indeed, until quite recently, the major function of tests was to differentiate student from student on a common scale. The statistics used to determine test reliability and test validity required that all students be given the identical tasks so that differentiation among students could be made, variances computed, and reliability determined. Such practices, built into the technology of test construction, undermined any educational inclination to cultivate the student's positive idiosyncracies or to use forms of assessment that were different for different students. Under the press of such instruments, a truly individualized form of teaching could hardly take place.

Fourth, under such assumptions, little or no role can be given to the pupil for participating in the creation of his or her educational program because the provision of such opportunities would make the system difficult to control, hard for educators to manage, and complex to evaluate. It would be like giving workers on an automobile assembly line the option of making choices about the upholstery or paint to be used on the cars that come along; such options would, in a technological view, create chaos. The result of such assumptions in educational practice is to regard the pupil as an essentially passive material to be molded by the impact of the treatment. Indeed, the language of research is revealing in this regard. One applies treatments to subjects in order to secure responses that yield statistically significant main effects.

Fifth, the consequences for curriculum of the interest in control and measurement have been to break up complex tasks into small, almost microunits of behavior and in the process to render much of the curriculum meaningless to children. If one is primarily interested in control and measured outcome, the best way to do it is to disallow the adventitious, to focus attention on highly discrete and highly defined tasks, and to assess after each task in order to determine whether the objectives of the tasks have been achieved. One model of such approach is the Distar Reading Program, which not only prescribes what students are to do and say, but also prescribes exactly what teachers are to do and say. The prescriptions in that program are to be followed scrupulously. A second model is the programs used in computer-assisted instruction. In such instruction, each frame must be defined and focal attention ensured. This is done by blocking the student's peripheral vision, by having the student wear earphones, and by keeping the student 12 to 18 inches away from the cathode-ray tube. The aspiration is for an errorless program. These models serve well as examples of connectionist psychology, and although they are extreme in form the tendency in curriculum and other areas shares many of their features. The tacit image is that of an assembly line.

Finally, one is struck by the sober, humorless quality of so much of the writing in the field of curriculum and in educational research. The tendency toward what is believed to be scientific language has resulted in an emotionally eviscerated form of expression; any sense of the poetic or the passionate must be excised. Instead, the aspiration is to be value neutral and technical. It's better to talk about subjects than students, better to refer to treatment than to teaching, better to measure than to judge, better to deal with output than with results. And if one is to do research, it is much more objective to speak in the third person singular or the first person plural than in the first person singular. Cool, dispassionate objectivity has resulted in sterile, mechanistic language devoid of the playfulness and artistry that are so essential to teaching and learning.

Now the reason for the paucity of scientifically based educational practice is not that teachers are ignorant or recalcitrant or unwilling to use what's new and effective, but that there is little that conventional forms of educational research have to offer educational practitioners. At the very minimum, as Dewey himself said, scientific conclusions have to be artfully interpreted and applied to particular educational situations, even if we grant that there is something to apply. What I think is beginning to occur is that more and more of the really bright, courageous students of education are beginning to look elsewhere to find ways of dealing with the problems of practice. The line of former educational scientists that are engaged in this search is growing longer. Donald Campbell, Lee Cronbach, Gene Glass, Philip Jackson, Lou Smith, and Robert Stake are a few of those whose more recent work raises serious questions about the utility and limits of science in the study of education. There are others within the curriculum field itself who have long held this view; Mike Apple, Mike Atkin, Herbert Kleibard, Steve Mann, Jim McDonald, Joseph Schwab, Decker Walker, and myself. In Europe people like Torstein Harbo in Norway, Ulf Lundgren in Sweden, Lawrence Stenhouse and Barry Moore in England, and Hartmut von Hentig in Germany, represent individuals whose views of curriculum, teaching, and evaluation are considerably more complex than can be encompassed by a simple means-ends model of educational practice.

Now the significance of this discontent is the promise it provides for the development of new ways of conceptualizing educational problems, formulating educational questions, and pursuing educational aims. What we badly need are models that are heuristic and useful, ways of talking about educational problems that are clear but not stilted. We need to avoid the pitfall that so many progressives fell into, both in the 1930s and in the 1960s: namely, the tendency toward romantic obscurantism, the infatuation with vague rhetoric that has little intellectual rigor. In a certain sense, we need to become hard-nosed about what has often been regarded as soft-nosed thinking. What I believe we need are approaches to the study of educational problems that give full range to the varieties of rationality of which humans are capable, that are not limited to one set of assumptions about how we come to know, that use methods outside of *as well as* inside the social sciences to describe, to interpret, and to evaluate what occurs in schools. Orthodoxy often creates blinders to new possibilities, and I believe the field of education has worn such blinders for too long.

I believe that we need evaluation methods that exploit the variety of expressive forms through which we understand and make public what we know. So much of the current evaluation methods emphasizes written language and ability in mathematics; yet, these forms of expression in no way exhaust the ways in which conception and expression occur in the culture at large. We need evaluation methods that give students the opportunity to use, for example, artistic forms of expression as intellectually legitimate and that cease penalizing students whose aptitudes and interests motivate them to work in such areas. Evaluation methods should be instrumental to the ends we seek; they should not, as so many of them do now, impede the realization of such ends.

I believe we need theory that unapologetically recognizes the artistry of teaching and that is useful in helping teachers develop those arts. The model of the teacher as a scientist who first hypothesizes before he or she acts may fit some aspects of teaching but certainly does not fit all of teaching. In what sense is teaching an art? How do teachers and school administrators use qualities of expression, timing, and the perception of expressive forms as a basis for action? What aspects of teaching can be routinized and what aspects require ingenuity and inventiveness? Questions such as these need to be dealt with in any adequate theory of teaching or school administration. The study of the arts of teaching might help us elucidate the basis for such theory.

I believe we need to be willing to recognize the interaction between the character of the curriculum and the kind of teaching that occurs, and the ways in which the school is organized and how the reward structure of the school is employed. For too long we have operated as though decisions about school organization were one thing and decisions about curriculum were something else. All of us who work in schools, whether elementary schools or universities, work and live within a culture. This culture functions as an organic entity that seeks stability yet reacts to changes in one part from changes made in others. We need to try to understand these interactions if we seek intelligently to bring about significant change in schools. The study of curriculum in isolation from the rest of schooling is not likely to reveal the ecology of the school.

Finally, I believe we need to develop methods that will help us understand the kinds of experience children have in school and not only the kind of behavior they display. The behavioristic-positivistic tradition in American educational research tended to regard experience as unknowable and focused therefore on what children did. Although such an approach has its virtues operationally, behavior does not tell the whole story. As students of the hidden curriculum have told us, students learn more than they are taught and teachers teach more than they know. Attention only to what the school explicitly teaches or to what students do may be misinformative with respect to what they are learning and experiencing.

To deal with the newfound appreciation of experience will require methods that differ markedly from those of behavioristic psychology. In this realm one can use the ideas of Simmel, Dilthey, Schutz, and others who are concerned with experience and meaning. The precedent for such inquiry already exists and is found largely in the work of continental philosophers. I believe its potential utility for the study of educational phenomena is quite promising.

Also promising is the tradition of ideographic inquiry and the analysis of the practical in education. The fertile but unplowed field of art criticism is also available to us. Art criticism, in particular, has much to offer to help us understand the arts of teaching and the qualities of the particular situations in which curriculum decisions must ultimately be made and applied. It is ironic that although most people regard both teaching and educational administration as arts, the conceptual tools for studying the arts and criticizing them have seldom been used to assess them in education.

What I believe we are seeing is the emergence of new models, new paradigms, new sets of assumptions that are finding increasing acceptance in the professional educational community. Whether the salient model will turn out to be a literary form of ethnography, the legal adversary model of evidence, or the model of art criticism is not yet clear. I believe the field has more than ample room for these three models and for scientific models, as well. For what I believe the study of education needs is not a new orthodoxy but rather a variety of new assumptions and methods that will help us appreciate the richness of educational practice, that will be useful for revealing the subtleties of its consequences for all to see. It is the function of this book to contribute to the work that has been going on. This work provides, I believe, a fresh vantage point from which new questions can be asked about the design and evaluation of educational programs.

REFERENCES

1. Carlton Washburne, "The Individual System and Curriculum," *The Elementary School Journal* (75th Anniversary Issue), Vol. 75, 1975, pp. 43–44.
2. Leon M. Lessinger, "Accountability in Public Education," in *Proceedings of the 1969 Invitational Conference on Testing Problems*, Educational Testing Service, Princeton, N.J., 1969, p. 110.
3. Ibid.
4. Lou Nash, "The Politics of Education in California," in *The Arts, Human Development and Education*, McCutchan Publishing Co., Berkeley, Calif., 1976.
5. See, for example, Joseph Schwab, "The Practical: A Language for Curriculum," *School Review*, Vol. 78, November 1969.
6. Edward L. Thorndike, "The Contribution of Psychology to Education," *Journal of Educational Psychology*, Vol. I, 1910, pp. 6, 8.
7. John Dewey, *The Sources of a Science of Education*, H. Liverwright, New York, 1929.
8. John Dewey, *Art As Experience*, Minton, Balch and Co., New York, 1934.
9. Franklin Bobbitt, *How to Make a Curriculum*, Houghton Mifflin, Boston, 1924.
10. W. W. Charters, *Curriculum Construction*, Macmillan Co., New York, 1923.
11. Henry Harap, *The Technique of Curriculum Making*, Macmillan Co., New York, 1928.
12. Ibid.
13. See Geraldine Joncich, *The Sane Postivist: The Biography of Edward L. Thorndike*, Wesleyan University Press, Middletown, Conn., 1968.
14. Ralph Tyler, *Basic Principles of Curriculum and Instruction*, University of Chicago Press, Chicago, 1950.
15. Ibid., p. 40.

16. Robert Mager, *Preparing Instructional Objectives,* Fearon Publishers, Palo Alto, Calif., 1962.
17. James Popham, *Instructional Objectives,* Rand McNally, Chicago, 1969.
18. Robert Glaser, "Instructional Technology and the Measurement of Learning Outcomes," *American Psychologist,* Vol. 18, 1963, pp. 519–521.
19. Carl Bereiter, "Schools Without Education," *Harvard Educational Review,* Vol. 42, No. 3, August 1972.
20. Ibid.
21. Kenneth Strike, "The Expressive Potential of Behavioral Language," *American Educational Research Journal,* Vol. 11, No. 2, Spring 1974, pp. 103–120.
22. Lewis Mumford, *Technics and Civilization,* Harcourt, Brace and Co., New York, 1938.
23. Raymond Callahan, *Education and the Cult of Efficiency,* University of Chicago Press, Chicago, 1962.

2

Social Forces Influencing
The Curriculum

For those who have eaten of the tree of knowledge, paradise is lost.

K. R. POPPER

In the previous chapter some of the ideas that have historically animated the field of curriculum were identified. These ideas have served and serve today as the ideological hubs around which curriculum planning revolves. These hubs provide a sense of coherence to those that hold them. They confer order on what would otherwise be a formless array of competing forces. However, the shape and direction the curriculum of the school takes are not only the product of the intentions of curriculum planners. The curriculum is also shaped by an array of social forces over which curriculum planners have no control. Like a giant gyroscope that strives to maintain its upright position in a wind-blown sea, the school and the programs it offers attempt to withstand or adapt to outside forces. This shifting set of conditions is one of the factors that makes educational planning so challenging. It is what differentiates educational planning from the kind of planning that is possible when working with materials that are unresponsive to social forces or that respond identically to identical stimuli. What educational planners have to cope with is a kind of organism whose contours are influenced by and which in turn influence the context in which the organism functions.

SIX FORCES INFLUENCING THE CURRICULUM

Consider the forces that are at present shaping the curriculum of American schools and giving direction to their aims and priorities. There are six forces that appear to be of such major importance as to warrant special attention. Perhaps first among these is the decline in student enrollment. According to the best projective data available, we can expect the decline in enrollment at the elementary school level to continue.[1] Given 1970 as a baseline, the drop in enrollment by 1980 is expected to be about 16 per cent.[2] At the secondary school level the decline has also occurred, and is expected to continue. Given 1970 as a baseline, the drop in enrollment by 1984 is expected to be about 9 per cent.[3] Now it was not considered at the time the birth control pill was introduced to the public and campaigns on Zero Population Growth were mounted that a smaller student population would have important consequences for what schools teach and for the priorities they embrace. It was not considered that a decrease in school-age population would have consequences for how teachers regard unionization. Yet such consequences have occurred. The availability of "the pill" has resulted in smaller families and fewer school-age children. With fewer children going to school, the amount of money coming from the states to local school districts has also declined because most states provide funds to school districts on the basis of average daily attendance. Yet the cost of maintaining the schools does not decline in proportion with the decline in enrollment. Fewer students does not mean proportionally fewer teachers. Heating and maintenance costs do not decline. The economies of volume are diminished when a 10 per cent decline in enrollment occurs.

Given this decline in enrollment, and the reduction in funding, school boards and communities must either tax themselves more or reduce expenditures by reducing educational services. What occurs in most school districts is that educational priorities are operationalized through program reduction, through reduction of staff, and through the redefinition of the criteria that teachers need to meet to secure sabbatical leaves. Because approximately 90 per cent of a school district's budget goes into salaries, it is from this area that most of the savings must come.

One way that districts can reduce or diminish escalating costs is to provide smaller salary increases for teachers. Another way is to reassign teachers from curriculum areas that are not regarded as essential to those that are. The curriculum begins to be redefined as budget constraints force school boards to operationalize their educational values in terms of dollar allocations.

At the same time that budgets are being reduced because of the fewer numbers of students enrolling in schools, the public is being told that students are not doing so well as they once did on standardized achievement tests. This is interpreted by the public as an indication that the schools are failing. Teachers are no longer assumed to be competent, at least not if one judges schools and teachers by the test performance of pupils. To determine who is and who is not competent, the logic that applies to students is extended to teachers and administrators. The way for the public to find out if teachers and administrators are competent is through careful evaluation of teaching and administrative performance. Because of the need to be "objective," specific criteria need to be developed and objectively applied. What happens in the pursuit of objectivity is that, for the most part, only the most superficial forms of teaching and administration are assessed: those aspects that require little or no judgment. In cases where judgment is required, the grounds for a negative appraisal by an administrator of a tenured teacher are so demanding that only the grossest forms of incompetence are likely to be identified publicly. Meanwhile, the relationship between those evaluated —teachers—and those who evaluate—supervisors and administrators—becomes increasingly strained. To protect their interests, teachers join unions and union like professional associations. Such membership heightens their identity as a group separated from management. In the expectation of lowered increments, the teachers' unions assume a more militant posture and submit pay packages that define their salary and other professional demands for the coming academic year. These demands are usually resisted by school boards and communities that believe that teachers should not act that way, that militancy is not, or at least should not be, a characteristic of the teaching profession.

The unions counter by claiming that the quality of education is increased when teachers have good salaries and good working conditions. Without good salaries the profession cannot attract high-caliber people and without good working conditions good teaching cannot occur. The counterpositions of teachers and school boards often result in some form of arbitration in which each side appoints or hires negotiators to arrive at an agreement that is mutually satisfactory. The ultimate threat from teachers takes the form of a strike, a threat that became an actuality in 184 school districts in the 1974–1975 academic year.[4]

In this little scenario that I have sketched, a variety of social forces are at play. First I identified the decline in enrollment as an important force in shaping the character of school programs. When enrollment declines, it influences the ways in which the public regards teachers and the ways in which teachers regard school administrators. It is not surprising when a group feels threatened by either the loss of pay or the loss of position that it unites in order to gain the strength that comes from solidarity. When one is living in an economy in which there is nearly double-digit inflation, the threat of no pay raise is effectively a threat of a cut in salary. Within a few years, one's economic position relative to the cost of living can diminish by 20 to 30 per cent. Thus, the reduction of funds a school district receives inadvertently exacerbates the conflict between school administrators and teachers by creating an adversary relationship. This relationship is also aggravated by the public's demand to hold teachers and administrators accountable in terms of so-called objective performance. These public expectations are first felt by administrators, even more than by teachers. School administrators are more visible, and they bear a greater formal public responsibility for the stewardship of schools. Because they are especially vulnerable—very few school administrators have tenure as administrators—they experience a great deal of pressure to perform as expected. This pressure is then shifted to teachers because a school administrator can look good only if teachers look good. Thus, we have, as a second force in this scenario, unionization.

We also have a third force, one so ubiquitous that we often fail to recognize its existence. That force is scientism: the faith in measured performance and so-called objective procedures for evaluating schooling and appraising competence. Scientism influences teachers because it influences the criteria used to determine professional competence. Even if it omits from its purview the intangibles in education that it is impossible to measure, it at least provides some teachers and administrators with the "objectivity" that they believe will protect them from capricious supervisors. As a fourth factor, the public, which demands that schools be held accountable, comes to regard test scores as a demonstration of such accountability. And even where parents and others in the community recognize the fact that tests assess only a slender portion of what children learn and experience, they realize that, regardless of their limitations, performance on tests will have an important bearing on the educational and economic mobility of students. Scientism as well as unionism and declining enrollment are potent forces affecting schooling.

These are not the only important forces operating, but before the others are identified it should be made clear that these forces are not *necessarily* deleterious.

Consider, for example, the unionization of teachers. Unionization among teachers is growing in the United States. In 1950 a total of 41,000 teachers belonged to unions.[5] In 1962 there were 71,000.[6] By 1970 there were 1,735,951 teachers who belonged.[7] This trend, as far as I can see, is not going to stop. Twenty years ago there was little a teacher could do to protect himself or herself against having classes that were too large or a teaching schedule that did not provide adequate time for preparation. One could, if one had the courage, complain to the principal, but if the principal chose to do nothing, that usually was the end of it. Today classes beyond a certain size constitute a violation of a contract. Administrators and school boards know this, and are often reluctant to deal with the grievance that would surely follow if the contract were violated. In this respect, there is truth in the assertion that better working conditions for teachers tend to improve the educational conditions for students. The problems emerge when union demands are so one-sided that meeting them in fact diminishes the quality of education children receive. For example, in some schools, even teachers who elect to teach an extra class or who choose to stay late to work on materials or projects they need for a class will have a grievance filed by the union representative in that school. In addition, the union members may make it difficult for such teachers to put in the extra effort, even if they want to. To provide "extra" service without extra pay is regarded as poor professional judgment: a form of economic liability for other teachers who are not so inclined.

Thus we do not have a black or white, clear-cut position regarding the virtues and liabilities of unionization but rather a picture filled with subtle complexities. Unions can ensure teachers that their rights as professionals will be safeguarded, that they will no longer need to occupy the role of a servant whose position in the community is low and whose prerogatives are few. Teachers need no longer agree to "carry the coal pail and be off the street by 9 P.M.," as they were once expected to do. Professional affiliation, whether in formal unions such as the American Federation of Teachers (AFT) or in unionlike professional organizations such as the National Education Association (NEA), provides a professional solidarity that can protect decent educational conditions for students as well as for teachers.

At the same time, unions and unionlike organizations can become so preoccupied with the financial well-being of their members that in their efforts to achieve greater economic benefits the educational well-being of students suffers.

Similar complexities pervade the situation with respect to declining enrollment. There was a time, not so long ago, when school districts such as Los Angeles had such a growth in student population that they had to open the equivalent of a new elementary school every four weeks. In such situations, attention to substantive educational improvement is likely to be marginal because teachers as well as school administrators are simply trying to keep their heads above water by finding places for new students who are entering each day. New buildings must be built, movable classrooms must be set up, new teachers must be hired, and in some cases split shifts must be instituted to cope with the increasing numbers of students. The major efforts and energies of the professional staff are devoted to organizational maintenance.

Now, for the first time in many years, school districts do not have these pressures bearing on them. Now there is time—at least theoretically—for reflection, for attention to substantive educational matters: what shall be taught, what ends shall be pursued, what kinds of programs shall be offered? For the first time, there is space available in schools to offer students opportunities to work in areas that previously were unavailable: art studios, science laboratories, teacher curriculum materials centers, photography workshops, and the like. Now there is time to engage in a professional dialogue on what is genuinely educational for students—and for the professional staff as well. Yet paradoxically, now that the time is available, the climate is not right. There are few school administrators who at present are inclined to be "innovative," a word overused and often abused in the past. Today the risks for serious innovation are too great for many school administrators. The climate is a conservative one; major concerns are expressed in demands for the so-called basic education. Thus, the educational opportunities that more space and fewer students provide are foregone in an educational climate that has little desire for experimentation.

What is fascinating when one looks at the social forces affecting schooling is the fact that these forces do not operate independently. As in a living organism, they interact with each other as various groups and beliefs come into contact and into conflict. Educational consumerism—the public's demand to participate in educational policy formation and its demand that teachers and school administrators be held accountable—finds expression in legislation requiring that pseudoscientific methods be used to appraise teaching and learning. Teachers and administrators, although often skeptical about the appropriateness of such methods, believe that scientific objectivity is preferable to the tyranny of personal subjectivity. Meanwhile, teachers defend themselves through new forms of professional solidarity represented by unionization. The triangle is formed: school boards represent one apex, administrators a second, and teachers a third. In some communities, parents are forming "learners' associations" because they believe that school boards are too political, too responsive to a handful of vocal parents, too weak before powerful teacher groups, and therefore not sufficiently independent to protect the educational interests of their children. The plot thickens. The population decline exacerbates the situation further by reducing opportunities for mid-career teachers who once hoped for professional mobility through opportunities to become supervisors or administrators. At present those opportunities are vanishing. Finding increasing pressures in the environment and publicity from the press, teachers often look forward to sabbaticals, but, of course, these too are less available than they once were.

The logic of these interactions is clear, and from the standpoint of each group of players understandable. Groups who feel under attack are well advised to unify to protect their interests. Adults who are led to believe that there are clear-cut answers to complex questions (consider presidential debates and other political analyses provided by aspiring politicians) extend these expectations to the realm of schooling. When there are more teachers than needed and less funds than were once available, expectations for performance rise and the real educational priorities emerge.

These forces—the decline in student population, unionism, scientism, and educational consumerism—do not exhaust the major social forces affecting schooling. Two other forces must also be considered.

The enormous influence of the textbook cannot be left out when the forces influencing education are being identified. Regardless of what one might want to create with respect to curriculum materials, at present the textbook holds a place of unparalleled importance in influencing what shall be taught in the schools. The reasons for its importance are not difficult to determine. Consider the range of subject matters and tasks with which elementary school teachers must deal. The typical teacher teaching, say, the fourth grade in a self-contained classroom is responsible for the following: reading, language arts, arithmetic, social studies, science, music, art, and physical education. In addition to these areas, many elementary school teachers are responsible for health education, career awareness education, human relations education, and environmental education. Within language arts education they are responsible for penmanship, grammar, punctuation, spelling, creative writing, as well as library skills. Given the variety of these demands, is it any wonder that many teachers—perhaps most—would welcome textbooks and other kinds of workbooks that in effect decide for them what children shall study, in what order, for what ends? Combine these demands with the expectation that teachers individualize instruction and there is even less wonder that prepackaged delivery systems should be regarded as timesavers; besides, it is consistent with our culture's proclivity for fast-food service and TV dinners. I say this not to be snide, but because it is reasonable to expect that the values that pervade the culture at large should manifest themselves in our schools. In fact, to expect otherwise would be unreasonable.

The textbook and its partner, the workbook, provide the curricular hub around which much of what is taught revolves. Their utility is straightforward. First, they provide a level of content expertise that few teachers possess. Second, they organize that content around topics that usually have some logic; in other words, the task of sequencing material for educational purposes is largely done—or at least believed to have been done. Third, the textbook provides both teachers and pupils with a kind of security: it lays out the journey that students and teachers will take; one knows what follows what and where it all ends. The coverage of this content becomes important because implicit in the textbook is the idea that if the children do not cover all of the material they are being cheated. Fourth, the textbook, which usually has a teacher's version, gives teachers the questions they should ask students, provides test items they can use, suggests activities students can engage in, and provides teachers with the correct answers. The workbook that frequently accompanies the textbook provides a simple way to keep children engaged, and if the culture of the classroom is such that using a workbook is an expected aspect of the school day, it is not likely that the teacher will meet with much resistance. In addition, individualization can be achieved by allowing all of the students to work toward the same ends using the same means at different grades. Individualization is thus converted into a form of depersonalized isolation for many students.

The importance of textbooks in defining content for students and teachers should not be underestimated. The inclusion of, say, the Westward movement means the exclusion of other topics, issues, or themes that might otherwise have been included. In addition, inclusion of a body of content in a textbook means, at the least, that students will have the opportunity to encounter it, and it is this opportunity that has the greatest impact on what is learned as a part of a formal curriculum. The absence of a content area increases the probability enormously that students will not learn "x," assuming that "x" is not likely to be learned in the culture outside of school.

The textbook not only defines a substantial proportion of the content, sequence, and aims of the curriculum, it also influences the way in which certain topics will be regarded. The most obvious illustration of this is found in the ways in which textbooks have treated women's and minorities' rights and other controversial issues. The kinds of biases subtly conveyed to young children about sex roles and minority groups have been so egregious that some states require that all state-provided texts be specifically screened for biases with regard to sex, race, ethnic group, religious orientation, and the like. Awareness of sex stereotyping and racial bias as far as white middle-class Americans is concerned is relatively recent. Thirty years ago one did not hear much about the covert messages in *Dick and Jane.* We have to thank the courage of vocal men and women who raised our consciousness regarding these matters. The initiation of change did not emanate from publishers, but from the kind of social pressure that groups supporting human rights brought to bear on the consciousness of America.

Yet, even today, sensitive issues are frequently defused or avoided altogether by textbook publishers seeking a wide market. Stockholders' investments are not to be jeopardized in the service of education. Darwin's theory of evolution is still approached with great caution among many publishing houses that seek to sell their books in communities whose religious beliefs are fundamentalist. Perhaps this is the way it ought to be. Perhaps there should be a compliant attitude toward the educational marketplace on the part of those in the education business. Yet I cannot help believe that a nation's capacity for growth is determined, at least in part, by the scope of intellectual tolerance it provides those whose beliefs deviate from the mainstream. The society that seeks stasis also seeks conformity. More, it seems to me, should be expected, even from those whose major motives are profit.

If reliance on the textbook and the workbook cultivates a form of pedagogical dependency on the part of teachers, if it inadvertently fosters stock curricular responses, and if at the same time the textbook meets real needs growing out of a situation that perhaps demands too much from teachers, what can be done about it? Perhaps under present-day conditions very little. If the expectations of educational ingenuity for a teacher teaching eight or nine subject areas in a self-contained classroom or for a high school teacher teaching five or six classes of 180 students are unrealistic, then what kinds of changes need to be made if teachers are to be pedagogically ingenious? It seems obvious that piecemeal, ad hoc changes are not likely to redefine or restructure the conditions that make the textbook a necessity. What is needed is a large, comprehensive view, one that appreciates the organic relationship between the schools and those who work in them plus those who provide the resources and support to make schooling possible in the first place. Furthermore, I believe that individual teachers and school administrators can make important differences in the educational lives that students lead. I do not believe that either teachers or school administrators must take to the streets to bring about improvement in the conditions of schooling. However, this is not to say that teachers should not be political; education itself is a political undertaking. It is to say that the larger picture should be appreciated and that incremental change can be brought about within the context of the larger views that one holds. In a society such as ours, there will always be a variety of images of the good educational life. The task is to understand the range of factors that influence their particular realization.

The sixth major social force influencing the curriculum and schooling are those influences emanating from court decisions and state and federal legislation. Undoubtedly, the most significant of these is 1954s *Brown v. the Topeka Board of Education*. The importance of the court's judgment that separate schools, defined in terms of legal segregation, could not provide equal education to children was a landmark in social influence, but not because it rapidly desegregated schools; it didn't. It was a landmark because it initiated the era in which the legal segregation of school children was considered a violation of constitutional rights by the highest court in the land. From this judgment, a host of other legal decisions was rendered that has served to generate other forces affecting schools and, hence, the programs that they provide. For instance, the busing of school children for purposes of racial desegregation could not have occurred without the Supreme Court's 1954 decision. The decision of the Los Angeles City Schools to assign teachers to schools on the basis of racial mix stems from the judgments made first in 1954.

There is little question that the desegregation of schools through busing, supported by legal decisions of the courts, has increased white flight from the cities to the suburbs. In 1950 the proportion of whites living in the ten largest cities in the United States was 86.5 per cent.[8] By 1970 it was 56.9 per cent.[9] It is as though the effect of the 1954 decision in practice was contrary to what the court intended. Because of the segregated character of housing in urban areas, schools have become increasingly segregated. Busing for purposes of desegregation is seen by the court as a way to remedy the school segregation created by such housing patterns.

For blacks and for other racial minorities, the creation of all-black schools in all-black communities in urban areas has meant the opportunity to take hold of policies determining what such schools teach. In many black communities, the call for curricular change has been twofold. First, blacks want programs that help children recognize and appreciate the high achievements of members of their race; they want their children to know something about their cultural heritage both in this country and in Africa. The commercial achievements of the Ibo, the art of Benin and Ife, the high cultural achievements of ninth-century Africa, as well as the works of Marcus Garvey, Booker T. Washington, W. E. B. Du Bois, and Martin Luther King, Jr., must have a place in the school curriculum. Second, many blacks want their children to have what they regarded as a solid academic education. They do not want the school to provide a watered-down or condescending curriculum. They do not want second-class programs that lead to educational dead ends.

I will not attempt to discuss the distinctive aspirations and consequences of the legal decisions for each racial and ethnic group. I use the preceding example simply to illustrate how one kind of legal decision, a decision aimed at the desegregation of schools, had consequences for what schools teach and how they are staffed. Legal decisions about desegregation are by no means the only kinds of legal and legislative decisions affecting minorities and the schools.

Recent legislation that also pertains to minorities deals with the school districts distinctive legal obligation to offer bilingual forms of instruction. Describing AB 1329, the *Legislative Counsels Digest* says:

This bill would require each limited-English-speaking pupil, as defined, enrolled in the California public school system in kindergarten through 12 to receive instruction in a language understandable to the pupil which recognizes the pupil's primary language and teaches the pupil English. The specific type of instruction or program a school district is required to provide would depend on the presence of a specified number of non-English-speaking or limited-English-speaking pupils, as defined, in a school with the same primary language in the same grade level or with the same primary language, in the same age group, in a multigrade or ungraded instructional environment. The pupil's parent, parents, or guardian would have the right not to have their child or ward enrolled in such an education program. Limited-English-speaking pupils in kindergarten through grade 12, who are not enrolled in one of these specified programs would be required to be individually evaluated and receive instructional services in an individual learning program.[10]

Obviously such legislation has important consequences in terms of who shall be hired as teachers, what types of materials shall be provided, and how the effectiveness of the school shall be determined. What schools provide and the mode of instruction teachers use must now take into account the linguistic and cultural backgrounds of the students the schools serve. To do less is to deny children and their parents the equal protection provided by the Constitution.

A decision rendered by the Court, one that will have profound consequences in California and elsewhere, is the Serrano-Priest decision. This decision holds that the range of financial resources among school districts in the state of California is so great as to deny children living in poor districts an opportunity to secure an education commensurate with that obtained by their peers living in districts whose tax base is strong. The court said:

It is an inescapable fact that under SB 90 and AB 1267, the high-wealth school districts, with far greater funds available per pupil than are available to the low-wealth school districts, have the distinct advantages of being able to pay for, and select, the better-trained, better-educated and more experienced teachers, the ability to maintain smaller class sizes by employing more teachers, the ability to offer a wider selection of courses per day, the ability to provide better and a greater variety of supportive services such as more counselors and teacher aides, the ability to obtain the latest and best educational materials and equipment, and the ability to keep the educational plants in tip-top shape. These are the kinds of items that go into the making of a high-quality educational program that benefits the children of a school district that has a relatively high level of expenditures flowing from high assessed valuations of property.

Therefore, the court held that California's financing system for public elementary and secondary schools, including the changes made by SB 90 and AB 1267,

constitutes a violation of the California Constitution's equal-protection-of-the-laws provision. This violation results from the fact that, even though SB 90 and AB 1267 have made significant improvements in the foundation-program system of financing public schools, including the narrowing of expenditure differentials between school districts, there remain substantial disparities in per pupil revenues and expenditures between school districts because of the substantial variations in assessed valuations of taxable property between school districts. Under these circumstances, such per pupil expenditure differentials between school districts constitute a denial of equality of education and uniformity of treatment to the children of the low-wealth school districts and does not comply with the *Serrano* court's demand for statewide educational equality and uniformity of treatment for *all* the school children of California.[11]

The range in pupil expenditure among the one thousand school districts in California is from $1,030 to $2,874.[12] To rectify what the courts regard as an educational inequity, they have decreed that, after 1977, school districts in California that spent more than 150 per cent of the state-guaranteed foundation per child must share their locally voted tax increases with lower-wealth school districts. Equalization of educational opportunity will occur by diminishing the range and by raising the median levels for each child attending the public schools.

One potential consequence of this decision may be to motivate parents who can afford to send their children to private schools to do so. No fiscal limit is prescribed for such schools. Thus, parents who have the resources may very well elect to have their children go to schools that can afford to offer the class size, the curricular scope, and the personal attention that the public schools cannot afford. Should large numbers of children from affluent families leave the public schools for the anticipated benefits provided by private schools, important curricular consequences are likely to occur. The public school will serve the lower, the upper lower, and the lower middle classes, and the upper middle and upper classes will be elsewhere. Another form of segregation will have been inadvertently created.

My task here is not to provide a substantive analysis of legal decisions bearing on education, that would require both another book and a set of skills I do not possess. I identify these legal decisions for illustrative purposes. The courts have always influenced educational practice: the laws of 1642 and 1647 in the Massachusetts Bay Colonies mandated reading instruction; the Morril Act established land grant colleges; *Plessy v. Ferguson* established equal but separate schools; the child labor laws increased enormously the number of children attending the public schools. But during the last two decades, the number of significant decisions has increased. As the attitude of the nation has moved toward a greater concern, at least judicially, for the rights of individuals and minorities, court decisions supporting those rights have been rendered. These decisions, in turn, affect the schools. They influence where people choose to live, what monies will be made available, what schools are obliged to teach, how schools will be populated, and where teachers will be asked to work. Clearly, no one concerned with the planning of school programs or interested in the study of curriculum decision making can afford to neglect the parameters that court decisions establish. Combined with state legislation, such decisions constitute the sixth major social force influencing the character of school programs today.

I have thus far attempted to identify and describe some of the influences these six major social forces have on what schools teach and what priorities and aims they hold. At present these six forces—decreasing enrollment, unionization, scientism, educational consumerism, textbooks, and court decisions—are the salient forces. But this does not mean that they are the forces that will always have a major impact on the content and direction of schooling. If the Russians land a person on Mars, we might very well have, as we did in 1957, a deluge of funds and a congressional mandate for more work in the sciences and mathematics. If drug abuse gets out of control, we may very well see a new emphasis in school programs dealing with the effects of drugs on individuals and on society. As an organ within a larger system, schools can isolate themselves from that system about as much as the liver can isolate itself from the heart and lungs. We cannot easily or accurately predict what new developments, crises, and the like will occur, either within our nation or outside of it; thus there will always be a need for those planning educational policies and programs to make judgments in context and to exercise practical wisdom. Such wisdom consists in part in being able to distinguish between the kind of data and information that one can get and reasonably depend on and the kind that one is not likely to be able to secure. The hunt for recipes, rules, formulas, and other nostrums to solve educational problems is a hopeless one. Contexts change and the configurations of schooling within those contexts also change. Sophisticated educational planning needs to consider both and to anticipate that "final" solutions will always be temporary at best. To say this is not to argue for slipshod thinking, bootstrap judgments, or seat-of-the-pants analyses. I am not arguing for innocence on the part of educational scholars or professionals. I am arguing against unrealistic aspirations, pseudo science, and the host of other bandwagons, bad analogies, and panaceas that emerge in the field each year. We need, I believe, to recognize the contingent character of educational practice, to savor its complexity, and to be not afraid to use whatever artistry we can muster to deal with its problems. For the curriculum planner this means a life of continual uncertainty: the contingent is inherent in educational planning; yet these emerging contingencies need not provide a sense of discomfort but an array of opportunities to exercise one's imagination, to cope with new problems, to make qualitative judgments as well as theoretical ones. What one uses to deal with these contingencies are not pat procedures, but ideas, concepts, frames of reference. One must work with such tools as means guided by a flexible form of intelligence. In the next chapter some of those tools are presented, first by asking what *curriculum* means and then by examining some of the assumptions on which this book is based.

REFERENCES

1. Harriet Fislow, "Demography and Changing Enrollments," unpublished manuscript, School Finance and Organization Symposium, 1976.
2. Ibid.
3. Ibid.
4. *Time* Magazine, October 4, 1976.
5. T. M. Stinnet, *Turmoil in Teaching: A History of Organizational Struggle for America's Teacher*, Macmillan Publishing Co., Inc., New York, 1968.
6. Ibid.
7. Lorraine McDonnell, "Teacher Collective Bargaining and School Governance," working paper for the Rand Corporation, June 1976.
8. Joel S. Berk and Michael Kirst, *Federal Aid to Education*, Lexington Books, Toronto, 1972.
9. Ibid.
10. Assembly Bill No. 1329, California, 1976.
11. Thomas A. Shannon, "The Second *Serrano* Case—Important Implications for California School Finance," *Special Report*, Association of California School Administrators, Vol. 3, No. 15, n.d., p. 9.
12. Bureau of School Appointments and Reports, California State Board of Education, n.d.

3

Some Concepts, Distinctions, and Definitions

It is the creative image, vital and burgeoning, that we see before us in the work of these artists, and the new reality that takes shape is not the inhuman world of the machine but the passionate world of the imagination.

HERBERT READ

Just what is the field of curriculum? How wide is its scope? What do its practitioners do? What kinds of problems do its scholars study? What methods of inquiry are appropriate to it? And does it claim any special terrain within education as a whole?

Perhaps the best way to begin is with some concepts and some distinctions. Take, for example, the concept *curriculum*. As a term in educational discourse, *curriculum* is used in a wide variety of ways. It has a common-sense meaning as broad as "what schools teach" to as narrow as "a specific educational activity planned for a particular student at a particular point in time." Yet, the term itself warrants analysis. Initially, the word derives from the Latin word *currere*, meaning "the course to be run." This notion implies a track, a set of obstacles or tasks that an individual is to overcome, something that has a beginning and an end, something that one aims at completing. This metaphor of a racetrack is not altogether inappropriate. Schools have historically established "courses" of study through which a student is to pass. Successful completion of the course warrants a diploma or degree certifying competence. In other ways, too, the idea of a curriculum as a course filled with increasingly difficult obstacles is an appropriate metaphor. Schools have functioned historically as institutions that serve as a type of educational sieve, selecting the more from the less able at each higher level of schooling. Thus at the various levels of schooling there were —and are—increasingly difficult examinations to pass that open or close the doors to further schooling. The concept of the curriculum as the course to be run is one that fits one of the school's historical functions.

Curriculum has also been conceived of and defined as "all of the experiences the child has under the aegis of the school." This conception of curriculum was created by progressive educators during the 1920s to emphasize several beliefs that they considered central to any adequate conception of education. First, they wished to remind other educators that the reality of a curriculum for a child was determined by the quality of the experience that the child had in the school and was not simply a piece of paper on which lesson plans were prepared. Although some degree of planning was considered appropriate and important, the real curriculum for the child, the one that made a difference in his or her life, was the curriculum that he or she experienced. Second, because children differ from one another in background, aptitudes, interests, and the like, the curriculum was never identical for different children. In a sense, one could have a curriculum only *after* it was experienced by a child. The curriculum was, one might say, to be discovered by looking backward. To their credit, these same progressive educators recognized that what children learn in school is wider than what goes on in classrooms and more varied than what teachers intend to teach. The experiences secured in the hallways and the playgrounds of the school were also influential aspects of educational life and should not, in their view, be separated from the responsibility educators should assume for guiding the child's experience in other aspects of school life. It was educational folly to care about the child's experience in the classroom but to disregard it in the playing fields. Indeed, progressive educators felt so strongly about the need to focus on the kind of experience the child had under the aegis of the school that they made a formal distinction between the curriculum, which was that experience (and hence each child had a different curriculum because his or her experience was never the same as another's), and the course of study, which was a written document that outlined the content, topics, and goals that a teacher was to use in planning the curriculum for a class or a child.

Whatever the conception of *curriculum*—and each of the two conceptions described has important consequences for the way in which one thinks about educational planning—it is clear that a school cannot function without some kind of program that it offers to its students. Whether that program is conceived as a preplanned series of educational hurdles over which the students must jump or the entire range of experiences a child has within the school, the school as an institution has some mission, some set of general aims or direction, and must provide some activities, programs, or means that engage those who work and study there. The design and evaluation of those activities and programs are what we are attempting to understand.

In considering such a plan or program, there are some distinctions we can make regarding the scale or scope of our attention and the location of our planning over time. In Figure 1 two continua are outlined, one dealing with *scale* and *scope*, the other dealing with *time*.

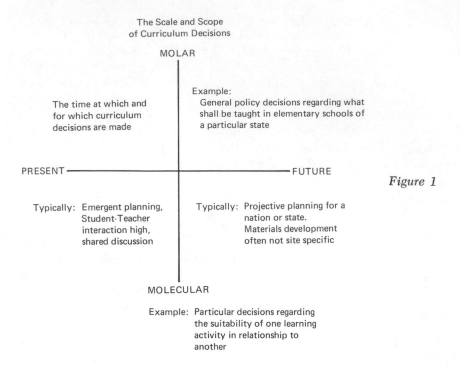

The Scale and Scope
of Curriculum Decisions

MOLAR

The time at which and
for which curriculum
decisions are made

Example:
General policy decisions regarding what
shall be taught in elementary schools of
a particular state

PRESENT ——————————————————— FUTURE

Figure 1

Typically: Emergent planning,
Student-Teacher
interaction high,
shared discussion

Typically: Projective planning for a
nation or state.
Materials development
often not site specific

MOLECULAR

Example: Particular decisions regarding
the suitability of one learning
activity in relationship to
another

The design of an educational program is influenced by a wide variety of decisions that range from the broadest types of educational policy bearing on the aims or content of educational programs to those decisions that have to do with very specific, highly focused aspects of a particular program. Take, as an example, decisions about what the schools of a state should be required to teach. Virtually all states have in their education code a section that prescribes the content of instruction. In California, for example, it is required that schools teach reading, writing, arithmetic, social studies, art, music, physical education, and science at various grade levels.[1] The decisions that led to these policies were curriculum decisions. Some group (in this case the state board of education) decided that schools should devote their attention, energy, time, and resources to a particular array of subject matters. And in California books or the resources to purchase books to ensure adequate attention to these field are also provided. This type of decision, like other large-scale decisions bearing directly on the program that the schools provide, exemplifies large-scale, molar curriculum decisions. The creation of a Career Education Program, the decision to emphasize the so-called basic skills, and the formulation of policy bearing on the development of new approaches to the teaching of science all represent molar types of curriculum decision making. The point here is that when one talks about curriculum planning or about the design of educational programs, one might be referring to planning at this level: the planning of curriculum policy or curriculum priorities. Obviously, such policies do not exhaust the decisions that need to be made, nor are they adequate for operating programs within schools, but they do establish the directions and boundaries for other decisions.

At the other end of the continuum are highly specific molecular decisions bearing on a particular educational situation or a specific set of curriculum materials. Does *this* particular curriculum activity build on what has preceded it? Are *these* examples likely to be meaningful to *this* group of students? Does *this* content adequately exemplify the generalization the students are expected to learn? Does the visual quality of the material stimulate interest or is it dull and unimaginative? Questions such as these are asked by anyone or any group concerned with the creation of curriculum materials. Obviously, such decisions are almost always made after more general, molar curriculum decisions have been made, after one decides, for example, that a social studies program dealing with sex role socialization is to be created.

The point here is that when one asks what kinds of problems curriculum decision makers encounter or curriculum scholars study, one can point to a range dealing with the most broadly based molar types of policy bearing on the shape and character of educational programs to the specific, molecular decisions that must inevitably be made within particular educational contexts.

In some countries, there is a formal separation between those who make the large-scale molar decisions about the content and aims of the curriculum and those who work within the parameters set by those decisions to create specific learning activities and teaching materials. In Norway, for example, a national board will appoint a national educational committee made up of prominent lay persons and scholars from various disciplines to outline the basic topics, content, and aims of the curriculum for children in primary and secondary schools. This committee, representing the views of the polity and the specialized scholarly competence of the school-related subject matter disciplines, is responsible for formulating directions and priorities in school programs. By using lay people, the broad interests of the public are believed to be served, and by utilizing scholars from school-related subject fields the most up-to-date and important ideas within the subject matter fields are likely to be identified. Once these molar decisions have been made, it is up to others to translate them into specific programs suitable for the interests and abilities of, say, ten-year-olds. The curriculum work here is to translate "new subject matter" into materials that will become useful for creating educational events in the classroom, something for which neither a university scholar nor a lay person has any particular preparation.

What we see here is not only a division of labor but also a political separation based on perceived areas of competence. Educators responsible for curriculum development perform an essentially technical role in attempting to actualize the collective decisions of selected lay people and scholars. Educational expertise in such an arrangement is aimed at the translation and implementation of educational policy.

The horizontal axis in Figure 1 extends from decisions made in the present for the present to those that are made to serve as a kind of blueprint or guideline to be followed in the future. Some examples will be useful. Much curriculum work consists of the creation of curriculum materials that are intended to be used by teachers to help students acquire more sophisticated skills or ideas. Typically, such materials are developed for use over one or more academic years. *Man: A Course of Study*, the Physical Sciences Study Committee's materials, and *Science: A Process Approach* are curriculum materials designed to improve the quality of teaching and learning in elementary and secondary schools. These materials have been developed largely through federal funds by curriculum development groups and are intended for students and schools throughout the country. The general assumption underlying the work of these groups is that teachers would welcome such materials, that national groups having funds and access to nationally known scholars would be able to provide teachers with a higher quality of materials than teachers could create on their own, and that use of such materials over extended periods would result in a higher quality of learning in the fields represented by those materials.

The creation of such materials represents an effort to influence the educational futures of students and teachers for a substantial period of time. Content and sequence are determined; the roles of the teacher and students are defined well in advance of the particular context in which the materials are to be used. Like the minister of education in France who was said once to have boasted that at 11:00 on any morning he knew what all the children in French schools were studying, nationally developed materials often tend to formulate long-term educational plans that are intended to become the course to be run.

At the other end of the continuum is another image of curriculum planning, one that is not so well defined or so long term in character. That model is perhaps best exemplified by the kind of curriculum planning that goes on in some progressive schools. This model conceives of planning as a joint effort between teacher and student, one that cultivates shared responsibility and that exploits emerging educational opportunities when they occur. At this end of the continuum, the teacher is likely to see his or her role as providing the kind of environment where new, unexpected interests can emerge and where "flexible purposing," to use Dewey's phrase, is both possible and desirable.[2]

The point here is simply that curriculum planning does not need to be long term and preplanned weeks or months before engagement with students is to occur. The teacher who decides that in the next hour his or her class might find a discussion about the emergence of national socialism in Germany stimulating is engaged in curriculum planning, even though such decisions do not result in the creation of written plans, elaborate visual illustrations, or well-designed boxes of self-instructional materials.

In making this observation I am not writing a brief either for no planning or for elaborate materials. I am attempting to point out that the planning of curricula is something that everyone does who provides an educational program for students. Such planning may be short term or long term, shoddy or careful, tasteful or ugly, appropriate for students or inappropriate. Whatever the quality of the planning, we all decide what we will do or allow to occur. The extent and scope of such planning depend on the context in which one works and on the view of curriculum and teaching that one holds.

Let me review the major points I have tried to make thus far. First, I have tried to show how curriculum planning spans a range that extends from the broadest types of decision about the content, scope, and aims of programs serving millions of students to highly specific, molecular decisions made by curriculum development specialists wrestling with problems of sequence in a particular mathematics curriculum or by a teacher deciding on a particular project for a class or a student. Curriculum planning is not limited to a single level of specificity along the continuum.

Second, I have tried to show that the planning of curriculum is an inevitable aspect of schooling; it *must* occur. The significant question is how well it is done. One need not have long-range plans or printed materials to have an educational program. Teachers can use the present situation to develop short-term plans with or for their students. Time is a variable that will vary in relation to the context or the view one holds about what constitutes an appropriate teaching role.

Thus, if someone asks what curriculum specialists do, given these distinctions, it is possible to respond by saying that their responsibilities extend from the shaping of educational policy bearing on the aims and content of educational programs to work dealing with the design of specific elements within particular educational programs. Where and when are such decisions made? They are made by groups developing materials or creating educational policy intended to serve a large educational constituency as well as by teachers deciding on the value and appropriateness of a specific project or task for a particular group of students.

Let's return for the moment to the concept *curriculum* and redefine it. *The curriculum of a school, or a course, or a classroom can be conceived of as a series of planned events that are intended to have educational consequences for one or more students.* In formulating this conception, or definition, of curriculum, I am not claiming to formulate a "real" definition. Curricula are not natural entities whose necessary and sufficient properties are capable of being discovered once and for all. What I am doing is formulating a concept of curriculum that I believe to be useful. Let's examine this concept more closely. A curriculum is a series of planned events. This implies that there will be more than one event planned, and this is typically the case, although theoretically one could have a single event constituting curriculum (but that likelihood is small). A second feature of the conception is that curricula are planned; someone must do something that has some aim, some purpose, some goal or objective, even though it might be highly diffuse or general. A third feature is that the intention be educational in character. Now this qualification, I readily admit, need not be a part of the definition of curriculum; one could formulate a curriculum designed to train bigots, burglars, or murderers, but within the context of this book and my purposes the qualification that the consequences are intended to be educational is important, if for no other reason than to highlight the fact that schools are supposed to be educational institutions. A fourth feature of this concept deals with the term *consequences*. Educational events or activities do much more than what is intended; they influence people in a wide variety of ways. Furthermore, I want to leave room for the teacher or curriculum developer to plan activities or events that do not have specific, highly predictable goals or objectives. I want to leave room for planning of events that appear to be educationally fruitful but whose specific consequences for different students might not be known in advance. The term *consequences* is sufficiently wide to allow for such planning. In other words, a curriculum is a program that is intentionally designed to engage students in activities or events that will have educational benefits for them. Some of these benefits might be delineated or specified in advance in operational terms; others will be general, broad, and diffuse, but in part capable of being recognized subsequent to the activity. Like other issues in this book, this issue—the character of educational goals—will be discussed in greater detail later.

When one is engaged in long-term planning and has formulated an array of goals or objectives, designed materials of various sorts, created learning activities to be used in the classroom, and prepared visual and auditory resources, it is possible to inspect the curriculum to see what its contents are and how they have been related. The curriculum in this context has a physical existence, it is embodied in a set of materials. These materials can be the subject of analysis and criticism in a measure similar to the criticism applied to books, paintings, symphonies, architecture, and the like. To be sure, the criteria will differ, but the principle of being able to criticize what has been created is the same.

The physical existence of such materials also means that they can be transported; the same curriculum can be used in different classrooms and in different schools. School administrators can discuss the strengths and weaknesses of the curriculum. Parents can inspect it and students can use it.

But curriculum planning need not result in the creation of physical materials. The teacher whose plans are in his mind alone might have planned a curriculum of an excellent sort, but because the plans are not public, they can neither be shifted about, inspected, nor shared with others. The only way to appraise the quality of the curriculum is to watch the teacher and the students in the class. One must attend to the attributes as they unfold, make judgments about the significance of the content as it is revealed, and appraise the quality of the resources as they are used. One must make one's judgment by observing the curriculum in use. For the teacher who does not make extensive or long-term plans, even of a mental sort, the curriculum may in fact be planned in process. In this situation, it is not simply that plans have been made but have not been written down, in this situation the teacher plans in process. What the teacher uses are initiating activities, but such activities are employed simply to get the ball rolling, to begin a process whose course is shaped in the conduct of teaching.

It is in this model of curriculum planning that the distinction between curriculum planning and teaching is particularly difficult to draw. What constitutes a teaching decision and what constitutes a decision about curriculum becomes very difficult to identify. Nevertheless, the general distinction between curriculum and teaching is useful, as I will discuss later in this book, even though there are cases in which the distinction between the two is not clear.

It might be noted that the planning of a curriculum on a long-term basis with clear specifications regarding its use can be compared to the creation of a score written by a composer or the plans prepared by an architect. Although these two examples are much more specific and detailed than what most curricula provide, the relationship between the composer and the pianist or the architect and the builder has similarities to that between the curriculum planner and the teacher. In each case the planner designs, and the performance is executed within the constraints of the design. And in each case the performers have degrees of freedom with which to interpret the plans that have been made. One can inspect the score, the architectural specifications, and the curriculum as planned and assess the ways in which those plans have been executed.

For those using a more emergent model of curriculum planning, that model in which plans are created in process, activities are much closer to the work of the painter or poet. In this model, decisions to do one thing rather than another are decisions that can be made only by considering options as they develop, by "reading" the situation, by exploiting the adventitious, and by allowing intentions to grow out of action rather than requiring them to precede it. This is the way a great many artists as well as teachers work. To work this way is not necessarily a mark of incompetence but could be the result of a preference for a particular way of working, the result of a considered view of one's professional role, a sign of commitment to a particular image of education. In such a model of curriculum planning one must place a good deal of faith in the ability of the teacher.

To work this way requires, I believe, a great deal of experience, competence, and confidence as a teacher. While the availability of a curriculum that has been well planned and accompanied by interesting and attractive resources for in-classroom use breeds confidence that what will be offered will be worth the student's time and effort, curriculum materials and particularly that species of materials called curriculum guides are often disregarded by teachers. The existence of a well-planned body of curriculum material is no guarantee that they will be used effectively or with enthusiasm in the classroom. To know that, there is no substitute for direct observation in the classroom.

Thus, when we talk about "the curriculum" we can mean that body of materials that is planned in advance of classroom use that teachers use to promote students' ability to learn some content, acquire some skill, develop some beliefs, or have some valued type of experience. The curriculum can also refer to those activities used in classrooms by teachers to facilitate student learning, whether or not those activities or that content has been specified. Appraisal of the former can be made by inspecting the materials that embody the curriculum. Appraisal of the latter can be made only by direct observation of the classroom itself.

NORMATIVE AND DESCRIPTIVE CURRICULUM THEORY

When we speak of theory we can distinguish between two types. Normative theory is concerned with the articulation and justification of a set of values. Its aim is to provide a persuasive case for the value of a particular end or state of being. In education, normative theory argues the case for certain educational goals on the basis that the goals themselves are intrinsically valuable. Thus, a theory of education that argues that education should aim at fostering the growth of the individual and that defines growth as the development of those modes of intelligence that enable individuals to secure meaning from experience is normative in character. Such a statement or position becomes theoretical as it presents to the world a coherent set of reasons and concepts that justifies its claims. Although one could ask for further justifications for the claim that education should be conceived of as a process concerned with fostering growth, once having received such justification, further justification leads either to an infinite regress or to a circular argument. Eventually, one arrives at value assumptions that are made rather than justified.

In educational theory in general, and in curriculum theory in particular, normative ideas are central. Education itself is a normative enterprise—that is, it is concerned with the realization of aims that are considered worthwhile. Thus, educational activities are not simply concerned with learning because what a person learns might have negative consequences for his or her development. What makes experience educational is its participation in a set of values. To the extent to which those experiences participate in those values, they are educational. To the extent to which they contradict those values, they are miseducational.

For the planning of curricula, normative commitments are also crucial. Such commitments, or images of educational virtue, influence what is regarded as relevant in planning and what data are considered important in making curriculum decisions. Without such values, neither education nor curriculum has a rudder. Now it should be noted that "theoretical" in the context of normative theory is not the same as a bald statement of values or belief: it is the coherent articulation of a view and a presentation of the grounds for holding it. Such theory is not necessarily predictive and need not employ scientifically verified facts to sustain it. What one looks for is coherence. The value orientations to curriculum that will be presented in the next chapter are examples of such theoretical views.

In saying that normative theory is not simply a bald statement of what someone values, I am not implying that there are necessary and suffecent conditions that can be used as criteria for determining whether a statement is theoretical. Normative theory extends from general statements and beliefs to highly elaborate efforts to justify a view of what is good or beautiful. Thus, the roots of such theory begin as humans speculate on what is good in life and worth achieving. Commonsensically, we call such speculation philosophies of life, and although few philosophers would consider such commonsense speculation philosophical in the technical or professional sense, the difference is one of degree rather than kind.

To say this is not to equate the commonsense theorizing that all of us do with the heady work of a Paul Tillich, Plato, Boyde Bode, or John Dewey. It is to recognize that the theoretical construction of value is not the sole province of those who are professional philosophers but is a part of the intellectual activity of ordinary men and women. The differences between the two reside in consistency, subtlety, scope, and coherence. These are differences that distinguish levels of quality rather than differences in kind.

I said earlier that normative theory is critical for education, and this point is worth emphasizing. Education is not the same as schooling, nor is it the same as learning. One can learn many things that are personally and socially dysfunctional: to become neurotic, fearful of people, a torturer, a racist, and the like. In each case, learning has taken place, but whether one considers such learning an instance of education depends on a normative theory of education. The claim that some groups or individuals do or would regard such learning as educational is not in dispute. This might be true, but to make such a claim is not to make a value statement but to describe a social fact. The question is whether one ought to regard such forms of learning as educational. Would you, given your normative theory of education, regard becoming neurotic or becoming a torturer an instance of education? I would not.

Without some view of what counts as education, one is in no position whatsoever to make judgments about the educational quality of the processes of schooling or their consequences. One cannot know whether research conclusions have any relevance to educational practice. One has no basis for appraising the educational merits of teaching. John Dewey makes this point very well, when he says:

That a man may grow in efficiency as a burglar, as a gangster, or as a corrupt politician, cannot be doubted. But from the standpoint of growth as education and education as growth, the question is whether growth in this direction promotes or retards growth in general. Does this form of growth create conditions for further growth, or does it set up conditions that shut off the person who has grown in this particular direction from the occasions, stimuli, and opportunities for continuing growth in new directions? What is the effect of growth in a special direction upon the attitudes and habits which alone open up avenues for development in other lines? I shall leave you to answer these questions, saying simply that when and only when development in a particular line conduces to continuing growth does it answer to the criterion of education as growing. For the conception is one that must find universal and not specialized limited application.[3]

Dewey goes on to distinguish between three types of experience: those that are *educational, noneducational,* and *miseducational.*[4] Education experiences are those, as I have suggested earlier, that contribute to the individual's growth. Growth, for Dewey, represents the extension of human intelligence, the increase in the organism's ability to secure meaning from experience and to act in ways that are instrumental to the achievement of inherently worthwhile ends. Noneducational experiences are those that are simply undergone and have no significant effect on the individual one way or the other. There are many such experiences undergone each day—the activities of habit—that punctuate our lives. Such experiences are had but without significant effect one way or another on our growth. We tie our shoes, walk across the room, drive our car, without contributing to or detracting from our growth.

Miseducational experiences are those that thwart or hamper our ability to have further experiences or to intelligently cope with problems in a particular arena of activity. In schooling, many students develop disinclinations to encounter certain fields of study. Their experience, say in mathematics, has been so unfortunate and uncomfortable that they avoid that field of study whenever it is their option to do so. For such students, mathematics was miseducational. It closed rather than opened them up to the intellectual and aesthetic possibilities of the field.

More radical examples of miseducational experience are found in the acquisition of phobias that children acquire because of the anxieties of their parents. Such phobias might deal with animals, airplanes, failure, and sex.

Children learn to become fearful and become incompetent in the areas in which these phobias function. Their experience constrains rather than expands the possibilities that life makes available. In these areas, miseducational experience results in a deep sense of personal discomfort.

Dewey's writings are a prime example of normative theory. He conceptualizes a value, namely growth, and then justifies its significance in argument. He locates the sources of growth in experience and then indicates the relevance of different types of experience for education. The position is thought through, well argued, and has practical consequences for teaching and curriculum planning. Such theory, rooted as it is in a metaphor of a growing organism, shapes our view of what is appropriate and inappropriate in educational practice. The appeal of Dewey's theory has been extraordinary for educators throughout the world, but it is not only the normative theory that appeals, and in the following chapter other conceptions of educational value will be presented.

Thus far, I have spoken of normative theory in education and curriculum, but what of descriptive theory, those statements or concepts that attempt to explain, usually through their power to predict, the events of the world? Descriptive theory with respect to the sciences is perhaps best exemplified in the natural sciences: they have provided the model that the social scientists have attempted to emulate. In the natural sciences, the task has been both to give an account of and to account for a set of phenomena. "What has occurred and how?" are major questions theorists ask. With a theory that is useful, one can anticipate the future; one knows what to expect given some set of conditions or circumstances. In some cases, such theory has made it possible not only to predict, but to control—although this is not always achieved. While scientists are able to land a spacecraft on Mars, astronomical theory is not yet able to control the path of stars. In the field of curriculum, theory in no way approaches that level of power, and for good reasons. Educational matters are value laden in ways that physics is not. In education, what one seeks is not the explanation of what is, but the achievement of what ought to be. Nucleii, as far as anyone knows, do not form purposes or have intentions: people do. Increasingly, social scientists are coming to appreciate the distinctive characteristics of theory in dealing with the human as a social creature and the institutions humans create. Lee Cronbach, a social scientist who recognizes this difference, writes:

Social scientists are rightly proud of the discipline we draw from the natural science side of our ancestry. Scientific discipline is what we uniquely add to the time-honored ways of studying man. Too narrow an identification with science, however, has fixed our eyes upon an inappropriate goal. The goal of our work, I have argued here, is not to amass generalizations atop which a theoretical tower can someday be erected (cf. Scriven, 1959b, p. 471). The special task of the social scientist in each generation is to pin down the contemporary facts. Beyond that, he shares with the humanistic scholar and the artist in the effort to gain insight into contemporary relationships and to realign the culture's view of man with present realities. To know man as he is is no mean aspiration.[5]

What I believe descriptive theory in curriculum has to provide primarily are concepts that enable us to make more subtle and powerful distinctions. At times, such theory might lead to empirical generalizations that can be considered in making particular decisions for specific circumstances, but such generalizations always need to be applied and interpreted with caution, not as rules but as considerations. No set of generalizations will adequately treat the particular characteristics of specific situations.

In the field of curriculum, descriptive theory has largely been borrowed from psychology. Theories of reinforcement, cognition, perception, learning, sequence, problem solving, and the like have influenced the ways in which curriculum theorists have conceptualized curriculum. Indeed, Dewey himself was greatly influenced by the descriptive theoretical work of Darwin. Dewey's conception of man is biological, as is Piaget's, whereas Bobbitt, particularly in his early work, attempted to apply the theories of scientific management to curriculum and teaching in order to increase the efficiency of schools. What we see both in Dewey and in Bobbitt is the influence descriptive theory has had on their normative theory of education. Once norms are formed, these norms in turn influence the kinds of descriptive data one uses to support one's norms. In short, a dialectic between the normative and the descriptive occurs.

To talk about the differences between normative and descriptive theory implies that the two are wholly distinctive. This is not the case. Normative theory is buttressed by descriptive claims emanating from descriptive theory: Dewey's theory of education is a case in point, as I have indicated. The way in which we understand the world to be influences our conception of its possibilities and therefore shapes our aspirations.

Descriptive theory is in a subtle but important sense pervaded by normative theory because the methods of inquiry we chose and the criteria we chose to apply to test truth claims reflect beliefs about the nature of knowledge. These beliefs are basically value judgments. Those embracing a different conception of knowledge will employ different methods of inquiry and may therefore come to different conclusions about the world. In short, epistemological commitments reflect a set of values. Theory in curriculum is therefore of two types, each of which penetrates the other: normative and descriptive. Normative theory articulates the values to which the educational program is directed and descriptive theory provides the concepts and generalizations that are taken into account in planning the school program.

Theory, however, is ideational and problems of curriculum development practical. It is important to distinguish between the ideas one works with and the practical act of constructing an educational program. Curriculum development is the process through which those ideas are transformed by

an act of educational imagination. I say imagination because no theory—
either normative or descriptive—prescribes what is appropriate for different
students. Ideas are guides, they are not recipes. One works with them, one
does not follow them. To engage in curriculum development, one must put
together much more than any of the theories can provide either individually
or collectively. Schwab makes this point well when he writes:

A curriculum grounded in but one or a few subsubjects of the social sciences is
indefensible; contributions from all are required. There is no forseeable hope of
a unified theory in the immediate or middle future, nor of a meta-theory which
will tell us how to put those subsubjects together or order them in a fixed hierarchy of importance to the problems of curriculum.[6]

It should also be noted that the competencies needed to design curricula
are not identical with those needed to create sophisticated and useful
curriculum theory. Aptitude differences exist among individuals, and the
kind of experience one needs in each realm of activity differs. Theoretical
training requires intensive study of relevant disciplines within philosophy
and the social sciences and the critical analysis of one's written work by
competent critics. The skills of curriculum development are acquired in the
act of designing curricula and in experiencing firsthand the problems of
transforming ideas into educational materials and events. Those skills include the ability to work with others, the ability to deal with the complexities of practical deliberation, the ability to establish distance between
one's work and oneself in order to see it more clearly, and the ability to
envisage the way in which activities might function within a classroom.
It requires the ability to appreciate the demands that a task makes on
teachers and students and to be able to judge how much guidance they
might need to engage in that task. Such skills are not trivial, nor are they
nonintellectual. They are demanding, they require a sense of taste and
style and the ability to deal with frustration.

What would a comprehensive, scientifically descriptive theory of curriculum look like if we had one? Such a theory would identify relevant phenomena in the planning of a curriculum. It would provide guidelines for
relating these phenomena to each so that they were maximally effective
with a group of students, given a description of the student's characteristics.
And it would provide a credible explanation of why the relationships between the curriculum and the student were effective for realizing particular
ends. Such a theory would, in short, enable the curriculum developer to
design curricula that were optimally suited to particular students, given
some view of what was educationally desirable. In addition, such theory, if
it were necessary for its efficacy, would specify the context conditions that
would need to obtain if the theory were to operate. If the theory were entirely comprehensive, it would provide such guidance for different subject
matters, disciplines, or fields of study, and it would be able to accommodate

the developmental levels and other relevant personal characteristics of students.

One does not have to exhaust the literature in curriculum to recognize that such theory is nowhere to be found. Instead, we have concepts, rules of thumb, perspectives, and frames of reference. We have theoretical ideas that are to be used flexibly rather than the equivalent of Boyle's Law or Bohr's atom. I believe man's ingenuity and need for forming his own purposes, his curiosity, and his irascibility foreclose on the possibility of developing a theory of curriculum comparable to that of atomic particles. We are "condemned" to a life of exciting uncertainty in which the flexible use of intelligence is our most potent tool.

CURRICULUM DIFFUSION

Once curricula have been designed and the materials embodying them produced, the problem of their diffusion to schools still exists. Curriculum diffusion is the process of moving curriculum material into the purview of teachers. There are many routes that one can take. One can attempt to design materials that need little or no form of inservice education, materials that move toward the "teacherproof" end of the spectrum. One can design materials and then work with supervisors or consultants within the school district to provide workshops or institutes to help teachers use the materials. One can establish teacher centers, as some educational laboratories have, that provide inservice education for teachers in the use of new curriculum materials (one can use materials as prototypes for teachers to develop their own materials).

The dissemination stage of the process is not a marginal one. It is simplistic to assume that teachers will adopt materials that they have been inadequately exposed to and which, initially at least, make demands on them that familiar materials do not. Quite often, new curriculum materials also require the use of new teaching skills. Curricula that are discovery oriented suffer from didactic teaching methods. Curricula that engage students in the examination of controversial issues need teachers who can guide rather than dominate discussions. Inappropriate teaching can scuttle the most well-intentioned and handsomely designed curriculum materials.

The need for the interpretation of new curricula has been recognized not only by educational laboratories, but by county education offices, among whose major functions is the diffusion of such material and the provision of inservice education. It is also recognized by commercial companies that produce and market such materials. Most of the larger companies have a cadre of former teachers and curriculum specialists who provide in-service programs to school districts that purchase their products.

The dissemination or diffusion of curriculum materials is a crucial step in the complex process of bringing about changes in schools and classrooms, the places in which change must occur if curriculum development is not to be an empty enterprise. In the last analysis, it is what teachers do in classrooms and what students experience that define the educational process. The character of this process might initiate with a vague image of a new way of teaching biology or art or the study of American political behavior. That image might eventually get transformed into a body of handsome resources, well-written prose, and imaginatively conceived opportunities for learning. But such materials, like a brilliantly composed musical score, need skillful and sensitive interpretation and a group of people who can interact mean-- ingfully with what has been created. If any of these components is missing, the process fails. If the score is poor, it is not worth playing. If the performance is poor, it will be poorly received. If the audience is ill-prepared to deal with it, it will fall on deaf ears. Composers need competent performers and performers need an appreciative audience. In education, similar relationships hold. The teacher might be, in some models of education, his or her own composer, but the need for competent performance, if not an artistic one, still exists. And the fit between the teacher's "score" and the students remains as critical in the classroom as it is in the concert hall— probably even more so.

REFERENCES

1. California Education Code: Statutes (1976), Sacramento: Department of General Services, Documents Section, 1967.
2. John Dewey, *Experience and Education,* Macmillan Publishing Co., Inc., New York, 1938.
3. Ibid, pp. 28–29.
4. Ibid, passim.
5. Lee Cronbach, "Beyond the Two Disciplines of Scientific Psychology," *The American Psychologist,* Vol. 30, No. 2, February 1975, p. 126.
6. Joseph Schwab, "The Practical: A Language for Curriculum", *School Review,* Vol. 78, No. V, November 1969, p. 10.

4

Five Basic Orientations to the Curriculum

The subject which involves all other subjects, and therefore the subject in which education should culminate, is the Theory and Practice of Education.

HERBERT SPENCER

The content and aims of school programs have long been the subject of debate. In these debates, differences seldom emerge in the form of abstract issues or bald-face confrontations of competing ideologies. Most often they emerge in the form of differences about specific practical matters: Should children be given letter grades? Should children be assigned to tracks according to their ability in school subjects? Should corporal punishment be used or threatened in school? Should the three R's be emphasized, and should children be kept back if they do not achieve grade-level standards?

Although the arguments that these questions elicit seldom broaden into an examination of principles, it is important for those concerned with designing educational programs to see behind the issues, to go beyond the immediate controversy, to penetrate the current debate in order to locate the values and premises behind the questions.

It is my contention that through such analysis the contending parties will have a clearer and more adequate basis for dealing with what is at issue. Furthermore, an awareness of the various orientations to schooling expands one's options in curriculum planning and thus contributes to one's degree of professional freedom. In this chapter, a framework is presented for the description of five important curriculum orientations. In addition, it provides examples to indicate how these orientations manifest themselves in the classroom.

DEVELOPMENT OF COGNITIVE PROCESSES

One major orientation to schooling emphasizes the belief that the curriculum provided and the teaching strategies used should foster the development of the student's cognitive processes. In this view, the major functions of the school are (1) to help children learn how to learn and (2) to provide them with the opportunities to use and strengthen the variety of intellectual faculties that they possess.

In this view, the mind is conceived of as a collection of relatively independent faculties or aptitudes: the ability to infer, to speculate, to locate and solve problems, to remember, to visualize, to extrapolate, and so on. It is these faculties that must come into play in order to adequately deal with the problems that individuals inevitably have to cope with during the course of a lifetime. For the school to emphasize the mere acquisition of information, the accumulation of fact, or even the dissemination of theory is not in the long run useful, for surely both facts and theories change, and at an alarming rate. If what is already known is emphasized; the student is in a poor position to deal with problems and issues that will inevitably arise in the future, many of which cannot at present even be envisioned. The most effective way to deal with such problems is not by storing bodies of knowledge in one's memory but rather by strengthening those cognitive processes that can be used later to deal with them. For this to occur, the curriculum used in the school and the forms of teaching employed are crucial. The curriculum is not to emphasize content, but process. Teaching is not to impart, but to help students learn to inquire.

The roots of this orientation to curriculum go back to the work of the phrenologists and faculty psychologists of the nineteenth century and to the progressive era in American education, particularly during the 1920s. For the phrenologists, the mind consisted of a collection of thirty-seven muscles that were located in different parts of the brain. Each section of the skull showed the location of these intellectual muscles. Following the phrenologists' lead, the faculty psychologists emphasized the importance of strengthening these mental faculties through practice, especially practice that was tough and demanding. Their slogan might be said to have been, "It doesn't matter much what a student studies in school, as long as he doesn't like it." In short, what was important was that the tasks encountered exercise the relevant faculties so that through exercise they became "strong."

Although it was believed that content, per se, was not the crucial issue in building a curriculum, it was believed that some subject matters were particularly useful for the development of specific faculties. Mathematics, for example—subjects such as algebra, geometry, trigonometry, and calculus —was justified not because it imparted content but rather because it fostered mental discipline, it strengthened the student's ability to reason. Mathematics was justified because of its contributions to the development of a rigorous mind rather than because students need to know the meaning of Euclid's first theorem.

It should be noted that in this view the criteria for the selection of curriculum content have an elegance and economy. If tasks or subject matters could be identified that strengthen the muscles of the mind, then it would be possible to accomplish a great deal with relatively little effort. For example, if the ability to deduce were a product of processes strengthened through exercise on particular tasks, then one's deductive ability could be strengthened with the expectation that those processes would be useful for tasks unlike those used to strengthen them. This view assumes, in short, general transfer. What transfers is not content, but process: the ability to use the variety of processes that the curriculum strengthened through exercise.

It was this belief that the work of Thorndike and Woodworth in 1901 undermined.[1] Testing for the transferability of learning, Thorndike and Woodworth demonstrated that transfer was not general but specific. What one learned transferred only insofar as the elements constituting the second task were identical with those of the first. Thorndike's theory of "identical elements," and the psychology of learning that he promulgated had a great impact on beliefs about how the curriculum was to be built.

One such impact was that it could no longer be assumed that the student would automatically learn to perform tasks not taught specifically, or at least taught in a way that encouraged the transfer of training. Thus, in preparing a curriculum in arithmetic, it was not assumed that if a student learned that three times four equaled twelve he or she would also know that four times three equaled twelve, or that two times six equaled twelve. One could not safely assume general transfer or the use of "reason" as a way of coping with new tasks. As a result, arithmetic textbooks placed heavy stress on the catch phrase of connectionist psychology—"practice makes perfect"—and "recency," "frequency," and "intensity" became the guiding principles of effective pedagogy.

The modern-day resurrection of process-oriented psychology emerged in part in the work of J. P. Guilford,[2] a psychologist whose major efforts have been devoted to the empirical articulation and assessment of a model of the structure of the intellect. The model that Guilford conceptualized—a complex structure that distinguishes over one hundred independent intellectual operations—could, in principle, be used to define the variety of tasks that could constitute a process-oriented curriculum. For example, if ideational fluency and ideational flexibility using figural material were considered important educationally, programs in schools could be designed to give children opportunities to use such processes on tasks that were intentionally designed to elicit them. What is important here is that specific mental operations are thought to be strengthened through activities especially designed to require their use. It is on the ability to use such processes that the individual must eventually depend. The major mission of schooling, in this view, is to increase the probability that maximum realization of those processes occurs.

Related to this conception of mind are the various levels of cognitive operation in the *Taxonomy of Educational Objectives: Cognitive Domain.*[3] The six levels that are identified—possession of information, comprehension, application, analysis, synthesis, and evaluation—represent increasingly complex forms of thinking. The tacit value position embedded in the taxonomy is that educational objectives should be developed so that they traverse the entire range of cognitive processes and not simply remain at the lower level of cognitive functioning. Implicit in this view is the belief that cognitive processes can be cultivated, that educational objectives should be derived from levels of cognitive functioning, and that test items should be designed to assess the levels of cognitive achievement that students have reached.

Within the curriculum field, a variety of programs have been designed that are directly related to the belief in the primacy of cognitive development as an aim of education. One such program, *Science: A Process Approach,*[4] emphasizes the use of those operations that are central to scientific inquiry but are also justifiable in their own right. *Elementary School Science*[5] is another program that places heavy emphasis on the cultivation of those intellectual abilities that are consistent with the spirit of scientific modes of thought. Jerome Bruner's seminal work *The Process of Education*[6] is an example of a hybrid orientation that marries forms of inquiry used in the natural and social sciences with the central concepts and generalizations within specific academic disciplines. What these curriculum orientations have in common is their emphasis on using curriculum tasks as a means of fostering processes that presumably will outlive the problems or concepts they were developed from. The major aim of these programs is the development of intellectual power rather than the simple dissemination of a body of ideas or information.

Given this orientation to the aims of educational programs, what might be expected of a teacher working within this framework? What might we expect to see in the way of teaching, curriculum content, and evaluation procedures? How might the values embedded in a cognitive process orientation to the curriculum manifest themselves in the conduct of schooling?

First, the curriculum used in the school would generally be problem centered; that is, students would be encouraged to define problems they wish to pursue, and with the teacher's help the appropriate materials and guidance would be provided. Some of these problems would be those defined by individual students, whereas others would be the result of deliberations by the class or of small groups of students. The reason a problem-centered curriculum is attractive to those emphasizing the development of cognitive processes is that the opportunities to define and solve problems are among the most critical intellectual abilities the school can foster. Without the opportunity to conceptualize, to analyze, to deal with ambiguity, to locate relevant resources, to evaluate the results of one's efforts, the child is unlikely to use his or her sophisticated abilities. What matters most is not the particular content on which these processes are employed—the repair of a carburetor can be treated imaginatively, while the reading of *Othello* can be done mindlessly—but the exercise of the intellectual faculties. And for this to occur, content that is meaningful to the student and problems that are intellectually challenging are critical.

Teaching in this orientation requires not only the ability to generate problematic situations for students, but also the ability to raise the kinds of questions with students that direct their attention to levels of analysis they would not be likely to use without the teacher's aid. The teacher has a positive role to play in cultivating "the higher mental abilities" by virtue of the tasks provided in the curriculum, the materials that are used, and the kinds of questions he or she raises while teaching.

A classification of the kinds of questions teachers and students raise in class ideally reveals a wide range of types and levels. Similarly, the kinds of problems and materials with which students work would include not only the verbal and mathematical but also visual and auditory modes of conception and expression. Students might be asked, for example, to transform ideas held in one conceptual modality, say a visual mode, into their verbal or mathematical "equivalents." The contrary would also occur. Concepts framed in linguistic or mathematical terms would be transformed into visual or auditory "equivalents." The point here is that the focus of curriculum content is derived from a conception of mental operations; the curriculum is essentially an investment to bring those processes into play and to strengthen them.

ACADEMIC RATIONALISM

One of the oldest and most basic orientations to curriculum goals and content may be called academic rationalism. This orientation argues that the major function of the school is to foster the intellectual growth of the student in those subject matters most worthy of study. The argument proceeds that schools are special places; their mission as social institutions should not be subverted by attempting to meet every social need or personal whim that might arise. Schools that devote their time and resources to problems of social adjustment, driver training, and drug education are depriving students of the intellectual tools they need to cope with life's most pressing problems—justice, wisdom, duty—as well as of the concepts and techniques that careful study in academic disciplines provides.

But what are the subjects most worthy of study? Who is to determine which subjects are best? Are there intrinsic differences in the value of various academic disciplines? The answers to these questions for those holding an academic rationalistic position are clear: not all disciplines are created equal. Some disciplines—biology, for example—deal with processes that inform one about the nature of life, a topic so important that the achievements in biological inquiry should be a part of the intellectual repertoire of all educated people. Furthermore, if biology or the sciences more generally are not taught in school, it is not likely that their ideas will be learned. Unlike driver training or home economics, education in the sciences is the special province of the school.

This position is argued in several ways. First, it is argued that biology (I use biology only as an example) as a branch of science not only represents a particular discipline having its own content, concepts, and patterns of inquiry, but it also represents a special mode of thought—science. Science is a fundamental form of human understanding and as such should be made available to students. In this argument, biology is a special case of a more general and powerful paradigm of human understanding that the school should foster, especially because an understanding of its concepts and procedures requires specialized forms of instruction. If it is not fostered by the curriculum, it is not likely to be learned.

The second ground on which academic rationalists argue is that all children should be introduced to basic fields of study because it is only in this way that they can discover if they have any interest in or aptitude for an area. It is through contact with the various disciplines that interests and aptitudes are stimulated. Part of the task of the school is to enable students to discover these interests and aptitudes.

It is clear that the latter argument is not as strong as the former. The number of subjects within the various modes through which humans come to know are extremely large. If biology should be taught, why not paleontology or meteorology? Interests and aptitudes could be revealed by those areas of study, as well. The school must make certain choices; it cannot teach everything. But if that is true—and it certainly seems true—what is the basis on which choices are to be made? The academic rationalist believes that the basic fields in the arts and sciences are important because they best exemplify and exercise the human's rational abilities. Their study is what education is basically about. Furthermore, within the various fields to be taught, the very best content, the most intellectually significant ideas, should be what students encounter. The greatest ideas created by the greatest writers, exemplified by the greatest works humans have produced, are the proper objects of educational attention.

An academic rationalist view of the curriculum has been admirably argued by one of its chief proponents, Robert Maynard Hutchins. When he was chancellor of the University of Chicago he established an undergraduate program that emphasized the study of the great books, the use of primary source materials, and the tradition of teaching in the context of small-group discussion. Hutchins was interested in helping students secure what he regarded as a basic liberal education, a form of education that enables students to ask basic questions about life, truth, justice, and knowledge and to read the works of individuals who have provided powerful and lasting answers to such questions. Of this form of education, Hutchins writes:

Liberal education consists of training in the liberal arts and of understanding the leading ideas that have animated mankind. It aims to help the human being learn to think for himself, to develop his highest human powers. As I have said, it has never been denied that this education was the best for the best. It must still be the best for the best unless modern times, industry, science, and democracy have made it irrelevant. The social, political, and economic changes that have occurred have not required that liberal education be abandoned. How could they? It is still necessary to try to be human; in fact it is more necessary, as well as more difficult, than ever.

Liberal education was the education of rulers. It was the education of those who had leisure. Democracy and industry, far from making liberal education irrelevant, make it indispensable and possible for all the people. Democracy makes every man a ruler, for the heart of democracy is universal suffrage. If liberal education is the education that rulers ought to have, and this I say has never been denied, then every ruler, that is every citizen, should have a liberal education. If industry is to give everybody leisure, and if leisure, as history suggests, tends to be degrading and dangerous unless it is intelligently used, then everybody should have the education that fits him to use his leisure intelligently, that is, liberal education. If leisure makes liberal education possible, and if industry is to give everybody leisure, then industry makes liberal education possible for everybody.[7]

What Hutchins and other academic rationalists argue is that schools should develop man's reason so that life can be critically examined and led intelligently. For reason to be optimized, the most appropriate pedagogical mode is dialectic discussion. Reason develops best when it is used, and if it is to be used, it should be used on the problems that are most fundamental to human existence. Because such problems have been addressed by humans of every generation and because the products of their work vary in quality, only the very best should be studied by students today. For practical purposes, this means that the curriculum should consist of not just the major academic disciplines in the arts and the sciences, but the very best, the most powerful, the most profound, the grandest of man's intellectual works within those disciplines. For the period of the past 150 years, the works of Darwin, Marx, Freud, Einstein, Ghandi, Stravinsky, Picasso, Louis Sullivan, Corbusier, Joseph Conrad, Camus, Paul Tillich, and Max Weber would receive attention. And they would receive attention in a dialectical mode: through discussion, analysis, and comparison. The central aim is to develop man's rational abilities by introducing his rationality to ideas and objects that represent reason's highest achievements.

Some might argue that such an education is fit only for a few, perhaps the "top" 10 or 15 per cent of the student population. Academic rationalists —at least those like Hutchins and Mortimer Adler—believe that all men are concerned with essentially the same fundamental questions, questions that deal with what is true, what is good, what is beautiful, how life might be examined, and the like. Although there will certainly be individual differences among students with respect to the rate at which they deal with such material and the depth to which it is penetrated, such an education, once reserved for rulers, is the right of every free person. The substitution of skimmed milk for rich educational cream is not the way to deal with individual differences when it comes to the content and aims of education.

Furthermore, the differentiation of content for students of different intellectual abilities ultimately leads to a kind of social stratification that makes it increasingly difficult for people to communicate with each other. Because no common educational grounding has been provided in the schools, the ideas people can discuss are those provided through the experiences they share. Increasingly, such experiences are provided by the mass media, and the mass media, the academic rationalists argue, have very little intellectual substance. Thus the absence of a common educational program in the long run undermines the very foundations of a social democracy. It undercuts the common intellectual base that a nation needs. But perhaps most importantly, differentiation of programs for individuals of different ability creates a self-fulfilling prophecy that sets limits to aspiration, forecloses one's options in life, and provides only a small portion of the total population with the kind of intellectual repertoire that optimally fosters the development of rationality.

PERSONAL RELEVANCE

A third orientation to curriculum is one that emphasizes the primacy of personal meaning and the school's responsibility to develop programs that make such meaning possible. In operational terms, this requires that teachers develop educational programs in concert with students rather than from a mandate handed down from the staff of a central office who don't know the child. The curriculum is to emerge out of the sympathetic interaction of teachers and students within a process called teacher-pupil planning.

A major argument supporting this orientation to curriculum is that for experience to be educational students must have some investment in it—

must have some hand in its development—and that without actual participation or the availability of real choices within the curriculum schooling is likely to be little more than a series of meaningless routines, tasks undertaken to please someone else's conception of what is important.

For a meaningful form of educational experience to occur it is critical that teachers regard children as individuals and not as mere members of a class or a group. Furthermore, the teacher must be able to establish rapport with students; he or she must understand how the child actually feels when engaged in activities in school. Without rapport it is not likely that the teacher will be in a position to understand the character of the child's experience, and unless this occurs both student and teacher are likely to deal with each other as role incumbents rather than as living creatures attempting to broaden and deepen the quality of their experience.

Another major argument underlying this view of the curriculum is that human beings from birth on are stimulus-seeking organisms, not stimulus-reducing organisms. The task of the school is to provide a resource-rich environment so that the child will, without coercion, find what he or she needs in order to grow. The metaphor is biological: growth is the aim of life.

In developing this view further, it is argued that organisms develop not so much from the outside in as they do from the inside out. Education is regarded as a process of leading forth from the native ability that the child possesses; thus, the image of the teacher is not so much that of a sculptor, someone who gives shape to formless clay, but rather that of a good gardener who cannot change the basic endowment children possess but who can provide the kind of environment that can nurture whatever aptitudes they bring with them into the world. Out of the interaction of aptitudes and environment, interests and intelligence develop. Once having discovered such interests, the teacher is to foster them by the artful construction of educational situations in which those interests can deepen and expand. Another way of identifying interests is to talk to children about their interests and thus to be in a position to provide for their development through the curriculum.

The admonition to build on the child's interest is often made as a corrective for educational programs that neglect them as sources of curriculum aims and content. Traditional educational programs are developed out of principles that identify educational value within particular subject matters or disciplines. Becoming educated means learning how to use the ideas within these disciplines. This approach, it is argued, has two educationally devastating consequences. First, it is often irrelevant to the child. Second, it fails to cultivate the child's idiosyncrasy by providing few opportunities that are of particular importance to the individual child.

In the last decade or so, A. S. Neill [8] has been a leading advocate of the philosophy that the child should play a major role in determining what he or she shall study. In the United States, the emergence of "free schools" represents a similar orientation; the child is to be given the "freedom" to choose. The teacher's responsibility is not to coerce but to facilitate. John Holt, a leading and articulate spokesman for this view of curriculum makes the case this way:

as a friend of mine put it, we teachers can see ourselves as travel agents. When we go to a travel agent, he does not tell us where to go. He finds out first what we are looking for. Do we care most about climate or scenery, or about museums and entertainment? Do we want to travel alone or with others? Do we like crowds or want to stay away from them? How much time and money do we want to spend? And so on. Given some idea of what we are looking for, he makes some suggestions. Here is this trip, which will take so long and cost so much; here is this one, here is that. Eventually, we choose, not he. Then, he helps us with our travel and hotel arrangements, gets us what tickets and information we need, and we are ready to start. His job is done. He does not have to take the trip with us. Least of all does he have to give us a little quiz when we get back to make sure we went where we said we would go or got out of the trip what we hoped to get. If anything went wrong he will want to hear about it, to help us and other clients plan better in the future. Otherwise, what we got out of the trip and how much we enjoyed it is our business.[9]

What one senses from the metaphor of teacher as travel agent is a conception of the teacher's role and of curriculum that values above all else the child's freedom to choose, and thus the opportunity to learn how to choose as a central aim of educational programs. Holt and others who share this view believe that in the process the child's talents will be cultivated; such a school allows the child to become his or her own person.

One can, of course, question the premise that the greatest of all educational goals resides in allowing children to choose what they think best. For one, choice is possible only when one has options *and* knows of their existence. Do children have the experience that will enable them to consider alternatives? If experience is limited, won't choice be limited? How can children follow their interests if they haven't had an opportunity to learn about possibilities, ideas, skills, and materials they have never dreamed of? Do children of eight, ten, twelve, or fifteen really know what's in their best interest in the long run?

What is it that children need? And who should decide? It can be and has been argued that "needs" are products of adult judgments of the gap existing between the ideals that adults hold and the state at which children are during their schooling. Schooling as an institutionalized form of education is intended to eliminate or at least reduce that gap. Furthermore, the belief that each child is so different that there can be no common educational program suitable for the vast majority is wrong to begin with. And so the counterarguments proceed. Boyd Bode, an influential American philosopher of education during the 1930s and honorary vice-president of the Progressive Education Association, underscored this point when he chastized his fellow progressive educators for overemphasizing the "needs" of children:

> The point is far more than the verbal question of how the term "need" is to be employed. It concerns the question of what education should be primarily concerned to achieve. The failure to emancipate ourselves completely from Rousseauism and the instinct psychology is responsible for most, if not all, the weaknesses of the Progressive movement in education. The attitude of superstitious reverence for childhood is still with us. The insistence that we must stick like a leech at all times to the "needs" of childhood has bred a spirit of anti-intellectualism, which is reflected in the reliance on improvising instead of long-range organization, in the over-emphasis of the here and now, in the indiscriminate tirades against "subjects," in the absurdities of project planning, and in the lack of continuity in the educational program. It has frequently resulted in an unhealthy attitude towards children, an attitude which suggests that there is no such thing as a normal child, and that we must be everlastingly exploring his insides, like a Calvinist taking himself apart day after day to discover evidence of sin.[10]

Even some of the most ardent progressives began to recognize limits of "needs" as a basis for the design of educational programs. Alas, we have yet to learn their lessons a generation later, as we search for needs not in the child but in the community through a process called needs assessment.

At present, the personal relevance orientation to curriculum is not popular. Except for a few private elementary schools and even fewer public schools, this orientation to curriculum is, in general, regarded as too laissez-faire. The demands by the American public for a return to "basics" has resulted in the creation of more structured forms of elementary and secondary schooling and more discipline. Corporal punishment is increasingly regarded as an appropriate means for dealing with unruly students.

Personal relevance as an orientation to education places a tremendous responsibility on the teacher. Prescribed content and predetermined routines and testing procedures in many ways lighten the teacher's load. They also lighten the intellectual load students must bear. A teacher who must establish rapport with students and who must create curricula that are especially suited to the aptitudes and interests of students has no small task with which to cope. Similarly, a student who must have a hand in defining the problems or projects he or she wants to undertake has a difficult intellectual problem to deal with. In this regard, it is easier to do what is expected, even if what is expected has little meaning or personal relevance. The major task in schooling for many students is to discover just what they need to do in order to get through at a level of performance they regard as acceptable for themselves. One major consequence of schools is that they often foster a form of learning that has little to do with the intellectual content of the subjects the student studies.

It is partly because the students' orientation to schooling is regarded as largely governed by extrinsic sources of motivation that those emphasizing personal relevance believe it to be so important. Schooling, they believe, is not likely to provide intellectual experience that becomes internalized unless students participate in the formulation of their goals. The elective system that most secondary schools offer is largely a hoax. In the first place, much too much of the student's program is determined by the timetable rather than by his or her choices. In the second place, institutions of higher education usually prescribe such a large number of required courses that few real choices are left for students. Students, therefore, too often find themselves waiting for the last half of their senior year when all of the required courses are out of the way to take the courses in which they have genuine interest. Their dues are paid beforehand so that they will have the freedom to pursue their education just before they are about to graduate.

What would we expect to find in a school that emphasized a personal relevance orientation to curriculum? How would time be used? How would students be evaluated? What modes of teaching would be employed? What kinds of content would be studied?

In the first place, we would probably find schools that are considerably smaller than the ones we have at present, at least smaller than those in urban areas. Size, especially when schools exceed seven or eight hundred students, often becomes an obstacle to flexibility. When one is dealing with hundreds of faculty members and thousands of students, the differentiation of programs for individuals becomes difficult. The machinery of organization takes over, despite the claim that large schools can better provide a wide array of options for students with special needs or interests.

What we would find in schools that were genuinely concerned with personal relevance is a place where interests and the demands of the tasks define the amount of time students spend in a course. We would also find small classes—perhaps with fifteen students—that were organized around a common set of interests and included students of different ages who shared that interest. Thus, for example, students of ages eleven through fourteen interested in astronomy, in weaving, in geology, or in the care and feeding of animals might work together in the same situation. It would not be assumed that all children of the same age would have to study the same content at the same rate, for the same aims, for a uniform period of time.

The role of the teacher would be one of providing sufficient structure and guidance for the child's experience to be educationally productive, but it would not be prescriptive or coercive. The teacher would be expected to stimulate and guide, to introduce the child to new materials and ideas, but the specific tasks and aims would be developed in a shared relationship. It would not be the kind of bureaucratized relationship that often occurs in forms of contract learning. Neither the student nor the student's parents would need to sign pseudolegal documents in order for commitments to be honored. Indeed, the use of such procedures would be anathema, because they exemplify many of the features in our society that those advocating truly personalized forms of education seek to ameliorate.

Evaluation would pay great attention to the processes in which students were engaged. How meaningful was the task to the child? What did he learn from it? How well, given where the child is, has the task been accomplished? What does the student believe she has learned from what she has done? How does he think the work could have been improved? What ideas did she formulate that might be pursued in forthcoming projects?

These are some of the questions that might guide an evaluation process within a personal relevance orientation to curriculum. The major focus is on the educational development of the individual child, because it is believed that it is his or her development by means of a personally relevant curriculum within a noncoercive environment that really promotes the realization of psychological freedom.

SOCIAL ADAPTATION AND SOCIAL RECONSTRUCTION

A fourth orientation to curriculum is one that derives its aims and content from an analysis of the society the school is designed to serve. In this orientation it is argued that schools are essentially institutions created to serve the interests of the society. As such their mission is to locate social needs, or at least to be sensitive to those needs, and to provide the kinds of programs that are relevant for meeting the needs that have been identified.

It is precisely in the identification of social needs that differences among various groups become most acute. One segment of the society regards the manpower needs of society as most salient, another segment the need for conformity to existing values, still another the need for children to take their place in the social order. The conception of needs among all such groups is essentially conservative; the role of the school is to maintain the status quo. If the society needs more engineers, doctors, physicists, skilled blue-collar workers, the school is regarded as the agency through which they will be provided.

Perhaps the classic case of using schools to meet social needs was the response made by Americans to Sputnik I. When on October 4, 1957, the Russians sent an unmanned satellite circling the earth, critics lambasted American schools for being lax, for failing to provide rigorous programs in mathematics and science, and even for being the prime cause of our second place in space technology. The schools were urged to remedy these deficiencies by emphasizing the teaching of mathematics and the sciences in the curriculum. The National Science Foundation, whose attention to education had preceded the rise of Sputnik I, embarked on a major funding program to support curriculum development in these areas. It was clear to many that the Russian success in space was ample evidence of our failure to offer the kind of educational program that the nation needed. From 1958 to 1968 over one hundred million dollars of federal funds was spent to sponsor curriculum development projects and to establish summer institutes for teachers of science and mathematics.

More recently people have become alarmed that many students are leaving school at age eighteen without a clear conception of the kind of vocation they wish to pursue. Children should be helped—some people believe—from the beginning of schooling at age five or six to the point at which they graduate to reflect about the world of work and to gradually develop the skills and attitudes that will increase their employability. Partly as a result of this concern, career education programs were developed. Funded by the National Institute of Education, career education curricula have been promulgated in schools in every state of the nation.

The point here is not simply to emphasize curriculum development projects in mathematics or the sciences or in career education but rather to illustrate the historical use that society has made of the schools, namely, as mechanisms for meeting what is regarded as critical needs within society.

The conception of these needs often emanates from what are regarded as particularly pressing social ills. Drug abuse, sex education, parenting programs, and ecological studies represent areas of concern for some groups, whereas black studies, sexism studies, and Chicano and Native American programs represent efforts to provide attention to what other groups believe to be important. What we see in these programs are the results of problems or deprivations that influential individuals or groups believe to exist. The curriculum becomes the vehicle for remedying such situations.

For a substantial proportion of those concerned, the needs that are perceived are not radical in nature; that is, they seek no fundamental change in the basic structure of the society. The development of a career education program, for example, seeks largely to raise the consciousness level of students to the world of work as it exists. Career education programs are not intended to encourage children or youth to consider alternatives to work as it is now generally defined or to seriously question the premises and values that give work such a central place in our lives.

A radical social perspective leads to the social reconstructionist orientation to the curriculum. This orientation is basically aimed at developing levels of critical consciousness among children and youth so that they become aware of the kinds of ills that the society has and become motivated to learn how to alleviate them. Programs having this orientation will frequently focus on controversial issues, what some writers in the social studies have called the closed areas of society: religious values, sexual preferences, political corruption, race prejudice, and the like. The aim of such programs is not primarily to help students adapt to a society that is in need of fundamental change but rather to help them to recognize the real problems and do something about them.

During the Vietnam war students in many high schools became politically involved for the first time. They felt strongly about what they believed to be moral inequities within the society—the drafting of high school dropouts while their college-going peers were exempted—and protested what they regarded as an unjustifiable war. Many of those students demanded and received in their school programs attention to the politics of the day. They demanded and received opportunities to design courses of study that they believed to be socially significant and to invite speakers to the campus who had messages that were unpopular in the general society.

At the college level, the revolt against courses that were prescribed and believed to be irrelevant to acute social needs was even stronger. The major theme in both cases—at least for some of the protesting students—was that a different view of what the school or the university should be was needed. In particular, such students argued the need to redefine their role and responsibility within the academic community. Their conception of relevance was derived not from the desire to adapt to what many of them regarded as a sick society but rather to build a new, healthier, and more just social order. The program of the school, in principle, was to support the achievement of such an end. Describing the situation during the late 1960s, Stephen Mann writes:

> A fundamental difference in world view is reflected here, and it is by virtue of this difference that the various protests blend into one. But this blending ought not to obscure what I believe is a matter of fact: that the center of gravity of student protest is nausea and rage over the way they are treated in school in the name of education. Nor is this fact mitigated by another equally apparent fact: that what passes for education is a consequence of very much the same forces as what passes for foreign policy. Protesting students are engaged in a struggle against many forms of oppression, but they are willing to put a good deal of their considerable energy and talent to work in the struggle against the oppression most immediate to their own experience, and that is the oppression of schooling.[11]

What we see here is an attack on schools and, hence, on curriculum, because of the roles students are forced to occupy. For some, who take their cues from the society, the relationship of the school to the society is essentially one of accommodation. The society orders and the school obeys. For others, educators such as Mann, the school should cultivate those attitudes and skills that will enable the young to build a better nation—indeed a better world—than the one in which they live. This means, at least for some arguing this view, that the school will have to change its structure so that it becomes *in form* what it hopes its students will learn. Thus, if bureaucratized, hierarchical social structures foster social inequities and if the school is organized on such a model, it must alter its structure in order to be effective. If it cannot change within the existing structure of state-funded schooling, alternative private schools must be established. Indeed, some individuals holding the social reconstructionist view of the curriculum are not at all sanguine about the likelihood that public schools can actually convey to students the kind of social message that they believe students need to hear. They fear that rather than the message changing the school, the school will change the message. The only viable route to the kind of curriculum that they believe significant is the establishment of alternative schools beyond the control of the existing power structure. John Galtung, a leading advocate of peace education, an orientation that is social reconstructionist in its social aims, says

First a few general remarks about the form of peace education. It has to be compatible with the idea of peace, i.e., it has in itself to exclude not only direct violence, but also structural violence. Only rarely is education nowadays sold with direct violence; the days of colonialism and corporal punishment are more or less gone. But the structural violence is there, and it takes the usual forms: a highly vertical division of labor which in this case expresses itself in one-way communication; fragmentation of the receivers of that communication so that they cannot develop horizontal interaction and organize and eventually turn the communication flow the other way; absence of true multilaterality in the education endeavor. All this relates to form; and if in addition the content of education is included, the structural violence becomes even more apparent.[12]

The curricular implications of social reconstruction for specific subject fields are profound. Content for the social studies, for example, is to be drawn from pervasive and critical social problems and from the hubs of social controversy. One does not learn how to cope with problems or controversy by systematically avoiding them in school. Content in the science curriculum is not exclusively to be drawn from the problems with which scientists work but from the individual and social problems for which scientific inquiry has some relevance: the causes and consequences of stress, community mental health, the implications of the right to die, eugenics, environmental pollution, the location of nuclear energy plants. In the arts, curriculum content might focus on the hidden forms of persuasion in advertising, the impact of new technology on the character of art forms, the ideals conveyed to the young by the mass media. What we see here is an emphasis on the questions that citizens have to deal with or that in some significant way affects their lives. One does not avoid dealing with such questions by retreating to the abstractions of the academic disciplines; one uses the knowledge provided by the academic disciplines as a tool for dealing with what is socially significant.

The other side of the social reconstruction–social adaptation orientation is aimed not primarily at preparing students to improve the social order by focusing on its problems but rather at helping students acquire the skills needed to fit into the society, largely as it is. Thus, social reconstructionism and social relevance are at opposite poles, but what they have in common is that both look to the society to decide what the aims of the school's program should be. The social reconstructionist looks at the society to locate its difficulties. Once they have been found, the program of the school is designed to help children understand these difficulties and to be able to cope with them. The person concerned with social relevance looks to society to find out what students need in order to get ahead and builds a curriculum that aims to achieve that goal.

The analysis of society as a basis for the formulation of curriculum content and goals is not as modern as one might believe. Its first formal use in American education was in the school survey movement initiated in around 1910. The major effort here was to use scientific methods to identify the strengths and weaknesses of school programs. The field of education during that time was in the process of establishing and testing its new-found scientific approach to education. University professors such as Elwood Cubberley and Jesse B. Sears were called on to provide services to schools while refining the methodology used in such work. Sear's book *The School Survey* [13] described the theory and methods of such work and appeared in 1928.

But in the field of curriculum the seminal work was done by Franklin Bobbitt, who argued that education should prepare for the fifty years of adult life the child eventually would lead and not merely be concerned with childhood, per se. To prepare for this life, "the curriculum discoverer," to use Bobbitt's term, was to identify the various areas of life for which schools should prepare the young. Bobbitt identified ten such areas. The next step, according to Bobbitt, was to identify those people in the community who displayed excellence in each of the ten areas. Their behavior, their understanding, and their attitudes, once analyzed by curriculum specialists, would constitute the goals of curriculum:

> The central theory is simple. Human life, however varied, consists in its performance of specific activities. Education that prepares for life is one that prepared definitely and adequately for these specific activities. However numerous and diverse they may be for any social class, they can be discovered. This requires that one go out into the world of affairs and discover the particulars of which these affairs consist. These will show the abilities, habits, appreciations, and forms of knowledge that men need. These will be the objectives of the curriculum. They will be numerous, definite and particularized. The curriculum will then be that series of experiences which childhood and youth must have by way of attaining those objectives. [14]

Bobbitt's view was a conservative one. But the point of his work was neither the virtue nor the vice of being conservative, it was his assumption that goals for education reside in the society and that the analysis of that society (in his case, successful adults) would provide the basis for the curriculum. Those who aim at social relevance of an adaptive variety as well as those seeking to reconstruct the social order share with Bobbitt the inclination to look to the world to find out what schools should teach. This aim they share; the images of the world that they see and the aims that they espouse, however, could not be farther apart.

CURRICULUM AS TECHNOLOGY

A fifth orientation to curriculum is normative in a way that the preceding orientations are not. It conceives of curriculum planning as being essentially a technical undertaking, a question of relating means to ends once the ends have been formulated. The central problem of the technological orientation to curriculum is not to question ends but rather to operationalize them through statements that are referenced to observable behavior. Once this task has been performed adequately, the problem is essentially one of designing appropriate means. This means-ends model of curriculum planning has the virtue of systematizing educational planning; it reminds educators to formulate purposes and to use those purposes as criteria for evaluating the efficiency and effectiveness of the plans that were made. It is argued that schools should be purposive; they should have meaningful goals, and it should be possible to determine—indeed measure—the extent to which they have been achieved. The curriculum is the course to be run; the obstacles or hurdles are the learning tasks that have been formulated. It they are well formulated, if they provide appropriate challenges and are neither too difficult nor too easy, the lessons to be learned will be learned and the objectives will be attained.

This orientation to curriculum planning, as I have already indicated, has a long history in education. Benjamin Bloom, Franklin Bobbitt, John Dewey, Virgil Herrick, Hilda Taba, Ralph Tyler, and other important educational planners and theorists have used such a model or have advocated its use. In addition, the means-ends orientation to planning is consonant with the Western world's efforts to control human activity. By conceiving of curriculum planning and teaching as technological problems, the power and precision of "applied science" could be employed in the schools, the vagaries of romanticism could be excised, and the uncertainties of art could be replaced by the replicability of the science of curriculum development and instruction.

The offshoots of this way of conceiving of proper curriculum planning are apparent in several of the major educational movements in the United States. One of these is called the accountability movement and is often associated with program-planning-budgeting systems. Although accountability can be conceived of in many ways in educational practice, it is often regarded by school administrators and members of school boards as essentially a problem of demonstrating that educational investments yield educational payoffs. The curriculum of the school is to be so designed and evaluated that teachers will be able to provide evidence of educational effectiveness. Expectations that operate in industry are transferred to the school. Because schools are intended to have a product—learning—there is no reason why the procedures used to increase the efficiency and effectiveness of factories should not also be applied to schools. Furthermore, the application of such criteria and the use of industrial management techniques give school administrators greater control over the system. Within such a rationale for curriculum, quality-control procedures are conceived of not just as a possibility but as an educational necessity.

Other spinoffs of the technological orientation to curriculum include contract teaching, programmed instruction, precision teaching, and laws such as California's Stull bill, which was designed initially to identify incompetent teachers through mandated evaluation.

What is often neglected or underestimated by those who regard the tasks of curriculum development as essentially technical ones is the way in which a technical orientation influences the values the curriculum emphasizes. Technique is never value neutral. And techniques patterned after scientific models are particularly likely to produce specific consequences for the form, content, and aims of schooling. For example, the position that curriculum development is at base a technical undertaking and the curriculum has no value position to offer regarding educational ends deprives the people with whom the specialist works of judgments about the ends to which he or she has a professional commitment. In fact, to take no position regarding ends *is* to take a value position, but it is one of absence rather than of presence, as far as educational goals are concerned.

A second consequence is the impact that a scientific technology has on the form of schooling. Scientifically based technologies place high priority on the specification of objectives, the development of units of performance that can be evaluated after relatively short time intervals, and the standardization of those features that lead to the ends that have been specified. The general tendency is to try to increase efficiency and effectiveness by the creation of routines that are common across the enterprise. In many situations, such efficiencies do emerge.

The cost of such routines, however, is not trivial if one embraces a view of education that regards the cultivation of productive idiosyncrasy a virtue. The personal relevance orientation described earlier, for example, would offer serious objections to the putative virtues of standardization within a technological orientation to curriculum.

What happens when method becomes a salient consideration is that method, or technique, becomes the criterion that defines what is acceptable. It is not at all unusual for those in school districts who review the behavioral obectives that teachers formulate to pay no attention to the substance of the objective; the concern is whether it has been stated properly—i.e., in conformance with the criteria for stating behavioral objectives. Those aims that cannot be so stated fall by the wayside. Form sets the boundaries within which the substantive goals of education can be articulated.

What would we expect to see in schools and classrooms in which the orientation to the curriculum was technological? How would teaching occur? How would students be evaluated? How would the aims of the curriculum be expressed?

One thing we could expect to see is that each teacher would have specific measurable goals for each subject area being taught. They would be, as Franklin Bobbitt said, "numerous, definite, and particularized." Furthermore, each objective would have some quantitatively defined test or test item that would be used to determine whether the student had achieved the objective. The students might be given a list of these objectives at the outset of each project or curriculum activity in order that they would fully understand what they were expected to accomplish. As far as possible all ambiguity with respect to goals would be eliminated.

At the beginning of the school year or at the beginning of a section of the curriculum, students would be pretested to determine their level of entry behavior. The measurement of these behaviors would be considered important because it would define the educational development the student had attained and would be used to prescribe the content and tasks he or she needed in order to move toward the achievement of curriculum objectives.

After this had been done, units of work would be laid out for each student or for groups of students and tests would be administered after each unit of work to monitor the achievement of students over time. When a treatment was ineffective, the student would be recycled into another set of tasks or the tasks would be revised by the teacher so that they were pedagogically more effective.

A curriculum having these features would be very sequential. Each task would build on what preceded and would prepare for what was to come. The implicit image of the curriculum is that of a staircase with few landings and no hallways feeding into it. The aim of the staircase is to increase the efficiency with which one arrives at the top floor. In a technologically oriented classroom, curriculum activities would often be available in workbooks or in boxes of sequential instructional materials. Students would come to regard it as their responsibility to proceed through the workbook or curriculum materials box on their own, although when they needed the teacher's assistance they could ask for and get it. More often than not, the materials would be color coded, so the students could know visually where they were in the program. Students would also be able to compare their location in the work to be done by comparing their colors.

Students as well as teachers would record the progress they had made by maintaining charts or records of the scores derived from their tests. In some classrooms these records would be publicly posted, particularly in the elementary grades. At the high school level, each student would record his or her score in a notebook and would be responsible for determining the final grade by calculating the average of the test scores. Specific scores would be assigned a specific meaning so that the students would know what scores they needed to achieve A, B, C, D, or F. Deviation from these standards by the teacher would be regarded as a social inequity by the students. The point in having such standards is to objectify the assessment of performance and the rewards that are provided. The tacit image of such a classroom is the efficient and effective machine.

THE IMPORT OF THE FIVE CONCEPTIONS

Again, what we find is that the dominant framework for viewing curriculum has consequences for the practical operation of schools; each orientation harbors an implicit conception of educational virtue. Furthermore, each orientation serves both to legitimize certain educational practices and to negatively sanction others. It also functions as an ideological center around which political support can be gathered.

It is difficult to overemphasize the importance of the various orientations to curriculum that have been described. Rather than being "mere abstract" philosophies that have little bearing on the conduct of educational practice, these orientations are permeated through and through with values that shape one's conception of major aspects of practice. What the teacher's role is to be is not separable from what one believes the content of the curriculum to be. If one views optimal educational practice as the form that yields predictable and measurable consequences, the teacher's' role and the character of the curriculum are partly defined. It's no good talking about nonempirical outcomes to be realized long after a course is completed if results are to be demonstrated in June. If one believes that the problems of the society should be the focus for identifying the contents of the curriculum, the likelihood of classical studies being important is remote. If one believes that the major function of the school is to ensure acquisition of the three R's, it is not likely that inductive or discovery learning will be given high priority as techniques for instruction.

Furthermore, each of the five basic orientations has specific implications for the goals and content of specific subject matter curricula. For example, *Science: A Process Approach*, a science curriculum for elementary-age children, was developed to foster certain cognitive process skills. Each unit of this curriculum is designed to sharpen children's ability to classify, to observe, to measure, and so forth. Cognitive processes play a critical role in determining what counts in scientific learning. The evaluation of the units that are taught is intended to determine whether children can employ these processes.

The significance of each of the five orientations to curriculum also becomes apparent if one considers the importance of content inclusion–content exclusion as an influence on what students learn in school. Each of the orientations emphasizes a particular conception of educational priorities. Each set of priorities defines the content and influences the climate within which students and teachers work. Thus the formulation of these priorities has a direct bearing on the kinds of opportunities for learning that students are provided. If one believes that students should learn to form their own purposes, to seek the resources with which they will work, to speculate on and consider alternative routes to an end-in-view, the ability to perform these functions and to use the modes of thought that they require is enhanced if the curriculum provides students with a climate and content to practice such skills and attitudes. A process-oriented curriculum establishes the boundaries within which such learning opportunities will be made available to students. ·

If one believes that students need to learn how to cope with the political system used in the community and that the best way to learn how to cope with it is to focus on real social problems, then it becomes important for the curriculum to provide those opportunities to students. A social reconstructionist view of the curriculum influences what shall be made available to students and what shall be regarded as of marginal educational worth.

The same ramifications exist for each of the other orientations to curriculum. Each has a consequential effect on what is included in and what is excluded from school programs as those programs operate both informally and formally. The general environment and educational climate as well as the specific content as such are influenced by the orientation to curriculum that one embraces. Because the provision of learning opportunities is probably the single most important factor influencing the content of learning in school, the importance of an orientation to curriculum can hardly be underestimated. We make a major decision about what shall be taught when we decide what image of education is most appealing.

What stance with respect to these orientations should the student of education take? Is one orientation better than the other? Are some orientations unjustifiable? There are two caveats that must be entered with respect to each of the orientations. One is the fact that they have been described independently of the context in which they are to function. They have been described as models or paradigms of educational virtue. In practice they are seldom encountered in their pure form, although in many forms of educational practice one of the five views dominates. Furthermore, because they have been described without reference to context, it is extremely difficult to determine which view is most appropriate to a particular population of children. Thus, although in general one might find one orientation closer to one's educational values than another, one might be willing to employ another view under particular circumstances.

The second caveat has to do with the problem of justification. It is my position that what distinguishes lay opinion from professional judgment with respect to the values guiding curriculum decisions is the extent to which the assets and liabilities of particular positions are recognized, as well as those of competing positions. Thus, what is reasonable to expect from a student of education are good grounds for the position or orientation embraced. This includes not only knowing what has been accepted for practice, but what has been rejected as well.

To provide such grounds in the course of argument requires a fine conceptual analysis of the problems or decisions that one encounters. It means learning how to look at a problem or decision from different perspectives and being satisfied with partial data and incomplete answers. It means knowing what research has to say, if anything, about different forms of practice. The ability to be content with inadequate data for making educational decisions is a condition of educational life. The data are never adequate to completely justify a practical decision, especially if the proposal for educational change is "innovative." In such cases, there is virtually no possibility that data will already have been provided to scientifically justify the use of a particular technique or program.

I have attempted in the preceding pages to characterize five major orientations for dealing with problems of content, aims, organization, teaching roles, and the like in designing educational programs because I believe that much of the controversy over what schools should be, how they should function, and what teachers should teach arise from conflicting assumptions and images of schooling. What we encounter at the point of controversy and contention are often the symptoms of more deep-seated differences.

I am not taking the position that one of the five orientations is better than another. Indeed, one thesis of this book is that educational decisions always must be made with an eye to the context in which the decisions are to operate. Different contexts may justify emphasis on different orientations. Furthermore, it is unlikely that any school will have only one orientation; one may dominate, but it is far more likely that schools will be somewhat eclectic in what they do. The five orientations I have described are intended to function as tools for the analysis of existing school programs and as foundations for a sharpening of discourse about the planning of new programs.

REFERENCES

1. Edward L. Thorndike and Robert S. Woodward, "The Influence of Improvement in One Mental Function Upon the Efficiency of Other Functions," *Psychological Review,* Vol. 8, 1901.

2. J. P. Guilford, *The Nature of Human Intelligence,* McGraw-Hill, New York, 1967.
3. *Taxonomy of Educational Objectives: The Cognitive Domain* (Benjamin Bloom, ed.), Longmans, Green and Co., 1956.
4. *Science: A Process Approach,* Commission on Science Education, American Association for the Advancement of Science, Washington, D.C., 1965.
5. *Elementary School Science Project,* University of California Printing Department, Berkeley, Calif., 1966.
6. Jerome Bruner, *The Process of Education,* Harvard University Press, Cambridge, Mass., 1961.
7. Robert Maynard Hutchins, *The Conflicts in Education in a Democratic Society,* Harper, New York, 1953.
8. A. S. Neill, *Summerhill,* Hart Publishing Co., New York, 1960.
9. John Holt, *What Do I Do Monday?* Dell Publishing Co., New York, 1970, pp. 70–71.
10. Boyd H. Bode, "The Concept of Needs in Education," *Progressive Education,* Vol. 15, No. 1, 1938, p. 9.
11. Stephen Mann, "Political Power and the High School Curriculum," in *Conflicting Conceptions of Curriculum* (Elliot W. Eisner and Elizabeth Vallance, eds.), McCutchan Publishing Co., Berkeley, Calif., 1974, pp. 148–149.
12. John Galtung, "On Peace Education," *Handbook on Peace Education* (Christoph Wulf, ed.), International Peace Research Association Frankfurt-Main, 1974, p. 155.
13. Jesse B. Sears, *The School Surveys,* Houghton Mifflin, New York, 1925.
14. Franklin Bobbitt, *The Curriculum,* Houghton Mifflin, Boston, 1918, p. 42.

5

The Three Curricula That All Schools Teach

Perhaps the greatest of all pedagogical fallacies is the notion that a person learns only the particular thing he is studying at the time.

JOHN DEWEY

THE EXPLICIT AND IMPLICIT CURRICULA

In the preceding chapter five basic ways were described in which the goals, content, and methods of curriculum have been conceived. These five orientations provide a way of rationalizing what schools teach. But schools teach much more—and much less—than they intend to teach. Although much of what is taught is explicit and public, a great deal is not. Indeed, it is my claim that schools provide not one curriculum to students, but three, regardless of which of the five curriculum orientations a school follows. The aim in this chapter is to examine those three curriculums in order to find out how they function.

One of the most important facts about schooling is that children spend a major portion of their childhood in school. By the time the student has graduated from secondary school, he or she has spent approximately 480 weeks or 12,000 hours, in school. During this time the student has been immersed in a culture that is so natural a part of our way of life that it is almost taken for granted. In that culture called schooling there are certain publicly explicit goals: teaching children to read and write, to figure, and to learn something about the history of the country, among them. There are, of course, other aims, many of which are associated with the explicit curriculum that the school offers to the students. There are goals and objectives for the sciences, the arts, physical education, social studies, and foreign language instruction. Not only do these goals appear in school district curriculum guides and the course-planning materials that teachers are asked to prepare, the public also knows that these courses are offered and that students in the dis-

74

trict will have the opportunity to achieve these aims, at least to some degree, should they want to do so. In short, the school offers to the community an educational menu of sorts; it advertises what is is prepared to provide. From this advertised list, students have, at least in principle, an array of options from which to choose.

But is this all that schools offer? Does this advertised menu exhaust what schools teach? The answer to these questions is clear: no. Work by Dreeben [1], Jackson[2], Sarason,[3] and others provides an extensive analysis of what has come to be known as the "hidden curriculum." Dreeben focuses on the sociological dimensions of the hidden curriculum, whereas Jackson and Sarason attend largely to its psychological aspects. Schools socialize children to a set of expectations that some argue are profoundly more powerful and longer-lasting that what is intentionally taught or what the explicit curriculum of the school publicly provides. Take, for example, that form of human behavior called initiative. It is possible to create a school environment in which the taking of initiative becomes an increasingly important expectation as children mature. In such an environment, as children got older they would be expected to assume greater responsibility for their planning; they would be expected increasingly to define their goals and determine the kinds of resources that they will need to pursue the ends they have formulated. One general goal of such an institution would be to enable children to become the mappers of their educational journey, so that when they leave school they are in a position to pursue goals and interests that are important to them. If this were an important aspiration of schools, schools would make it possible in dozens of ways for initiative to be developed; it would be a part of the culture of schooling.

Critics of schooling point out, however, that rather than cultivate initiative, schools foster compliant behavior. One of the first things a student learns—and the lesson is taught throughout his or her school career—is to provide the teacher with what the teacher wants or expects. The most important means for doing this is for the student to study the teacher, to learn just how much effort must be expended for an A, a B, or a C grade. How long should the term paper be is a question heard not only in secondary school, it is heard in graduate school, as well. Of course, such a request for information is not entirely unreasonable; one does want to know something about the general expectations. Yet, too often, the issue becomes the expectation and the need to meet it in the most expeditious way possible. This tendency to foster compliant forms of behavior is often exacerbated by programs that use behavior modification techniques. I was in one third-grade classroom in a wealthy San Francisco suburb where I noticed that on the wall of the room there was a chart on which each student's name was listed. Next to each name was a set of twenty boxes and in every fifth box was a picture of a smiling face. I asked one of the children what the chart was for, and he replied that after they completed reading a book they colored in one of the boxes. I then asked what the smiling faces were for. He replied that when they had read five books and therefore reached a smiling face, they got a goldenrod ticket, three of which were good for leave to go to lunch five minutes early.

There are a host of educational issues that could be identified and discussed concerning the use of such a reward system, but for now the point will remain with the fostering of compliant behavior. Such a reward system holds out to children something they apparently want and fosters a willingness to perform. In using such a system, the teacher or the school can, of course, increase or decrease the size or attractiveness of the reward to bring out the desired behavior at the lowest cost. Regardless of the type or size of the reward, the point remains the same: the school seeks to modify the child's behavior to comply with goals that the child had no hand in formulating and that might not have any intrinsic meaning.

Now, in some respects, the use of rewards to reinforce or control behavior is a ubiquitous part of our culture, indeed of all cultures. Insofar as there are conventions, mores, customs, sanctions, and the like in culture, there will be forms of behavior that are positively rewarded and others that are sanctioned negatively. The question is not whether there should or could be a cultural institution without procedures for monitoring, rewarding, and punishing those who are a part of that institution. The major question deals with the pervasiveness of such conditions and their appropriateness, given the institution's explicit mission. If an institution utilizes expedient means for the management of students that, while doing so, interferes with the realization of some of its primary purposes, there is reason for questioning such "expedient" means.

I would not like to give the impression that the use of such rewards is the primary way in which compliant behavior is elicited and sustained. The factors that sustain such behavior are in a significant sense built into the ways in which roles are defined in schools. Take, for example, the expectation that students must not speak unless called on, or the expectation that virtually all of the activities within a course shall be determined by the teacher, or the fact that schools are organized hierarchically, with the student at the bottom rung of the ladder, or that communication proceeds largely from the top down. What does such a system teach the young, who must spend up to 480 weeks of their childhood there? What does it mean to children to engage in a wide array of tasks that often have little or no intrinsic meaning to them in order to cope with the school successfully?

For those who have analyzed the implicit curriculum of the school and what it teaches, these lessons are among the most important ones that children learn. It is pointed out that most children will not have jobs in adult life that are intrinsically interesting. Most jobs do not afford an individual the opportunity to define his or her purposes. Most jobs depend on the use of extrinsic motivation to sustain interest. Most jobs do not provide for high degrees of intellectual flexibility. Most jobs depend on routine. From the standpoint of the type of work that most Americans will engage in during the course of their careers, one could argue that schools provide excellent preparation. Schools prepare most people for positions and contexts that in many respects are quite similar to what they experienced in school as students: hierarchical organization, one-way communication, routine; in short, compliance to purposes set by another.

Compliant behavior is only one of several kinds of behavior that schools foster. Some of these might be considered positive. I use compliance here simply for illustrative purposes. Take as another example competitiveness. Do schools teach children to compete, and do they encourage competitiveness? One way, and perhaps the most obvious way in which competitiveness is fostered, is through athletic competition. Athletic leagues engender a need to win by beating the other person or team. The metaphor is apt. One succeeds only at a price paid by another. But there are other forms of competition that are not so obvious that are also at work in schools. One of these is formal grading practices. When students are assigned grades based on the expectation that the distribution of scores or performance will be statistically normal, the relationship students are forced into is one of competition. If only students with the highest 10 per cent of scores can receive an A grade, then clearly one student's A is another student's B. Again, one wins only at the cost of beating another. When the stakes are high, as they are when students are seeking admission to universities, medical schools, and law schools, it is not unheard of for some students to destroy the work of others or to check out or mutilate books needed by other students to successfully compete. Knowing well what will count, some students use whatever means necessary to gain an advantage.

Because it is extreme, such behavior is not characteristic in schools and universities and, depending on one's social vision, competitiveness, could be viewed as the engine of human progress, something that schools would be well advised to encourage.

Competitiveness is not only fostered by the grading system, it is also fostered by the differentiation of classes into ability groups. For example, most comprehensive secondary schools and even a large percentage of elementary schools differentiate students into three or more ability groups, in, say, mathematics or English. Students who successfully compete for grades are rewarded not only by grades, but also by admission to honors classes. This assignment to classes in which one is honored by being in an honors class often becomes something highly valued by parents and students. Yet, why should students whose background or genetic makeup is advantageous be rewarded in this public way? Is it the case that the less able are less honorable or less worthy? This is not far from a cultural truth. The word *virtuoso* means someone who is good at something. The word *virtue* means good. The association historically and culturally between being good at something and being good is of long standing. Thus, combined with the Calvinist tradition of associating failure with sin and success with goodness, it is not surprising that quicker students are honored by being assigned to honors classes.

Consider as still another example of the implicit curriculum the impact of time on the students' perception of what counts in school. In planning school programs one of the decisions that must be made is when various sub-ects will be taught and how much time will be devoted to them. Although such decisions are not intended to reflect to students' value judgments about the significance of various subject areas, in fact, they do. Students learn in school to read the value code that pervades it. One of these coded qualities is the use and location of time. Take as a specific example the location and amount of time devoted to the arts in school programs. Virtually all ele-mentary school programs devote some attention to the arts. But if one asks about how much and compares it to the amount of time devoted to, say, social studies, reading, mathematics, or the sciences, the proportion is quite small. But if one looks further to determine when the arts are taught, one will find that they are generally taught in the afternoon rather than in the morning and often on Friday afternoon.

What this conveys to the student is that the arts are essentially forms of play that one can engage in only after the real work of schooling has been finished. In the morning, students are fresh; they can cope at this time with the rigors of reading and mathematics. In the afternoon, the arts can be used as a reward, as a break from the demands of thinking. This reinforces the belief that the arts do not require rigorous and demanding thought and that they are really unimportant aspects of the school program. The idea that the arts deal with feeling and that reading and arithmetic deal with thinking is a part of the intellectual belief structure that separates cognition from affect, a structure whose consequences are as deleterious for educa-tional theory as they are for psychology.

The major point I am trying to make here is one of illustrating the fact that schools teach far more than they advertise. Function follows form. Fur-thermore, it is important to realize that what schools teach is not simply a function of covert intentions; it is largely unintentional. What schools teach they teach in the fashion that the culture itself teaches, because schools are the kinds of places they are.

The recognition of the impact of the hidden, implicit curriculum is rela-tively new. Aside from Willard Waller's *The Sociology of the School*, there was little interest in the educational consequences of schooling, per se, until the 1960s. It was during that decade that work by Dreeben, Jackson, and Sar-ason was first published. What students of education began to recognize was what Lewis Mumford was talking about in 1934 in his *Technics and Civiliza-tion*. At that time Mumford wrote:

One may define this aspect of the machine as "purposeless materialism." Its particular defect is that it casts a shadow of reproach upon all the non-material interests and occupations of mankind: in particular, it condemns liberal esthetic and intellectual interests because "they serve no useful purpose." One of the blessings of invention, among the naive advocates of the machine, is that it does away with the need for the imagination: instead of holding a conversation with one's distant friend in reverie, one may pick up a telephone and substitute his voice for one's fantasy. If stirred by an emotion, instead of singing a song or writing a poem, one may turn on a phonograph record. It is no disparagement of either the phonograph or the telephone to suggest that their special functions do not take the place of a dynamic imaginative life, nor does an extra bathroom, however admirably instrumental, take the place of a picture or a flower-garden. The brute fact of the matter is that our civilization is now weighted in favor of the use of mechanical instruments, because the opportunities for commercial production and for the exercise of power lie there: while all the direct human reactions or the personal arts which require a minimum of mechanical paraphernalia are treated as negligible. The habit of producing goods whether they are needed or not, of utilizing inventions whether they are useful or not, of applying power whether it is effective or not pervades almost every department of our present civilization. The result is that whole areas of the personality have been slighted: the telic, rather than the merely adaptive, spheres of conduct exist on sufferance. This pervasive instrumentalism places a handicap upon vital reactions which cannot be closely tied to the machine, and it magnifies the importance of physical goods as symbols—symbols of intelligence and ability and farsightedness—even as it tends to characterize their absence as a sign of stupidity and failure. And to the extent that this materialism is purposeless, it becomes final: the means are presently converted into an end. If material goods need any other justification, they have it in the fact that the effort to consume them keeps the machines running.[4]

Mumford was concerned with the quality of life that technologically advanced societies were rapidly developing and believed that technology would get out of hand, become master rather than servant to man. Forty years later we find Ivan Illich expressing a similar concern.

Speaking of the distinction between convivial and anticonvivial tools, Illich holds that most tools used in industrial societies restrict rather than expand human freedom. He believes their impact on society to be socially devastating and calls therefore for a reconstruction of society in a form that would make convivial life possible:

A convivial society should be designed to allow all its members the most autonomous action by means of tools least controlled by others. People feel joy, as opposed to mere pleasure, to the extent that their activities are creative; while the growth of tools beyond a certain point increases regimentation, dependence, exploitation, and impotence. I use the term "tool" broadly enough to include not only simple hardware such as drills, pots, syringes, brooms, building elements, or motors, and not just large machines like cars or power stations; I also include among tools productive institutions such as factories that produce tangible commodities such as those which produce "education," "health," "knowledge," or "decisions." I use this term because it allows me to subsume into one category all rationally designed devices, be they artifacts or rules, codes or operators, and to distinguish all these planned and engineered instrumentalities from other things such as basic food or implements, which in a given culture are not deemed to be subject to rationalization. School curricula or marriage laws are no less purposely shaped social devices than road networks.[5]

Illich, a leading critic of formal schooling, is concerned with what he believes are the pervasive use of anticonvivial tools. He believes such tools—and the term *tool* refers to anything that can be used—impose themselves on the lives of individuals and groups in such a way as to close rather than open options, divide rather than unify the polity. The tool becomes a master that manages the lives of people. Furthermore, tools interlock and reinforce their power to control. If one is caught in a traffic jam, one misses one's plane at the airport. If this happens, the connection in Denver is also missed, which means that one cannot make an obligatory meeting in New York, which, in turn, will have other consequences.

Although Illich is writing about technological societies at large, the points he makes about them can be applied to schools. We divide time to create schedules that produce a degree of neatness and predictability for the use of school resources. When a school has two thousand students, as many schools have, it is important to develop an organizational pattern that avoids chaos. The timetable and computerized class schedule regulate operations. At the same time, such procedures impose a kind of rigidity that requires that regardless of what one is doing, regardless of how well it is going, one must stop working and move on to the next class. Another class is waiting to move in. Every fifty minutes, an entire school population of two thousand students and sundry teachers plays musical chairs.

Now, clearly, one must weigh the benefits of using time this way against the costs. It might very well be that the benefits outweigh the costs. I am not arguing now that they do not. The point, however, is not whether such a schedule constitutes an educational vice or virtue, it is that the structure of the school day itself has educational consequences for both students and teachers. The timetable teaches. What the timetable teaches is interesting to speculate about. For one thing it may teach students to be cognitively flexible, to be able to shift problems and adapt to new demands on schedule. It may teach students not to get too involved in what they do because to become too involved is to court frustration when time runs out. Such a schedule may teach students the importance of punctuality: they need to be where they are supposed to be, on time, eight times a day.

These aspects of the culture of schooling no school district advertises; indeed, there are few teachers or school administrators who conceptualize the latent lessons of school structure this way. The culture one is immersed in is often the most difficult to see. Yet, because these aspects of the life of schooling are so pervasive, their effects might be especially important. After all, the westward movement is studied for only a few weeks in the fall of the fifth grade, but the impact of school structure does not cease until one leaves graduate school.

It is trendy, or at least it has been, to consider the implicit curriculum as having an entirely negative impact as far as education is concerned. But this is not necessarily true. The implicit curriculum of the school can teach a host of intellectual and social virtues: punctuality, a willingness to work hard on tasks that are not immediately enjoyable, and the ability to defer immediate gratification in order to work for distant goals can legitimately be viewed as positive attributes of schooling. They form no formal part of the curriculum, yet they are taught in school. Indeed, I believe that parents know they are taught, not perhaps at a critically conscious level, but more or less intuitively. This is perhaps best illustrated by two examples: the attractiveness of prestigious universities and the recent interest in more structured forms of elementary education.

What is it that makes Princeton, Yale, Harvard, Stanford, Swarthmore, Smith, and Radcliffe attractive places for so many aspiring middle-class students? A part of the reason is undoubtedly the excellence of the faculties at such institutions. The extensiveness of the libraries might also play a role. But one cannot easily discount the tacit appreciation of the general culture that pervades these schools. Colleges and universities with lesser reputations also teach most of the courses offered at these institutions. Indeed, the explicit curricula across universities in the United States are very much the same. But what does differ is the recognition that universities also present students with a way of life, a set of standards, a distribution of students coming from particular social classes, and levels of academic achievement that will have an important impact on entering students. If one visits university campuses across the country, one is struck by both their sameness and their differences. Some universities monitor or attempt to monitor students' behavior in much the same way as some high schools. Others give the impression that within their hallowed walls reside the seeds of social revolution. Still others have a kind of cool intellectual pride, a sense of scholarly self-esteem that sets the institution aside from the more prosaic forms of cultural life. Such environments, developed through tradition, have selection procedures for staff as well as students that provide an implicit curriculum whose specific goals are not articulated and might not even be consciously recognized. It is something one senses. Many parents as well as students recognize such qualities and guide their children to places whose implicit curriculum is compatible with their values and with the levels of social, economic, and academic achievements to which they aspire.

Similar factors are at work in the motivation among parents to create within school districts more structured forms of elementary education. Although the return to the so-called basics movement is a part of this motivation, the back-to-basics movement cannot be easily separated from larger, more general values. For example, in a suburb near Stanford University a small group of parents petitioned the school board to create a structured elementary school for their children. As a result of this petition and because some school board members were supportive of the proposal, the board offered to make a part of one elementary school a structured school, with a principal who was sympathetic to such a program. However, the board said that parents who did not want their children in such a program would have the option of having them attend parallel, nonstructured classes within the same school, This proposal by the board was not good enough. The parents seeking a more structured elementary school argued that is was necessary for the entire school to be structured, not just a part of it, because "what happens to students on the playground is as important as what happens in classes." What the parents were correctly pointing out was that in order for the school to be optimally effective, in their terms, the entire environment needed to be taken into account. They did not want the values they thought would be fostered within the classroom vitiated by those that their children would encounter in the schoolyard.

The implicit curriculum of the school is not only carried by the organizational structure of the school and by the pedagogical rules that are established in school—in some high schools students must carry a pass to show hall guards that they have permission to use the washroom—but is also manifested in more subtle ways. Consider for a moment school architecture and the design of school furniture. Most school rooms are designed as cubicles along corridors and have a kind of antiseptic quality to them. They tend to be repetitive and monotonous in the same way that some hospitals and factories are. They speak of efficiency more than they do of comfort. Where, for example, aside from the teachers' lounge, can one find a soft surface in a secondary or junior high school? Schools tend not to be designed with soft surfaces. They tend to look like most of the furniture that goes into them. Most of the furniture is designed for easy maintenance, is uncomfortable and is visually sterile. Plastics can be used in attractive ways, but instead wood-grained formica is used to make desks that restrict the ways in which one can sit and that yield to no form of body pressure. Rooms seldom have a soft relief; there are few places for enclosure or for privacy. The point here is not so much to chastise school architects but to point out that the buildings that we build do at least two things: they express the values we cherish, and, once built, they reinforce those values. Schools are educational churches, and our gods, judging from the altars we build, are economy and efficiency. Hardly a nod is given to the spirit.

Thus, the implicit curriculum of the school is what it teaches because of the kind of place it is. And the school is that kind of place through the ancillary consequences of various approaches to teaching, by the kind of reward system that it uses, by the organizational structure it employs to sustain its existence, by the physical characteristics of the school plant, and by the furniture it uses and the surroundings it creates. These characteristics constitute some of the dominant components of the school's implicit curriculum. Although these features are seldom publicly announced, they are intuitively recognized by parents, students, and teachers. And because they are salient and pervasive features of schooling, what they teach may be among the most important lessons a child learns.

THE NULL CURRICULUM

There is something of a paradox involved in writing about a curriculum that does not exist. Yet, if we are concerned with the consequences of school programs and the role of curriculum in shaping those consequences, then it seems to me that we are well advised to consider not only the explicit and implicit curricula of schools but also what schools do *not teach*. It is my thesis that what schools do not teach may be as important as what they do teach. I argue this position because ignorance is not simply a neutral void; it has important effects on the kinds of options one is able to consider, the alternatives that one can examine, and the perspectives from which one can view a situation or problem. The absence of a set of considerations or perspectives or the inability to use certain processes for appraising a context biases the evidence one is able to take into account. A parochial perspective or simplistic analysis is the inevitable progeny of ignorance.

In arguing this view I am not suggesting that any of us can be without bias or that we can eventually gain a comprehensive view of all problems or issues. I do not believe that is possible, nor do I believe that we would be able to know whether our view was comprehensive, for to know that would require that one know everything that was applicable to the problem. Such a perspective requires omnipotence. Yet if one mission of the school is to foster wisdom, weaken prejudice, and develop the ability to use a wide range of modes of thought, then it seems to me we ought to examine school programs to locate those areas of thought and those perspectives that are now absent in order to reassure ourselves that these omissions were not a result of ignorance but a product of choice.

In identifying the null curriculum there are two major dimensions that can be considered. One is the intellectual processes that schools emphasize and neglect. The other is the content or subject areas that are present and absent in school curricula.

Consider first the intellectual processes that are now emphasized in school programs. Discourse in education, both in the public schools and in University schools and departments of education, has placed a great deal of emphasis on the development of cognitive processes. Cognition is supposed to be contrasted with affect, which in turn is contrasted with psychomotor activity. This trilogy is believed to exhaust the major parameters of mind. Cognition, the story goes, deals with thinking, affect with feeling, and psychomotor activity with acting or skill performance. Once these distinctions are made, they tend to become reified, a process that is encouraged by the use of taxonomies for the formulation of behavioral objectives within each of the three "domains": cognitive, affective, and psychomotor. Aside from the problems inherent in the reification of distinctions among thinking, feeling, and acting, cognition itself has come to mean thinking with words or numbers by using logical procedures for their organization and manipulation and not thinking in its broadest sense. The term *cognitive* originally meant the process through which the organism becomes aware of the environment. *The Dictionary of Psychology* offers this definition: "a generic term used to designate all processes involved in knowing. It begins with immediate awareness of objects in perception and extends to all forms of reasoning." [6] Yet, in the literature of education the term has been impoverished, and in the process what we consider to be thinking has also been diminished. Thus there is the irony of cognition becoming increasingly important in educational discourse while it is being robbed of its scope and richness.

What school programs tend to emphasize is the development of a restricted conception of thinking. Not all thinking is mediated by word or numbers, nor is all thinking rule abiding.

Many of the most productive modes of thought are nonverbal and alogical. These modes operate in visual, auditory, metaphoric, synesthetic ways and utilize forms of conception and expression that far exceed the limits of logically prescribed criteria or discursive or mathematical forms of thinking. When attention to such intellectual processes, or forms, of thinking is absent or marginal, they are not likely to be developed within school programs, although their development might take place outside of school. But the consequences within schools for students when such modes of thought and expression are absent or given low priority are significant. The criteria that are employed for assessing intellectual competence must of necessity focus on the forms of thinking and experience that are available and salient. Thus, not only does the neglect or absence from school programs of nondiscursive forms of knowing skew what can be known and expressed in schools, it also biases the criteria through which human competence and intelligence are appraised.

When we look at school curricula with an eye toward the full range of intellectual processes that human beings can exercise, it quickly becomes apparent that only a slender range of those processes is emphasized. When one also considers the fact that some of the most interesting work going on in the field of brain physiology is pointing out that the hemispheres of the brain are specialized, that the right and left hemispheres perform different intellectual functions, and that those functions can atrophy or strengthen with use or disuse, the neglect of what are erroneously referred to as affective processes is particularly significant. Researchers studying brain functions have demonstrated that the left hemisphere is the seat of speech—a fact known since the nineteenth century. But they have more recently demonstrated that what in previous years has been regarded as the minor hemisphere is not minor at all. The right hemisphere provides the location for much of the visualization processes, it is the seat of metaphoric and poetic thought, and it is where structure-seeking forms of intellectual activity have their home. Writing cogently about research on hemispheric specialization, Gabrielle Rico says:

These findings bespeak a partial redundancy in the two halves of the brain, operating to prevent the individual from being totally incapacitated should disaster strike one or the other hemisphere. But beyond redundancy of function, such evidence lends credence to Bogen's suggestion that a more fundamental distinction between the two hemispheres is not so much a distinction between material or content specificity (speech or faces) as between process specificity. How, then, can these differing processing capacities best be characterized? A question certainly far from resolved. But there are signs pointing the way:

1. If the left hemisphere is better able to process sequentially ordered information, the right is better at simultaneous patterning. Special tests by Levy Agresti (1968) show a right hemisphere superiority for matching spatial forms, suggesting to her that it is a synthesis in dealing with information. Furthermore, one of the most obvious symptoms to follow right hemisphere damage is the patient's inability to copy block designs (Bogen, 1970) or to arrange blocks in a required pattern. There is also evidence that the left hemipsphere tends to classify objects according to related linguistic categories, whereas the right tends to connect objects which are structurally isomorphic. Nebes (1975) writes, "the left hemisphere tends to choose items which are similar in their use—i.e., if shown a cake on a plate it might pick out a fork and spoon, while the right selects objects unrelated in use but structurally similar—a round straw hat with a brim" (p. 16).

2. If the left is better able to cope with familiar, learned, habitual configurations, the right is better able to handle unfamiliar configurations: in tests those which were unfamiliar and therefore not susceptible to verbal labels—random shapes, unusual textures—were processed by the right hemisphere, totally baffling the left. Furthermore, shapes easily categorized by language, such as ♡ or → were readily processed by the left (Nebes, 1975, p. 14).

In addition, the right hemisphere is better able to reconstitute the whole of a figure after being exposed to only a small number of its elements (Bogen, 1972, p. 52).

3. If the left hemisphere is better able to handle time-ordered stimulus sequences, the right is superior for processing time-independent stimulus configurations (Gordon and Bogen, 1975). Carotid amytal injection is a method in which a drug is injected into one or the other hemisphere to immobilize it for 3–5 minutes. This method has confirmed that the left is specialized for time-ordered sentences, paragraphs, phrases which were retrieved according to grammatical rules and ordered into a specific temporal arrangement. In contrast, the right hemisphere was better able to retrieve songs and melodies which are remembered and produced as intact wholes (presentationally), not as units pieced together tone by tone, word by word. Gordan and Bogen suggests that the ability to store and recall intact such large units may be an important aspect of those tasks for which the right hemisphere of most individuals is dominant.[7]

What Rico is pointing out are some of the major conclusions of a body of research on the functions of the brain that has been going on over the last twenty years. This research provided a useful perspective for examining what school programs provide, what they cultivate, and what they neglect. If we are concerned in schools with the development of productive thought, if we are interested in strengthening those processes through which invention, boundary pushing, and boundary breaking occur, then it seems reasonable that school curriculum should provide children with the opportunities to use those processes in the course of their work. It is not beyond the realm of possibility that every course that now occupies a position within schools could foster such processes. This would, of course, require that the curriculum activities planned, and particularly the kinds of tests that are used, elicit and reward such processes. The cultivation of imagination is not a utopian aspiration.

The neglect of such processes within schools, assuming they are not adequately fostered outside of schools, can lead to a kind of literalness in perception and thought that impedes the appreciation of those objects or ideas that best exemplify metaphorical modes of thinking. Take as an example the reading of poetry or literature. What will a strictly literal construction of the following poem render?

> you shall above all things be glad and young,
> For if you're young, whatever life you wear
> it will become you; and if you are glad
> whatever's living will yourself become.
> Girlboys may nothing more than boygirls need;
> i can entirely her only love
> whose any mystery makes every man's
> flesh put space on; and his mind take off time
> that you should ever think, may godforbid
> and (in his mercy) your true lover spare:
> for that way knowledge lies, the foetal grave
> called progress, and negation's dead undoom.
> I'd rather learn from one bird how to sing
> than teach ten thousand stars how not to dance[8]

Now take the last couplet in that poem,

> I'd rather learn from one bird how to sing
> then teach ten thousand stars how not to dance.

To penetrate the meaning of that couplet, to grasp the allusions it contains, requires one to free oneself from literal perceptions of meaning and to apprehend the import of the images in the poetry itself. Although these images are not literally translatable, there are a lot of things we can say about them.

Learning is a humble thing compared to teaching. To teach puts one in a superordinate position, to learn in the position of a subordinate. Learners are seldom philanthropists. But who would the poet rather learn from: not Einstein, or Marx, or Darwin, but from a bird. And what would he rather learn: to understand the universe, to be able to turn dross into gold, to be able to create atomic fission? No. He'd rather learn to sing. He'd rather learn to do something that gives joy to life from one of the most fragile of God's creatures than to teach the largest bodies of our universe itself how not to dance.

But who teaches stars not to dance? How does one teach stars not to do something. Astronomers do. Astronomers teach us that stars do not dance. What we see are simply the light waves that flicker as they traverse the atmosphere. The poet E. E. Cummings chooses joy over knowledge. But to know *that,* no liberal reading will do. An ability to allow one's imagination to grasp and play with the qualitative aspects of Cummings's impression is a necessary condition for recovering the meaning the poet has created.

Schools have a role, it seems to me, to offer the young an opportunity to develop the kinds of intellectual processes that will be useful for dealing with the likes of E. E. Cummings and other poets who have given the world its poetry.

Such processes are not restricted to poetry; they function in any sphere of human activity in which new patterns must be perceived, where literal perception will not do, when multiple meanings must be understood, where intimation, nuance, and analogy are at work. Consider the following passage from Aleksandr Solzhenitsyn's *Gulag Archipelago:*

Spring promises everyone happiness—and tenfold to the prisoner. Oh, April sky! It didn't matter that I was in prison. Evidently, they were not going to shoot me. And in the end I would become wiser here. I would come to understand many things here, Heaven! I would correct my mistakes yet, O Heaven, not for them but for you, Heaven! I had come to understand those mistakes here, and I would correct them!

As if from a pit, from the far-off lower reaches, from Szerzhinsky Square, the hoarse earthly singing of the automobile horns rose to us in a constant refrain. To those who were dashing along to the tune of those honkings, they seemed the trumpets of creation, but from here their insignificance was very clear.

In the first place, it was very interesting to try to figure out the layout of the entire prison while they were taking you there and back, and to calculate where those tiny hanging courtyards were, so that at some later date, out in freedom, one could walk along the square and spot their location. We made many turns on the way there, and I invented the following system: Starting from the cell itself, I would count every turn to the right as plus one, and every turn to the left as minus one. And, no matter how quickly they made us turn, the idea was not to try to picture it hastily to oneself, but to count up the total. If, in addition, through some staircase window, you could catch a glimpse of the backs of the Lubyanks water nymphs, half-reclining against the pillared turret which hovered over the square itself, and you could remember the exact point in your count when this happened, then back in the cell you could orient yourself and figure out what your window looked out on.[9]

To understand this passage requires an ability and willingness to make the connection between spring and promises, to recognize its sense of growing life, and to appreciate how the experience of an April sky can be caught in "Oh, April sky!"—the tempo of the passage, the contrast of life and death, of heaven and prison, of the cacophony and the din of motor cars outside where life bustles and the cool systematic efforts to sustain that life in one-self by counting the turns en route to one's cell. An educational program that provides little or no opportunity for students to refine the processes that make such understanding possible is likely to yield a population ill prepared to read the world's great literature. But, perhaps even more importantly, it is likely to withhold from students the joys of intellectual discovery.

The major point I have been trying to make thus far is that schools have consequences not only by virtue of what they do teach, but also by virtue of what they neglect to teach. What students cannot consider, what they don't know, processes they are unable to use, have consequences for the kinds of lives they lead. I have directed my attention in the preceding section to the school's general neglect of particular intellectual processes. Let me now turn to the content or subject matter side of the coin.

Why is it that the vast majority of schools in the United States at both the elementary and secondary levels teach virtually the same subject matters? Let us assume for the moment that basic reading skills, basic arithmetic skills, and basic skills of writing, including spelling, grammar, and punctuation, are necessary parts of virtually all elementary school programs. But even given this assumption, why are time, space, and energy given over to advanced forms of mathematics, history, the sciences, and physical education? Why do most secondary schools require three years of English, two years of mathematics, and one or two years of science? Why do they require two or three years of U.S. history or social studies? Why is it that law, economics, anthropology, psychology, dance, the visual arts, and music are frequently not offered or are not required parts of secondary school programs? Why do so few schools offer work in filmmaking, in the study of communication, in the study of war and revolution? In raising these questions I am not now making a brief that these particular subject matters replace those that now occupy a secure place in school programs. I am trying to point out that certain subject matters have been traditionally taught in schools not because of a careful analysis of the range of other alternatives that could be offered but rather because they have traditionally been taught. We teach what we teach largely out of habit, and in the process neglect areas of study that could prove to be exceedingly useful to students. Take, as an example, economics.

Economics is presently taught in less than 10 per cent of all secondary schools in the United States. Now economic theory is not something one is likely to learn simply through the process of socialization. One does not encounter economic theory as one might encounter various forms of social behavior. Yet economics provides one of the frames of reference that enables one to understand how our social system operates. Indeed, to take advantage of the economic opportunities that this nation affords, it is useful to know something of the economic structure of the society, to understand how capital can be used to increase income, to know how to read a stock market report—in short, to have what is needed to make the most out of the resources one has. Yet such problems and the subject matters within which they appear seldom receive attention within schools, say, in comparison to sentential calculus or advanced forms of geometry. The null curriculum includes the study of economics.

Take as another example the study of law. What does a lay person need to know about the law to understand his or her rights, the basic ways in which our legal system works, the rights and obligations incurred in the signing of a contract? What does it mean to be arrested? What is the difference between a criminal and civil suit? What is a tort and when has a crime been committed? Although I realize that such seemingly simple questions are extraordinarily complex, the same holds true for virtually all other fields in which a student works. Students could be introduced to the study of law first because the problems that it poses are interesting and rich—there is much that could be related to their lives in a fairly direct fashion—and second because it is important for citizens to know something about the legal system under which they live so that at the very least they will be in a position to understand the obligations of a contract and the remedies for its violation. At present, such knowledge is almost entirely within the province of the legal profession.

Take as still another example the study of what might be called the vernacular arts. In our society, a wide variety of visual forms are used to shape values, to influence aspirations, and in general to motivate people to do or not do certain things. The design of shopping centers, the forms of the displays that are created, the kinds of images that are shown in the mass media, on television and on film, those images are, as Vance Packard aptly called them, the "hidden persuaders" in our culture. They are designed with skill and serve the interests of the manufacturer and merchant, politician, industrialist, builder, and salesman. How do these images work? In what ways do they impose themselves on our consciousness? Are we or can we become immune to their messages, or do we delude ourselves into thinking so? Are there ways students could be helped to become aware of such forms and how they function? Could they be enabled to learn to "read" the arts of the vernacular, to understand how they themselves use such arts to persuade and motivate? Is there a grammar to these images, a syntax that, although not following the forms of logic used in verbal and written discourse, nevertheless exists and can be revealed through analysis?

The study of popular images, the arts of the vernacular, could of course be offered as a part of the school's program. The study of such arts would, at least in principle, help develop a level of critical consciousness that is now generally absent in our culture. Yet, as ubiquitous and as powerful as such popular images are, there are hardly any schools in the country that pay serious attention to them or help students learn to read the messages they carry at a level that subjects them to critical scrutiny. Writing about these images, Edmund Feldman says:

One reason for this difference between the perception of visual and verbal imagery lies in the fundamentally sequential structure of speech and writing as opposed to the almost simultaneous perception of visual forms. Second, because of our phylogenetic heritage, the visual image established connection with different—one might say "older"—portions of the brain than verbal structures. The feelings experienced in the presence of visual images are more difficult to control or resist than those dependent on language. Because language (especially the complex linguistic forms of modern man) evolved after the development of visual perception in the phylogeny of our species, we are equipped with older, possibly less sophisticated, biological equipment for the apprehension of images. We cannot so readily defend against what a picture seems to tell us to do or feel. Third, our knowledge systems and our educational institutions have been organized almost exclusively for the transmissions and reception of linear structures. It is obvious that these institutions find themselves in crisis when nonlinear, that is, visual, sources of imagery are perfected and made cheaply and instantly available. To complicate the problem further, it is possible that the most technically sophisticated mental operations on which an advanced civilization depends cannot be learned execept through linear, sequentially organized meaning structures. But for the engineering of public assent, the encouragement of nonreflective behavior, visual imagery is ideal.

If visual images are relatively invulnerable to logical and semantic scrutiny, how can we account for the extraordinary influence of verbal slogans in religion, politics, and advertising? The explanation is simple, and it reinforces our argument concerning the compelling power of the visual image: the effectiveness of a slogan depends on repetition, and the function of repetition is to convert a logical sequence into an image. In fact, the repeated slogan becomes a motor image—one that we find difficult to forget, like the lyrics of a bad song or a frequently heard advertising jingle. So long as a slogan can be analyzed semantically it can be resisted. But once it has been drilled into the popular consciousness in the form of a patterned reenactment, there is no way to prevent many compelling transactions, that is, automatic acquiescence, from taking place. Thus the slogan becomes part of our involuntary behavior.[10]

It becomes clear that what we teach in schools is not always determined by a set of decisions that have entertained alternatives; rather, the subjects that are now taught are a part of a tradition, and traditions create expectations, they create predictability, and they sustain stability. The subjects that are now taught are also protected by the interests of teachers who view themselves as specialists in particular fields. There is no national lobby of teachers of law, or of communications, or of anthropology. Indeed, in the words of one individual who tried to bring an anthropology curriculum into secondary schools, it was necessary to fly under false colors. In order for anthropology to be taught; it has to come disguised as history, a field already established and serving a well-defined professional interest group.

The strategy that we finally elected was chosen because it looked as though it might work, because it was consistent with our definition of the faults of the traditional social studies, and because it made sense in terms of what anthropology as a discipline had to offer. We decided to subvert a course very commonly taught in the ninth or tenth grade—the world history course. More specifically, we intended to offer materials that could be rationalized as world history and which would, in effect substitute for a substantial segment of the traditional course. Many supporters of anthropology in the high schools urged us to design a high school level anthropology course. We resisted this advice; we knew that such a program would never become a required course and we knew what happened to elective courses. The elective route was no way to bring large numbers of students into a meaningful encounter with anthropology.[11]

Take as still another example the general neglect of the arts in elementary and secondary schools. Although elementary schools are generally supposed to provide programs in the arts, few well-thought-out and competently taught art programs exist at this level. Elementary school teachers have little background in the arts and, in general, are not well prepared to teach them.

At the secondary level, where there are arts specialists, the arts are taught in about half of all secondary schools and only 20 per cent of the school population enrolls for as little as one year. This neglect of the arts, compared to, say, the sciences, leaves students unable, by and large, to deal meaningfully with sophisticated forms of the serious arts. One need not have special tuition to appreciate "Gunsmoke," "Maude," or "Truth or Consequences." When it comes to the music of Stravinsky, the films of Bergman, the paintings of Matisse, the architecture of Corbusier, the sculpture of Brancusi, the dance of Cunningham, tuition is needed. Yet, schools do not provide programs that develop such abilities, and, because such abilities do not develop on their own, millions of students leave schools each year without access to what such artists have contributed to the world. If in hundreds of years some archeologist wanted to understand something of the aesthetic level our culture had achieved, no more representative artifacts could be dug up than the Sears Roebuck catalogue and the TV Guide.

Law, anthropology, the arts, communication, economics, these are just a few of the fields that constitute the null curriculum. I am not here making a brief for these particular fields or subject matters, for in fact I believe that there can be no adequate conception of appropriate curriculum content without consideration of the context in which it is to be provided and the students for whom it is intended. I identify these fields and subject matters for purposes of exemplification and to highlight the point that what we offer the young in schools is largely bound by tradition. One could hope for more.

When we ask, therefore, about the means through which schools teach, we can recognize that one of the major means is through the explicit curriculum that is offered to students. But that is not all. Schools also teach through the implicit curriculum, that pervasive and ubiquitous set of expectations and rules that defines schooling as a cultural system that itself teaches important lessons. And we can identify the null curriculum—the options students are not afforded, the perspectives they may never know about, much less be able to use, the concepts and skills that are not a part of their intellectual repertoire. Surely, in the deliberations that constitute the course of living, their absence will have important consequences on the kind of life that students can choose to lead.

Thus far we have examined not only the major orientations that have guided thinking about what shall be taught in school, but we have also examined what schools teach that teachers do not realize they are teaching and what they neglect teaching, as well. The consequences of school programs emanate from values that are explicit and operational as well as those that are tacit and covert.

In the following chapter, we will deal with the problem of how curriculum objectives can be formulated, a problem that has been the center of great controversy during the last fifteen years.

REFERENCES

1. Robert Dreeben, *On What Is Learned in School*, Addison-Wesley Publishing Co., Reading, Mass., 1968.
2. Phillip Jackson, *Life in Classrooms*, Holt, Rinehart and Winston, Inc., New York, 1968.
3. Seymore Sarason, *The Culture of the School and the Problem of Change*, Allyn and Bacon, Boston, 1971.
4. Lewis Mumford, *Technics and Civilization*, Harcourt, Brace and Co., New York, 1938.
   20–21.
5. Ivan Illich, *Tools for Conviviality*, Harper & Row, 1973, pp. 20–21.
6. *The Dictionary of Psychology* (Warren, Howard, and Crosby, eds.), Houghton Mifflin, Boston, 1934.
7. Gabrielle Rico, *Metaphors and Knowing: Analysis, Synthesis, Rationale*, Doctoral Dissertation, Stanford University, 1976, pp. 41–44.
8. E. E. Cummings, *Collected Poems*, Harcourt, Brace and Co., New York, 1926, p. 315.
9. Alexander Solzhenitsyn, *Gulag Archipelago*, trans. by Thomas P. Whitney, Harper & Row, New York, 1973, p. 212.
10. Edmund Feldman, "Art, Education and the Consumption of Images," in *The Arts Human Development and Education* (Elliot W. Eisner, ed.), McCutchan Publishing Co., Berkeley, Calif., 1976, pp. 137–148.
11. Robert Hanvey, "The Social Studies, the Educational Culture, the State," in *Confronting Curriculum Reform* (Elliot W. Eisner, ed.), Little, Brown and Co., Boston, 1971, pp. 143–153.

6

Educational Aims, Objectives, and Other Aspirations

Finally, there should grow the most austere of all mental qualities; I mean the sense for style. It is an aesthetic sense, based on admiration for the direct attainment of a foreseen end, simply and without waste. Style in art, style in literature, style in science, style in logic, style in practical execution have fundamentally the same aesthetic qualities, namely, attainment and restraint. The love of a subject in itself and for itself, where it is not the sleepy pleasure of pacing a mental quarter-deck, is the love of style as manifested in that study.

ALFRED N. WHITEHEAD

No concept is more central to curriculum planning than the concept of objectives. The argument for its importance is straightforward. I will try to provide it.

Objectives are the specific goals that one hopes to achieve through the educational program that is provided. In order for educational planning to be meaningful not only must goals be formulated, they must also be formulated with precision and with clarity. To formulate them with precision and clarity it is best not to use words that have referents that are difficult to observe. Words such as *understanding, insight, appreciation,* and *interest,* refer to qualities that cannot be observed directly; they require one to make inferences about their existence through the observation of manifest behavior Thus, useful objectives should be stated in behavioral terms or, in more current jargon, performance terms. When objectives are stated behaviorally, it is possible to have specific empirical referents to observe; thus, one is in a position to know without ambiguity whether the behavioral objective has been reached. An objective that seeks to help students appreciate the insights of great poetry needs to be recast into terms far more specific and precise. What would a student *do* to demonstrate that such appreciation has occurred? What behavior would he or she display? What task is he or she to perform?

It should be noted, as it is by those who advocate the use of specific behavioral objectives in curriculum planning, that the objective is to be stated in terms of desired *student behavior*. It should not describe what the teacher is to do. If an objective stated that "The objective of the course is to introduce students to great ideas of the Western world," not only would the behavior be obscure—the term *introduce* for a behaviorist is vague—the objective would logically be achieved when the teacher introduced the material to the students. The objective in this case is stated in terms of teacher behavior, not in terms of the desired behavior of the students.

A further condition for formulation of meaningful behavioral objectives is that both the behavior and the content be identified. Appreciation, for example, is always of some thing or idea. Understanding always has a subject matter. One does something to something else and in some context. Thus, objectives that are adequately behavioral will not only refer to student rather than teacher behavior, will not only minimize the need for inference—the closer to manifest behavior the better—but meaningful objectives will also identify the particular subject matter in which the behavior is to take place. For example, the student will be able to identify the major causes of the Westward movement in the United States during the period 1840–1870.

Even with these criteria, for hard-line behaviorists, the foregoing objective is still too diffuse. What is missing is a statement of the specific criterion level the student will have to meet in order to demonstrate that the objective has been attained. There might be five major causes for the Westward movement. How many of these must a student identify—one, two, three, four, or all five? Thus, not only must an objective have the characteristics I have already described, but also, perhaps most importantly, it must specify the criterion level that must be achieved to demonstrate competency in reaching the objective. Perhaps the best spokesman for this view is Robert Mager:

An objective is an *intent* communicated by a statement describing a proposed change in a learner—a statement of what the learner is to be like when he has successfully completed a learning experience. It is a description of a pattern of behavior (performance) we want the learner to be able to demonstrate. As Dr. Paul Whitmore once put it, "The statement of objectives of a training program must denote *measurable* attributes *observable* in the graduate of the program, or otherwise it is impossible to determine whether or not the program is meeting the objectives."

When clearly defined goals are lacking, it is impossible to evaluate a course or program efficiently, and there is no sound basis for selecting appropriate materials, content, or instructional methods. After all, the machinist does not select a tool until he knows what operation he intends to perform. Neither does a composer orchestrate a score until he knows what effects he wishes to achieve. Similarly, a builder does not select his materials or specify a schedule for construction until he has his blueprints (objectives) before him. Too often, however, one hears teachers arguing the relative merits of textbooks or other aids of the classroom versus the laboratory, without ever specifying just what goal the aid or method is to assist in achieving. I cannot emphasize too strongly the point that an instructor will function in a fog of his own making until he knows just what he wants his students to be able to do at the end of the instruction.[1]

What Mager and others holding this view are trying to do is to develop a highly precise technology for statements of objectives that they believe will improve the quality of teaching and learning. For many behaviorists, one of the major problems of goal statements is that they are vague, and because they are vague they tend to be educationally meaningless. To have a meaningful objective, and by inference a useful one, one should be able to determine, usually through measurement, whether it has been achieved. To the extent that there is ambiguity in the statement, its meaningfulness and utility are diminished. Furthermore, if a curriculum planner knows exactly what kind of behavior he or she wants students to display, it is easier to select content and formulate activities that are instrumental to the desired end.

The tendency toward high levels of behavioral specificity is, of course, not new in American educational planning. Franklin Bobbitt, whose ideas we encountered earlier, listed ten areas for such objectives in his book *How to Make a Curriculum*, which was published in 1922. Although Bobbitt's objectives, too, are vague by today's standards, the spirit of behavioral specificity is the same. Indeed, the general thrust toward the study of behavior rather than experience has been characteristic of American educational psychology since the turn of the century. Thorndike, Watson, Hull, and Skinner participate in that tradition, and it provides the theoretical backdrop for this approach to the formulation of behavioral objectives.

There are two other traditions associated with the behavioral specification approach to objectives; one of these is found in industry, the other in military training. They have two features in common: the characteristics of the performance to be produced are known in advance, and, ideally, the specifications of the objectives and characteristics of the individual performance are isomorphic—i.e., a perfect match between objective and behavior is desired. In industrial settings, such as in automobile production, the same conditions hold. A prototypical form is created for the cars to be assembled. This form is described both physically and mechanically for each model. Subsequently, a component analysis is made of the prototype, a task analysis follows that prescribes the steps to be taken in production and their sequence, and production begins. The manager of the assembly line has the task of ensuring that all operations are performed in the order specified. The goal to be achieved is the creation of an isomorphic relationship between the original prototype and each car coming off the line. If these cars do not match, there is a call-back, and the problem is identified and readjustments are made. An efficient and effective assembly line produces identical cars day after day that in every aspect match the model that was originally created.

Military training programs have similar features. New recruits are processed through a program that specifies in almost every detail what is to be done and how. The slogan "There is a right way, a wrong way, and an Army way" is not altogether inappropriate. When one has a training program, a program that intentionally attempts to help another acquire a known, specific performance system to be used to achieve a known goal, the acquisition of known behavioral routines might be appropriate. Personal ingenuity and idiosyncratic behavior are discouraged both on the assembly line and in the boot camp. The armed forces justify such an approach on the basis that it is of paramount importance for soldiers to learn to follow orders: prediction and control of troops are required in time of war. Industry employs such an approach because it is efficient; more cars can be produced in better fashion when systematic, routinized procedures are followed.

It is interesting to note that the earliest efforts at specifying goals and prescribing the methods through which those goals could be attained occurred during the so-called efficiency period in American education from about 1903 to 1925.[2] During this period, school administrators were being criticized in the press for running slack schools, schools that had much waste, that did not give the public a fair return on its investment. These men, vulnerable as they were (and are), sought what they could to make schooling more rigorous and in the process discovered the work of Frederick Taylor, an industrial management consultant and the father of time and motion study. Taylor would go into industrial plants with a team of colleagues and study the movements of the work force, measure the current level of productivity, and then prescribe minute steps to be taken by workers to eliminate excess waste in movement. By utilizing his methods, companies such as Bethlehem Steel were able to significantly increase their level of productivity. Raymond Callahan, a historian noted for his work pertaining to this period, writes:

> The first element in the mechanism of scientific management listed by Taylor was time and motion study and the development of unit times for the various components of any job. This Taylor regarded as "by far the most important element in scientific management," and it was the basic element in achieving his first principle of the development of a true science for a particular job. Frank Gilbreth testified on this point by stating that "any plan of management that does not include Taylor's plan of time study cannot be considered as highly efficient. We have never seen a case in our work where time study and analysis did not result in more than doubling the output of the worker." Not only was time and motion study thus conceived by the engineers themselves, but also it was apparently identified in the mind of the average American as the key element of the system. Milton Nadworny notes, "Although scientific management employed many identifiable and characteristic mechanisms, its most prominent tool was a stopwatch, the popular symbol of the scientific management movement. The stopwatch symbolized the new approach to management: 'management based on measurement.' "[3]

It is not surprising when one is in a vulnerable position, as superintendents of schools were and are, that one should embrace any new idea that promises to reduce that vulnerability. Scientific management, as Taylor called it, appeared to provide the mantle of scientific respectability that schoolmen needed and wanted. By wrapping themselves in a scientific cloak, they believed they could protect themselves from the criticism that they were inefficient stewards of the schools. One superintendent said:

One may easily trace an analogy between these fundamentals of the science of industrial management and the organization of a public school system. For example: (1) The state as employer must cooperate with the teacher as employee, for the latter does not always understand the scieince of education; (2) the state provides experts who supervise the teacher and suggest the processes that are most efficacious and economical; (3) the task system obtains in the school as well as in the shop, each grade being a measured quantity of work to be accomplished in a given term; (4) every teacher who accomplishes the task receives a bonus, not in money, but in the form of a rating which may have have money value; (5) those who are unable to do the work are eliminated, either through the device of a temporary license or of a temporary employment; (6) the differential rate is applied to the teacher, quantity and quality of service being considered in the rating; (7) the result ought to be a maximum output at a low relative cost, since every repeater costs as much as a new pupil; (8) the teacher thus receives better wages, but only after demonstrated fitness for high position; (9) hence we ought to have the most desirable combination of an educational system—relative cheapness of operation and high salaries.[4]

It is, I think, particularly important to take note of the language that was used during this period. The society was viewed as the consumer of the school's products. The children were the raw material to be processed according to specifications laid down by the consumer. And the teachers were the workers who were to be overseen by supervisors. All of this was to take place under a superintendent. Although the modern concepts of quality assurance and quality control were not used then, a similar spirit was at work in those "good" old days.

The analogy between industrial processes and educational processes is a deceptive one. When one is working with inert material for ends that are uniform and prespecified, the task of determining effectiveness and locating inefficiency or ineffectiveness is comparatively simple. After all, when one thousand pounds of pressure is placed on thirty-gauge steel within a one-inch diameter, the reaction of the steel to the pressure is quite predictable. As long as there is no human error or mechanical failure, the results will be the same time and time again. Industrial managers bank on it. Such conditions, however, seldom obtain in the classroom. Children are far from inert, so are teachers. They respond differently to the "same" stimuli, because how the stimuli are perceived—indeed, *whether* they in fact stimulate—depends as much on the characteristics of the student as it does on the objective characteristics of the stimuli themselves. Furthermore, the realization of outcomes that are common to all students, the production of educational products all having identical features, at best suits only a small array of those aims that most educators seek in the course of teaching. One major problem I see in the admonition to teachers and curriculum planners to specify their aims in behavioral terms is that the limitations of such objectives are seldom acknowledged. They are offered as though one were not really professionally competent without a list of objectives that one could pull out for each set of curriculum activities formulated.

In identifying what I believe to be an oversimplified view of the character of educational aims, I am not taking the position that there is no place for clearly defined behavioral objectives in a school curriculum. When specific skills or competencies are appropriate, such objectives can be formulated, but one should not feel compelled to abandon educational aims that cannot be reduced to measurable forms of predictable performance. Conceptions of method should serve as tools and as heuristic devices for improving the quality of educational experience, not as constraints on teachers, teaching, or what students have an opportunity to learn.

Let me provide a description of some other limitations behaviorially defined objectives have in the design of educational programs. I identify these limitations not as a wholesale condemnation of their use but as an attempt to increase the sophistication of the dialogue about them.

One limitation of discursively defined behavioral objectives deals with the limits of discourse itself. Much, perhaps most, of what we aspire to and cherish is not amenable to discursive formulation. Take, for example, our image of human sensitivity. Although we could describe discrete behaviors that were intended to characterize a sensitive human being—say, one who was responsive to the feelings of others and compassionate—discrete forms of human performance would ultimately fail to capture what we are able to recognize in others. Language is, after all, a surrogate for experience. We try to articulate in words what we know in nonlinguistic ways. For much of our experience, discursive language performs rather well. But for the subtleties of human experience, for our knowledge of human feeling, for modes of conception and understanding that are qualitative, discourse falls far short. How many words would it take to describe insight, perceptivity, integrity, self-esteem? How would one describe how water tastes? How would one describe the qualities of a late Beethoven quartet in precise, unambiguous, measurable terms?

The point here is not an effort to inject the mystical into educational planning but rather to avoid reductionistic thinking that impoverishes our view of what is possible. To expect all of our educational aspirations to be either verbally describable or measurable is to expect too little.

A second problem with the use of specific behavioral objectives is that those who evaluate them often fail to distinguish between *the application of a standard* and *the making of a judgment*. Dewey makes this distinction quite clear when he says,

There are three characteristics of a standard. It is a particular physical thing existing under specified physical conditions; it is *not* a value. The yard is a yardstick, and the meter is a bar deposited in Paris. In the second place, standards are measures of definite things, of lengths, weights, capacities. The things measured are not values, although it is of great social value to be able to measure them, since the properties of things in the way of size, volume, weight, are important for commercial exchange. Finally, as standards of measure, standards define things with respect to *quantity.* To be able to measure quantities is a great aid to further judgments, but it is not itself a mode of judgment. The standard, being an external and public thing, is applied *physically,* The yard-stick is physically laid down upon the things measured to determine their length.

Yet it does not follow, because of absence of a uniform and publicly determined external object, that objective criticism of art is impossible. What follows is that criticism is judgment; that like every judgment it involves a venture, a hypothetical element; that it is directed to qualities which are nevertheless qualities of an *object;* and that it is concerned with an individual object, not with making comparisons by means of an external preestablished rule between different things. The critic, because of the element of venture, reveals himself in his criticisms. He wanders into another field and confuses values when he departs from the object he is judging. Nowhere are comparisons so odious as in fine art.[5]

Standards are crisp, unambiguous, and precise. A person can swim five lengths of the pool or cannot. Someone can spell *aardvaark* or cannot. Someone knows who the twenty-seventh president of the United States was or does not. Someone can multiply two sets of three-digit figures correctly or cannot. For such performances, standards are specifiable and applicable by anyone or by any machine that "knows" the rules through which the standards are to be applied. But what about the rhetorical force of a student's essay? What about the aesthetic quality of her painting? What about the cogency of his verbal argumentation? What about her intellectual style, the ways she interprets the evidence in a science experiment, the way in which historical material is analyzed? Are these subject to standards? I think not.

But to say that such qualities cannot be measured by standards is not to say that judgments cannot be made about them. It is not to say that one can have no criteria through which to appraise them. Judgments can say much about such qualities, not by the mechanical application of prespecified standards, but by comparison of the qualities in question to a whole range of criteria that teachers or others making the judgment already possess. How much weight does one give to insight and how much to logical argument? How does one compare this essay, or this statement, or this project, or this painting, to the one or ones the student did before? Judgments about such qualities are not will-of-the-wisp, cavalier, irresponsible conclusions, they are complex appraisals that use an extraordinarily wide range of knowledge to arrive at what, on balance, is a warranted human judgment. The multiple-choice test is simply not adequate for everything.

A third problem with the demand that all objectives be behavioral and defined in advance deals with the assumption that the prespecification of goals is the rational way in which one must always proceed in curriculum planning. This assumption is rooted in the kind of rationality that has guided much of Western technology. The means-ends model of thinking has for so long dominated our thinking that we have come to believe that not to have clearly defined purposes for our activities is to court irrationality or, at the least, to be professionally irresponsible. Yet, life in classrooms, like that outside them, is seldom neat or linear. Although it may be a shock to some, goals are not always clear. Purposes are not always precise. As a matter of fact, there is much that we do, and need to do, without a clear sense of what the objective is. Many of our most productive activities take the form of exploration or play. In such activities, the task is not one of arriving at a preformed objective but rather to act, often with a sense of abandon, wonder, curiosity. Out of such activity rules may be formed and objectives may be created.

The relationship between action and the formation of purpose is well known to artists. In a particularly telling passage describing the work of the abstract expressionists, Harold Rosenberg, one of America's leading art critics, writes:

> At a certain moment the canvas began to appear to one American painter after another as an arena in which to act—rather than as a space in which to reproduce, re-design, analyze or "express" an object, actual or imagined. What was to go on the canvas was not a picture but an event.
> The painter no longer approached his easel with an image in his mind; he went up to it with material in front of him. The image would be the result of this encounter.[6]

What Rosenberg describes of the abstract expressionists is to some extent an echo of Aristotle's remarks more than two thousand years ago. "Art," he said, "loves chance." "He who is willing to err is the artist." What both Aristotle and Rosenberg point out is that purpose need not precede action. Purposes may grow out of action. Unfortunately, our cultural tendency to eschew play and praise work makes it sometimes difficult to explain why play is justified in its own right and why in a broad sense it may be among the most productive forms of human activity.

PROBLEM-SOLVING OBJECTIVES AND EXPRESSIVE OUTCOMES

What would a broader, more generous conception of educational aims look like? Are there ways of thinking about objectives and outcomes that are not constrained by the kinds of criteria that are prescribed for behavioral objectives? I believe there are. But before describing two other ways of conceptualizing educational aims let me reiterate that I believe behavioral objectives to be appropriate for some types of educational aims, even though

I recognize that they are in no way adequate for conceptualizing most of our most cherished educational aspirations. When it is appropriate to formulate specific types of educational exercises that aim at particular definable skills, the use of such objectives may be warranted: one must be able to swim four laps of the pool to be able to swim in the deep end. But one should not, in my view, attempt to reduce all of our goals into such forms. To do so robs them of the very qualities of mind one may be seeking to foster.

In Figure 2 two types of objectives and one kind of outcome are presented that can be planned in the design and evaluation of educational programs. The first of these, the behavioral objective, has already been described, and I will not restate its feature here. The problem-solving objective differs in a significant way from the behavioral objective. In the problem-solving objective, the students formulate or are given a problem to solve—say, to find out how deterrents to smoking might be made more effective, or how to design a paper structure that will hold two bricks sixteen inches above a table, or how the variety and quality of food served in the school cafeteria could be increased within the existing budget.

In each of these examples the problem is posed and the criteria that need to be achieved to resolve the problem are fairly clear. But the forms of its solution are virtually infinite. Some students might increase food quantity and variety by finding new sources of supply or by establishing a student volunteer system to work with the kitchen staff. Others might decide that the most effective solution would be for interested students to set up their own kitchen facilities on school premises, and others might formulate an ordering system so students could place orders for some good Chinese and Italian food at a local inexpensive restaurant.

The point is that the shapes of the solutions, the forms they take, are highly variable. Alternative solutions to problem-solving objectives could be discussed in class so that the students could begin to appreciate their practical costs.

This form of objective is not unknown in the design field and in science laboratories. Designers, for example, are almost always given a set of cri-

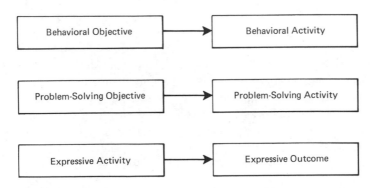

teria or specifications and asked to create a product that will satisfactorily meet those criteria. Often they are asked to create several solutions so that the client can compare alternatives and decide which suits his or her needs best.

In architecture, the client provides the architect with a set of specifications—budget, site, personal life-style, preferred architectural style—and the builder and municipal code present others. Finally, engineering requirements impose their demands: the building has to stand, the cantilevered deck must not fall, the foundations must not sink. Within these design constraints, the architecture must create viable and constructive solutions.

In such situations the potential answers are not known beforehand. What is known is the problem; what constitutes appropriate solutions remains to be seen after the work has been done.

In the sciences this type of problem-solving activity is characteristic, at least for most scientists. The concept of "normal science," a term coined by Thomas Kuhn, aptly describes the work of the typical scientist. Such a person works within a given theory, a theory that he or she does not question. The problem is to find solutions to problems posed within the terms of the theory. Kuhn writes:

Mopping-up operations are what engage most scientists throughout their careers. They constitute what I am here calling normal science. Closely examined, whether historically or in the contemporary laboratory, that enterprise seems an attempt to force nature into the preformed and relatively inflexible box that the paradigm supplies. No part of the aim of normal science is to call forth new sorts of phenomena; indeed those that will not fit the box are often not seen at all. Nor do scientists normally aim to invent new theories, and they are often intolerant of those invented by others. Instead, normal-scientific research is directed to the articulation of those phenomena and theories that the paradigm already supplies.[7]

Like the architect, the scientist tends not to redefine the givens, in this case the basic theoretical premises by which he or she has been professionally socialized and that serve to define not only the problem, but also the scientist's expertise.

One very important difference between the problem-solving objective and the behavioral objective is that the solution to the problem in problem-solving objectives is not definite. The problem is, in a significant sense, a genuine one. Behavioral objectives have both the form and the content defined in advance. There is, after all, only one way to spell *aardvaark*. Given the same set of behavioral objectives for a class of students, the successful teacher elicits homogeneous behavior at the end of an instructional period that is isomorphic with the objective. This is not the case with a problem-solving objective. The solutions individual students or groups of students reach may be just as much a surprise for the teacher as they are for the students who created them.

The issue concerning the form statements of objectives are to take is far wider than the character of the forms themselves. Although it is said that form follows function, the opposite is equally true: function follows form. The form, in large measure, reflects an underlying set of assumptions that might not themselves have been examined. The idea that goals should be specifiable in advance and that success in teaching consists primarily of bringing about predictable outcomes are themselves what is at issue. Such a set of beliefs, fostered not through an explicit educational rationale but rather embedded in the very techniques that one is encouraged to use, can have significant effects on the way the teacher's role is conceived and what educators believe they are after. Surreptitiously but inexorably, techniques that go unexamined with respect to the ideology that they reflect can be debilitating. Training comes to be substituted for education.

The use of problem-solving objectives places a premium on cognitive flexibility, on intellectual exploration, on the higher mental processes. It tends toward the formulation of curriculum activities that are likely to be taken seriously by scholars. The reason I make these claims is that not only have I seen this happen in classes where students had such objectives, but also it is reasonable to expect that when students have a set of clear criteria and are free to meet those criteria in ways that require ingenuity, they will take a deeper interest in coping with the problem. The opportunity to use ingenuity breeds interest.

EXPRESSIVE OUTCOMES

A third type of educational aim is what I have called, in previous writing, expressive objectives.[8] Because I now see that the term *objective* implies a preformulated goal, something out of reach but to be attained, I think it desirable to change the term to *expressive outcomes*. Outcomes are essentially what one ends up with, intended or not, after some form of engagement. Expressive outcomes are the consequences of curriculum activities that are intentionally planned to provide a fertile field for personal purposing and experience. Take, for example, much of our ordinary activity—say, going to the movies. There is no one I know who formulates specific behavioral objectives before going to a movie. Nor do I know anyone who formulates a problem-solving objective. Most of us go to the movies because we think something interesting or exciting will happen to us there. We do not formulate specific goals that describe what our behavior will be after we leave. We do not establish criteria that the director and actors will have to meet in order to be successful. The fact of the matter is that we already have such criteria in ample abundance and retrospectively select from the ones we have those that appear appropriate for the particular movie we have just seen. If the movie is a comedy, we apply comedic criteria, if an adventure, dramatic criteria, and so forth.

But the problem of appraising the qualities of expressive outcomes is more complicated than I have just described, even in life outside of schools. If the movie we have just seen was billed as the year's funniest comedy or if it is being shown in the finest first-run theater charging the highest prices in town, we come to expect more than we would otherwise. If our favorite actor or actress is in the film or if it was directed by Fellini, Bergman, or Houston, we might make a more complex appraisal. If we have had the bad fortune of seeing a series of poor films during the last two months, our receptivity toward a somewhat better than mediocre film may be higher than it would otherwise be. The point here is that the appraisals we make as a result of activities we engage in are clearly complex and highly rational, employing a wide range of criteria that, although not explicit, operate in our judgments. The same holds true in classrooms.

I believe that it is perfectly appropriate for teachers and others involved in curriculum development to plan activities that have no explicit or precise objectives. In an age of accountability, this sounds like heresy. Yet surely there must be room in school for activities that promise to be fruitful, even though the teacher might not be able to say what specifically the students will learn or experience. Parents do this all the time. The trip to the zoo, weekends spent camping in the woods, the bicycle ride after dinner; no specific objectives or problems are posed prior to setting out on such activities, yet we feel that they will be enjoyable and that some "good" will come from them.

Curriculum planning and schooling in general need not always be single-minded in their pursuits, forever focusing on objectives that are by definition always out of reach. Purposes need not precede activities; they can be formulated in the process of action itself.

In Figure 2 not only is a distinction made among educational objectives, problem-solving objectives, and expressive outcomes, they also are related to different types of curriculum activities. What we see in Figure 2 is that in both behavioral objectives and problem-solving objectives the formulation of the objectives precedes the curriculum activity. In this respect, they both participate in the standard means-ends approach to planning. However, expressive activities precede rather than follow expressive outcomes. The tack taken with respect to the generation of expressive outcomes is to create activities that are seminal; what one is seeking is to have students engage in activities that are sufficiently rich to allow for a wide, productive range of educationally valuable outcomes. If behavioral objectives and behavioral activities constitute the algorithms of curriculum, expressive activities and expressive outcomes constitute their heuristics.

These are not the only forms of language that are significant. The modifiers around the word *objective* have themselves changed significantly. In Tyler's curriculum monograph published in 1948, *objective* was preceded by the word *educational*. Thus, what one was to formulate was an *educa-*

cational objective. Later the term was shifted by other writers to *instructional*. Still later the word became *behavioral,* and even later it was a *performance* objective that was to be formulated.

This shift in modifier is not an accident, it reflects an increased emphasis on the manifest behavior of the student and on discrete forms of student activity. It gradually moves from the general to the specific. But it is significant in other ways, as well. An educational objective supposedly has something to do with *educational* outcomes. An instructional objective, although not strongly normative, still participates in the context of education. But behavioral or performance objectives may or may not be educational; the normative aspect of education no longer is a part of the term. One can have a behavioral objective that aims at creating racists or paranoids. Such an aim could hardly be regarded as educational, unless, of course, racism and paranoia were part of one's conception of education.

These shifts in language are, in my opinion, no mere minor modifications. Words, of course, have connotations as well as denotations, and it is often the connotative meanings that influence significantly the way we come to think about things. For new students of education, students who do not have the benefit of perspective, the new term, normatively void as it is, might appear as a natural entity. History sustains our memory and provides for depth of field.

It would be erroneous to assume that some fields, such as the fine arts, have a monopoly on the use of expressive activities. This is not the case. Any activity—indeed, at their very best, activities that are engaged in to court surprise, to cultivate discovery, to find new forms of experience—is expressive in character. Nothing in the sciences, the home or mechanical arts, or in social relationships prohibits or diminishes the possibility of engaging in expressive activities and in the process of achieving expressive outcomes. The educational problem is to be sufficiently imaginative in the design of educational programs so that such outcomes will occur and their educational value will be high.

SOME GENERAL QUESTIONS ABOUT THE USE OF OBJECTIVES IN DESIGNING EDUCATIONAL PROGRAMS

After all of the analyses of the various types of objectives and the criteria that each should meet, one is still left with some basic questions about their utility in curriculum development and teaching. One of the questions deals with the matter of specificity and the educational "unit" for which they are appropriate or necessary. How specific should objectives be? Should they be formulated for the entire course, for parts of a course, for each curriculum activity that is formulated? It is clear that answers to these questions will differ depending on the view of educational planning that one holds. If one views curriculum planning and teaching, as, in their idealized form, an error-free type of program that moves a student as swiftly as possible from one condition at entry to another at exit—I use the technical jargon intentionally—it is likely that specificity in objectives and a large number of objectives would be desired. Yet I believe that in general one would do well to think through a set of objectives in some detail, particularly when one is not clear about the purposes or aims of teaching or when one needs for matter of public record a set of specific statements of educational goals. In other words, on the whole I see no compelling need for a teacher to formulate or to have formulated for him or her a highly specific set of behavioral objectives. For one thing, such a list, especially if prepared at the level of specificity that would satisfy a behaviorist, could easily run into hundreds of items for an elementary school teacher in a self-contained classroom. Assume for a moment that a teacher taught seven subject areas each week. Suppose further that the teacher divided the class into three ability groups and had one objective each week for forty weeks during the school year for each of the three groups in each subject area taught. Such a teacher would have $7 \times 3 \times 40 = 840$ objectives. Obviously no teacher is able to make explicit 840 objectives or be in a position to remember them if they were presented in the form of a guide or manual. How many objectives are feasible? Which ones should be omitted? For what scope of curriculum content are they appropriate? At present there are no quantitative research data that are adequate for answering such questions, nor do I believe there are likely to be.

What I want to claim is that teachers during the school year deal with far more than 840 obectives in the classroom. These objectives are not found in lists. They are not written (although some school districts have compiled such lists of objectives in notebooks the size of the New York City telephone directory). These objectives are a part of the personal and psychological repertoire that teachers draw on each day when working with students.

What I am referring to is the kind of intelligent activity that teachers typically employ in working with students, the kind of intelligence that gives motive and purpose to their teaching, that tells them when they should help a child feel better about himself, when she needs to work harder, when he needs a richer set of resources to work with, when a closer analysis of the text is appropriate. In thousands of ways, teachers draw on images of human virtue as criteria for the direction of their activity as teachers and for the directions they should take with their students. The storehouse of such images is large, and it needs to be. It is modulated according to circumstance and context and with regard to the particular student with whom the teacher interacts.

From this point of view, 840 objectives is a paltry sum. Consider for a moment the range of problems, content, contexts, and individuals with which a teacher must deal. Not only must there be some sense of purpose or direction to the activities in which teachers are engaged, but also the priorities among those projects must be considered, altered, or sustained. When does a teacher, for the time being, wisely forget about the goal of helping a student learn to spell a set of words correctly or learn how to punctuate an adverbial clause and instead attend to other aims, aims that are also a part of his or her aspirations for the student but not an explicit part of that particular segment of the curriculum? When does a teacher choose to make educational capital out of unexpected opportunities in the classroom—an offhand remark by a student or a keen insight by another— and in so doing depart from his or her previously specified objective? All of these happen in classrooms, at least those that are not rigidly tied to a set of single-minded aims. In particular, elementary school classrooms often acquire their own tempo; the students become immersed in what was to be a casual short-term project, and teachers often yield to such tempo, recognizing the need for an organic as contrasted to a mechanical treatment of time.

Thus, from one point of view, 840 objectives are far more than any teacher can reasonably be expected to focus on—420 would be equally difficult. Yet, at the same time, teachers operate with thousands of objectives in the form of their aspirations for the students with whom they work. The major difference is that their latter aims are implicit and contextual rather than explicit and prepared prior to the specific context in which they are to teach.

REFERENCES

1. Robert Mager, *Preparing Instructional Objectives*, Fearon Publishers, Palo Alto, Calif., 1962, p. 31.
2. See Raymond Callahan, *Education and the Cult of Effluency*, University of Chicago Press, Chicago, 1962.
3. Ibid., p. 28.
4. Ibid., pp. 103–104.
5. John Dewey, *Art As Experience*, Minton, Balch and Co., New York, 1934, pp. 307–308.
6. Harold Rosenberg, *American Painting Today*, Horizon Press, New York, 1965, p. 25.
7. Thomas Kuhn, The Structure of Scientific Revolutions, University of Chicago Press, Chicago, 1962, p. 24.
8. Elliot W. Eisner, "Instructional and Expressive Objectives: Their Formulation and Use in Curriculum," in *AERA Monograph on Curriculum Evaluation: Instructional Objectives* (W. James Popham, ed.), Rand McNally, Chicago, 1969, pp. 1–18.

7

Dimensions of Curriculum Planning

We need, that is, both a way of passing from naked propositions and their logical connections to the human activities that give them their sense, and beyond those activities to the features of the world and human life within which they are at home; and also a reverse road, back from "forms of life" in the world to the specific activities in question, and so eventually to the original propositions again.

STEPHEN TOULMIN

Thus far, a variety of ideas, concepts, and theories have been discussed pertaining to the design and evaluation of educational programs. The ultimate test of these ideas is determined by the extent to which they make educational planning more intelligent. As I have already indicated, education is not a field that will yield to simple prescriptions or recipes. Each situation in which educational decisions are made is significantly unique, not simply unique in the sense of time and place—all situations are unique in that sense—but unique in the sense that the goals, methods, people, and context differ from each other in important ways and must be treated with respect to those differences if decision making is to be effective. What we can expect of ideas about curriculum planning is not that these ideas provide formulas, but that they sophisticate our deliberations in planning programs and, hence, contribute to educationally richer programs than might otherwise be provided. In short, we ought to view ideas as tools, not as blueprints; they are things to use, not things to follow.

There are five basic questions that we can ask about the process of curriculum development. What is it? When is it done? Where is it done? How is it done?

Curriculum development is the process of transforming images and aspirations about education into programs that will effectively realize the visions that initiated the process. I use the term *images* and *aspirations* intentionally. The initiating conditions of curriculum development are seldom clear-cut, specific objectives; they are, rather, conceptions that are general, visions that are vague, aspirations that are fleeting. Much of what we value, aspire to, and cherish is ineffable; even if we wanted to, we could not adequately describe it. Furthermore, what we value and seek is often riddled with contradictions—even within the context of schooling—and must be compromised or negotiated in context. We want children to master "the basic skills"; we would like them to be supportive and cooperative with their peers and with adults, yet we also would like them to take initiative, to be able to compete and not feel bound by rules that might stifle their imagination, curiosity, or creativity. Our images of virtue are in flux; because images can never be translated wholly into discourse, to that degree they are always beyond the grasp of written or verbal expression.

Curriculum development in the context of education is, in this sense, a process that seeks the realization of certain ineffables. It is a process that is engaged in by anyone who attempts to make that translation. One group continually engaged in that process are teachers. Teachers inevitably have a range of options that they can exercise in the selection, emphasis, and timing of curricular events. Even when they are expected to follow certain guides or books in which activities and content have already been determined, there are still options to be considered and choices to be made by teachers with respect to how those materials will be used and the ways in which what is done in one particular area of study will or will not be related to what is done in other areas of the curriculum. These decisions are, of course, decisions bearing on the curriculum; they influence the kind of opportunities for learning and experience that children will have.

But more typically the scope of teachers' freedom regarding what skills are to be taught, when, in what order, and how is far wider than what the most highly structured programs provide for. Typically, the teacher will have a general guide of topics in a subject field, a sequence among topics, a general set of aims, textbooks, and other instructional resources. With these materials and within the constraints set by time, school culture, and the characteristics of the students, the teacher builds an educational program. The decision making for that program may be a species of long-term, highly systematic planning; a teacher might try to develop a calendar of topics and activities that extend throughout the year, or the teacher might plan on a week-to-week basis, without making any attempt to follow a specified timetable. The extent to which one or the other plan is selected can depend on the teacher's need for order and predictability and on the teacher's view of the educational process. For example, if a teacher believes that students should play a central role in the development of curriculum, that they should have significant opportunities to decide what they study and what ends they seek, then it is not so likely that it will be possible to predict where a class or an individual student is likely to be a month or two in the future. The point in such a view of educational planning is to encourage the student to develop increasing amounts of competence, and initiative and thus to assume greater responsibility for planning his or her educational program. The control of student progress and the prediction of learning at specific intervals over time are, in a sense, beside the point. But even so, the teacher plays an important role in curriculum decision making, because it is the teacher who decides to give or not to give students the opportunity to assume curricular responsibility, and it is the teacher who decides what kind of encouragement and guidance to provide in the selection of topics and areas of study.

In contrast to such a curriculum plan, consider the increasing tendency among school districts to specify particular performance objectives for students at intervals within each grade level. In such a system the scope for teacher or student flexibility in curriculum decision making is reduced significantly because the specified objectives define expected levels of student performance. The teacher and the students, if they are old enough, know what these expectations are, they know that they (both students and teacher) will be tested to determine their success in meeting these objectives, and hence their choices are circumscribed by the objectives. Options that might have otherwise been pursued are relinquished in favor of school- or districtwide goals.

Whether one works within a system that encourages truly individualized educational programs and that supports high levels of student planning or within one where grade-level expectations and curriculum content are specified in great detail, the role of the teacher in curriculum decision making is always important. It is important because the teacher serves as the interpreter of educational policy and because the teacher is the major mediator of what shall be taguht—if not learned—in the classroom.

Although curriculum development can and often does take form in the creation of materials, curriculum development more frequently yields no materials but, rather, plans that might be no more than sketchy notes. For example, a teacher might decide that a particular activity would be educationally beneficial in a classroom, say, a discussion of a book or film that students have read or seen. And the teacher might also decide that after the discussion he will ask the students to express their ideas about what they have read or seen in a painting or short story, a poem or a play. What the teacher wants to do is to help children recognize that ideas can be expressed in different ways and that they can have a choice in the way in which they choose to express what they know. Suppose further that the teacher thinks that it might be interesing and useful to follow up this activity by having a poet or a painter visit the class to talk with the children about her work. In this episode, the teacher is engaged in curriculum planning, but no materials are being created. It might be that the teacher prepares some notes to himself or develops a fairly elaborate lesson plan, but the latter is not a necessity. Teachers engage in such planning most of the time, and to do so is to make curriculum decisions, to engage in a form of personal curriculum deliberation. This, too, is one way in which curriculum development occurs. Indeed, it would not be possible to have a school without some form of curriculum development. The form might be as "loose" as is used in a neoprogressive school or as "tight" as a highly systematic training program that leaves virtually nothing to chance. The point here is not the form that curriculum planning takes, but the fact that it must occur.

A second group involved in curriculum development is that working under the aegis of school districts. Many school districts appoint committees made up of subject specialists and teachers to work jointly in the creation of curriculum materials that are considered particularly suitable for their particular school district or some portion of it. A school district under the leadership of the assistant superintendent for curriculum and instruction might decide as a result of the activities of a lay group that curriculum materials are needed in the area of human relations. The district serves a community that has a wide array of ethnic and racial minority groups and after having conducted a national search for available curriculum materials decides to create its own materials, materials that will draw on the talents and resources of people living in the community. A committee is appointed by the superintendent to work on such a project, and a budget is made available to compensate teachers and others for the additional work that they will be required to do.

Such a group might work two afternoons each week after school for six months to develop the structure and format for the curriculum, to create the activities, and to secure the necessary materials so that what is created can be used in the classrooms. At the end of its work this committee will have prepared written, visual, and perhaps audio material relevant to the children living in the community the school district serves. Such work might be followed up with in-service education programs for principals and selected teachers, so that the aims of the project are gradually realized. If as a result of such a trial the materials are found to need revision, revision will occur. The expectation is that these materials, especially created for this particular school district, will become a regular part of the curriculum of each school. The materials represent the vehicles through which the initial aspirations of the lay group will be realized.

It is obvious that it is one thing to create plans for oneself and quite another thing to create plans and materials that others are to use. All teachers do the former; relatively few do the latter. What one can consider in developing materials for others to use will be described in detail later. For now it is important to recognize the difference.

A third major group to engage in curriculum development are the staffs of state departments of education or the committees that work under the aegis of the chief state school officer.

Curriculum development at the state level can take the form of specific curriculum materials to be used in the classroom, or, as is more typically the case, it can take the form of curriculum outlines that can be used as guides by local school districts. In California, for example, the state superintendent of schools appoints committees to develop new state guidelines, or, as they are called in California, State Curriculum Frameworks, for the teaching of particular subject areas prescribed in the state education code. These committees, made up of representatives from professional groups in education and lay people, might be appointed for a one- to three-year period to meet, say, monthly, and to carry out the deliberations, consultations, and preparation of a new framework for teaching mathematics, social studies, art, music, the humanities, and so on.

The function of such statewide curriculum committees is to make use of knowledgeable people in the subject field in order to upgrade the quality of educational programs in the various fields of study. It provides an opportunity for the state to update what it offers school districts and in the process be instrumental in guiding the direction of educational change.

In developing a statewide framework for a field, a curriculum committee is faced with a variety of difficult decisions. How specific should the materials be? If they are highly specific, they might be inappropriate for particular populations within the state. If they are very general, the translation from the guidelines to practice might be very difficult. Who should be consulted in preparing such guidelines? In a statewide framework committee on which I served, a circuit of hearings was held throughout the state with relevant professional groups. We wanted reactions to the ideas we as a committee had created and we wanted the groups to feel that they, too, participated in the process of planning the framework they would eventually use. As it turned out, this process was a form of in-service education for those of us on the committee as well as for those who participated in twenty-odd meetings that were held throughout the state. We learned a great deal about what teachers and university professors regard as appropriate goals and content, and they had the opportunity to reflect on some ideas about the content and goals of curriculum that they might not have otherwise considered.

This planning process lasted about three years, at the end of which a statewide framework for the visual arts was published by the state department of education and disseminated to all public schools and colleges in California. In addition, the work of the state curriculum framework committee was given a central place in regional and statewide conventions in art education. What occurred was a spinoff whose effects were much wider than the work that the committee did on the written document itself. The position the committee developed with respect to the curriculum for teaching art in the state had an intellectual set of consequences for the way in which art education was conceptualized.

One should not underestimate the importance of state-endorsed programs or curriculum materials. The ultimate legal responsibility for education belongs not to the local school district but rather to the state. The constitutions of the various states assign that responsibility to the state board of education, which in turn develops a state education code that provides the guidelines, standards, and mandates for local school districts. The state superintendent of schools, through his or her staff, and with the assistance of the county school superintendent, is responsible for monitoring local school districts to assure that the requirements of the state education code are met. Although relatively few county superintendents execute primarily a monitorial function, the authority of the office and that of the state department of education carry weight. In many states, the withholding of funds to local school districts is possible if the mandates provided in the state education code are not heeded.

The point of all of this is to underscore the importance of state sanctions in the area of curriculum policy, particularly when a statewide educational policy is backed up by funding options that the state department of education holds.

It should be noted also that the state board of education is in some degree guided by the advice of the state superintendent of public instruction, particularly with respect to matters dealing with what should be taught and for what amount of time. In some states, the education code specifies which subjects will be taught at each grade level and how many minutes of instruction will be provided for these subjects each week. In addition, the state prepares a list of acceptable textbooks or provides state-adopted textbooks for the local school districts. Because many teachers build their programs around them, these resources have a great impact on the content with which students come into contact. If a textbook in science devotes three chapters to ichthyology, students using that textbook study ichthyology. If a textbook on the social studies presents a black perspective on the civil rights movement, students study that material. Because access to content is a condition to learning that content, questions of content inclusion–content exclusion are extremely important. In effect, they define much of the opportunity students will have within the school to deal with certain topics and ideas.

A fourth group that engages in curriculum development are those working in university research and development (R&D) centers and in regional educational laboratories supported by the National Institute of Education. Research and development centers, all of which are affiliated with universities, conceive of their mission as conducting research and facilitating educational development by devising products and programs that are primarily experimental and, in principle, related to ongoing research. Educational laboratories do, however, engage in the creation and testing of curriculum materials, the marketing of which is handled by commercial publishers.

Educational laboratories such as CEMREL engage in the development of curriculum materials in mathematics and in the area of aesthetic education. The main function of educational laboratories is to use federal funds to pioneer new methods and programs that require the skills of sophisticated curriculum specialists and others and the kind of risk capital that commercial publishers would be unwilling to provide. Thus, with average annual budgets of millions of dollars, the laboratories conceptualize, develop, test, and document these materials for use in classrooms throughout the country. In addition, some laboratories have created teacher centers to train teachers in the use of the materials they have designed. The materials once produced are often published commercially, and school districts, with the aid of federal funds, may purchase from a commercial publisher what has been developed through the support of federal funds at the laboratory or the university-related R&D center.

Educational laboratories are generally larger and have larger budgets than R&D centers; they occupy often elaborate and at times sumptuous quarters and have a staff that consists not only of curriculum specialists, but also social scientists, designers, photographers, managers, secretaries, and the like.

In their ideal form, educational laboratories and university R&D centers should undertake programs of curriculum development that are high risk, forward looking, and based on the highest professional standards of the field. Agencies supported by the taxes of citizens have a special obligation that, in my view, exceeds that of commercial publishers. Unfortunately, the competition for federal funds has created in both laboratories and R&D centers a need to "look good," to project an image of success that too often hampers candor. Laboratories and R&D centers should be places where it's all right to fail. Indeed, a laboratory without failure is a contradiction in terms.

A fifth group, and in many respects the most influential group aside from the classroom teacher in the area of curriculum development, are commercial publishers. And the most influential material published is the textbook. Textbooks are not typically looked on as curricula, but they are certainly important curriculum materials. In the first place, textbooks are, for many teachers, the hub around which programs are built. When a school or school district adopts a textbook in social studies, science, or mathematics, this book, de facto, defines a significant portion of the content of what students will study. Textbooks in these areas also contain suggestions to students and teachers for supplementary activities and in this way further define what students will do in the classroom. In addition, teacher guides are prepared for many textbooks that provide guidance to the teacher regarding the kinds of questions or issues that can be used for discussion, and some contain tests that can be used to determine if the students have learned what the textbook taught.

Increasingly, however, publishers are developing not only textbooks, but also multimedia kits designed to teach what publishers believe will sell in schools. Most of these materials—and they come in video cassettes, film-strips, audiotapes, graphic displays, and educational games—are designed to provide short-term units rather than semester or year-long programs. The creation of these materials originates from at least three factors: the possibilities that new technology provides, the marketability of the materials to schools and hence their profitability for publishers, and the realization that the channels through which students learn are multiple and the range of sensory modes that can be used for facilitating learning is wide. Yet, despite the plethora of such materials—a visit to a national convention of teachers and school administrators will provide a mind-boggling array of such materials displayed by publishers—the single most important resource influencing what children study in school, aside from the teacher, is still the textbook.

What we find when we look at who does curriculum development and where and when it is done are a variety of groups engaged in the task. Teachers develop curriculum when they plan for their classes, school districts engage in curriculum development through the creation of materials to be used in classrooms, professional and lay groups develop curricula when they create state frameworks for teaching in particular subject fields. Finally, educational laboratories, R&D centers, and commercial publishers engage in curriculum development through the production of materials such as *Man: A Course of Study*, SRA Reading Kits, DISTAR, CEMREL's Aesthetic Education Program, and SWIRL's Basic Reading Series. All of these groups and individuals engage in curriculum development as they attempt to transform aspirations and images of educational virtue into plans and methods they believe are useful for realizing such ends.

DIMENSIONS OF CURRICULUM PLANNING

What are the factors that one might consider in the design of an educational program? What can one take into account in curriculum planning? As I have already indicated, I do not believe it possible in the field of education to prescribe formulas that one is to follow, but it is possible to provide concepts and generalizations that can heighten one's sensitivity to issues, problems, and possibilities to which one might attend. What follows is the identification and discussion of some dimensions of curriculum planning that can be considered by those attempting to design educational programs. The sequence of these dimensions is, to a large degree, arbitrary. One need not begin or end with the factors or aspects as they appear here. Because for the purposes of writing some ordering is necessary, the sequence that follows seems to me to be reasonable, but one may proceed in curriculum development with a very different order.

It should be noted at the outset that the study of the processes of curriculum development as it actually occurs for individuals or groups is rare. It has only been quite recently that the process has been studied empirically. The reason for the general neglect is fairly clear. Individuals and groups interested in developing curriculum materials or formulating curriculum policy have had those goals as their major priorities. The study of the processes through which decisions are made is seldom a part of their mission. Hence, what groups actually do in different contexts and circumstances is at present largely known through recollection rather than through, say, naturalistic observation as an ethnographer might study the process. What is clear from the case studies of curriculum decision making that have been published is that the process is far more convoluted, circuitous, and adventitious than one might be led to believe by reading the formal literature on curriculum planning. In the next chapter, a description of the planning processes of one curriculum development group will be described in some detail. For the present, we will examine some of the aspects that can be considered in the creation of a curriculum.

GOALS AND THEIR PRIORITIES

Perhaps the area in curriculum planning that has received the most attention in the literature is that of how objectives should be formulated. If one looks into the literature in curriculum, one will find distinctions that are made among aims, goals, and objectives. Aims are the most general statements that proclaim to the world the values that some group holds for an educational program. "The aim of this school is to help students learn to participate effectively in the democratic way of life." From aims we sense a direction, a point of view, a set of values, to which the community or group subscribes. These statements form a kind of educational manifesto of cherished values, and, although such statements have been regarded by many as meaningless, if one were to contrast the statement of aims made in school districts in the United States with those found in the written material produced in China, Cuba, or the Soviet Union, one would note significant differences in the spirit and outlook of what has been written. What such statements provide is an articulation of educational faith, in a sense in the way in which the Preamble of the Constitution or the Declaration of Independence expresses general but still meaningful beliefs about the individual and his or her relationship to the society.

A second kind of aim is referred to as a goal. Goals are statements of intent, midway in generality between aims and objectives. Goals describe the purposes held for a course or school program. "The goal of this course is to help students understand the causes of social revolution." "The goal of the course is to develop skills in copper enamel jewelry making." These statements are considerably more specific than aims, but insufficiently specific for, say, instructional objectives. Goals are intended to provide a greater focus on anticipated outcomes and to provide curriculum planners with the basis for the selection of curriculum content. In the standard curriculum literature, goals are supposed to be deduced from aims. Having deduced goals, one then deduces objectives. Having deduced objectives, one then proceeds to formulate curriculum activities. The planning process is supposed to be a step-by-step process from the general to the specific; from ends to means. The problem with this view, as I have indicated earlier, is that it assumes that curriculum activities that are educationally significant always have explicit goals or objectives, which they do not, and that the formulation of goals must precede activities, which is not always true.

Objectives are typically specific statements of what students are to be able to do after having experienced a curriculum or a portion of one. Objectives of the instructional variety are supposed to state with little ambiguity what particular forms of behavior the student will be able to display. Thus, "The student will be able to create a clay bowl on a potter's wheel that is at least twelve inches high, having walls no thicker than one-half inch," would be an example of an instructional objective.

Now the thrust of these comments is not essentially to restate the forms in which educational intentions are couched or even to describe their levels of generality but rather to point out that intentions are appropriate to consider in the development of an educational program and that priorities among goals must be determined.

The determination of priorities is influenced by the context in which programs are to function. For example, a school board, a community, or a school faculty might be convinced that a particular set of goals is of the utmost importance but at the same time recognize that the realization of those goals in this particular context is not possible at this time. Thus, goals, even those holding high status, are shifted in their operational importance. A faculty might believe that the critical study of local politics is crucial to the sound education of adolescents but might also recognize that the community would not allow such studies to be taught, or that there is in fact no one on the faculty who has the professional competence to teach such a course well. In this case, other areas and goals become practically more important.

Thus far I have discussed goals as they relate to and across subject matters, but within fields, too, there is a host of competing goals. What kind of goals should be emphasized in mathematics: comprehension of the structure of mathematics as a system or skills in computation? What kind of social studies should be provided: those that emphasize history or those that emphasize the methods of inquiry of the social sciences? What sort of art program should be offered to students: one that enables them to appreciate the most significant works of art that have been created or one that aims at the development of skills needed to create art? Competent curriculum deliberation will consider the options within as well as between fields of study. In such consideration, educational values obviously come into play, and it is here that basic orientations to curriculum emerge among those who deliberate. But the ultimate resolution of these priorities always takes place within the constraints of the context. What one finally puts into practice is a function of the interaction of aspirations and existing constraints.

Although acquiescing to existing constraints in educational planning can lead to an inert form of educational conservatism, regard for the constraints of the context is necessary for an intelligent form of curriculum deliberation. Curriculum planning cannot adequately be treated in a simple piecemeal fashion; there are always tradeoffs in time, expected outcome, human and fiscal resources, community support, and the like. To neglect "the big picture" is to court disaster, yet to regard the context only as a set of constraints rather than a set of opportunities is to embrace a maintenance model of educational management. Negotiating the balance between the desirable and the possible is one of the arts of school administration as well as curriculum planning.

THE CONTENT OF THE CURRICULUM

Because goals seldom prescribe the content that can be used in their realization, attention to the selection of content is always an important curriculum consideration. If a curriculum development group working on the development of a curriculum in, say, biology agrees that the major aims of the program are to help students understand (1) that scientific inquiry always yields conclusions that are tentative and (2) that living organisms depend on the environment to survive, the specific content as well as the teaching methods that may be instrumental to such purposes is still not yet given. What the group must do is to identify the variety of potential content areas within biology or within the students' experience outside of biology that will help them grasp these ideas. A curriculum development group might, for example, choose a variety of content ranging from simple forms of plant life to complex forms of human behavior for exemplifying the relationship between organism and environment. Or the group might decide to create some analogies to nonbiological entities such as cities or nations in order to illustrate how similar principles operate in "nonliving phenomena."

The point here is that groups concerned with curriculum planning have options in content selection. The problem is one of deciding which of the possible content options should be selected. One possible criterion for content inclusion, in addition to whether there is some relationship between the content and the aim, is whether the content is likely to be meaningful to the children for whom the program is intended. Children bring to school a wide variety of experience that originate from the homes and communities in which they live. The kind of biological content that children living in a rural area might find meaningful can differ significantly from that which inner-city urban youngsters might find meaningful. One way of dealing with such diversity is to include in one's curriculum material options from which teachers and students can themselves choose. In other words, by providing different kinds of content to make the same point, the flexibility of the materials is increased.

There are, of course, limitations on the number of options that can be provided. The physical size of the syllabus, for example, is not a trivial consideration—nor is the amount of materials teachers should be asked to read. More will be said about these considerations later; for now, the major point to be made is that goals do not prescribe content. Content selection, like goals, can be considered against a backdrop of options. Furthermore, curriculum developers, within the limits that seem reasonable, can provide teachers with the content of options that are related to the aims of the curriculum.

TYPES OF LEARNING OPPORTUNITIES

Goals and content are necessary but not sufficient for the development of a curriculum. The educational imagination must come into play in order to transform goals and content to the kinds of events that will have educational consequences for students. This transformation requires that an event be conceptualized and have sufficient educational promise for students to be used in an educational program. I say that the educational imagination comes into play because it is this task—educational transformation—that draws most heavily on the expertise of the teacher or curriculum designer.

If a group of citizens wanted to know what the most significant concepts and generalizations were in some branch of biology, the individuals most likely to provide such information would be biologists who knew their field well and who were aware of the most recent developments within it. But to acquire such information from biologists is not sufficient for the creation of an educational program. Some educationally appropriate means must be created to enable students to interact with problems or situations that will yield an understanding of these concepts and generalizations. A biologist who has not worked with adolescents, who does not understand what teachers are able to do in a secondary school classroom, is not necessarily the best person to make such a transformation. It is here that curriculum expertise is crucial. For it is here that educational events must be planned and curriculum materials prepared to enable teachers and students to grasp those concepts and generalizations and to do it in a form that is consistent with one's view of education. For example, if one believes that the major mission of the school is to introduce students to the products of the best inquiry in the arts and the sciences, one might decide to use a moderately didactic approach to instruction in, for example, the biological sciences. Such an approach would emphasize the big ideas and theories that biological greats have created. In such a view, the work of Mendel, Darwin, Wall, Muller and Dobzhansky would play a prominent role in content selection. The thrust of the curriculum would be to help students understand the theories and concepts these biologists created, say, within the context of their time. To do this one might provide lectures and films, and perhaps have students read excerpts from primary source material. But if one were interested in having students understand the relationship between biological ideas and the methods through which those ideas were created, if one wanted to help students appreciate the tentativeness of scientific conclusions, then the type of learning opportunities one might use would give students experience in the conduct of biological experiments. The transformation of the "same" content would take different forms because the basic orientation to education would differ significantly.

The options available to the curriculum designer are numerous with virtually any body of content, and in the curriculum field, as in education at large, there has been a longstanding controversy on the relative importance of process as compared to product. Those who emphasize the importance of process tend to formulate learning opportunities that stimulate children to active inquiry. Such individuals want the student to inquire, to think, to act, and in the process to learn. The outcomes of the process are what children learn from the engagement. It is to be hoped that the product of such activity will be consistent with valid substantive knowledge in the field in which the inquiry occurred. But that is not necessarily the major aim. The main aim is to teach children to think, to act, and to learn from the consequences of one's action.

Those who emphasize the product are more interested in what children learn of the conclusions of mature inquiry in specialized fields. Does the student understand the relationship between random mutation and natural selection? Does the student grasp the concept of dominant and recessive genes?

These views of what counts educationally have an extraordinarily important bearing on the kinds of learning opportunities that are created in the curriculum. The advocate, for example, of learning by discovery will frequently be interested in helping children "learn to think like scientists." For such people the curriculum should be built around problems. The task of the curriculum designer is to create activities that help children either formulate problems or try to resolve the problems posed within the materials.

Although I have emphasized the relationship between one's orientation to curriculum and the kinds of learning opportunities that might be provided, in practice the relationship between activities and goals is neither linear nor unidirectional. Indeed, teachers are more inclined to focus on what they might *do* than on what goals they intend to accomplish.[1] This is because practical decisions always relate to the utility of action. What teachers want and need are ideas that have practical payoffs; ideas that for the most part lead to action. Projects that appear interesting, activities that seem heuristic, events that will be attractive and engaging to students are valued by teachers. Once students are fully engaged in such activities, one can guide them so that various goals and aims are achieved.

But goals and aims, unless they can be transformed into educational events within the classroom in a form that is interesting to students, and within the capacity of teachers, are only empty hopes that have little educational reality. One means through which types of learning opportunities might be created is a matrix of intellectual processes. One such matrix has been formulated by J. P. Guilford, a psychologist long interested in creative thinking and in the structure of the human intellect. What Guilford has done is to conceptualize the variety of aptitudes or processes that the human mind is capable of. His scientific ambition has been not only to conceptualize these mental processes, but also to create instruments that can be used to assess them. We need not for our purposes try to evaluate the scientific validity of these instruments, but we can examine his model of intellect for its potential utility in the creation of learning opportunities within a curriculum. That is, we can use Guilford's model as a kind of mnemonic device to help us—if we so choose—to create learning opportunities that elicit different forms of thinking. These forms, once identified, could then be related to bodies of content considered important so that sophisticated forms of thinking could be used to deal with educationally significant content.

Related to Guilford's structure of the intellect are the intellectual processes identified in the taxonomy of educational objectives in the so-called cognitive domain. The cognitive taxonomy lists, not 120 mental processes, as does Guilford, but six. They are (1) possession of information, (2) comprehension, (3) application, (4) analysis, (5) synthesis, and (6) evaluation. Although these terms refer to kinds of objectives that one can formulate and to the kind of test items or tasks on tests related to those objectives, the taxonomy can also be used to formulate types of learning opportunities that can be made available to students. For example, one could design learning opportunities that were intended to elicit each or all of these processes. Of course, there can be and often is a gap between intention and reality, but nevertheless the taxonomy can help focus attention to enable one to convert a learning opportunity from one that is parochial and prosaic into one that has intellectual significance.

A word must be said about the potential hazards of classification systems, taxonomies, theoretical models, and the like. Such conceptual devices can be extremely useful for helping one differentiate and classify. In performing this function, they increase intellectual precision by helping us bracket the world in useful ways, but one must not forget that such bracketing is a construction of mind, that there are other ways to classify, and that one should take care not to reify concepts into realities that eventually constrain our understanding. Some of this has already occurred in the case of the taxonomy of educational objectives. These taxonomies differentiate the cognitive from the affective, the affective from the psychomotor, and the psychomotor from the cognitive. Although these distinctions were originally considered nominal in their ontological status, individuals in education and psychology sometimes conclude that so-called cognitive activities are independent of affective ones, or that psychomotor activities are neither cognitive nor affective. In actual experience, there is no clear line between cognition and affect, except within the definitions of the taxonomy. For example, to have a feeling and not to know it, is not to have it. To think about a feeling is to know it. In short, the affective and cognitive pervade each other. Although in our culture we do find it useful to talk about our thoughts and our feelings, in education such talk can lead to theoretically devastating ideas and to practically questionable results. Some schools, for example, teach "cognitive" subjects in the morning and "affective" ones in the afternoons. My point here is not to argue that conceptual devices should not be used in the formulation of types of learning opportunities but rather to state that unless they are treated as limited tools such devices can interfere with the ways in which aims and activities are conceptualized.

THE ORGANIZATION OF LEARNING OPPORTUNITIES

All educational programs occur over time. How events are planned within a period of time is one of the decisions curriculum planners can make. There are two images of curricular sequences that it may be useful to distinguish between. One of these is the "staircase" model already mentioned, the other is a "spiderweb" model.

The staircase model conjures up the image of a series of independent steps that lead to a platform from which one exits. This conception is one that conceives of curriculum activities as building on what preceded them, preparing for what is to come. The movement, as is true in the climbing of a staircase, is always upward.

This conception is metaphorically consistent with terms such as *entry skills* and *exit competencies*. The route is well defined, mechanical in construction, and efficient. There is little room for wasted motion or exploratory adventures. Perhaps the most pristine example of such a model in curriculum is to be found in linear programs used in computer-assisted instruction. The same image was used in teaching machine programs that were available several years ago. The task of the curriculum designer is to create a sequence of frames, that, like the staircase, leads the student to a predetermined destination whose features are known by the curriculum designer and the teacher.

The spiderweb model is one in which the curriculum designer provides the teacher with a set of heuristic projects, materials, and activities whose use will lead to diverse outcomes among the group of students. The assumption used in this mode of curriculum organization is that what is needed are projects and activities that invite engagement rather than control. With engaging projects or activities students will create ideas and develop skills that they want to pursue. The task of the teacher is then to facilitate the interests and goals that students develop as a result of such engagement. As children bring with them different experimental backgrounds, it is reasonable to expect that the kind of meaning they make will also differ. This is seen as a virtue rather than a liability, for it is in the cultivation of those interests that truly personalized education resides.

To be sure, the kind of personalized education that is implied in a spiderweb model of curriculum organization places great demands on the inventiveness of the teacher. In this model the teacher cannot rely on stock responses to identical problems or tasks among students. Some students will work independently, others will work in small groups, but all will require a teacher who knows what kinds of problems and interests the students have and who is prepared to provide or point them to the resources that they need to develop those interests or to resolve those problems.

I do not believe it possible to conclude that one mode of curriculum organization is more educationally beneficial than the other. It depends on one's view of education and on the readiness of students—regardless of their age—to cope with different types of problems or tasks. It requires, as Whitehead implied, attention to the rhythm of education:

Life is essentially periodic. It comprises daily periods, with their alternations of work and play, of activity and of sleep, and seasonal periods, which dictate our terms and our holidays; and also it is composed of well-marked yearly periods. These are the gross obvious periods which no one can overlook. There are also subtler periods of mental growth, with their cyclic recurrences, yet always different as we pass from cycle to cycle, though the subordinate stages are reproduced in each cycle. That is why I have chosen the term "rhythmic," as meaning essentially the conveyance of difference within a framework of repetition. Lack of attention to the rhythm and character of mental growth is a main source of wooden futility in education. I think that Hegel was right when he analysed progress into three stages, which he called Thesis, Antithesis, and Synthesis; though for the purpose of application of his idea to educational theory I do not think that the names he gave are very happily suggestive. In relation to intellectual progress I would term them, the stage of romance, the stage of precision, and the stage of generalisation.[2]

Yet, notwithstanding the argument that there is no intrinsic value in the abstract for either of these models of curriculum organization, I think that it is fair to say that the spiderweb model has more appeal to the progressives among educators, whereas the staircase model has appeal to those with the more conservative educational bent. Those holding a progressive, or child-centered, philosophy tend to emphasize the differences among children and the belief that children should be given ample opportunity to formulate their own educational aims. The image of the teacher in such a view is like that of the travel agent described earlier. The teacher is not to "stuff the duck" but rather to facilitate the achievement of aims born out of the interaction children have with the stimulating resources the teacher pro-vides.

Those with a more conservative view of education believe that there is a body of content that children should learn and that the sequential organi-zation of this material is the best assurance that it will be learned. The staircase model fits the view nicely because it is systematic, well organized, and linear. When this view prevails, providing for individual differences usually means varying the pace through which children proceed to climb the same stairways rather than building different stairways leading to different goals for different children.

Historically these alternative models or conceptions of curriculum organi-zation have been the subject of much dispute. In his classic book *The Child and the Curriculum,* John Dewey describes these camps this way. One group says:

Subdivide each topic into studies; each study into lessons; each lesson into specific facts and formulae. Let the child proceed step by step to master each one of these separate parts, and at last he will have covered the entire ground. The road which looks so long when viewed in its entirety, is easily traveled, considered as a series of particular steps. Thus emphasis is put upon the logical subdivisions and consecutions of the subject-matter. Problems of instruction are problems of procuring texts giving logical parts and sequences, and of presenting these portions in class in a similar definite and graded way. Subject-matter furnishes the end, and it determines method. The child is simply the immature being who is to be matured; he is the superficial being who is to be deepened; his is narrow ex-perience which is to be widened. It is his to receive, to accept. His part is fulfilled when he is ductile and docile.

Not so, says the other sect. The child is the starting-point, the center, and the end. His development, his growth, is the ideal. It alone furnishes the standard. To the growth of the child all studies are subservient; they are instruments valued as they serve the needs of growth. Personality, character, is more than subject-matter. Not knowledge or information, but self-realization, is the goal. To possess all the world of knowledge and lose one's one self is as awful a fate in education as in religion. Moreover, subject-matter never can be got into the child from without. Learning is active. It involves reaching out of the mind. It involves organic assimilation starting from within. Literally, we must take or stand with the child and our departure from him. It is he and not the subject-matter which determines both quality and quantity of learning.[3]

For Dewey, the solution to the problem of how to sequence learning opportunities was to be found not in orthodoxies or in dogmas but rather in the concept of experience itself. The central question for Dewey was, "What kind of experience is a mode of curriculum organization likely to yield for students?" For Dewey, the experience was to be educative, rather than non- or miseducative.[4] Yet differences of view as to what educational experience is and what conditions are likely to produce it still generate a considerable degree of acrimony in the field. Different parties may agree that students should have experiences in school that educate rather than its contrary, but they may differ radically in their conception of educational experience and in their judgment of what will bring it about. One task of the curriculum specialist is to facilitate the critical deliberations of such issues so that the choices that are ultimately made will rest on considered alternatives.

THE ORGANIZATION OF CONTENT AREAS

One task of the curriculum specialist is to help curriculum planners consider the ways in which content areas within the curriculum should be defined. One can, of course, maintain the traditional subject matter fields and make decisions about content within these boundaries. One might continue to teach arithmetic, history, art, music, science, reading, and the like. But one could also choose to teach communication, the humanities, the social studies, or ecological studies, problems of contemporary society, popular culture, and other areas that redefine or cut across the traditional subject matter fields within the curriculum.

The definition of these areas of study is a matter of what Bernstein calls "classification." Classification can be strong or weak, it can invite integration or discourage it. Bernstein writes:

> Classification, here, does not refer to *what* is classified, but to the *relationships* between contents. Classification refers to the nature of the differentiation between contents. Where classification is strong, contents are well insulated from each other by strong boundaries. Where classification is weak, there is reduced insulation between contents for the boundaries between contents are weak or blurred. *Classification thus refers to the degree of boundary maintenance between contents.* Classification focuses our attention upon boundary strength as the critical distinguishing feature of the division of labour of educational knowledge.[5]

If the model from which the curriculum is drawn is what is usually found among academic disciplines that occupy so central a place in the university, then it is likely that its classification will have strong boundary strength.[6] Discrete subject matters will constitute the content and organization of the curriculum. But if the curriculum of the secondary school is considered not primarily as preparation for the university or as an effort to prepare students to become scholars in discrete fields of learning, then it is more likely that other forms of content organization will be considered. To develop programs that depart from traditional subject matter disciplines is easier to say than to do. In the first place, certification requirements may deter the educators of teachers from preparing prospective teachers who can deal with a range of fields or with problems that are not within single disciplines. Second, there may be no individuals on existing school faculties who are interested in cross-disciplinary teaching or teaching in areas that do not closely approximate the fields in which they have been trained. Third, the political situation of professional educators often parallels disciplinary lines, and they may not wish to have competition for time and resources coming from programs outside of their particular fields. Finally, testing programs might penalize students who did very well in, say, the study of mass media in high school, but who knew little about English literature. In short, there are many social, political, and intellectual impediments to the development of new forms of content organization within the curriculum.

Yet, notwithstanding the practical difficulties of developing new forms of content organization, this is an area in which theoretical options exist. If the grounds for developing new modes of content organization are sufficiently compelling, one could try to make the changes or secure the resources to support it.

It is interesting to speculate on the possible grounds for such change. One of the arguments that has supported conventional approaches built around the disciplines is related to the so-called structure of the disciplines argument.[7] It is argued that each formal discipline has a distinctive structure. The syntactical aspect of the structure of a discipline defines the mode and criteria through which inquiry proceeds. The conceptual or substantive structure defines the concepts and subject matters inquired into. Because disciplines have a history and are well defined compared to general fields of study and because they offer the student organized concepts and theory, knowledge in these disciplines is easier to acquire, to store, and to retrieve than that available in fields that are less well organized. The order disciplines provide, the methods they employ, the criteria they use, make intellectual precision possible.

Yet it can be argued that the problems that citizens confront in their daily lives seldom come in the forms with which the disciplines can deal. Most practical problems of life are "messy." They require the use of diverse kinds of knowledge; they demand the application of practical judgment that is not rule governed or accessible, using criteria that might be suitable for a single discipline. The argument proceeds that school programs, both elementary and secondary, should not be controlled by a propaedeutic theory of education. Schools should not decide what to teach or how to organize what they teach on the basis of what universities teach. What follows represents one secondary school's effort to offer courses that traverse disciplinary lines:

Courses in the upper two years are generally available to both junior and seniors. Very few requirements are placed upon upper class students since they are expected to exercise mature judgment in choosing their areas of specialization. Students are expected to sign up for approximately 30 units of courss per year, except by special permission with the faculty scheduling committee.

Science

300   How To Fix It

Simple maintenance and repair of household items.   1 unit

301   Student Teaching In Science—3 W's or TBT (senionrs only)

Students will teach science classes in consultation with science teachers. Credit for maini-teaching.   2 units per trimester

303   Intermediate Biology

An inquiry into life and a study of the basic structures and functions of micro-organism, plants, and onimals with emphasis on evolutionary steps, patterns of heredity, animal behavior, and ecosystems.   4 units

304   Advanced Biology   4 units

305   TBT I—(theories behind technology)
Inter-disciplinary course of physics and chemistry. Emphasis on scientific processes rather than accumulation of facts.   4 units

306   TBT II
An advanced continuation of TBT I   4 units

Social Sciences

310   Rebel
A study of the rebel in contemporary society—his reasons and his strategies.
                                                                                   4 units

311   Survival
Practical ways of understanding and surviving in the modern city.   2 units

312   Which Way America
An in-depth approach to key events and people that shaped America   2 or 4 units

313   Backgrounds of Contemporary America
Course starting with contemporary events as a springboard into their root causes. Use of historical factual data along with American literature to capture the American consciousness of today. Will include some emphasis on means of communicating these ideas. Can be used in partial fulfillment of State History and English requirements.   4 units

314   Black Humanities   To be announced
A study of the writing of the Afro-American people with emphasis on the period

from 1900 to the present, oral interpretation of recent Black writing in America and the African nations. (Course design could be a project of the interested students and faculty.) A Black teacher is being sought for this course.   2 units

MODE OF PRESENTATION AND MODE OF RESPONSE

One of the least-considered options in curriculum planning deals with the modalities through which students encounter and express what they learn. For the vast majority of subject fields in schools, the mode of presentation that students encounter is either verbal or written language. The teacher talks or students read textbooks containing the information and ideas they are to acquire. To demonstrate what they have learned, the students are expected to write or to take examinations that are also presented in written form. Out of traditional expectations we have inadvertently allowed one mode to so dominate how expression is to occur in school that we have come to believe that to have any understanding at all the student must be able to demonstrate it in verbal or written terms.

Yet the forms through which knowledge and understanding are constructed, stored, and expressed are considerably wider than verbal or written discourse. What can be known, say, about autumn can take form in scientific propositions that deal with chemical changes in trees, in astronomical propositions about the location of our planet in relation to the sun, in poetic expression disclosing the smell of burning autumn leaves, in visual images that present to our consciousness the color of a Vermont landscape, in auditory forms that capture the crackle of leaves under our footsteps. Autumn, in short, is known in a variety of ways and the ways in which it can be known are expressible in a wide range of expressive forms.

Now the significance of this fact for the development of educational programs is considerable. What it implies it that educational programs that aim to help children gain an understanding of the world need to recognize that understanding is secured and experienced in different ways. What one is able to know through forms of musical expression cannot be known in discursive form, and vice versa. Humans employ different knowledge systems to acquire, store, and retrieve understanding, and they use different performance systems to express what they know about the world. For the curriculum designed, this implies that if students are to understand phenomena in the variety of ways in which they can be understood, they need to have the opportunity to encounter forms that express ideas about those phenomena in different ways. Furthermore, it implies that if teachers are to understand what students know about something, then students should be given options in the ways in which they can express what they know. In short, students need not be restricted to one way of expressing what they have learned; curriculum designers need not use verbal or written forms of expression as the only means of presenting ideas to students.

When one also recognizes that there are aptitude differences among students with respect to the knowledge and performance systems they use best, the grounds for using diverse modes of presentation and reponse become even stronger. One could argue that by withholding such opportunities from students a significant proportion of them are denied equal educational opportunity and that certain modes of presentation and forms of response deny them the opportunity to display what they have learned in the forms that most suits their aptitudes.

Although this might seem farfetched, I do not believe it is. We have created a culture in schooling that is so heavily pervaded by verbal and written performance systems that we take such performance systems for granted. In the process we forget that the culture at large depends on a much wider array of human competencies. We regard alternatives that are nondiscursive as "enrichment activities." We assign them to the margins of our concerns; they are events that are "nice to have" but not really of educational significance. Furthermore, we do not often recognize the unique epistimological functions that different expressive forms make possible.

The appreciation of this epistemological diversity allows the curriculum designer to create activities that may be experienced in one mode and expressed by the student in another. For example, a student might read a short story and express what she has learned or experienced from it in a painting, film, or poem. Or, conversely, a student might see a film and express his reaction in a short story. Although such activities do occur at present, they are seldom created intentionally and are seldom based on a realization of the interaction between knowledge and performance systems. What I am suggesting here is that curriculum designers can intentionally exploit the variety of modalities humans use to conceptualize and experience the world and to express what they have learned about it.

It is true, of course, that fields do have indigenous expressive modalities. Historians write prose, physicists express what they have learned in equations, musicians perform with voice or instrument, painters create visual images. To know whether someone knows history, we ask the the person to speak or write. To determine whether someone knows physics, we ask the person to explain physical theory or to do a physics experiment. To the extent to which we would like students to express themselves within the mode that is indigenous to the discipline, *that* mode should dominate. But ideas secured from a discipline need not necessarily be limited to the mode indigenous to it. A study of history can lead to ideas that are best expressed by some students within the context of poetry rather than prose or within film or music. Ideas dealing with historical phenomena can be expressed in modes that are nonverbal. In addition, ideas that are not historical, per se, can be stimulated by the study of history, and, of course, these too can be expressed in modes that do not make use of what is indigenous to historical scholarship.

I use history only as an example. Other fields fit, a fortiori. Now this way of thinking about expression and response has some very interesting epistemological implications. We take history to be what has been written that meets, roughly, the criteria accepted within that field. By convention, historians expect history to be written and they expect historical scholarship to contain evidence, if not proof, of historical veracity. But such conventions need not necessarily foreclose other ways in which historical insight or generalization can be conveyed. Indeed, one might argue that written expression is a surrogate for what the historian knows in other ways, ways that often are not verbal. What I am suggesting is for curriculum designers to consider the potential of allowing students to use modes of response to historical ideas or experiences that might take shape in forms that are not indigenous to history as it is now conceived. I believe the exploitation of such possibilities has considerable potential for the education of the young. Indeed, to dramatize the limited scope of our expressive options, one has only to look at graduate programs. We seem to operate on the belief that the written word is the only means through which one can legitimately demonstrate that one knows something.

TYPES OF EVALUATION PROCEDURES

Closely related to the type of presentation and response available to students is the type of evaluation procedures that are used to identify and assess what students have learned and experienced. Although subsequent chapters treat the problems of educational evaluation in detail, some preliminary remarks about the relationships between evaluation and curriculum development seem appropriate here.

In the first place, evaluation is a process that pervades curriculum decision making. Evaluation is not simply an activity that occurs after students have completed a unit of study. The very act of deciding on content, activities, aims, sequence, or mode of presentation or response requires one to consider the options and to evaluate the utility of the alternatives. Because more options exist than can be employed, selection is necessary. Selection requires choices, and choices require appraisals concerning strengths and liabilities of the alternatives with respect to some set of values; hence, evaluation occurs. The main issue with respect to evaluation centers around the care, the complexity, and the comprehensiveness with which the choices are made. In this sense, evaluation is a necessary part of any deliberative process. What we seek is that it be competent. Evaluation in the more traditional view often refers to the measurement of student performance. Here, too, there are important options that curriculum can consider. In terms of what I said earlier about the relationship between modes of presentation and response and student aptitudes, we may infer that how a student is able to express what he or she has learned will influence what the student can make public. What is made public in turn influences what conclusions teachers and others come to regarding how well the student has done. Although the provision of different student performance options for purposes of summative evaluation creates problems for classical test theory, I do not believe that the requirements of classical test theory should determine how we try to find out what students have learned and experienced at school. Let the test and measurement specialists follow our needs in education rather than we follow theirs.

With respect to the procedures for evaluation in the curriculum development process, groups often go through several steps or stages. As I have already indicated, evaluation occurs throughout the process of curriculum development. The determination that a new program is needed is, in part, the consequence of having judged that a lack exists or that some new program holds promise for significant educational gain. Needs assessment, the process through which educators and others determine exiting needs, is itself pervaded by value judgments in the selection of items used on questionnaires and tests, of the format that is employed, and in the populations that are selected for assessment, not to mention the value-saturated process of interpreting the information once it is secured.

But even after the initial judgment has been made about the need for a new program, the selection of activities, goals, content, and the the like require, as I have indicated, some form of evaluation. Any form of decision making requires judgment, and judgment requires evaluation of choices, options, and alternatives.

Taking this as a given, we can identify the stages or steps that many curriculum groups employ in the process of evaluating materials that are being developed. One such process is referred to as hothouse trials. In this stage, a group of curriculum developers will work with an evaluator to locate classrooms in which prototype materials may be tried. These prototype materials are usually in rough form, having enough finish for the teacher or, as is sometimes the case, a member of a curriculum development team to use them in a classroom. The purpose of the hothouse trial is to identify any major problems with the material, to determine if some important oversights have been made: Are the problems suitable for children of this age? Can a teacher have easy access to the materials the way they have been designed? Do the tasks take longer than was expected?

To engage in hothouse trials, a curriculum development group, say, one working within an educational laboratory, will have established a network of schools around the laboratory that have agreed to cooperate with the laboratory in testing new material. For the school, such cooperation provides stimulation to teachers and creates a form of in-service education. In addition, some laboratories give cooperating schools free materials after they have been tested. For the laboratories, the schools provide the field site that they need to reality-test the materials. A network of schools with which the laboratory has a good relationship diminishes the need to locate and contact new schools each time materials have to be tested. Thus, the relationship can be viewed as a kind of symbiotic one: all concerned appear to benefit by meeting the needs of the others.

The evaluator attached to the curriculum development group observes the materials being used in the hothouse trial. The evaluator's function is to locate difficulties that the teacher might not recognize and to feed back such information to the curriculum development team. Sometimes a member of the curriculum development team will actually teach with the materials in order to get a firsthand view of how the materials function, but even when this occurs, the evaluator may still be present to observe what the teacher might not see.

The function of the hothouse trials is to permit the curriculum team the closest possible scrutiny of how materials function in classrooms. The rapport between the member of the team and the teachers of the schools should be good: ideally they should see each other as colleagues. Although this rapport and relationship do not typify the field at large—teachers and curriculum developers are seldom seen as colleagues and they typically have no rapport—such a relationship is helpful for purposes of formative evaluation.

After hothouse trials have been completed and the necessary revisions made, the materials are then offered to a limited number of school districts for field testing. Field testing is done on a larger scale and is more impersonal in character than hothouse trials. In this stage of evaluations school districts agree to return to the laboratory their appraisal of the materials after they have had the opportunity to use them. Such appraisals might consist of evaluations that teachers complete or instruments that measure students' performance on achievement tests that the laboratory supplies. The function of the field testing is to approximate more closely the conditions under which the materials will be used but still to be in a position to modify the materials prior to their publication and dissemination. The materials at the field trial stage of development are often in a mimeographed or offset-printed form: they lack the kind of finished quality that they will receive when they are to be marketed.

As a result of field testing, final modifications of the material are done, and subsequently the materials are sent to a publisher who then mounts an advertising program to make their purchase possible by the 17,000 school districts in this country. This advertising program includes display of the materials at conventions attended by teachers and school administrators, mailing of brochures to school districts, placement of ads in journals read by teachers, and visits by salesmen to the school districts to demonstrate the materials at in-service meetings.

These procedures might give one the idea that testing curriculum materials is like testing new drugs before they are marketed, but the resemblance is slight. In drug testing, it is possible to isolate the relationships between the chemistry of a drug and the chemistry of individuals. For the testing of curriculum materials, the context and manner in which they are used by the teacher make a crucial difference in how they will be experienced by children. Poor teaching can render even the most attractive materials dull, and teaching that is imaginative can convert even the most banal materials into experiences that are stimulating. Curriculum materials are always mediated by the context, and the teacher plays a crucial role in that context. This is one reason why the notion of developing "teacher-proof" curriculum materials is suspect. Not only does it demean the teacher and the profession of teaching, it also simply cannot be done in educational situations: training programs, perhaps, but educational programs, no.

I make a point of this because I do not believe that we can have standards for the evaluation of curriculum materials as we have standards to appraise food and drugs. We can use criteria, but criteria imply judgments that are flexible, that consider relationships between the materials and the context in which they are to function. What might be right for one situation will be wrong for others. The creation of a bureau of standards for curriculum materials could work only for the identification of their most egregious faults; such a bureau might function as a screening agency but not as a selection agency. What I believe we can provide through the evaluation of curriculum are judgments concerning the qualities the materials possess, information about some of their effects in a particular context, but not guaranteed results or even the implication of such results. In educational situations we do not have the luxury of substituting rule for judgment.

What I have tried to do thus far is to identify some of the factors that one can take into account in the process of curriculum development, in particular in the design of materials that may be of help to the teacher in his or her work. These factors, or considerations, are to be viewed as heuristic: they are tools to be used, not rules to be followed. There are no rules or recipes that will guarantee successful curriculum development. Judgment is always required, and if this task is a group effort, sensitivity to one's fellow workers is always necessary. To provide a sense of how one such group actually functioned, I have prepared a description of Stanford's Kettering Project, a curriculum development project in elementary art education that I directed at Stanford University. I hope it provides you with a sense of the adventitiousness and flexibility curriculum development requires.

REFERENCES

1. This point has been made with particular force by James McDonald. See his article, "Myths about Instruction," *Educational Leadership*, Vol. 22, No. 7, May 1965, pp. 613–614.
2. Alfred North Whithead, "The Rhythm of Education," in *The Aims of Education and Other Essays*, Macmillan Co., New York, 1929, p. 29.
3. John Dewey, "The Child and the Curriculum," in *Dewey on Education* (Martin S. Dworkin, ed), Bureau of Publications, Teachers College, Columbia University, New York, 1959, p. 95.
4. For a discussion of the differences among educative, noneducative, and miseducative experiences, see John Dewey, *Experience and Education*, Macmillan Co., New York, 1938.
5. Basil Bernstein, "On the Classification and Framing of Educational Knowledge," in *Knowledge and Content* (Michael Young, ed.), Collier-Macmillan Publishers, London, 1971.
6. Ibid., p. 49.
7. Joseph J. Schwab, "The Concept of the Structure of the Discipline," *Educational Record*, Vol. 43, July 1962, pp. 197–205.

8

Some Observations on a Curriculum Development Project

༄༅༅

There is a simple job to be done. The task can be stated in concrete terms. The necessary techniques are known. The equipment needed can easily be provided. Nothing stands in the way but cultural inertia. But what is more characteristic of America than an unwillingness to accept the traditional as inevitable? We are on the threshold of an exciting and revolutionary period, in which the scientific study of man will be put to work in man's best interests. Education must play its part. It must accept that fact that a sweeping revision of educational practices is possible and inevitable. When it has done this, we may look forward with confidence to a school system which is aware of the nature of its tasks, secure in its methods, and generously supported by the informed and effective citizens whom education itself will create.

B. F. SKINNER

༄༅༅

The intention in this chapter is to provide an intimate view of the work of one curriculum and development project.[1] Although this work was done several years ago, it is included in order to offer the reader some concrete examples of the way in which ideas are used, altered, tested, and discarded in the course of curriculum development.[2] Some of the assumptions and ideas that are described are not ones I would use today, but because this work represents my first effort to create a body of curriculum materials for use on a national scale, I believe it appropriate to describe that work so that its assumptions can be compared and contrasted with those presented in earlier chapters of this book. Despite Professor Skinner's confidence in the state of educational technology, our work was not the assured execution of a set of known and tested procedures, but a halting and exploratory effort to give form to a vision.

In the first section of this chapter are described some of the salient characteristics of the field of art education at the time the project was started. In the second section of the chapter the specific purposes of the project and the way in which the work was organized are described. In the third section the theories and beliefs that gave direction to the curriculum development work are addressed and the limitations of theoretical ideas in the practical context of curriculum development are pointed out. Finally, the potential virtues of alternative approaches to the curriculum development process are discussed.

THE BACKGROUND AND AIMS OF THE KETTERING PROJECT

In September 1968, with the support of the Charles F. Kettering Foundation, I initiated a two-year project aimed at developing an art curriculum that would improve the quality of art education in American elementary schools. Although in 1968 the curriculum development movement was more than ten years old, the formal and systematic development of curriculum in the field of elementary art education was hardly begun. In mathematics, in the sciences, in the social studies, and in English, large-scale national projects had been launched. Yet in art education no national project had as yet been funded.

The need for curriculum development programs in art was, I believed, apparent to anyone familiar with the general quality of art education at the elementary school level in the United States. Most school districts in the country employed few or no elementary school art teachers, and the large urban districts that had trained art teachers used them as itinerants who had limited contact with both children and teachers. Thus, most of the art teaching provided in elementary schools was handled by teachers who possessed little skill or understanding in this area.

Because of their obvious lack of background either in art or art education, I was interested in developing resources—both written and visual—that elementary school teachers could use to improve the quality of art education they provided.

In the proposal to the Charles F. Kettering Foundation, a number of ideas that were to provide guidance in the development and organization of the curriculum development efforts were made explicit. First, it was made clear that the curriculum that was being proposed included what I have called in previous writing the productive, the critical, and the historical aspects of art.[3,4] The productive realm focused on helping children acquire the skills necessary for converting a material into a medium for artistic expression. The critical realm focused on developing students' ability to see what they looked at, to develop their ability to encounter visual forms from an aesthetic frame of reference and through such a frame to acquire aesthetic experience. The historical realm attempted to help students understand that art is created in the context of a culture that influences the form and content of art, and art in turn influences the culture.

A second feature of the proposed curriculum was that it was to have a sequential character, because it was recognized that few elementary art programs provided continuity. Itinerant art teachers work with a class only occasionally and very often initiate class projects that can be completed in "one sitting." Regular classroom teachers tend to believe that the wider the variety of projects and materials they allow children to work with the better; hence they, too, offer children not so much an art program as a collection of unrelated art "activities" that are so brief in duration that children seldom have the time necessary for developing the skills that make artistic expression possible.

A third feature of the curriculum proposed to the foundation was that it should contain a wide variety of visual materials especially designed to develop the skills identified in the written curriculum guide. It was quite apparent that in the physical sciences, for example, curriculum developers had provided devices that visually illustrate, say, Newton's third law; why could not similar devices be prepared for teaching the visual arts? It seemed ironic that in a field concerned with vision so few especially designed visual materials were available. It was one of the goals of the project to prepare such materials and to relate them directly to tasks and objectives that appeared in the written curriculum guides.

A fourth feature of the proposal was its attention to the development of evaluation devices or procedures for each of the lessons and units that were to be created. I took the view—not one widely shared at that time in the field—that it was possible to determine the extent to which artistic learning had occurred. Evidence of such learning is manifested not only in the quality of products children create, but also in the insight, sensitivity, and relevance of their remarks about works of art and other aspects of the environment. In addition, I believed that it was possible to create exercises or tests that would in specific ways elicit such skill if it had been developed in the first place.

In sum, the Kettering Project was an effort to develop a sequentially ordered curriculum in art that contained both a written syllabus and a wide array of visual support materials that elementary school teachers could use to increase the quality of the art programs they provided to their students.

HOW WORK ON THE PROJECT
WAS ORGANIZED

Because the grant for the project covered a two-year period, it was within that period of time that a number of tasks had to be undertaken and completed. These included refining the ideas presented in the proposal, creating a structure for writing the syllabus, appointing a staff, creating and field testing lessons, constructing the visual materials to accompany the lessons, evaluating and revising both written and visual materials on the basis of field testing, locating schools wishing to participate in the project, constructing evaluation instruments, and preparing a final report to the foundation. Had I, as project director, fully appreciated the complexity and magnitude of the curriculum development task, I would have requested funds to cover a five- rather than a two-year period. At that time, I did not, and it was with the two-year time frame that work was planned.

The first thing I did after being notified that support would be forthcoming was to select eight doctoral students, five in the field of art education and three in general curriculum at Stanford University, who were to work on the project during the two-year period. These students were joined by a student in product design who was to provide some of the artistic expertise for the construction of visual materials. The doctoral students and I formed the primary core responsible for the major decisions during the life of the project. This group of nine people would meet regularly each week to consider, for example, the way in which the curriculum would be structured, to write lessons, and to critique what each had created. I tried, during the two-year period, to fulfill two responsibilities: first to provide the leadership necessary for the project to succeed; second, to make the project one that could contribute to the education of graduate students. This meant that decisions I might have made on an arbitrary basis were made less efficiently with respect to action but more effectively in relation to the contributions that group deliberation made to the education of the students who worked with me. Furthermore, I wanted the students to feel that this was *our* project, not simply my project; hence, collective decision making was something that I encouraged. Only when perseveration became acutely frustrating or grossly unproductive did I attempt arbitrarily to resolve an issue being discussed.

Once the core group had been formed, I shared with each member of the group the proposal that was submitted to the foundation and I described in detail the rationale for the project and some of the goals I hoped an effective curriculum would achieve. These sessions were used to orient members of the group to the kind of work that was ahead of us and to reemphasize and clarify through discussion the leading ideas constituting my thinking about the teaching of art at the elementary school level. It became clear to me that the kind of understanding I wanted the core group to secure could not be compressed and secured within three or four staff meetings. Such understanding needs time to grow and would, I hoped, occur during the course of the curriculum development work. Yet, I did want to lay enough groundwork concerning what the project was after and why, so that members of the group would feel intellectually secure in what they were trying to accomplish.

The work for the project was divided in two phases. Phase I was devoted to (1) conceptualizing the format, or structure, to be used for writing lessons and designing instructional materials, (2) writing lessons and having them critiqued by the group, (3) designing instructional materials to accompany the written materials, (4) securing teachers and classrooms for initial field testing, and (5) revising the materials, both written and visual, as a result of initial field testing. Phase II was devoted to the local dissemination of the use and effects of the materials developed.

The core group decided that it would be a good idea to invite four elementary school teachers to join the group as consultants and to use their classrooms as the places where the initial testing of the materials would take place. Four teachers, each of whom worked in a different elementary school near Stanford University, were subsequently employed as consultants to the project. Their role was to read the material that had been prepared and to let us know what aspects of the work were clear, foggy, useful, relevant, or irrelevant. The teachers were, in a very real sense, our contact with educational reality, and, although we did not expect or want them to function as experts on art, they were informed about and sensitive to children and to life in their classrooms and were in a position to tell us whether what we were developing had any chance of succeeding in an elementary school classroom.

Thus, the staff of the Kettering Project for the first year of its existence consisted of a project director, five doctoral students in art education, three doctoral students in general curriculum, one master's degree student in product design, and four elementary school teachers. Meetings of the project director and the students were held two to four times per week, whereas meetings that included the teachers were held once every month to six weeks.

One of the first tasks that needed to be undertaken after the initial staff orientation session was completed was the development of a structure, or format, that could be used to organize our lesson writing and that could be read easily by elementary school teachers. Although the rationale for the project and the three realms of artistic learning had been formulated, the specific format that would provide the architecture within which our curriculum writing would occur had not been developed. I now believe, although I did not appreciate it at the time, that decisions about the character and structure of this format are crucial for the curriculum development process. This conceptual architecture reveals implicity the assumptions and values embedded in a project and provides the constraints within which curriculum writers must work. It is clear that when eight to ten people come together to prepare written materials that are to constitute a syllabus for others to use, some common framework must be developed that all members of the group can use if the syllabus is to have continuity and cohesiveness. The first month of the project was devoted to the development of the categories that would constitute the format for our work. The categories for this format are as follows:

1. Concept
2. Principle
3. Objective
4. Rationale
5. Introductory motivating activity
6. Learning activity 1, 2, 3
7. Evaluation procedures
8. Materials needed

Concept refers to an idea, such as color or line, that was to be the focus of a unit. A unit consisted of seven to ten lessons. *Principle* refers to a general proposition about the concept that the curriculum was designed to help children understand in some way. Thus, "Color can express feeling" is a principle in which the concept color is embedded. *Objective* refers to instructional objectives that the children were intended to attain. *Rationale* provides the teachers with reasons that justify the importance of the concept, principle, and objective we had formulated.

The *introductory motivating activity* was a procedure we suggested could be used by the teacher to help the students get ready for the lesson. *Learning activity 1, 2, 3* refers to the fact that each lesson contained one to three learning activities, each of which we believed was instrumental in achieving the objective for that lesson. The availability of three learning activities was intended to provide teachers with choices regarding the learning activity that seemed most suitable for their particular class. *Evaluation procedures* describes how the effectiveness of the lesson or unit could be evaluated, whereas *materials needed* was a list of materials that we provided and those that the teacher needed to provide for use in the particular lesson.

As I have already indicated, each unit consisted of seven to ten lessons. This meant that once a teacher chose a unit he or she was committed to staying with it—to its culmination, we hoped. We did not want to encourage teachers to shift from lesson to lesson in different units, because we believed that this would vitiate any continuity that we were able to build into our materials. The organization of lessons into a unit is schematically illustrated in Figure 3.

By use of this curriculum format, seven units were selected for the development of lessons. In the productive realm, units focused on drawing, graphics, and painting. In the critcial realm, units dealt with line, color, and composition. In the historical realm, they focused on the general features of art history. Using these units, the core group of project staff produced sixty-seven lessons and about seven hundred pieces of specifically designed instructional materials that accompanied the lessons in the units. These

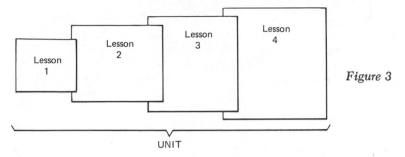

Figure 3

materials, both written and visual, are sufficient for over two years of art instruction assuming that a teacher allocates about two hours per week to the study or creation of art.

At the time the project was undertaken, I was very intent an specifying goals or objectives so that teachers would know where they were heading. I was also intent on developing a structured sequence among lessons to counteract the fact that most elementary classrooms had no sequentially organized art programs. Although the objectives that were formulated were more general than formal instructional objectives, I would today provide a much more open-ended approach to objectives, using instructional objectives much more sparingly and placing more emphasis on problem-solving objectives and expressive outcomes. Similarly, I would not attempt to provide a sequence longer than three lessons; we used sequences of from seven to ten lessons in our work.

HOW THE GROUP WORKED

To produce the lessons within each of the units, the core group was organized into teams of two members each. These teams were responsible for writing ten lessons in each of the units and for conceptualizing the type of visual support materials that they believed would increase the effectiveness of the lessons. Our working procedures provided for each team to write a draft version of the lesson and to have it reviewed by either the project director or the total group. After this initial review, the material was revised and reviewed by the teachers who served as consultants. Following their recommendations, the lesson was used in the classroom of the teacher-consultant and subsequently further revisions were made.

It is important to note here that the process of group planning and review of curriculum materials is a complicated and time-consuming enterprise. Even seemingly minor decisions, such as whether to use slides of works of art or cardboard reproductions of works of art for a particular lesson, could require a full hour or more of discussion. These discussions appeared to some to be inefficient and frustrating, but I am convinced they are a necessary part of curriculum planning.

As already indicated, the teams that wrote curriculum were also responsible for conceptualizing the instructional support materials to accompany their written work. In most cases, members of the team also constructed these materials and made seven copies of each of them so that eight complete sets of materials were available for testing in classrooms. When the materials were especially complex or could not be efficiently fabricated by a team member, the student who served as our product designer undertook the responsibility for production. As I have already indicated, the project produced about seven hundred pieces of visual instructional materials, each having a code number corresponding to a number found within a lesson in a particular unit.

Phase I of the project, which extended from October 1, 1968, to August 1, 1969, culminated with the production of two large syllabi containing the units for each of the three realms of artistic learning that the project was interested in fostering. Also produced were eight pairs of "Kettering Boxes," which contained sets of instructional support materials. These materials, both written and visual, had been revised at least twice, and most of the lessons had been tried in the classroom by teacher-consultants or by members of the team who developed the material.

Phase II, the second year of the project, was one in which the tryout of the materials expanded from four teachers to twenty teachers working in five schools in two school districts near Stanford University. During this phase of the project, units that were not completed during phase I were brought to completion and observations of the use of the curriculum and instructional resource materials were continued.

Because it was my aspiration as project director to develop materials that did not require extensive in-service education, only one formal in-service session was held for the twenty elementary school teachers who participated in the project during the second year. Whatever additional in-service education occurred was provided informally by the core staff as they observed teachers and students when they were using the materials in class.

This aspiration also reflected naiveté on my part. I had hoped to create material that needed little pedagogical expertise, but in retrospect—particularly in art—the need for in-service education in the use of the material cannot be circumvented. The teacher plays a crucial role in the ways in which materials are employed in the classroom.

In addition to the expanded field testing of the curriculum materials, phase II became the period in which evaluation procedures and instruments needed to be developed. With the bulk of the curriculum development work completed by March 1968, the attention of the staff shifted to the conceptualization of aspects of artistic learning that were to be evaluated in ways not provided for in the evaluation procedures suggested at the end of each lesson. This effort required for its successful completion as much time and support as went into the development of the curriculum itself. The project staff obviously had neither the same amount of time nor the kinds of resources that would have been optimal. Nevertheless, the types of competencies the staff sought to assess and the procedures that were conceptualized were, in my opinion, promising and ambitious. These materials included the appraisal of the visual products that children in the classes produced, interviews with teachers, and analyses of the written comments they made in the curriculum syllabus they were using. Evaluation procedures also employed tests of comprehension that had been especially prepared. The staff of the project made every effort within the time constraints to secure a wide variety of evaluative information that would be useful in determining the effects of the projects on the students as well as those aspects of the curriculum that needed further revision. The data from these procedures and instruments were collected in May and June of 1969 and analyzed during July and August.

As the final formal task of the project, a final report was prepared for the foundation. This report was divided into eight sections and each member of the core staff was asked to prepare a chapter or portion of the report. As project director, I prepared both the introductory and concluding chapters of the report and reviewed all of the material prepared by the staff. In addition to the final report that describes the project in detail and presents a critical analysis of its strengths and weaknesses, a collection of sample lessons was prepared that was intended to provide those interested in the project with material necessary for understanding the format of the lessons and the level of detail with which they were written. Thus, two final written products were prepared during the summer and fall of 1969, a final report and a collection of sample lessons from each of the units that had been written.

DISSEMINATION OF THE WORK

One might ask, after a substantial fiscal investment,[5] not to mention the investment in time and energy, how the results of the project were disseminated to the field of art education, aside from the information provided in the final report and sample lessons. To disseminate information about the project to the field, a wide variety of channels became available, most of which were neither consciously sought nor anticipated. These channels emerged in part because there was a growing interest in the work we had done and in part because the ideas in the project were a "natural" part of ideas I had worked with professionally in the field. For example, I prepared two articles for two major art education journals.[6,7] One of these was published when the project was initiated and described its goals and rationale; the other was published after the project had been completed and provided a description of what we had learned. Other channels for dissemination included invitations to speak about the project at conferences and conventions. The *New York Times* and the *Christian Science Monitor* had articles about the project. One of the largest school districts in the United States invited me to make a videotape dealing with the project for in-service training of teachers, and the state of Hawaii invited the core staff there to work with elementary school teachers to develop materials similar to those used in the Kettering Project that would be appropriate for Hawaiian schools. When I was in England and Israel I described the project to various groups of educators. In addition, people in art education from various parts of this country had visited schools where the materials were being used. The opening chapter in *Programs of Promise* [8] is devoted to a description of the Kettering Project, and my own book, *Educating Artistic Vision* [9] describes the project in some detail. Finally, the materials and ideas used in the project are being used in my own teaching and training of teachers. Regarding the last point, the *California State Framework for the Visual Arts* [10] recommends an approach to curriculum development that, in significant measure, grew out of the curriculum development work done on the Kettering Project.

As I have indicated, these channels for dissemination were not contrived at any point during the life of the project. I knew, of course, that a final report would be written, but I did not plan the events or opportunities that flowed after the work had been completed. It is important to point out that in disseminating information about the project there was no attempt to offer the curriculum as a completed or a flawless program. Indeed, whenever lectures were delivered or articles published, every effort was made to point out the difficulties and limitations of the work we had done as well as the kinds of benefits it could offer. We did not attempt to market the materials, either literally or psychologically, to the professional public. Our main concern, in addition to developing the best materials we could produce, was to acquire a more adequate understanding of the problems involved in curriculum development work and to share such understanding with members in the field.

THEORIES USED TO DEVELOP CURRICULUM MATERIALS

Thus far I have described the goals of the Kettering Project and the kinds of tasks that were undertaken in phases I and II of its life, in order to clarify how the project was organized. It is to the theories used in its development that we now turn.

When one talks about theories underlying or guiding curriculum development work, there are at least two aspects of the term *theory* that need clarification. If by *theory* is meant a systematic set of interrelated statements that explain, through their power to predict specific consequences flowing from certain conditions, then theory in education generally and in curriculum particularly can be used only in the loosest sense. If ideas that are used to guide action—if general beliefs about what children ought to learn—are considered theoretical, then this is much more like the status of theoretical ideas in curriculum work than the type of theory referred to earlier.

A second necessary clarification deals with the referent of *theory*. In curriculum development work, *theory* can refer to ideas about the nature of the subject matter being taught, about how children learn, or about how a particular enterprise might go about its work. For example, aesthetic theory deals with explanations concerning the defining characteristics of art, and behaviorism presents ideas that purport to explain the conditions necessary for learning, whereas organizational theory is supposed to explain why an organization functions the way it does and by implication what sorts of changes might make it more productive.

In the development of the lessons and the visual materials, there was one particular theoretical idea in psychology that guided a great deal of what we produced. That idea deals with the process of visual differentiation: seeing is not identical to looking. For example, in grammatical terms *seeing* is an achievement verb, whereas *looking* is a task verb.[11] Seeing is an accomplishment, something that is learned; it is not an automatic consequence of maturation. Hence, in the development of materials and tasks, we were intent on providing visual images that students could compare and contrast and in this process attain better skills in visual differentiation. That is, they would gradually become able to see visual qualities in visual form that previously went unseen. To do this required that we produce tasks and materials whose differences from a visual point of view were at first obvious. Gradually, the differences between visual images students were asked to look at and compare became increasingly subtle. Many of the materials we developed, such as transparent overlay boards that were used to alter the quality of reproductions of works of art, were intended to foster visual differentiation.

The point here is that both beliefs about what is desirable from an educational point of view (developing greater visual differentiation) and beliefs about the ways in which such learning can be fostered played an important role in providing direction to our practical work.

Another important idea had to do with the importance of time and practice in the acquisition of the skills necessary for artistic expression. In my writing in the field of art education I have differentiated between expression and what might be called self-disclosure.[12] The former requires that an individual have sufficient control over a material to be able to use it as a medium for expression. Expression requires the application of intelligence for the purpose of converting a material into a medium.[13]

To be able to achieve expressive ends with materials requires from an educational point of view that the student have sufficient time and opportunity to acquire, practice, and refine the necessary skills. In the language of curriculum discourse, both continuity and sequence should be provided for in the materials developed. In practical terms, these ideas about the meaning of expression and the conditions necessary for its achievement function as the intellectual justification for the development of units as compared with a grab-bag or an ad hoc approach to the development of learning activities.

The significance of these theoretical beliefs in our curriculum development work can perhaps be better appreciated if some theoretical ideas that we did not employ are mentioned. The concept of reinforcement, a central idea in behaviorism, was nowhere purposefully employed in the preparation of written materials. We did not want teachers to use, for example, secondary reinforcers to sustain interest or to motivate children. The idea of giving "brownie points" for work completed would have been abhorrent to the group, and at no time did it emerge as an idea for consideration. Another idea not employed was that of using immediate as compared to delayed feedback to guide or reinforce the students' learning. This psychological idea simply was not a part of the intellectual body of beliefs that gave direction to our efforts.

In identifying the theoretical ideas that were central to and those that were absent from the project, I do not want to imply that ideas about visual differentiation and those dealing with continuity and sequence provided recipelike prescriptions that were to be followed assiduously. Although some ideas were of greater significance than others, it is more accurate to say that these ideas were embedded in a constellation of more general ideas about art, education, and artistic learning that had permeated my writing for about a decade. These ideas formed what Decker Walker[14] has called a platform. They constituted a body of beliefs that were shared by members of the project staff and provided an almost unarticulated covenant that gave direction for our work.

It is both of interest and of significance to note that the beliefs that become a shared aspect of group endeavors often seem to be internalized by group members in a covert way, much in the way that social habits are learned during childhood. The language that becomes salient in a group, the way in which values are communicated, and the general intellectual style of the leading group members seem to create a climate—or a culture—to which group members adapt. In our case, there was no manifesto that presented the values and beliefs the group came to share. In the first place, an important characteristic of deeply held beliefs and values is their ineffable quality. Yet, this does not mean that they are not communicable, and I believe the total configuration of decisions within a group expresses and at the same time reinforces such beliefs and values.

Curriculum development on the scale with which we worked is inevitably a group enterprise; yet, despite this obvious feature, there is little in the literature that discusses curriculum development from the standpoint of group processes. In the types of theory that guide curriculum work, ideas about how people learn and about the nature of the subject to be learned often are prominent. For example, *Science: A Process Approach* is structured largely by ideas about the nature of cognitive operations and the conditions that will refine them, whereas *Man: A Course of Study* is based largely on certain large ideas believed important for children to learn and understand. These teaching ideas reflect the orientations to curriculum that each project embraces. When it comes to ideas that can be used to structure curriculum development groups in order to maximize their ideational fluency, social compatibility, or morale, little is available in the published material in the field of curriculum. Yet, for groups who organize their work as ours did, the importance of group process is enormous. We found that whereas psychological ideas, for example, could provide some general guidance when it came to making specific concrete decisions concerning a particular lesson or instructional support material, psychological ideas were too general to be of much use. Although we used such ideas as a general intellectual backdrop, sustained deliberation was required among members of the core group to arrive at a decision with which we could feel comfortable. There are several good reasons why these deliberations required so much time. First, we were trying to anticipate the likely effects of taking one course of action rather than another. Because theoretical ideas are by definition general, and because we were dealing with a specific instance, we could not confidently extrapolate from the theory to the consequence of the action we were considering. Consequently, we felt compelled to explore a wide range of possible consequences flowing from a particular action in order to avoid miseducational side effects. Blind alleys as well as direct routes need to be identified, and group deliberation is one way of doing this. Joseph Schwab's conception of the "practical" is, from our experience both accurate and apt as a way of characterizing the process of curriculum planning.[15]

Second, through group deliberation, a variety of perspectives are presented. This variety makes it possible to see the problem from different angles, and hence the decision reached is much more likely to arise from the comparison of a host of alternatives. Paradoxically, "inefficiency" in group deliberation can be more efficient than efficiency.

Third, it is often the case, as revealed in group deliberation, that more than one educational value attends to a variety of decisions being considered. In a sense, the decision finally reached is partly a matter of which group member has been most persuasive in the decision-making process. For example, there are assets and liabilities attached to the use of, say, cardboard reproductions of works of art as compared to colored slides. The former are easily movable, and there is no need to turn down the lights. However, the quality of such reproductions leaves much to be desired, and some might not possess the very qualities that one hopes children will learn to experience. Slides, although often of high visual quality, require a darkened room, a screen, and a projector. In addition, teachers might not want to take the time to set up this equipment if only a few slides are to be shown.

What happens in group deliberation is that the pros and cons, from an educational, practical, psychological, and social point of view, are discussed. The decision the group finally makes will depend not only on the "objective" evidence but also on the persuasiveness of a member who feels deeply and argues cogently about either slides or reproductions.

Because the actors in this drama are human, all of the human emotions come into play. Group members gradually learn how to couch their criticism in forms that are not so abrasive. There are times when someone's ego must be the primary consideration. In short, the viability of the group as a group is not a trivial consideration when curriculum development is undertaken as a group effort.

In an interesting way, the process of group deliberation in curriculum development has certain similarities to the kind of deliberation that goes on when juries decide the disposition of a case they have heard. In both situations, the evidence is weighed. And the metaphor *weigh* is a telling one. What is being considered and compared is not qualities or anticipations that can be put on a common yardstick and measured. Rather, it is more a comparison of incomparables. There are few curriculum problems that have one solution. For any problem there are usually several credible solutions; hence, the problem for the curriculum group is to weigh the various putative virtues *and* costs of each and finally to arrive at a decision that is then subjected to empirical test. This process includes not simply securing the facts—which are probably more difficult to secure in curriculum planning than in jurisprudence—it also includes assigning values to these facts. In both situations, the absence of recipelike solutions is notable.

The various rationales and concepts that are found in the literature of curriculum and the empirical generalizations that are produced in the behavioral sciences should not, as I have said so often, be considered blueprints for curriculum construction but rather as devices that enable a curriculum construction group in its more passive and reflective moments to remember what might be an important consideration. The concepts of objectives, continuity, sequence, integration, and formative and summative evaluation and the categories describing the changing cognitive structure of the child provide only the most general criteria against which decisions about the curriculum can be appraised. And none by itself is adequate to resolve the range of diverse and at times competing values that can be justly claimed for different courses of action. There is not now, and I do not believe there can be, a single theory of curriculum capable of resolving and integrating the conflicts in interpretation, fact, and value emerging from different theories within the several social sciences. Theoretical consistency in curriculum development, even if it could be achieved, might in fact be an educational pyrrhic victory.

If one uses three commonplaces in the curriculum literature—the student, the society, and the subject matter—as criteria with which to identify what considerations were most prominent in our own curriculum development, in retrospect it appears that attention to the subject matter was easily the most prominent of the three. The student, although important, was simply too remote during the course of curriculum development to play a really central role in our work. In addition, we believed—or took comfort in the thought—that the classroom teacher would make whatever adaptations of our material that were necessary to suit the particular child or class or situation in which the curriculum would be used.

As for the society, it simply never appeared in our deliberations, perhaps because our value commitment toward the visual arts already implicitly embraced the belief that the development of children's artistic abilities would be important for the improvement of society. Whatever the reason, once the group was launched into the process of curriculum development, focused attention to the needs of society did not seem productive for meeting our immediate need: that of creating learning activities and instructional support materials that would teach nontrivial artistic content to elementary school children.

POSSIBLE ALTERNATIVE APPROACHES TO CURRICULUM DEVELOPMENT

It is far easier for me to identify those aspects of the curriculum we created that need modification and improvement than it is for me to identify those aspects of the curriculum development strategies we employed that need improvement. We attempted to identify the strengths and weaknesses of the curriculum throughout the process of curriculum development and through "achievement testing." We did not try to identify the difficulties that might have resided within our style of curriculum development work. I do not believe that a style of work can be appraised legitimately outside the context, values, and purposes of the project for which it is an intrumentality. I believe that significant interaction occurs between the kind of orientation or platform one establishes for a curriculum and the working arrangements one formulates. The tool and the product are interdependent. What I sought was a program that would nurture the artistic development of children. I do not believe that such a program could be created within a set of working arrangements that were, for example, mechanical or authoritarian in nature. Furthermore, the context within which we worked was an educational one. I had an educational as well as an administrative responsibility for the people who worked in the core group. This educational responsibility necessitated, in my view, particular types of working relationships that might not be critical in, say, a regional educational laboratory.

In retrospect, I would not have made radical changes in the basic way in which we operated, given the conditions I laid down in the proposal that I prepared for the Kettering Foundation. Those conditions stipulated that there would be developed at Stanford University a set of curriculum materials, both written and visual, that could be used by elementary school teachers to increase the quality of art education in their classrooms. However, there are approaches to curriculum development that differ significantly from the model we employed. One of these, one that I used in the development of Kettering-like materials in Hawaii, is to bring groups of elementary school teachers together for workshops where examples of the lessons and visual instructional materials that have already been developed are presented and discussed. These materials are then used as prototypes for curriculum development by teachers. The teachers act as curriculum writers and as artists who produce instructional support material to accompany the written materials they prepare. As in the working arrangements used at Stanford, teachers can be grouped in teams of two or three, perhaps from the same elementary school. The major conceptual work—the format, its categories, and the development of exemplary lessons—will already have been completed. This aspect of curriculum development work is both difficult and time consuming, and I have found when working with teachers that they are able to produce a great deal of promising material quite quickly. Of course, the supervision of such teams must be close, and people competent in art need to be available for consultation, especially with respect to the separation of ideas and skills that are trivial from those that are significant.

One of the potential strengths of such an approach to curriculum development is that it takes the responsibility off of a single group of people for creating a complete "curriculum package." Instead, it uses the core team to conceptualize the basic curriculum structure to be used and to develop prototype materials. The structure and materials created are then resources for teachers to use in developing their own materials. In addition, the core team functions as consultants to the teachers.

This procedure for curriculum development also has the potential advantage of increasing the teacher's understanding of the project by putting him or her in the position of having to think through the project clearly enough to be able to prepare materials that others can use. This last condition for curriculum writing is an important one. Teachers must write their materials and develop their visual support devices with the criterion in mind that other people will need to be able to use such materials without direct consultation with the person who made them. Such a criterion provides a new frame of reference for teachers to use in curriculum writing.

This procedure for curriculum developments has, I believe, an important contribution to make to the in-service education of teachers. It has the virtue of being practical and concrete while asking teachers to consider concepts such as continuity and sequence as well as other matters that so often appear to teachers to be little more than educational slogans. In identifying this way of going about curriculum development as an alternative to the way our group worked, I am not suggesting that it is without liabilities. Our problems in education are not to be characterized as having ideal solutions. They are, rather, problems whose solutions are always imperfect and need to be weighed with respect to competing strengths and weaknesses. For example, although broadening the responsibility for curriculum writing is likely to yield products whose quality is uneven, at the same time, it is likely to increase motivation and comprehension of the project's objectives. What kind of tradeoff is most beneficial from an educational point of view? As far as I know, there is no metric that can be confidently applied to resolve such a problem: it's a matter of making a judgment rather than applying a standard. In making such a judgment, the image one holds of teachers and of schools comes sharply into play. If schooling is seen as a quasi-industrial venture and teachers as a workforce to be directed by management, the likelihood of being sympathetic toward a program that is "teacher-proof," one in which the teacher functions as a conduit for a totally prepackaged program, is higher than if one conceives of teachers as professionals who, with students and other teachers, jointly plan the educational program.

The work that we did in curriculum development was instructive because it provided an arena in which theoretical ideas could be employed and through use their utility and limitations appreciated. Some of the ideas that were embraced at the outset of the work were reaffirmed, whereas others were discarded. We erred in attempting to develop materials that needed little or no in-service education, that overemphasized instructional objectives, that payed too much attention to the development of technical skills and provided too little opportunity for the exercise of imagination, that were too prescriptive regarding sequence, and that underestimated the need for a syllabus to be attractively illustrated and printed. We also severely underestimated the amount of time needed to do work on the scale we aspired to reach. Yet, to be able to learn these things required the investment of time and energy that all those affiliated with the project expended. All in all, I believe that what we learned was worth the investment we made.

REFERENCES

1. A modified verson of this chapter appears in *Strategies for Curriculum Development*, (Jon Schaffarzick and David Hampson, eds.), McCutchcon Publising, Co., Berkeley, 1975.
2. The final report of the Project is entitled *Teaching Art to the Young: A Curriculum Development Project in Art Education*, Stanford University, School of Education, 1969.
3. Elliot Eisner, "Curriculum Ideas in a Time of Crisis," *Art Education*, Vol. 18, No. 7, October 1965.
4. Elliot Eisner, "The Development of Information and Attitude Toward Art at the Secondary and College Level," *Studies in Art Education*, Vol. 8, No. 1, Autumn 1966.
5. The amount allocated to the project by the Kettering Foundation for the two-year period was approximately $70,000.
6. Elliot Eisner, "Curriculum Making for the Wee Folk: Stanford University's Kettering Project," *Studies in Art Education*, Vol. 9, No. 3, 1968.
7. Elliot Eisner, "Standford's Kettering Project: An Appraisal of Two Years Work," *Art Education*, Vol. 23, No. 8, 1970.
8. Elliot Eisner, "Stanford's Kettering Project: A Radical Alternative in Art Education," in *Programs of Promise*, Al Hurwitz (ed.), Harcourt Brace Jovanovich, New York, 1972.
9. Elliot Eisner, *Educating Artistic Vision*, Macmillan Publishing Co., Inc., New York, 1972.
10. *California State Framework for the Visual Arts*, State Department of Education, State of California, Sacramento, 1971.
11. For this distinction, I am indebted to the work of Gilbert Ryle, *The Concept of Mind*, Barnes and Noble, London, 1949.
12. This distinction grows out of John Dewey's writing, especially Chapter 13 of *Art As Experience*, Minton, Balch and Co., New York, 1934.
13. Ibid.
14. See the following by Decker Walker, *Strategies of Deliberation in Three Curriculum Development Projects*, Ph.D. Thesis, School of Education, Stanford University, 1971.
15. Joseph Schwab, "The Practical: A Language for Curriculum," *School Review*, Vol. 78, November 1969. No. 19.

9

On the Art of Teaching

*First we see the hills in the painting, then we see the painting in the
hills.*

LI LI WENG

In the previous chapter and in those that preceded it, I have focused mainly
on the problems of curriculum planning. In this chapter I wish to address
myself to another central aspect of the educational process: teaching. It is
my thesis that teaching is an art guided by educational values, personal
needs, and by a variety of beliefs or generalizations that the teacher holds
to be true.

To argue as I will that teaching is an art is something of a paradox. We
live at a time when virtually the entire effort of those who have attempted
to study teaching has been devoted to the creation of a science of teaching.[1]
Yet, most of those who teach—indeed, even those who study teaching
scientifically—often regard their own teaching as an artistic activity. For
some, to say that teaching is an art is to say that it is poorly understood and
that when it is understood a science of teaching will have been developed.[2]
I will have more to say about this issue a bit later, but for the present let us
think about what it means to say that teaching is an art.

FOUR SENSES OF THE ART OF TEACHING

There are at least four senses in which teaching can be considered an art.
It is an art in the sense that teaching can be performed with such skill and
grace that, for the student as well as for the teacher, the experience can be
justifiably characterized as aesthetic.[3] There are classrooms in which what
the teacher does—the way in which activities are orchestrated, questions
asked, lectures given—constitutes a form of artistic expression. What occurs
is a performance that provides intrinsic forms of satisfaction, so much so
that we use the adjectives and accolades usually applied to the formal arts
to describe what the teacher does while teaching.

Teaching is an art in the sense that teachers, like painters, composers, actresses, and dancers, make judgments based largely on qualities that unfold during the course of action. Qualitative forms of intelligence are used to select, control, and organize classroom qualities, such as tempo, tone, climate, pace of discussion, and forward movement. The teacher must "read" the emerging qualities and respond with qualities appropriate to the ends sought or the direction he wishes the students to take. In this process, qualitative judgment is exercised in the interests of achieving a qualitative end.[4]

Teaching is an art in the sense that the teacher's activity is not dominated by prescriptions or routines but is influenced by qualities and contingencies that are unpredicted. The teacher must function in an innovative way in order to cope with these contingencies. To say that prescription and routine do not dominate the teacher's activity is not to say that they are not present or play no part in teaching. Teaching requires for its artistic expression routines with which to work; the teacher must have available repertoires to draw on. It is through repertoires or routines that the teacher can devote his or her energies and attention to what is emerging in the class. Without such routines, an enormous amount of energy would need to be spent by the teacher to develop skills to use in the classroom. Thus, the presence of well-developed routines or teaching repertoires enables the teacher to deal inventively with what occurs in class. It is precisely the tension between automaticity and inventiveness that makes teaching, like any other art, so complex an undertaking. Without automaticity and the ability to call on stock responses, energies are lost and inventiveness is hampered. Yet, if responses are too automatic or routine, if they become too reflexive, the teacher's ability to invent is hampered. Teaching becomes a series of routine responses rather than an opportunity for ingenuity.

Teaching is an art in the sense that the ends it achieves are often created in process. Craft has been defined as the process through which skills are employed to arrive at preconceived ends. Art has been defined as the process in which skills are employed to discover ends through action. H. W. Janson, the noted art historian has said, "Artists are people who play hide-and-seek but do not know what they seek until they find it."[5] In a similar sense, teaching is a form of human action in which many of the ends achieved are emergent—that is to say, found in the course of interaction with students rather than preconceived and efficiently attained. This is not to say that there are no situations in which preconceived ends are formulated; most of the arguments urging the clear specification of instructional objectives tacitly imply that the quintessence of teaching resides in the efficient achievement of such ends. It is to say that to emphasize the exclusive use of such a model of teaching reduces it to a set of algorithmic functions. Opportunities for the creation of ends in process or in the post facto analysis of outcomes require a model of teaching akin to other arts. Teachers do, at least in part, use such a model to guide their activities, not as a function of professional incompetence, but as a way of keeping their pedagogical intelligence from freezing into mechanical routine.

It is in these four senses—teaching as a source of aesthetic experience, as dependent on the perception and control of qualities, as a heuristic or adventitious activity, and as seeking emergent ends—that teaching can be regarded as an art.

Because teaching can be engaged in as an art is not to suggest that all teaching can be characterized as such. Teaching can be done as badly as anything else. It can be wooden, mechanical, mindless, and wholly unimaginative. But when it it is sensitive, intelligent, and creative—those qualites that confer upon it the status of an art—it should, in my view not be regarded, as it so often is by some, as an expression of unfathomable talent or luck but as an example of humans exercising the highest levels of their intelligence.[6] As Phillip Jackson has said, rather than complain about the art of teaching, we should try to try to foster whatever artistry the teacher can provide.[7]

THE ROLE OF THEORY IN TEACHING

If we conceive of teaching as an art, does theory have a role to play in the guidance and conduct of teaching? Does artistic teaching vitiate the use of scientifically grounded theory? Theoretical frameworks, scientific or otherwise, are frames of reference that perform two extremely important functions. First, they serve as a means for identifying aspects of the reality to which they address themselves. Theories remind us of what to attend to by calling our attention to the theory's subject matter. For example, theories in sociology make vivid the social structure of the classroom, they illuminate class differences among pupils, they describe friendship patterns and formal and informal sanctions. Psychological theory (depending on the specific theory being used) might address itself to questions of self-esteem or forms of reinforcement or the need to provide students with opportunities to practice the behavior they are expected to learn. What theories do in this regard is to help us focus attention on aspects of classroom life that we might otherwise neglect. They are tools that help us bracket the world so that we can bring it into focus.[8]

But theories, in the social sciences at least, do more than this. They also provide rough approximations of what we might expect of certain pedagogical arrangements by the kinds of generalizations that they provide. Although no single theory in any of the social sciences is likely to be adequate to deal with the particular reality with which an individual teacher must cope, theories do provide generalizations that can be considered in one's reflective moments as a teacher. These moments, what Jackson calls "pre-active teaching," [9] occur prior to actual teaching: planning at home, reflecting on what has occurred during a particular class session, and discussing in groups ways to organize a program. Theory here sophisticates personal reflection and group deliberation. Insofar as a theory suggests consequences flowing from particular circumstances, it enables those who understand the theory to take those circumstances into account when planning.

In all of this, theory is not to be regarded as prescriptive but as suggestive. It is a framework, a tool, a means through which the world can be construed. Any theory is but a part of the total picture. Joseph Schwab describes the limits of theory this way:

> If, then, theory is to be used well in the determination of curricular practice, it requires a supplement. It requires arts which bring a theory to its application; first, arts which identify the disparities between real theory and theoretic representation; second, arts which modify the theory in the course of its application, in light of the discrepancies; and, third, arts which devise ways for taking account of the many aspects of the real thing which the theory does not take into account. [10]

The point in Schwab's observation is not, as some seem to believe, to excise theory from curriculum planning or from teaching, but rather to hold appropriate expectations for its utility. What is dysfunctional is to regard it as a formula to be followed or as utterly useless. The former overestimates its function, the latter underestimates it.

In one sense, all teachers operate with theory, if we take theory to mean a general set of ideas through which we make sense of the world. All teachers, whether they are aware of it or not, use theories in their work. Tacit beliefs about the nature of human intelligence, about the factors that motivate children, and about the conditions that foster learning influence the teacher's actions in the classrooms. These ideas not only influence their actions, they also influence what they attend to in the classroom: that is, the concepts that are salient in theories concerning pedagogical matters also tend to guide perception. Thus, theory inevitably operates in the conduct of teaching as it does in other aspects of educational deliberation. The major need is to be able to view situations from the varied perspectives that different theories provide and thus to be in a position to avoid the limited vision of a single view.

Thus far we have talked about teaching as an art and about some of the functions that theory performs in teaching. But what of the concept *teaching* itself? What does it mean "to teach?" What are the ways in which the term can be construed?

For John Dewey the term *teaching* was regarded as similar in form to the term *selling*. [11] That is, one could not teach unless someone learned, just as one could not sell unless someone bought. Teaching and learning were regarded as reciprocal concepts. Although it was possible to learn without having been taught, one could not be said to have taught unless someone had learned.

The reason this view of teaching was embraced was because the term *teach* implied an end-in-view namely, learning. Teaching was goal-directed and represented, in Gilbert Ryle's terms, an achievement, not merely the performance of a task.[12] For example, to say that someone has run is to describe an activity—it is a task term. But to say that someone has won is to describe an achievement, it is an achievement term for Ryle. Thus, if a teacher attempts to teach but does not succeed in helping the student learn, then he or she may be said to have lectured, conducted a discussion, demonstrated, explained but *not* to have taught. To teach, in this sense, is known by its effects. Those effects are learning. Just as one could not be said to have sold something unless another bought, so too, one could not have been said to have taught unless another had learned.

When the study of teaching became a major interest among researchers in the early part of the 1950s, the view that teaching should be conceptualized in terms of its consequences presented something of a difficulty. To subscribe to this view of teaching means that one could study teaching only by first determining its effects on students, particularly with respect to the achievement of specified goals. This posed formidable problems in the study of teaching because it required that one must study two things: what teachers do and what students learn.

To simplify the research task, teaching was reconceptualized as a variety of acts performed by individuals called teachers as they work in classrooms with the intention of promoting learning. Whether they were successful was a matter to be studied separately. Thus, using this conception, it became possible to ask what teachers did in the classroom and to establish criteria, independent of their effects, that could be used to appraise the quality of what they did. Teachers, for example, lectured, demonstrated, explained, led discussions, introduced materials, and brought lessons to closure. All of these activities, regardless of their effects, could be evaluated by using criteria appropriate for each act. For example, the logic of lectures, the vividness of the examples provided, the coherence of expression, such considerations could be used to evaluate aspects of teaching. The ability to ask questions in a discussion, to help the discussion move forward, to engage many participants, and to foster critical and analytical skills could be applied as criteria to appraise the teacher's skills as a discussion leader. It was believed to be too much to expect that both the quality of the acts of teaching and their consequences be studied simultaneously in a field just beginning to study teaching scientifically.

What we see here are two radically different conceptions of teaching. One regards teaching as a form of achievement directly related to learning. The other regards it as a set of acts performed by people we call teachers as they attempt to foster learning. To which of these conceptions shall we subscribe? Which one is "correct?"

It is both interesting and important to recognize that if we consider how we use the term *selling* it becomes clear that we do in fact use it not in one way but in two ways. Nel Noddings has pointed out that when we talk about someone engaged in selling, we describe a series of acts and not necessarily a series of achievements.[13] Someone is a salesman, is in the selling game, is selling cars. We use such phrases without necessarily implying that the individuals so engaged are successful. One is selling even though one might not have sold any cars today or even this week. Selling here designates a variety of actions that are guided by a set of intentions, not by a set of achievements. Similarly, we can talk about teaching as a set of acts guided by intentions, not as representing achievements.

At the same time, we also talk about teaching in the sense that someone has fulfilled an intention. Teaching also refers to the achievement of intended learning. We say, for example, "I taught you or I failed to teach you," implying that if one had not succeeded, teaching did not occur.

What can we do about this duality? I suggest that we can appropriately conceptualize teaching both ways. We do at present and have in the past used both conceptions of teaching, and I believe that they have served us well. We discern the meaning of the term *teach* not by referring to some operational or stipulated definition, but by recognizing how it functions in a context of other meanings. Much of our language functions in the same way. If under certain circumstances the context is insufficient to provide clarity of meaning, we can then stipulate what we mean by teaching so that others will know how we intend to use the term. In most cases, I believe, we can use the term *teach* in both ways—as an achievement term and as a task term—without a serious problem in communication.

There is, however, a tendency in our discussions to use the *teaching* and *instruction* interchangeably. These terms, I would suggest, are not interchangeable. Their connotative meanings are sufficiently distinctive to warrant attention because what they connote can lead to different conceptions of education and educational practice.

Perhaps the best way to illustrate the differences between *teaching* and *instruction* is to relate an episode that occurred to me in 1972 [14] when I was studying English primary schools. I was having tea in a common room of a London primary school with a group of primary school teachers. We were talking about how the school day was organized and in the course of the conversation I said that I was interested in the way in which they provided instruction. A group of incredulous expressions appeared on their faces. "Instruction?" they asked. I said yes, I was interested in how they provided instruction to the pupils. One of them said, "We don't provide instruction in this school, we teach. Instruction is provided in the church and in the army, but in this school we teach."

What they were conveying to me, and it was the first time I had reflected on the distinction, was that instruction was concerned with forms of training; it was harsher, less organic, more mechanical than teaching. To "teach" is softer than to "instruct." Perhaps this is why the term *instruction* is more likely to be used by those whose orientation to curriculum is technological and who want to maximize effective control over the content and form of what children learn in school. *Instruction* is a term more suited to a manual than is the term *teach*. Instruction is less apt to be associated with the adventitious, with what is flexible and emergent, in short, and what is artistic, than is teaching.

Now this difference between terms might seem like quibbling, but it is not. It is precisely because we do not have clear-cut, stipulated definitions of these terms that their connotative meanings take on such importance. When terms are not formally differentiated, context and connotation significantly influence the kinds of meanings that individuals are likely to construe. To use the term *instruction* as an equivalent to the term *teach* is not to have an equivalent at all; each term carries its own conceptual baggage, and although there is some overlap, the significance of the terms reside in their differences because each implies a different image of what teaching should do.

It is significant, also, I believe, that the terms we use in educational discourse not only reflect different assumptions about the means and ends of education, but that terms cluster—that is, individual terms tend to have conceptual links to other terms. In combination, they generate a view of what is educationally desirable. Consider, for example, the term *individualized instruction*. Contrast this with *personalized teaching*. The term *individualized* is harsher and more bureaucratic in character than *personalized*. The latter is softer and more intimate. When combined with *instruction, individualized instruction* takes on a connotation that is more technological than *personalized teaching*.

Consider the following: "In this school system, individualized instruction is provided to learners after first having measured a learner's entry skills. Once these entry skills have been determined, appropriate exit skills are specified and measured at the end of the instructional period." Language of this sort communicates not only because of the specific denotations of the language used but because of the images that the language conveys. *Entry* and *exit* conjure up something of an assembly line in which products are processed according to specifications. Education in this context is something that one does to another through a process called instruction. When such terms permeate our discourse they shape our view of the character and aims of education.

When it comes to discourse about teaching, perhaps no concept has had greater currency than the concept of individualized instruction. I have already pointed out that the concept itself participates in a tradition that is more mechanical than organic. If we were to study the ways in which individualization is provided in classrooms, we would find that in many classrooms the variable that is individualized for students is time. Individualized instruction in a great many classrooms means allowing children to take different amounts of time to arrive at the same destination. Yet, individualization (or personalized teaching, if you prefer) can be provided by altering the teaching method so that it suits particular children, by altering content, and by altering the goals themselves. Time is but one factor of many that can be modified to accommodate the characteristics or aptitude of different children.

What is not recognized—even by teachers who provide it regularly—is that the use of different kinds of explanations for different children, the variety of questions and types of examples teachers provide, the different ways in which motivation is engendered, the modulation of one's tone of voice and one's tempo to suit individual children are examples of individualized instruction. To be sure, these forms of pedagogical adaptation use no mechanical means—no workbooks, test forms, color-coded boxes of reading material—yet they reside, I believe, at the heart of individualization, for they represent one person's effort to try to communicate with another. Each child, so to speak, is a custom job.

Because of our national tendency to seek prepackaged and field-tested devices to make education efficient, we sometimes fail to recognize the extent to which some of the teaching practices employed daily reflect the most straightforward examples of individualization. Mechanical images too often intervene and hamper our recognition of the excellent things we already do.

Artistry in teaching is not a common occurrence. It is an ideal. The reasons for its importance are not self-evident, and although I have described the senses in which teaching is an art, I have not said much about why artistic teaching is so important to the educational development of the young.

One of the reasons is that teachers who function artistically in the classroom not only provide children with important sources of artistic experience, they also provide a climate that welcomes exploration and risk taking and cultivates the disposition to play. To be able to play with ideas is to feel free to throw them into new combinations, to experiment, and even to "fail." It is to be able to deliteralize perception so that fantasy, metaphor, and constructive foolishness may emerge. For it is through play that children eventually discover the limits of their ideas, test their own competencies, and formulate rules that eventually convert play into games. This vacillation between playing and gaming, between algorithms and heuristics, between structure-seeking and rule-abiding behavior, is critical for the construction of new patterns of knowing. Play opens up new possibilities, whereas games exploit those possibilities within a set of defined parameters, something that mature intellectual models do with their work. Playing with ideas that are transformed and guided by rules is as prevalent in the art studio as it is in the science laboratory. Although each area has its own syntax, each its own form and rules, they share the need for play as a source of invention and discovery. But for such a disposition to be cultivated, teachers themselves need to feel free to innovate, to explore, and to play. Teaching is not an act modeled after the sequences of a highly efficient assembly line. Teaching is more like what occurs on a basketball court or on a soccer field. Let me develop this analogy.

Basketball is a game defined by certain rules in which its players seek an unambiguous outcome: to end the game with more points than their opponents. In the former characteristic, basketball and teaching are similar: both have rules that define the activities of their respective games. However, in the latter characteristic, having unambiguous goals, the teacher is generally unlike the basketball player. Goals change in teaching, they are not without ambiguity, and they are certainly not the same for all students. Still, basketball and teaching are alike in many ways. A basketball player must watch the court and understand emerging configurations: so must a teacher. A player must recognize productive possibilities and must know how to pass as well as to shoot: so must a teacher. The basketball player must also know how to slow down the pace, when to speed it up, and even when to stall for time: so must a teacher. He needs to know when to cut, how to slow down a pass, how to talk to his opponent, and how to provide support for his teammates: so must a teacher. The skills that he must have to play the game well require intellectual flexibility. Although good teams have a set of preplanned patterns, once they get on the floor they need to know both how to improvise within those patterns and when to give them up at a second's notice in order to exploit other options. Flexible purposing, Dewey calls it,[15] knowing when to alter the goal, when to explore new interactions and when to shift strategies. In this sense, neither basketball nor teaching is optimized by chaotic abandon or rigid adherence to prespecified plans. Fluid intelligence, intelligence in process, is the hallmark of effectiveness in both arenas. Unlike the automobile assembly line where systemization, orderliness, predictability, and control serve the goals of efficiency, effective teaching, like effective basketball, profits from flexibility, ingenuity, and personal creativity, the last things desired on the assembly line.

To say that excellence in teaching requires artistry implies that the teacher is able to exploit opportunities as they occur. It implies that goals and intentions be fluid. But in many ways this is contrary to the belief that single-mindedness and clarity of one's ends-in-view are required for rationally guided activity. To be rational, one must be intentional. But what is not adequately appreciated is the limitation that such a conception of rationality places on the ways in which teaching can be undertaken. If teaching is regarded—at least in part—as a form of inquiry, as a process of exploring problems that one cannot always define or predict—problems of a pedagogical and substantive variety—the limitations of such a conception of rationality begin to become apparent.

Furthermore, the mandate to operationalize aims has the effect of frequently restricting the aims of teachers in curriculum development to those for which a technology of measurement is available. If such a technology is absent, the likelihood of relinquishing valued aims increases. The ability to measure provides a formidable restraint on what teachers come to believe they ought to do.

But perhaps the most insidious aspect of belief that aims should always be clear and measurable is the coercive impact such a belief has on our conception of rationality and intentionality.

What counts as an intention? Must an intention be capable of linguistic formulation? Is it necessary that the aspiration one seeks be statable in discursive language? Given the admonition that teachers state their objectives behaviorally, it would appear that objectives that cannot be articulated in discursive form are not objectives. Such a view is naive on several counts. First, much of what we aim for is held "in the mind's eye" as an image rather than as a proposition. The image is a visual form of knowing that is in many ways clearer than its discursive representation. Imagine an architect have to discursively describe the features of the structure she intends to create. Such a description is likely to fall far short of the architectural qualities she is after. The images of excellence in the arts and the sciences, in the social studies, and in the conduct of practice are often extremely difficult to articulate—and at times are ineffable. To expect all of what we prize to be capable of being translated into discourse is to make a second conceptual blunder: namely, failure to appreciate the modes of conceptual representation humans are capable of using.

One must ask further whether intentions must always precede action. Is it not the case that action breeds intention as often as intention leads to action? Is it not the case that means and ends interact? Why should a static, unidirectional conception of intentionality and rationality dominate our conception of responsible teaching and curriculum development? Largely, I believe, because we have taken our image of rationality from technologies that emphasize standardization, routine, and efficiency. As long as we conceive of the school as an institution with a static and common mission whose goals must be clearly specified, the belief that effective teaching must lead to the efficient attainment of such goals follows. The task of school administrators, or "program managers," as they are being called increasingly, is to see to it that teachers perform in ways consistent with those goals. Rational planning consists of articulating those goals, subdividing them into units, and casting them into operational forms. The next step is to attempt to discover or to create procedures known to be instrumental to the achievement of those goals. Once this has been accomplished, a monitoring system can be employed to control the performance patterns of teachers who, in turn, can control the performance patterns of students.

The failure to distinguish between education and training, between the school and the factory, between the algorithms and the heuristics of teaching accounts for the simplistic nostrums that are promulgated as ways of improving education. Intentions need not be statable to be held. Intentions need not precede action, they can grow out of action. Rationality includes the capacity to play, to explore, to search for surprise and effective novelty. Such activities are not necessarily contrary to the exercise of human rationality, they may be its most compelling exemplification. What diminishes human rationality is the thwarting of flexible human intelligence by prescriptions that shackle the educational imagination.

ON THE RELATIONSHIP BETWEEN TEACHING AND CURRICULUM PLANNING

Just what is the relationship between teaching and curriculum planning? For some, the distinction between teaching and curriculum is blurred. The argument is that if curriculum constitutes the content of what children learn, then it is not possible to separate the forms through which that content is conveyed from the content itself because form and content interact. How one teaches and what one teaches are inseparable.

This argument is not without merit. Indeed, one of the aims of this book is to encourage students of education to consider curriculum planning and schooling as an entity because each aspect of schooling has a bearing on other aspects. The timetable of the school, for example, influences the way in which teachers must plan the curriculum, pace lessons, and organize learning activities. Evaluation practices influence educational priorities as much as they reflect them. Yet, to say that teaching and curriculum interact or influence each other is to make a distinction between teaching and curriculum. I believe this distinction is a useful one for several reasons.

First, we already have a tradition of discussion regarding the term *teaching*. In the English language—despite the difficulties and differences in conceptions discussed earlier—we do talk about teaching and regard it as something other than curriculum. In the simplest terms—too simple to be sure—curriculum is the content that is taught and teaching is how that content is taught. This simple difference is important because all curriculum planning, insofar as it precedes its actual use in the classroom, requires a transformation of a set of plans or materials into a course of action. This transformation is what we regard as teaching.

Now it should be noted that in this view not all of teaching takes place when teachers talk to a group of students or lead a discussion. Teaching includes the setting up of conditions that do not require the teacher to be in an interactive relationship with students. Thus, a teacher who arranges a set of conditions, say a terrarium or a selection of books or art material with which students may work, and who provides a modicum of guidance

Figure 4

to enable students to use these resources is engaged in teaching even though no lecture or discussion is provided. In short, teaching does not require either a didactic or a dialectic relationship between teacher and pupil. It can and does occur through the creation of an intellectually productive environment.

Earlier I pointed out that intentions and rational planning need not precede action, that intentions can develop out of actions as well as lead to it. How does such a conception bear on the relationship of teaching to curriculum?

The "standard" model of this relationship appears in Figure 4.

In this model, intentions are formed that set the direction and the constraints for curriculum planning. Once the curriculum is planned, it provides the aims, the content, and the resources that the teacher uses in order to teach. Teaching is that array of activities the teacher employs to transform intentions and curriculum materials into classroom conditions that promote learning. Although much pedagogical activity takes this route, not all of it does. Consider the diagram in Figure 5.

In this model, teaching, which always has a content because it is logically impossible to teach or to try to teach someone nothing, interacts with curriculum. One engages in teaching some content and out of action intentions develop that are then used as a basis for planning curriculum. In this model, action is the initiating agent that leads to the formation of intentions, which in turn leads to curriculum planning.

Both of the models presented here are unidirectional. One starts with intentions and terminates with teaching. The other starts with teaching and terminates with curriculum planning. Perhaps a more adequate representation of the process is found in Figure 6.

In this model, the process is circular—that is, one can enter the circle at any point in the model. Intentions lead to curriculum planning, which in

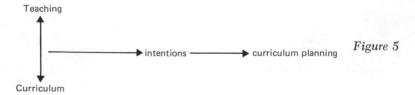

Figure 5

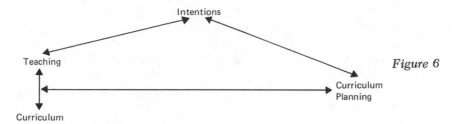

Figure 6

turn provides the content and structure for teaching, which through the course of action leads to the formation of new intentions. One might start with curriculum planning and through it provide the content and structure for teaching, which in turn leads to intentions; or one might start with teaching and through action formulate intentions, which in turn lead to curriculum planning.

With such a model, one can begin to study the sources of intentionality in teaching and speculate on the kinds of value orientations that are more likely than others to encourage teachers to use teaching to formulate intentions and vice versa.

There is another comment worth making about the relationship of curriculum to teaching that has to do with primacy of curriculum in this relationship. By this I mean that it is no virtue to teach well what should not be taught at all. Put another way, what is not worth teaching is not worth teaching well. Thus, if the content to be taught is without redeeming features, it makes little sense to worry about how well it is being taught; teaching matters, so to speak, when what is taught is worth the student's time.

Looking at it from another angle, a curriculum composed of high-quality content and imaginative activities and materials can be scuttled by poor teaching. If the teacher is unable to effectively use materials in the classroom, regardless of how well planned they are, the virtues of the materials as far as the students are concerned go unrealized. But if the curriculum materials are without intellectual virtue, effectively teaching them constitutes a vice.

The virtues and vices of teaching are not only related to the quality of what is taught, but are also determined by criteria that are appropriate to the form of teaching that is provided. For example, the kinds of skills one needs to be able to give a lucid and coherent lecture are not the same as those needed to conduct a discussion. A teacher who is good at the former may be poor at the latter. To attempt to apply a single set of criteria to a wide variety of types and forms of teaching is to overlook what is distinctive about each type. Consider not only the giving of lectures and the leading of discussions, but the organization of small-group activity, individual counseling and guidance, and the ability to maintain a wide array of diverse but productive activities in the classroom; each of these forms of teaching requires the use of different skills. The criteria that are appropriate for appraising the quality of one kind of teaching are not necessarily appropriate for appraising the quality of another.

This admonition to apply to an art form the criteria appropriate to it is well known in the fine arts. We do not use criteria appropriate for tragedy to appraise the quality of melodrama and vice versa. What constitutes excellence in surrealist painting does not constitute excellence in impressionistic work. In teaching, too, excellence is related to the form of teaching being employed. It is probably too much to expect a high degree of excellence in all of the major forms of teaching that can be provided in a classroom. What we probably do want is a high degree of excellence in some.

I make this point—although it may seem obvious—because we often talk about excellence in teaching as though it were a single set of qualities. We sometimes tend to evaluate teaching with a single image of pedagogical merit. And research in teaching has tended to underplay the distinctive differences of different forms of teaching as well as the normative frames of reference or orientations to education that any set of criteria must in some way reflect. Yet these orientations are, in the last analysis, the crucial criteria for appraising the educational value of teaching. Excellence as a lecturer or as a discussion leader is not sufficient to constitute educational virtue if either the lectures or the discussions are regarded as educationally inappropriate. No judgment can be made about the quality of teaching as an educational event or performance without reference to some theory of education. It is ironic that the most neglected aspect in research on teaching is the very framework that would have made it possible for the researcher to say something about the educational significance of the findings.

In all of this discussion about the art of teaching, about differences between teaching and instruction, and about teaching as an independent or reciprocal concept, it is easy to neglect the fact that teachers have needs that must be met through teaching. Because teachers are *people* who teach, it is important that, in our efforts to develop self-instructional materials for students and prepackaged procedures for instruction, we do not eviscerate the classroom of those opportunities that teachers need to gain satisfaction from teaching. When such procedures begin to dominate classroom practice, opportunities to gain satisfactions from teaching can be seriously diminished. The teacher who wants the pride and satisfaction that come from having designed a reading program may be restricted from using such a program. Although schools do not exist primarily for the benefit of teachers, teachers who receive little or no satisfaction from what they do are not, I believe, likely to be educationally effective. The human need for pride in craftsmanship and being able to put something of oneself into work is recognized even by companies that sell packaged cake mixes.

The need to get something out of what one does, aside from student achievement, is still very great for most of us. The school should provide the conditions where such needs can be met. Unless the school can provide the necessary life-space for the teacher's growth, the existence of optimal conditions for the educational growth of students is not assured.

REFERENCES

1. See, for example, the two volumes of the *Handbook of Research on Teaching*. (N. L. Gage, ed.), *Handbook of Research on Teaching*, Rand McNally & Company, Chicago, 1963; and Robert M. W. Travers, ed. *Second Handbook of Research on Teaching*, Rand McNally & Company, Chicago, 1973.
2. This is reflected in the phrase "The state of the art," which typically implies that a high state of refinement or understanding has not yet been attained.
3. That the quality of experience defines art is best argued by John Dewey in *Art As Experience*, Minton, Balch and Co., New York, 1934.
4. See David Ecker, "The Artistic Process as Qualitative Problem-Solving," *Journal of Aesthetics and Art Criticism*, Vol. 21, No. 3, Spring 1963.
5. H. W. Janson, quoted in *Meaning*, Michael Polanyi and Harry Prosch, The University of Chicago Press, Chicago, 1977.
6. Dewey writes of the role of intelligence in art as follows: "Any idea that ignores the necessary role of intelligence in production of works of art is based upon identification of thinking with use of one special kind of material, verbal signs and words. To think effectively in terms of relations of qualities is as severe a demand upon thought as to think in terms of symbols, verbal and mathematical. Indeed, since words are easily manipulated in mechanical ways, the production of a work of genuine art probably demands more intelligence than does most of the so-called thinking that goes on among those who pride themselves on being 'intellectuals.' " *Art as Experience*, Minton, Balch and Co., New York, 1934, p. 46.
7. Phillip Jackson, *Life in Classrooms*, Holt, Rinehart, and Winston, Inc., New York, 1969.
8. See especially, Morris Weitz, "The Nature of Art," in *Readings in Art Education*, (Elliot W. Eisner and David Ecker, eds.) Blaisdell Publishing Co., Waltham, Mass., 1966.
9. Jackson, op. cit.
10. Joseph Schwab, "The Practical: A Language for Curriculum," *School Review*, Vol. 78, November 1969, p. 12.
11. John Dewey, *How We Think*, D. C. Heath, Lexington, Mass., 1910.
12. Gilbert Ryle, *The Concept of Mind*, Barnes and Noble, New York, 1949.
13. Nel Noddings, in a personal communication.
14. For a report on this work, see Elliot W. Eisner, *English Primary Schools*, National Association for Young Children, Washington, D.C., 1974.
15. John Dewey, *Experience and Education*, Macmillan Co., New York, 1938, passim.

10

The Functions and Forms of Evaluation

Our discussion will be adequate if it has as much clearness as the subject matter admits of, for precision is not to be sought for alike in all discussions, any more than in all the products of the crafts. . . . for it is the mark of an educated man to look for precision in each class of things just so far as the nature of the subject admits; it is evidently equally foolish to accept probable reasoning from a mathematician and to demand from a rhetorician scientific proofs.

ARISTOTLE

Although many people regard evaluation as something analogous to the giving of grades, in fact evaluation is used in education to perform a wide variety of different functions. It is our purpose in this chapter to identify some of these functions and to describe the forms evaluation can take when directed toward various ends. Of the functions of evaluation in education, five seem especially important:

1. To diagnose
2. To revise curricula
3. To compare
4. To anticipate educational needs
5. To determine if objectives have been achieved

Let's examine each of these different functions. Evaluation can be used to diagnose—but what? Three subject matters, each of which will be discussed in detail later, can be identified now as being the potential focus of diagnosis. They are the *curriculum* itself, even before it is employed in a classroom, *the teaching* that is occurring, and *the student* and his or her learning and experience.

Diagnosis as an evaluative technique is most often used in the context of student learning, and the term itself has a medical connotation. Students are "diagnosed" in order to "prescribe" a "treatment" that is educationally effective. The medical analogy has its uses: it suggests that treatments will be employed that fit the nature of the student's difficulties. But there are limits to such metaphors. Students are not patients and they don't normally have illnesses to be treated. Furthermore, although there are standard forms of medical technique, controlled pharmaceutical formulas for medicines, and routine procedures for medical diagnoses, virtually none of these rigorous tools, treatments, or techniques available to the medical practitioner is available to the educational practitioner. To be sure, there are intelligence tests and diagnostic tests in reading and some other subject areas such as mathematics, but the confidence one can place in these tools is limited and, in addition, performance on them is greatly influenced by the cultural conditions in which students live. Having said this, we can still talk about diagnosis as a function in evaluation. To diagnose can represent the effort to locate or try to locate the sources of difficulties students are having with particular learning problems. In the field of reading, where many of the available diagnostic tools exist, it is possible to employ tests that assess word-attack skills, paragraph meaning, general comprehension, and vocabulary. The achievement profile secured from such instruments is designed to guide the teacher so that if a student is weak in a particular area instruction in that area can be provided.

It should also be pointed out that the diagnosis of learning difficulties does not require the use of tests, and at its most general level it is used by virtually all teachers to identify whether their students understand what is being taught. For example, an art teacher can look at a student's work or watch the student while working in class and "diagnose" the sorts of strengths and weaknesses that the student possesses. One student might, for example, be unable to control the material adequately to use it as a medium of expression, another student might be neglecting attention to his work's formal features, still another student might be inadequately wedging the clay with which she is working. In each of the foregoing cases, the type of problem the student has requires a different type of "solution" or educational "treatment."

But even more generally, any teacher attempting to explain something to students in class would attempt to determine whether the explanation was understood. To do so requires some form of diagnosis: a request by the teacher to a student to explain, to demonstrate, to draw relationships. The questions students themselves ask provide diagnostic information to the teacher. Indeed, if one looks at teaching dialectically, much of what teachers do will be seen as a result of their understanding of where students are and what they need. The use of an example to clarify a point that is not understood requires some conception of what is likely to make more sense to students than the explanation just provided. The good example provides the necessary bridge between the student's current level of comprehension, his or her experience, and the aims toward which the teaching is directed. The selection of the right example is, one might say, the result of a diagnostic evaluation.

Perhaps the classic example of such diagnosis occurs in the sixth book of Plato's Republic.[1] Glaucon, after he asks about the nature of knowledge, is given an image by Socrates in an effort to help him grasp the hierarchy of truth that is used in Plato's epistemology. Glaucon fails to grasp the meaning of the image (in this case, a line divided into four segments intended to represent various degrees of truth), and so Socrates proceeds in the beginning of Book Seven to tell Glaucon the famous parable of the cave, which even more graphically depicts the relationships Socrates tried to explain earlier. What Plato gives us here is a telling image of both teaching and diagnostic evaluation. When a teacher monitors his or her teaching tactics to suit students, a diagnostic form of evaluation has occurred. Thus, diagnosis in evaluation can be employed dynamically in the context of teaching or more formally in the context of specially designed tests that locate the students' strengths and weaknesses, and therefore it provides a basis for curriculum change.

A second function of evaluation is to revise the curriculum. If for the moment we conceive of the curriculum as a set of materials to be used by students or by the teacher in order to have educational consequences, then it becomes clear that such materials will need modification and improvements from the point of initial inception to the point where they are ready for general dissemination to the schools. This process—what Michael Scriven refers to as formative evaluation [2]—has as its major aim the improvement of the program or curriculum that is being developed. In educational laboratories that develop curriculum materials, such evaluation goes through a variety of stages before the final product—in this case a packaged curriculum—is disseminated. One of these stages focuses on an evaluation of the content and aims of the curriculum.[3] Before learning activities are created, there is some appraisal of the content that has been selected and the aims that have been formulated. This process, which itself is a part of the curriculum development process, lays the groundwork for transforming content and aims into promising learning activities: events that have as their intended consequences educational outcomes related to the subject matter or content employed in the first place.

Once the content has been appraised and learning activities have been formulated, the materials are "hothouse tested," as described earlier. Among other things, this affords schools the opportunity to have contact with a developing educational enterprise that is stimulating to the school. It provides a type of Hawthorne effect for those teachers who elect to try the new material.

If the curriculum developer and an evaluator visit the classroom on appointment to watch the class use the materials and to observe the teacher and talk with him or her about the materials, the developer can gain some insight into the problems that exist and how they might be remedied. The materials might be too sophisticated for children of a particular age to use, the learning activities might turn out to be dull, the teacher might have difficulty handling the materials physically, the explanations might be misleading and therefore likely to be misunderstood, and so on. After the materials have been revised as a result of hothouse testing, the materials will be disseminated for field testing. Ideally, these stages of evaluation will yield curriculum materials that do not have major educational faults.

When the curriculum development movement got under way in the early 1960s, there was talk about the desirability of creating "teacher proof" curricula. That aspiration has, through the years, given way to the more realistic view that teachers are not mere tubes for curriculum developers. They cannot and should not be bypassed. Materials guarantee nothing. What they do is to expand the range of resources with which teachers and students can work. They are not a substitute for teachers.

The use of evaluation to revise the curriculum is in my view one of the central functions of evaluation. It is a type of feedback mechanism for educational improvement that diminishes the tendency to use evaluation practices as a means of classifying students, rewarding them, or selecting the able from the rest. Although classification, selection, and reward have been historically important functions of evaluation, when evaluation is used this way the responsibility for performance shifts almost wholly to the student rather than the school. If students fail to perform, under conventional assumptions the fault lies with the students.[4] However, when student performance is viewed as an index of program effectiveness, the likelihood of curriculum improvement increases and a major contribution is made toward improving the quality of education.

A third function of evaluation is to compare programs, teaching, and other aspects of schooling such as forms of school organization. Educational policy is supposedly made with an eye toward improving the quality of educational experience the school provides. This means that when a school board decides that new school buildings will be designed on an open plan, there is implicit in that policy the belief that such a plan will have beneficial effects on the students for whom it is intended. Many, but not all, policy changes in schools are based on certain values that the new policy is intended to realize. Often the "new math" was adopted because people came to believe that it was important for students to understand the logic, or structure, of mathematics. The use of peer tutoring is embraced because it is believed that students teaching each other provide benefits that cannot be secured from a student-teacher relationship. Team teaching is used in schools because collaboration by teachers is thought to make it possible for them to exploit their strengths as teachers. Related arts programs are developed because such programs are considered to help students appreciate the common elements among the arts. Comparative approaches to evaluation ask whether these beliefs are true. Does the new math do more than the old math in helping students understand the structure of mathematics? Does peer tutoring have benefits that more typical teacher-pupil relationships fail to provide? And so forth. Insofar as educational policy rests on evidence concerning the effects of the alternatives being considered, the comparative evaluation of these programs, in principle, is one vehicle for making such evidence available.

There is, however, a set of paradoxes regarding the use of comparative methods for curriculum policy making. In the first place, educational materials and modes of school organization are not susceptible to the kind of standardization that can be assigned to, say, light bulbs. If the electric company says that a light bulb will burn for about 740 hours, nine times out of ten its life will be close to that mark. Educational materials and new forms of educational practice cannot be standardized with the precision possible with materials that are inert; hence, a program evaluated as effective in one setting is not guaranteed to be effective in other settings. Moreover, the new setting will assuredly differ from the others in which the materials were originally used. Thus, a policy to adopt a new curriculum, to employ a new form of school organization, or to use a new procedure for scheduling must to a large degree be based on the attractiveness of such materials, modes of organization, and procedures rather than on "hard data."

Even if such data could be obtained, it might take several years to evaluate programs adequately to the point where hard data were available. By that time, the desire to implement the innovation might have run its course; its most ardent advocates might have left the district, the need for such innovation might have changed, or some new and even more promising innovations might have emerged on the horizon. Thus comparisons of educational programs are difficult. They are difficult not only because of the reasons cited, but also because new programs most often tend to be aimed at the achievement of goals different from those that old programs were designed to achieve. It is seldom the case that the goals of existing programs are considered to be without merit. Hence, when one weighs the promise of a new program against that of an existing one, their effectiveness is found to be not strictly comparable. They aim at different ends. Because it is not a matter of one program doing better what another program does—that would be far easier—the problem of comparison is extremely complicated. Nevertheless, the effectiveness of different programs can be compared, if only in relation to their own goals and unanticipated consequences. Such a comparison will not provide simple and certain conclusions about what to adopt and implement, but it will expand the pool of considerations from which competent educational conclusions can be drawn.

A fourth function of evaluation is to anticipate or identify educational needs. The concept of educational needs is directly related to the practice of needs assessment, in which various modes of data collection are employed with a community or school population in order to identify appropriate educational goals. For example, the U.S. Office of Education and later the National Institute of Education frequently required the writers of proposals for educational innovations first to do a needs assessment to demonstrate the existence of the need to be met through the proposed project. Writers of proposals would then employ tests of achievement and of attitude, conduct interviews, and determine public opinion by collecting statements from community leaders that there was a need for the program for which funding was sought. Needs assessment became the process for justifying the educational importance of educational innovation.

The practice of studying the community or the school population for which a program is intended is not unreasonable. At the same time, it is wise to be aware of the fact that educational needs are not like the clouds or the grass. They are not simply out there to be discovered by interview or tests. Educational needs are the products of judgments about what counts in educational matters. What constitutes an educational need depends on the educational values one holds. In Chapter 4, some of the values that animate educational programs were identified. Clearly, someone who embraces academic rationalism will perceive educational needs differently from someone who is a social reconstructionist. The academic rationalist looks at the school population and concludes that the students are without an appreciation of the past, are ignorant of the major intellectual works of man, and cannot adequately reason. The social reconstructionist exclaims that students need to know that the environment is being poisoned, that bigotry and race hatred are rampant, and that the world needs a common government if it is to survive.

The influence of the values one brings to a situation is manifest in how one describes that situation. The selection of tests, the identification of relevant populations to study, the way in which data are secured and analyzed, these all reflect the values one considers important. If one values curiosity, imagination, and sensibility, it is possible to describe educational needs in these terms. If one values reading skill, arithmetical competency, and neatness, one looks for other types of data. In short, we look for data with which to determine educational needs by selecting subject matters to which we are already commited. In part, we find what we look for.

A fifth function of evaluation, and the one most traditionally employed in curriculum theory, is as a means for determining whether educational objectives have been attained. The theory underlying this function of evaluation is straightforward. Educational programs should be purposeful; therefore, they should have goals. To be meaningful, these goals should be sufficiently specific to make it possible to determine whether they have been realized. The objectives once formulated at a meaningful level of specificity are the criteria through which student performance is assessed. Evaluation in this function is designed to provide the tasks and identify the situations that make possible the acquisition of data relevant to the objectives. Evaluation therefore can be used as a type of feedback mechanism to "recycle" the student if he or she fails to achieve the objectives, to pass him or her on to the next level if the objectives have been attained, to revise the curriculum if it is not effective for a particular student or group of students, or to alter the objectives.

This emphasis on use of evaluation conceives of clearly formulated objectives as a central and necessary condition for meaningful evaluation. It is argued, erroneously in my view, that there can be no evaluation without a "clear" statement of objectives.[5] Objectives are the criteria for determining whether the program has been effective. Evaluation is the means of collecting the data and analyzing them.

There is, of course, a reasonableness in the desire to have objectives in order to evaluate the effectiveness of an educational program. Yet, the evaluative net one casts can and ought to be much wider than the particular objective or set of objectives specified by a particular curriculum. The outcomes of educational programs are not completely predictable, and hence to evaluate only for those goals one has intended can lead one to neglect equally important, and at times even more important, outcomes that were unintended. Using objectives to serve as criteria for evaluating educational programs has an important function to perform, but a conception of evaluation that limits itself to what has been preplanned in terms of goals or objectives is likely to be educationally thin.

It should be noted that the use of objectives as a basis for evaluation has given rise to particular conceptions of educational practice. Mastery learning[6] is one such practice. Mastery learning theory posits that schools should not be primarily concerned with sorting out people through instruments that compare students to each other. Schools have historically performed the sorting role for society, and the result has been both frustration for those students who did not succeed and a loss of talented resources that society could have otherwise secured. Rather than attempt to sort out the able from the less able through evaluation procedures that are designed to compare students to each other, the school should formulate specific levels of mastery—particular objectives—and should evaluate students in relation to their mastery of these objectives, regardless of the amount of time it might take for particular students to attain mastery. Such a theory of educational practice would give virtually all students a sense of achievement and, in the long run, would contribute to their mental health as well as to their competence.

In describing mastery learning, I am simply pointing out the function that evaluation performs in such a view of educational practice. In this view, the form of evaluation called for requires a specific, operationally defined conception of mastery; hence the need for a set of behavioral objectives.

The idea that evaluation should determine whether objectives have been achieved has given rise not only to the concept of mastery learning, but also to distinctions between two types of tests. These are *norm-referenced* and *criterion-referenced* tests.[7] In norm-referenced tests, of which IQ tests and most published achievement tests are examples, the performance of an individual or a group is compared to the performance of other individuals or groups. The test is constructed to discriminate between the performances of individuals and to enable the test maker or user to rank individuals within a group. Ranking can be individual or within groups, the most general being that of individuals whose performance places them in the upper half or in the lower half of a population of those who have taken the test. Rankings can be further refined into quartiles—the placement of individuals in the first, second, third, or fourth quarter of a population. Regardless of the particular scheme used, the distinguishing feature of norm-referenced tests is that the scores individuals achieve on such tests are reported and their meaning is interpreted in relation to the performance of others.

Criterion-referenced tests are designed to measure performance in relationship to some criterion.[8] The purpose is not to compare an individual with a group but to determine whether an individual can attain some criterion to which the test is referenced. An example might help illustrate this function.

When I was a boy of about nine years of age I attended a summer camp located on a small lake in Illinois. On that lake there three areas marked off by floats that were to be used for swimming by the boys in the camp. One area was for nonswimmers, a second for intermediate swimmers, and a third, which had a small wooden raft anchored to the bottom of the lake, for advanced swimmers. To get permission to swim to the raft that was in deep water, a boy had to be able to swim two laps of the intermediate section of the lake. If he could swim one and three-quarter laps, he had to use the intermediate section. It didn't matter whether a boy could swim three or three hundred laps, all he needed to be able to swim to use the raft was two laps. That task, defined clearly in terms of a measurable competency, is an example of a criterion-referenced task or test. The issue was not one of comparing the swimming skills of the boys (although that inevitably happened), it was to determine the presence of a competency.

Driver training programs, typing classes, and other skill-oriented courses use criterion-referenced tests. Indeed, contract learning—that form of educational practice in which teacher and student jointly form an agreement regarding the education task to be performed, the anticipated product, and the time of completion—is a not too distant relative of criterion-referenced testing, which itself is related to the use of defined objectives as a basis of evaluation.

THE MAJOR SUBJECT MATTERS OF
EVALUATION

As I have indicated earlier, evaluation is a process than can be directed toward three important subject matters: the curriculum itself, the teaching that is provided, and the outcomes that are realized. Attention to the curriculum is justified on rather straightforward grounds. Unless one appraises the quality of the content and learning activities that constitute the curriculum, one has no basis for determining whether it is worth being taught. To paraphrase Plato, "The unexamined curriculum might not be worth learning."

But what are the aspects of the curriculum that can be evaluated, even prior to its implementation in the classroom? First, one can make some judgment about the educational significance of the content to which students will be exposed. Now the significance of the content can be determined only with criteria that flow from a set of values about what counts educationally. But whatever these criteria are, and they will differ for different groups and individuals, the application of such criteria is important for appraising the value of the curriculum in the first place. Some example of how such criteria are applied might be helpful.

For years state boards of education and local school districts have engaged in the process of textbook selection. Textbooks, a fundamental element in most curricula, were adopted on the basis of attractiveness and feasibility as a teaching tool. It wasn't until the civil rights and women's liberation movements that states adopted specific criteria dealing with race and sexism to be used for evaluating textbooks and other curriculum material. Regardless of how attractive and significant the educational content of a textbook is, if it places minority groups in an unfavorable light or undermines the image of one of the sexes it is to be rejected as suitable material for children in the schools. In California, the state department of education guidelines regarding the content of educational materials, including textbooks, state:

Male and Female Roles—Ed. Code 9240(a), 9243(a)
In order to encourage the individual development and self-esteem of each child, regardless of gender, instructional materials, when they portray people (or animals having identifiable human attributes), shall portray women and men, girls and boys, in a wide variety of occupational, emotional, and behavioral situations, presenting both sexes in the full range of their human potential.
Emotions—for example, fear, anger, aggression, excitement, or tenderness—should occur randomly among characters regardless of gender.
Traditional activities engaged in by characters of one sex should be balanced by the presentation of nontraditional activities for characters of that sex.

Ethnic and Cultural Groups—Ed. Code 9240(b) and 9243(a)
In order to project the cultural diversity of our society, instill in each child a sense of pride in his or her heritage, eradicate the seeds of prejudice, and encour-

age the individual development of each child, instructional materials, when portraying people (or animals having identifiable human attributes), shall include a fair representation of white and minority characters portrayed in a wide variety of occupational and behavioral roles, and present the contributions of ethnic and cultural groups, thereby reinforcing the self-esteem and potential of all people and helping the members of minority groups to find their rightful place in our society.[9]

Obviously, these particular criteria, while important, represent only a limited range of those relevant to evaluate textbooks or curriculum. The intellectual significance of the content itself is, or ought to be, an important focus for appraisal. In the teaching of science, for example, what are the intellectual significance and validity of the concepts, generalizations, and subject matters with which students will deal? If the concepts are intellectually marginal and the generalizations trivial or so remote as to have little illuminative power for those other than specialists, it seems unlikely that schools should use their students' time to deal with that material. If ideas are being promulgated that are out of date, no longer valid, or simply insignificant, it makes little sense to spend a great deal of energy trying to help children learn such material. Some appraisal of the content of the curriculum in terms of its intellectual significance and the covert messages it might convey seems an appropriate focus for the evaluation of the curriculum.

But because curricula are intended for people and because people have different priorities, the appraisal of the curriculum needs also to be made with an eye toward its appropriateness for the population for whom it is intended. Determining the appropriateness of curriculum content takes at least two forms. First, it is important to determine whether the content and tasks the curriculum encompasses are within the developmental scope of the children who are to deal with it. Some kinds of content are inappropriate from a developmental point of view for the children of certain developmental levels. The concept of readiness, although at times abused in schools, can be employed to make judgments about the relationships between psychological tasks and content and the characteristics of the students.[10] Thus, content within a curriculum might fare well from the standpoint of its significance within a discipline and yet be rejected on the grounds that it is developmentally inappropriate for particular groups of children.

The second basis on which content may be evaluated deals with the experiential fitness of the content to the experiential background of the students. Curriculum content might be intellectually important and developmentally appropriate but still be ill suited to the background or interests of the students. The importance of this criterion will, of course, vary with the curriculum orientation one embraces. To someone holding an academic rationalistic orientation, the need for students to be interested in a particular subject matter is likely to be less important than it is to someone concerned with personal relevance as a central condition of meaningful education. Yet this criterion can never be completely neglected. If the experiential background of students is so remote from the content encountered as to make it essentially meaningless, it is obvious that the curriculum, regardless of how defensible on other grounds, is inappropriate for that population. The point to remember here is that in evaluating the curriculum the educational significance of the content is a primary consideration. If the content is misleading or invalid, subsequent evaluation is not necessary. But even if the curriculum has been adjudged intellectually impeccable, one still has to appraise it both developmentally and experientially with respect to its suitability to the population for whom it is intended.

I have in the course of my work in education visited classrooms in Nigeria where eight-year-old Nigerian children were studying the Battle of Hastings. One can only wonder why out of all the possible subjects that those eight-year-old children might encounter they were studying the Battle of Hastings? There are good reasons why a former British colony should continue its traditions, but one might question the appropriateness and the meaninfulness of such content for those children. One does not have to travel to Nigeria to find similar situations in schools.

There are, of course, other criteria that can be used to evaluate the curriculum aside from the three already identified. As a matter of fact, any of the dimensions identified as relevant for curriculum development are also relevant for evaluating the curriculum after it is developed. Two examples should suffice.

You will recall that the forms used to display content and tasks to students and the forms through which their responses were elicited were identified as dimensions to be considered in curriculum development. If it is true that different forms of presentation provide different types of information, and that different forms of expression convey different types of understanding and insight, and if it is further assumed that the nurture of a wide range of human abilities is an educationally desirable goal, then it seems reasonable that educational materials, those materials that constitute a central portion of the curriculum, should employ the range of means available for both display and expression. This means in practical terms that curriculum materials can be evaluated with respect to the extent to which they employ visual, auditory, and kinesthetic modes of presentation as well as linguistic ones. It means also that the forms through which the students' competency is to be displayed can have a similar range. There is no intrinsic reason, except tradition, why curriculum materials must require a verbal mode of presentation and a linguistic form of response. Once we are willing to grant that the forms one uses to express oneself influence what one is capable of "saying" and that individuals differ with regard to their aptitude for using different sensory modalities for processing and expressing what they know, feel, or believe, the first steps are laid for justifying the use of diverse modes of presentation and response in the curriculum and classroom. To the extent to which we value this diversity and try to nurture it, it becomes important not only to construct, but also to evaluate materials with an eye to these values.

The second major subject matter for evaluation is the quality of teaching that is provided. Although some educational theorists make no distinction between teaching and curriculum, I believe the distinction to be useful for several reasons. First, one can and usually does plan curriculum prior to using it in the classroom. Thus, curriculum development is a process, at least during some of its stages, that occurs outside of the classroom.[11] Second, and most important for the purposes of this chapter, the intellectual significance of the curriculum can be appraised independently of how well it is taught. A teacher might do a brilliant job of teaching, but the ideas or skills being taught might be trivial, biased, or invalid. Conversely, a teacher might be using a faultless curriculum with respect to its intellectual merit and its appropriateness both developmentally and experientially for students, but that teacher might be teaching so poorly that only confusion and frustration result for the students. The educational problem in each of these cases is different, and without a distinction between curriculum and teaching I fear they will fail to emerge.

To evaluate the quality of teaching is, of course, easier to say than to do. Efforts at identifying the qualities that make for effective teaching have been many but for the most part have not proved very illuminating. The approaches that have been taken to study and identify effective teaching have been scientific in character. The need for quantification, for explanation, for replicability, and for generalization have often led to a highly reductionistic approach to the study of teaching, one that attempts to locate specific causal relationships. The assumption is that by identifying specific causal units, eventually a holistic view of teaching will result. As yet this has not happened.[12] I will have more to say about the study of teaching later, but I would like to say now that there are aspects of teaching that can be evaluated by a sensitive student of classrooms: the type of relationships teachers establish with their classes, the clarity of their explanations, the level of enthusiasm they display, the kinds of questions they raise. Although these specific qualities have not been demonstrated through quantitative empirical research to make for effectiveness, I believe that they are relevant considerations in evaluating what teachers do when they teach.

In stating that I believe they are relevant for evaluating teachers even though quantitative empirical research has not as yet demonstrated their efficacy, we approach the hub of an epistemological issue in education. What is true? What counts as evidence? It is clear that scientific evidence about teaching or about most other aspects of educational practice is quite limited. There is very little in the way of hard data that can be used to justify educational practices, and even the little there is requires a non-scientific leap of faith because the sample from which the original conclusions were drawn is not likely to be identical to the population to whom the conclusion is to be applied. Indeed, if educational practitioners *had* to base their educational practices on hard data we would have to close our schools. Yet, to assume that the only source of understanding is the laboratory is to render oneself helpless. There is much—to provide a gross understatement—that is useful from seasoned experience and critical reflection on that experience. The aspects of teaching that I have identified are only a few of relevant dimensions that can be attended to and evaluated. Without evaluating teaching as well as the curriculum, one is not in a position to know, when there are difficulties, what their sources are.

The third major subject matter for evaluation and the one most characteristically attended to is the evaluation of student outcomes. The selection of the term *outcomes* as opposed to *objectives* was not a casual one. Objectives are intended goals; they are the destinations one hopes to arrive at through the educational program. But roads taken do not always lead to the destination one intends, and even when they do, much can be learned en route. Thus, *outcomes* is a broader term than *objectives*. The achievement of objectives can be included in the outcomes, but there is often much more to include as well.

Figure 7 presents a simple trichotomy of the kinds of outcomes that might be realized in a classroom. One segment of the circle deals with the outcomes that are subect specific; a second segment deals with outcomes that are teacher specific, and a third segment refers to outcomes that are pupil specific.

Subject-specific outcomes are directly related to the content that is taught. Such outcomes can be, but are not necessarily, related to the objectives for the course. There are several reasons why subject-specific outcomes need not necessarily be related to course objectives. First, many courses in a field of study have no articulated objectives yet are educationally effective. Second, even when objectives are specified, outcomes may be realized that, al-

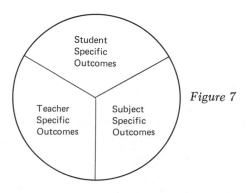

Figure 7

though within the context of the subject studied, are not defined by the objectives. To evaluate with respect to subject-specific outcomes means to focus one's evaluation on the learning of the subject matter of a course or segment of the course. This is often done through the use of standardized or teacher-made achievement tests. Generally, such assessment focuses on outcomes within a subject that are common across students. A multiple-choice test, for example, presents to a population of students a common set of test items. Such items allow no scope for a personally constructed response; the alternatives are provided in the distractors from which the student must select. Thus, what such a test reveals is determined by the choices the test maker made during test construction. Hence, what one finds out about student understanding when such tests are used is what has been selected by the test constructor as being relevant. These are items sampled from the universe of content that the course has provided. And because in "objective" or multiple-choice tests little or no scope is provided for students to demonstrate their understanding of aspects of the course or content not sampled, those aspects simply fail to emerge for consideration.

Attention to what students learn about specific content within a course has been a primary and traditional concern of achievement testing. To find out what students have learned has almost always meant to find out what about the content taught they have learned. Such a focus is useful for evaluation, but it represents only one segment of a much more complex picture. Students learn not only what was intended, they learn not only what is related to the content of what has been studied, they also learn because of the unique intellectual relationships they make between the content and their other interests. They may be stimulated by the content of a course to learn things that are only tangentially related to the content. These outcomes, outcomes that are ripe for educational evaluation, are student specific.

If one raises the question "What has a student learned in my class or course that is not about what I have been teaching?" one begins to move into student-specific domains. And if one begins to develop procedures for obtaining some understanding of such outcomes, one is engaged in a student-specific mode of evaluation. Obviously, so long as the options presented to a student or group of students present no opportunity for the display of what might be called personalized learning, such outcomes will not be manifest. If we want to know what the personal spinoff is from the content or courses we teach, the tasks or methods used for evaluation have to be sufficiently open ended to allow such personalized learning to emerge. Interviews, open-ended essays, and projects whose parameters provide opportunities for students to reveal what personal meanings they have constructed for themselves need to be made available. Such procedures will, of course, not be focused on providing comparative data. They are focused on the revelation of idiosyncratic outcomes.

Procedures that elicit idiosyncratic outcomes—in other words, personalized learning—are methodologically distinct from procedures normally used in the construction of achievement tests. Typical procedures for the construction of achievement tests require not only that a common set of items be applied to a population of students, but also that items on which most of all students do well or items that systematically differentiate male from female performance be eliminated. The aim of typical achievement tests is to provide scores that make possible the differentiation of students. The type of differentiation sought arises from differences in performance on the same set of items for all students. In general, the closer the population's performance is to the normal curve, the greater the likelihood the test is statistically reliable.

Yet, applying a common set of items to assess a common content across a population of students can vitiate efforts to individualize teaching or to foster the development of students' aptitudes and interests. We often say that it is educationally desirable to encourage students to pursue particular interests within school and that teachers should be flexible and imaginative in developing programs particularly appropriate for the individuals with whom they work. However, the use of tests that seek only common outcomes from a content area common to all students can be and often is inconsistent with such aims. If we are really serious about curriculum differentiation for students, the need for student-specific forms of evaluation will become increasingly important.

The third segment of student outcomes is represented by those that flow from what the teacher teaches about him- or herself. The intellectual style the teacher displays, the standards that he upholds, his willingness to take risks, his tolerance for nonconformity, the type of precision and punctuality he values, these aspects of the teacher as a person are not necessarily trivial aspects of teaching. Indeed, because these features are likely to be more pervasive than the content studied, it might be that they have important consequences for what students learn. Studying with a really great teacher, whether in elementary school or at the highest levels of the university, can help a student more than exposure to some particular body of content.

What do the personal qualities of teachers mean for the elementary school age children with whom they spend five or more hours each day for forty school weeks? At present these questions are not answerable. Conventional conceptions of educational evaluation have seldom included them in the procedures used to assess the effects of schooling. Yet, these questions and others that could be raised, it seems to me, are nontrivial aspects of schooling. Unless one is aware of the possibility of educationally significant effects issuing from the characteristics, values, and interests of teachers it is not likely that answers to such questions will be obtained. It would be interesting to ask students to characterize the contributions, other than those provided by course content, that their teachers made to them. What would students say about those contributions? Do those who work with particular teachers over extended periods of time display particular characteristics, interests, attitudes, or styles of inquiry that derive from characteristics of their teachers? A comprehensive theory of educational evaluation would include teacher-specific outcomes as at least one of three that warrant examination.

HOW CAN EDUCATIONAL EVALUATIONS BE REPORTED ARTISTICALLY?

How can what occurs in a classroom or school be made vivid to a public that wants increasingly to know what it is getting for its investment in schools? The typical procedures for reporting the educational efficacy of schools have been twofold. First, parents have been led to believe that the grades their children receive adequately portray how well their children are doing in school and by implication how well the school is doing by the child. Good grades mean that the child is doing well; poor grades mean that the child is doing poorly, although as educational consumerism increases, poor grades might come to mean that the school rather than the child has done poorly.

The other major vehicle for reporting to the public how schools do is through the use of standardized testing. In many states, standardized achievement tests are mandated by the state legislature, and in some cities newspapers publish the mean performance by grade of students in schools within the school district.[13] Parents and other citizens read such reports and draw conclusions about the educational quality of the school or school district by the rank that a school or school district occupies in some regional or national distribution. These scores are usually "unencumbered" by socioeconomic considerations or by any other factors or conditions that could influence test scores. Thus, the public has before it an array of test scores that provide a deceptive sense of educational precision. Although no competent educator would claim that performance on standardized reading and math tests adequately represents educational quality, these test scores, for all practical purposes, have become the major indices the public uses to judge the effectiveness of schools. And because the public uses such scores, school administrators feel the need to focus their teachers' attention onto activities that are likely to lead to higher standardized test scores. A school that succeeds (and by extension an administrator who is effective) is one whose students receive high standardized test scores.

Thus, we have something of an educational irony. Most educators would say that neither letter grades nor standardized test scores capture the richness of educational experience, nor do they adequately disclose the quality of education provided and experienced in the school. Yet schools do reward students with honors classes and deans' lists based on such grades and therefore legitimize the importance of grades while recognizing their limitations. Although educators point out that standardized test scores do not necessarily represent what students are learning, the administration of such tests proliferates and the subsequent publication of their results has consequences that are as often as misleading as they are informative.

This state of affairs stems from several sources. First, the aspiration for precision in evaluation has manifested itself in the quantification of student performance, which in turn is translated into grades. Somehow a type of precise objectivity is implied when complex forms of learning are reduced to a single score or letter. Second, parents often want an unambiguous indicator of their child's or the school's performance. To suggest contingencies or qualifications concerning the performance of students or the school is for many parents to inject an uncomfortable degree of uncertainty and complexity. Simplicity, even if it is misleading, is often preferable to the kind of complexity that an educational connoisseur might perceive.

This preference for the simple and the neat is not unrelated to the correct assessment that parents make of the criteria that their children must meet if they are to have upward educational mobility. Admission to universities is heavily influenced by the rank students hold in high school. And class rank is a function of the grades received. In short, the criteria applied to students for purposes of selection and retention in the hierarchy of schooling reinforce the use of a grading system that can be easily translated into simple, numerical indices. Grade-point average, class standing, college board scores: these are far easier to compare in a competitive educational market than widely diverse, even if illuminating, forms of educational disclosure. We seek to reduce diversity in order to have a uniform scale on which comparisons can be made.

A third reason standardized test scores and grades have become the basis for judging educational quality is that we have not provided the public with alternatives. By neglect of such alternatives, a tradition of grading practices has been established. The public expects it. Yet, if we think about the reporting problem—helping parents and others to understand what has taken place in schools—a wide array of possibilities comes to mind.

The problem of disclosing the character of educational events and the quality of what children are learning can, I am arguing, be conceived as an artistic problem. How can the results of educational evaluation be communicated so that the complexity *and* ambiguity *and* richness of what happens in schools and classrooms can be revealed?

Part of the answer to this question depends on the recognition that people communicate through different expressive modalities and that each modality has the power to convey different types of understanding. Quantitative indices are useful for some purposes but not for all. Written descriptions are helpful for understanding some events, but they cannot duplicate visual images for some purposes. Statistically derived norms are helpful for locating trends but neglect the unique occurrence. In short, if one considers the range of ways through which people come to express and understand and compares it with the range used for reporting the results of educational evaluations, it becomes apparent that only a slender slice of educational life is likely to be captured by the forms of reporting that are typically used. To capture this richness and therefore to help the public understand and appreciate the problems as well as the achievements of a classroom or school requires the construction of an evaluational landscape. Such a picture will probably employ a wide range of information secured from a variety of sources and revealed through different types of reporting procedures.

One of these procedures is likely to be what I referred to as educational criticism.[14] Such criticism would be aimed at helping parents, let us say, understand what has happened during the course of a school year in a particular school. What were the key events in the school? How did they come into being? In what ways did students and teachers participate? What consequences for the school did such events have? How could such events be strengthened? What do such events enable children to learn?

What is Mrs. Jones' classroom like? In what sorts of activities have the children engaged? What does Mrs. Jones provide that is uniquely hers? What is the character of the school day for children in her class? What are children deriving from her class that is not likely to be revealed by standardized testing? Questions such as these, if answered by a competent educational critic, would give parents an understanding of the school and the classroom that most at present do not have. Even parents who value education very highly have only the vaguest ideas about the kind of educational experience provided by the school their children attend. In the first place, report cards, if they are used, give no indication of the sorts of events I have described. The major focus of report cards is on how "well" the child is doing according to some criterion that itself is vague. And if the school is one where parent-teacher conferences are held in lieu of formal report cards, even then the discussion between parent and teacher is more likely to focus on the student's performance than on the program in which he or she is participating.

Another vehicle for disclosing the richness of educational programs to parents is through the use of film and videotape. One can capture on film or tape aspects of educational life that give a vivid picture to parents and others of what the school actually provides. The creation of such tapes and films will of course demand skills that most evaluators do not at present possess. Yet, the absence of such skills is no argument against developing them. The use of film and videotape, even the use of still slides and photographs, can be extremely informative if they have been taken with an artistic, educationally informed eye. The task of making such visual materials the sources of educational disclosure has scarcely been touched.

There have been films made of schools, such as *High School* by Frederick Wiseman, that are powerful statements about the quality of life in an urban high school, and by extension in others. That film is extremely skillful in portraying certain aspects of high school life, but its strength is at the same time a source of its weakness. It exaggerates to make a point—it is a visual polemic. It does not attempt to disclose the strengths of the school it portrays, but instead accentuates its oppressive, mindless, military character. Informed educational criticism and the informed educational use of videotape and film would aim at a more circumspect view of educational life. Supplemented by critical narrative, such visual materials considerably expand the channels for communication.

The use of still photography is also potentially powerful in revealing aspects of educational life that measured achievement and even artful criticism cannot capture. Paradigm cases of such visual renderings already exist, perhaps the most notable being Alfred Stieglitz's *The Family of Man*. Since Stieglitz created that exhibition, numerous other portfolios of visual reporting have appeared. What these portfolios offer us, and what they could portray about the educational quality of life in schools, is a nondiscursive mode of disclosure capable, when artistically created, of helping us vicariously participate in the life that the school provides. At present, the use of such vehicles as an explicit form of educational reporting is virtually absent from the scene in American education. When it does occur, it is by accident, connected to a student yearbook or newspaper but not as part of formal resources the school uses to understand and report what it is doing.

Educational criticism and the use of videotape, cinematography and still photography can be supplemented with still other types of information that would provide a more comprehensive and adequate picture of school life. One of these supplements is tape-recorded interviews of both students and teachers that deal with their work and its aims, their satisfactions, the situations and problems they encounter, their ideas about educational improvement, their aspirations in the school, the outcomes they value most and least, and so forth. Taped interviews on cassettes could be produced and edited in a way that would deal with ideas, beliefs, and feelings that seldom get expressed on written questionnaires and are never possible to express on achievement tests. The spontaneity of the interview, when it is conducted by a skillful interviewer, one who knows both interview techniques and education theory and practice, could yield data that are present simply unavailable.

It should be noted that listening to tape-recorded interviews may itself require a type of connoisseurship that needs to be developed. What is said and what is not said, how something is said, the tone of expression, and so forth—all of the nonlinguistic cues that possess meaning—need to be penetrated if what one says is to be fully appreciated. Nevertheless, all of us have developed such skills to a considerable degree—they are survival skills—and even if they are not refined to an optimum level, we have learned how to listen sufficiently well to get much out of what others say.

Additional information that could be used to construct an adequate evaluation of a school or classroom would include an analysis of the work that children produce. In typical evaluation procedures, examination scores, grades received on essays, and ratings of projects undertaken and completed are the data that are reported to parents about the progress their children are making in school. When this is done, it is seldom clear whether, for example, a grade of B on an essay refers to the quality of the essay in relation to some external standard, whether it refers to the quality of the essay relative to other essays produced by students in the class, whether it is based on the efforts put forth by the student in writing the essay, whether it represents the amount of growth the student has achieved since the beginning of the semester, or whether it is based on a combination of all of these criteria. These procedures for grading are not the ones I am referring to as an analysis of what children produce in school. The problem with such procedures is that they provide conclusions rather than disclosures about the character of the work done and the sorts of progress and problems children encounter. To do the latter would require, first, close attention to what a given child or class has created. If the work is an essay, one might describe how a child has organized his essay, the quality of the arguments or evidence he employs, the extent to which his imagination has been used to create his work. These aspects of the work could be treated comparatively with other work created by the child or the class and could be accompanied by a critique that would help adults or children understand what has been accomplished. If, for example, one wants to help a school board or a group of parents understand that human development is uneven, that children of the same age are at quite different places with respect to skills or understanding, it would be useful to display the range of work—not just the best work—that the children in class create. The display of only the best conceals the range of differences and distorts the real educational picture with which teachers must work. The visual display of such range when critically described and analyzed would do much to make apparent to a school board, for example, some of the realities of classroom performance.

The major point I am attempting to make here is that the problem of communicating to some public—parents, school board members, students, state agencies—about what has happened in schools, the problem of making known what is strong and what is weak, what needs support and what does not, can be usefully conceived as an artistic problem. It is a problem of putting together an expressive, sensitive, and revealing picture of educational practice and its consequences. The construction of such a picture can exploit both the various modalities that people have always used to communicate and also the new technology that can capture and hold even the most evanescent happenings in classroom, life.

That this approach to educational evaluation is rare can be appreciated by examining evaluation studies. These studies virtually always are characterized by the attempt to be quantitatively "objective" and impersonal and to focus on measured achievement with no attention paid to the relationship between what was done (the process) and what ensued (the product). Conventional training in evaluation still bears the imprint of psychometrics. Although psychometric techniques are useful for describing some aspects of education performance, they by no means embrace the entirety of what counts educationally. When young evaluators are trained in psychometrics and neglect the normative and theoretical aspects of educational practice, the problem is compounded. Education is a normative enterprise. What counts educationally depends on one's educational values. The reduction of educational evaluation to a set of limited quantitative methods, ones that harbor their own values, which often go unacknowledged or unappraised, is to reduce educational evaluators to technicians and evaluation to a technical process. Educational evaluation is more than that, however. No narrow range of technical skills applied to educational settings is likely to reveal the richness of their context. To interpret the meaning of even that which is secured through parochial means requires some vision of educational virtue and some understanding of the history of educational practice.

It might seem strange to mention the importance of the history of education and educational theory in the context of discussing educational evaluation. These subjects are seldom found in such discourse, and when they occur as a part of the educational program of prospective evaluators, more often than not they are there to meet institutional requirements rather than because they are considered important. Yet I hope I have made the point that educational evaluation requires a sophisticated interpretive map not only to separate what is trivial from what is significant in educational settings, but also to understand the meaning of what has been seen. Without a normative and historical perspective, the interpretation and appraisal of educational events are impoverished.

REFERENCES

1. *The Republic, transl. by B. Jowett,* The Modern Library, New York, n.d.
2. Michael Scriven, "The Methodology of Evaluation," in *AERA Monograph Series on Curriculum Evaluation, No. 1,* Rand McNally, Chicago, 1967.
3. Not all development processes start with aims and content. Curriculum activities themselves can provide a starting point for aims.
4. This assumption is widely prevalent in England and on the continent, where evaluation practices are designed to select the most able for the assignment to different forms of secondary schools and for university admission.
5. This assumption is embedded in much of the material on evaluation sent to school districts by state departments of education.

6. Benjamin Bloom, *Human Characteristics and School Learning*, McGraw-Hill, New York, 1976.
7. For a description of norm- and criterion-referenced test theory, see Gilbert Sax, "The Use of Standardized Tests in Evaluation," in *Evaluation in Education: Current Applications* (W. James Popham, ed.), McCutchan Publishing Co., Berkeley, Calif., 1976, pp. 243–308.
8. Ibid.
9. *Guide Lines for Evaluation of Instructional Materials for Compliance with Content Requirements of the Education Code*, California State Department of Education, Sacramento, 1975.
10. The work of Jean Piaget is often used to support this view.
11. Phillip Jackson refers to this as "Pre-Active Teaching." See his book, *Life in Classrooms*, Holt, Rinehart and Winston, New York, 1968.
12. Barak Rosenshine and Norma Furst," "The Use of Direct Observation to Study Teaching," in *Second Handbook of Research in Teaching* (Robert Travers, ed.), Rand McNally, Chicago, 1973.
13. State-mandated achievement tests are used in fifteen states as of 1973. Source: Phyllis Hawthorne, *Legislation by the States: Accountability and Assessment in Education*, Report No. 2, Wisconsin Department of Public Instruction, August 1973.
14. Although Chapters 11 and 12 describe the theoretical aspects of educational criticism and provide examples of it, those wishing to consult other works should see Elliot W. Eisner, "On the Uses of Educational Connoisseurship and Educational Criticism for Evaluating Classroom Life," *Teachers College Record*, Vol. 78, No. 3, February 1977, and "The Forms and Functions of Educational Connoisseurship and Criticism," *Journal of Aesthetic Education*, Vol. 10, Nos. 3 and 4, July–October 1976. Also see the following doctoral dissertations completed at Stanford University.

   W. Dwaine Greer, *The Criticism of Teaching*, Doctoral Dissertation, Stanford University.

   Elizabeth Vallance, *Aesthetic Criticism and Curriculum Description*, Doctoral Dissertation, Stanford University, 1975.

   Gail McCutcheon, *The Disclosure of Classroom Life*, Doctoral Dissertation, Stanford University, 1976.

   Tom Barone, *Inquiring into Classroom Experiences: A Qualitative Holistic Approach*, Doctoral Dissertation, Stanford University, in process.

   Robin Alexander, *Educational Criticism of Three Art History Classrooms*, Doctoral Dissertation, Stanford University, in process.

   Leonard Davidman, *A Formative Evaluation of the Unified Science and Mathematics in the Elementary School Curriculum*, Doctoral Dissertation, Stanford University, 1976.

11

The Forms and Functions of Educational Connoisseurship and Educational Criticism

The transition from a paradigm in crisis to a new one from which a new tradition of normal science can emerge is far from a cumulative process, one achieved by an articulation or extension of the old paradigm. Rather it is a reconstruction of the field from new fundamentals, a reconstruction that changes some of the field's most elementary theoretical generalizations as well as many of its paradigm methods and applications.

THOMAS S. KUNN

It is the function of this chapter to identify and discuss some of the assumptions, principles, and procedures used in educational connoisseurship and educational criticism. This form of educational inquiry, a species of educational evaluation, is qualitative in character[1] and takes its lead from the work that critics have done in literature, theater, film, music, and the visual arts.

Interest in qualitative forms of research and evaluation have increased in recent years, but little of the work that has been done has been related to the fine arts. Most of those who have used qualitative approaches have related their work to ethnography. Yet, there is no area of human inquiry that epitomizes the qualitative more than what artists do when they work. Thus, it seems to me that if we seek to know what qualitative inquiry consists of, we can do little better than analyze the work of those for whom it is a necessary condition.

Artists inquire in a qualitative mode both in the formulation of ends and in the use of means to achieve such ends.[2] The result of their work is a qualitative whole—a symphony, poem, painting, ballet—that has the capacity to evoke in the intelligent percepient a kind of experience that leads us to call the work art. My claim is that the paradigmatic use of qualitative inquiry is found in the arts.

190

Another form of qualitative inquiry is found in the work of those who inquire into the work of artists, namely the art critics. The art critic finds himself or herself with the difficult task of rendering the essentially ineffable qualities constituting works of art into a language that will help others perceive the work more deeply. In this sense, the critic's task is to function as a midwife to perception, to so talk about the qualities constituting the work of art that others, lacking the critic's connoisseurship, will be able to perceive the work more comprehensively. "The end of criticism," wrote Dewey, "is the reeducation of the perception of the work of art." The critic's task in this view is not primarily the issuance of a judgment but rather the difficult task of "lifting the veils that keep the eyes from seeing." [3]

There are two important points to be made about criticism. First, criticism is an empirical undertaking. The word *empirical* comes from the Latin *empiricus,* meaning "open to experience." Criticism is empirical in the significant sense that the qualities the critic describes or renders must be capable of being located in the subject matter of the criticism. In this sense, the test of criticism is in its instrumental effects on the perception of works of art. It is not abstraction that one understands through criticism but rather qualities and their relationships.

It is interesting to note that the studies we usually call empirical are studies whose findings are couched in terms that are not in the strict sense empirical at all. Take, for example, studies that report significant differences in variances or in means between groups of students. What we have in such studies are conclusions that may be four or five orders removed from the empirical qualities from which the conclusions were drawn. We tend to forget that individual students confront individual test items and answer them correctly or incorrectly. From the individual's response to individual items, a raw score is calculated for each student. This raw score is itself an abstraction that significantly limits the information on each student's performance. Two students, for example, can receive the same raw score for entirely different performances on the same test. These raw scores are then summed and averaged, a second-order abstraction. Following this procedure, variances are computed and compared and a probability is calculated to determine the relationship between variances across groups. These represent third- and fourth-order abstractions. In no way is it possible to reconstruct an individual student's test score from knowledge of a mean or from the differences between means. These latter quantities are in fact abstractions that, although derived from empirical performances, are not themselves empirical. One cannot locate a mean by looking for it in the world.

The second point I want to emphasize with respect to criticism is that *anything* can be its subject matter. Once again, by *criticism* I do not mean the negative appraisal of something but rather the illumination of something's qualities so that an appraisal of its value can be made. Although *criticism* is a term that is most frequently used in the arts, it also is used in sports, in the assessment of research, in the appraisal of human behavior, particularly in social settings, and in a host of other areas in which humans have intercourse with the world. There is nothing, in principle, that cannot be the object of criticism.

Although teaching is frequently referred to as an art, and although in our vernacular we recognize the artistic aspects of educational practice—the beautiful lesson, the exciting discussion, the well-made point, the elegant exposition—when it comes to our attempts to describe or understand educational practice, criticism is almost never appealed to as a possible method or approach. The reason for the neglect of criticism as a potentially useful vehicle for the description, interpretation, and evaluation of educational practice is, I think, a result of the ways in which educators have been professionally socialized, particularly those holding doctorates and working in universities.

Doctoral programs socialize students to believe that the most dependable procedure one can use to obtain knowledge is through science and that respectable inquiry in education, at least respectable empirical inquiry, is scientific in character. To use other methods, to employ metaphor, analogy, simile, or other poetic devices, is to lack rigor. Jeffreys tries to make the point this way:

> No matter what the subject matter, the fundamental principles of the method must be the same. There must be a uniform standard for validity for all hypotheses, irrespective of the subject. Different laws may hold in different subjects, but they must be tested by the same criteria; otherwise we have no guarantee that our decisions will be those warranted by the data and not merely the result of inadequate analysis or of believing what we want to believe. . . . If the rules [of induction applied in scientific inquiry] are not general, we shall have different standards of validity in different subjects, or different standards for one's own hypotheses and somebody else's. If the rules of themselves say anything about the world, they will make empirical statements independently of observational evidence, and thereby limit the scope of what we can find out by observation. If there are such limits, they must be inferred from observation; we must not assert them in advance.[4]

Jeffrey's argument proceeds beyond the rejection of critical language; it also tends to include all forms of inquiry that do not translate the phenomena of interest into quantity. This is so pervasive a belief in educational research that educational research itself is identified not just with empirical inquiry but with quantitative empirical inquiry. For example, from Volume 11, Number 2, to Volume 13, Number 1, the *American Educational Research Journal* published 47 articles. Of these only one was nonstatistical in character.

I mention this not as a condemnation of statistically oriented inquiry in education but rather as an example of its pervasiveness and of the relative neglect of other forms of inquiry that could be useful to the field. I believe that the creation of educational criticism, a form of criticism not unlike that found in the arts but directed to educational matters, could provide a kind of utility that scientific studies and quantitatively treated phenomena neglect. Indeed, I hope that one day we will have journals of educational criticism and critical theory that will seek to refine the quality of educational criticism and the methods and assumptions with which those doing such criticism work.

THE RELATIONSHIP OF EDUCATIONAL CRITICISM TO EDUCATIONAL CONNOISSEURSHIP

Effective criticism, within the arts or in education, is not an act independent of the powers of perception. The ability to see, to perceive what is subtle, complex, and important, is its first necessary condition. The act of knowledgeable perception is, in the arts, referred to as connoisseurship. To be a connoisseur is to know how to look, to see, and to appreciate. Connoisseurship, generally defined, is the art of appreciation. It is essential to criticism because without the ability to perceive what is subtle and important, criticism is likely to be superficial or even empty. The major distinction between connoisseurship and criticism is this: connoisseurship is the art of appreciation, criticism is the art of disclosure. Connoisseurship is a private act; it consists of recognizing and appreciating the qualities of a particular, but it does not require either a public judgment or a public description of those qualities. The perception and appreciation of a particular requires a sensory memory. For example, if one is to develop connoisseurship of wine, one must drink a great deal of wine, learn how to attend to its qualities, and be able to recall from one's gustatory memory— and in the case of wine, the olfactory and visual memories also come into play—the qualities of other wines in order to have a backdrop against which the particular qualities of the wine being tasted can be compared and contrasted. In the case of music, the auditory mode provides the backdrop. A connoisseur could compare Arturo Toscanini's performance of Beethoven's Seventh Symphony with that of Herbert Von Karajan. Only after a range of experiences are had in a mode of expression will sophisticated levels of connoisseurship be developed.

The same considerations apply with respect to educational connoisseurship. One must have a great deal of experience with classroom practice to be able to distinguish what is significant about one set of practices or another.

In saying that experience counts in the development of connoisseurship, whether in education or in the fine arts, it is important to recognize that the length of time spent in a classroom or the number of museums visited or the frequency with which one attends sports events is not necessarily an indication of the level of connoisseurship someone has achieved. Let us distinguish between recognition and perception, and let us agree with Dewey that recognition is perception aborted: looking is engaged in simply to be able to see enough to classify.[5] That is an oak tree, the other is an elm, that was a half-gainer, that was a full twist with a somersault, and so forth. Perception based on recognition alone stops with assigning the particular to the class to which it belongs; it does not proceed to the sensory exploration of the ways in which *this* particular oak tree differs from other oaks, it does not locate the specific characteristics of *this* elm, *that* half-gainer, *this* full twist with a somersault. Recognition is not exploratory, it is focused on classification.

If one looks within a classroom primarily to recognize rather than to see, the number of years one spends in a classroom will contribute little to the development of connoisseurship. To develop connoisseurship one must have a desire to perceive subtleties, to become a student of human behavior, to focus one's perception. Looking is a necessary condition, but looking is essentially a task one undertakes; it is seeing that is an achievement.

It would be difficult to overemphasize the importance of connoisseurship in the creation of educational criticism. Connoisseurship provides the fundamental core of realization that gives criticism its material. Because it is so central to any understanding of practice, it is rather surprising that it has received so little attention. We tend to take it for granted, or we seem to believe that with the use of an observation schedule the problem of seeing what goes on in classrooms is cared for. This is simply naive. What is significant in a social setting might have little to do with the incidence of a particular activity or statement but a lot to do with a single act or statement or with the organizational structure of the classroom or with the character of an assigned task or with the way in which a reward is given. Observation schedules are tools that can guide one's attention, but their mechanical use can blind one to what is significant.

It may be that the neglect of connoisseurship is due to the fact that relatively few people doing educational research spend much time in classrooms. The general tendency in educational research is to use instruments that can be easily administered and scored and that are not susceptible to confounding through bias or long-term exposure to the vicissitudes of classroom life. The rigorous experiment in education is "clean." To achieve such cleanliness, experiments in educational research tend to be brief. The modal amount of time for educational experiments reported in two years of the studies published in the *American Educational Research Journal* is less than one hour. For fourteen experimental studies reported during this period, six used a treatment period of less than one hour, three from one hour to one day, three from one day to one week, and one for over one year. No time was reported for one study. It is my view that such a conception of clean experimentation in education is likely to lead to work that has little significance for educational practice.

The development of educational connoisseurship requires an ability not only to perceive the subtle particulars of educational life but also to recognize the way those particulars form a part of a structure within the classroom. Erickson's discussion of the chess game is most apt.[6] To understand a chess game, one must do much more than measure or even describe in qualitative terms the character of the physical movements made by each player. One must be able to perceive the structure of the game within which the physical movements take on social meaning. One must eventually be able to conceptualize the rules that give structure to the enterprise and define it as the game.

Similarly, the development of educational connoisseurship requires the ability to perceive the "rules" through which educational life is lived. Such a task is what Gilbert Ryle refers to as "thick description," about which more will be said later.[7]

The work that my students and I are doing at Stanford University is aimed at the development of educational connoisseurship and the ability to create useful educational criticism. Educational connoisseurship is to some degree possessed by virtually everyone who has spent some time in schools as a student or as a teacher, but it can be refined and developed. What is involved in the development of educational connoisseurship is, first, the opportunity to attend to happenings of educational life in a focused, sensitive, and conscious way. Second, it requires the opportunity to compare such happenings, to discuss what one sees so that perceptions can be refined, to identify events not previously perceived, and to integrate and appraise what has been seen. This is being done at Stanford through the direct observation of classrooms and through the careful viewing of videotapes of classroom life. When students jointly view such tapes, the basis for description and discussion is provided. Over time, descriptive language becomes less mechanical, more incisive, increasingly literary or poetic as students try to get at the essence of what is occurring. To talk about essences and significance in the observation of educational events requires, of course, not only a sensitivity to the emerging qualities of classroom life, but also a set of ideas, theories, or models that enable one to distinguish the significant from the trivial and to place what one sees in an intelligible context. This process is not serial: we do not see and then assess significance; the very ideas that define educational virtue for us operate within the perceptual processes to locate among thousands of possibilities what we choose to see. The essence of perception is that it is selective; there is no value-free mode of seeing.

Given the impact of our theories on our perception, the development of educational connoisseurship is much more complicated than simply a species of discrimination training. The problem of developing connoisseurship of the complex life of classrooms is not simply one of identifying the equivalent of Boeing 707s or DC-10s. Plane spotters have a comparatively simple task. The forms of such planes can be known in advance, and interaction effects are minimal. A 707 is a 707 is a 707. But in classrooms, interaction effects are the rule, not the exception. To discern what an event means requires an understanding of the context in which it occurs; that context requires not only some knowledge of the people involved and the circumstances within which the event occurs, but in many situations also something about the past, against which the particulars of the present can be placed. Again, memory is indispensable.

What we begin to recognize when we consider what connoisseurship entails is that the perceptual processes operate within an array of values and theoretical concepts that influence perception. Indeed, in both the social sciences and philosophy we use theories to organize our conception of the world. Individuals working with different theories—whether normative or descriptive—will attend to different phenomena within the "same" setting and interpret their significance differently. For the development of educational connoisseurship, an understanding of different social sciences, different theories of education, and a grasp of the history of education is not simply an intellectual ornament to be acquired within a graduate program but an essential working tool.

The cognitivist view that I am expressing with respect to the perception of educational practice has eloquently been expressed by a major American aesthetician concerning the role of theory in the perception and appraisal of art. Morris Weitz points out that although previous attempts to define the necessary and sufficient properties of art have been unsuccessful (because art is an open rather than a closed concept), the work of the great aestheticians is not useless. He writes:

> In spite of the fact that all of them [theoreticians] fail to accomplish what they set out to do—to give a true definition of works of art—these definitions are nevertheless helpful and well worth intensive study. For behind every one is a redefinition of "work of art"; i.e., an attempt to get us to concentrate on certain criteria or properties of works of art as against others. If we attend to these criteria or properties and forget the unsuccessful attempts as true, essentialist definitions, we can learn a great deal from the theories, especially as to what we should look for in works of art and how we should look at them. Indeed, the great contribution of theories of works of art is precisely in their teachings, not in their definitions, of art: each of the theories represents a set of explorable criteria which serve to remind us of what we may have neglected or to make us see what we may not have seen. To do this, I should think, is the primary job of teaching. Here, then, is the relation between teaching and the nature of art or, to use the title of your conference, the nature of art and its implication for teaching: that the great theorists of the nature of art have served as the great teachers as well, in telling us, through their definitions of art, what we are to learn from them about the arts.[8]

The same argument can be made—a fortiori—for theories of human behavior, culture, and education.

WHAT DO CRITICS DO?

As I have already indicated, educational connoisseurship is a necessary condition for doing useful educational criticism. But what is it that critics do? What do they write about? And what kind of validity and generalizability does criticism have? Criticism is the art of disclosing the qualities of events or objects that connoisseurship perceives. Criticism is the public side of connoisseurship. One can be a connoisseur without the skills of criticism, but one cannot be a critic without the skills of connoisseurship. In using language to make public qualities and meanings that are not themselves discursive, something of a paradox exist. How can words express what words can never express? The successful resolution of this paradox lies at the heart of the critical act. To accomplish this feat, critics do not aspire toward a translation of an event from one modality to another. For in fact no such translation, at least in the literal sense, can be made. It is one thing to translate from one language into another. And even between languages there are difficulties. But to expect to translate what is known in a visual mode into a discursive mode is to use the term *translate* metaphorically. A more appropriate word, coined by Kozloff, is *rendering:*

> For what criticism proposes to give, I think, is essentially an account of an experience, and never, as is sometimes supposed, a substitute for an experience. Though ideally it must be self-sufficient as prose, it can never be a stand-in for what has been perceived, lest it compromise a metaphorical with a literal fiction. Indeed, criticism's merit lies exactly in the fact that it is neither a work of art nor a response, but something much rarer—a rendering of the interaction between the two. Best, then, that it reconcile itself to virtual rather than actual meanings, the ambiguity of symbolic reference as opposed to the pidgin clarity of signs.[9]

What critics do or should try to do is not to translate what cannot be translated but rather to create a rendering of a situation, event, or object that will provide pointers to those aspects of the situation, event, or object that are in some way significant. Now what counts as significant will depend on the theories, models, and values alluded to earlier. But it will also depend on the purposes of the critic. For example, an educational critic focusing on the learning patterns of a particular student will attend to qualities and circumstances different from those he or she would attend to if interested in the critical rendering of the character of classroom discourse, the qualities of the classroom's visual environment, or the meanings embedded in the treatment of time in the classroom. The point here is straightforward: What is rendered by someone working as an educational critic will depend on his or her purposes as well as the kinds of maps, models, and theories being used.

Of particular importance in understanding how critical language is illuminative is the distinction between discursive and nondiscursive forms of knowledge and that between representational and presentational symbols.

The conception of nondiscursive modes of knowing is not a new distinction among those schooled in philosophy, but it is new to those raised in the traditions pervading American educational research and its offspring, educational evaluation. American educational research has, since the early work of E. L. Thorndike, been largely behavioristic in its psychology and operationalist in its philosophy. To "know" has meant to make statements couched in the form of propositions and that therefore can be apparaised by logical criteria. But because logic is essentially a tool for determining consistency between propositions, something more is needed if relationships between propositions are to be more than merely consistent. If propositions are to make true statements about the world, referents for those statements have to be located in the world. And because in empirical matters observation is subject to biases of one sort or another—biases in perception, in selection of population, and the like—observations need to be operationalized through standardized procedures that are reliable and quantitative and therefore supposedly least likely to suffer from unreliability and subjectivity. For generations, this conception of the meaning of knowledge has dominated inquiry into educational matters. Indeed, to do educational research has come to mean, by custom, to engage in inquiry having these characteristics. The idea that there are multiple ways in which things are known—that there is a variety of expressive modalities through which what is known can be disclosed—simply has been absent from the conversations that animate the educational research community.

A distinction between the respective contributions of the sciences and the arts to human understanding is made by Ernest Cassirer in *An Essay on Man*. Cassirer points out that a scientific perspective without an artistic one or an artistic perspective without a scientific one leads to monocular vision; both are necessary to have depth perception. Science, writes Cassirer, focuses on what is general and common across particulars, whereas art focuses on the unique characteristics of the particulars themselves.

The two views of truth are in contrast with one another, but not in conflict or contradiction. Since art and science move in entirely different planes they cannot contradict or thwart one another. The conceptual interpretation of science does not preclude the intuitive interpretation of art. Each has its own perspective and, so to speak, its own angle of refraction. The psychology of sense perception has taught us that without the use of both eyes, with a binocular vision, there would be no awareness of the third dimension of space. The depth of human experience in the same sense depends on the fact that we are able to vary our modes of seeing, that we can alternate our views of reality. Rerum videre formas is no less important and indispensable task than rerum cognoscere causas. In ordinary experiences we connect phenomena according to the ccategory of causality or finality. According as we are interested in the theoretical reasons for the practical effects of things, we think of them as causes or as means. Thus, we habitually lose sight of their immediate appearance until we can no longer see them face to face. Art, on the other hand, teaches us to visualize, not merely to conceptualize or utilize, things. Art gives a richer more vivid and colorful image of reality, and a more profound insight into its formal structure. It is characteristic of the nature of man that he is not limited to one specific and single approach to reality but can choose his point of view and so pass from one aspect of things to another.[10]

Cassirer's plea for binocular vision through complementary forms of inquiry is one that I would echo. One mode of conception and one form of disclosure are simply inadequate to exhaust the richness of educational life.

The notion that knowledge can be conceived and experienced in nondiscursive as well as discursive forms has been perhaps most eloquently expressed by an American aesthetician who was influenced by Cassirer's work, Susanne Langer. Langer argues that although propositions are among the most useful of cultural tools for expressing ideas about factual states of affairs, they are virtually useless when it comes to expressing what we know about the life of feeling:

> Yet even the discursive pattern has its limits of usefulness. An expressive form can express any complex of conceptions that, via some rule of projection, appears congruent with it, that is, appears to be of that form. Whatever there is in experience that will not take the impress—directly or indirectly—of discursive form, is not discursively communicable or, in the strictest sense, logically thinkable. It is unspeakable, ineffable; according to practically all serious philosophical theories today, it is unknowable.[11]

Discursive language, the type used in science and in much of our ordinary speech, is our most powerful tool for classification, but when particular qualities of life must be revealed we have to appeal to a language more intimate, or, in Langer's terms, a language that presents to our consciousness what the feeling of those qualities is. Literature, is, of course, a prime example of the nondiscursive use of language. So is poetry. What enables us to empathetically participate in the events, lives, and situations that the writer portrays is not mere factual description. If this were the case, everyone who could describe the facts would be a Doestoevsky, a Shakespeare, or a Bellow. What gives literature its power is the way in which language has been *formed* by the writer. It is the "shape" of language as well as the perceptive recognition of the metaphorical, connotative, and symbolic character of particular words and phrases that makes written language literature. What the writer is able to do, as is the painter, composer, dancer, or critic, is to transform knowledge held in one mode into another, namely the mode within which the artist or critic works. Somehow the artist finds or creates the structural expressive equivalent of an idea, a feeling, or an image within the material with which he or she works.

The material becomes the public embodiment—a medium, in the literal sense of the word—through which the life of feeling is shared. The arts are not a second-class substitute for expression, they are one of the major means people throughout history have used both to conceptualize and express what has been inexpressible in discursive terms.

Now the talk of the critic is in many respects similar to that of the artist. Both work within the limits of the material to create a form that expresses what has no name. The *particular* qualities of joy, grief, enchantment, irony, perseverance, or courage are never adequately revealed through the ordinary verbal classification of these terms alone. What was the character of this man's courage? What is the particular quality of her joy or grief? How does this classroom lead its life? What kind of personage does this teacher represent to his class? To reveal these particulars, to capture these "essences," one must not only perceive their existence but also be able to create a form that intimates, discloses, reveals, imparts, suggests, implies their existence. In this process of transformation, metaphor is, of course, a centrally important device. Metaphor breaks the bonds of conventional usage to exploit the power of connotation and analogy. It capitalizes on surprise by putting meanings into new combinations and through such combinations awakens our senses. Metaphor is the arch enemy of the stock response.

The use of metaphor is not restricted to the creation of literature and the writing of poetry and criticism; it plays an extremely important role in our vernacular language. Take, as example, slang. "Cool it," "right on," "hot-shot," "you know it," "into it," "heavy" are only a few examples of metaphorical usage. We don't ask of such language what it literally means because literally its meaning is either absurd or nonexistent. Yet we all sense the rightness of the phrase when used in an appropriate context. Indeed, we use such language not simply because it is more economical than its discursive "equivalent" but because it has no discursive equivalent. Fresh conceptions find their expression in the inventive use of language. Even our discursive language is filled with words that once were metaphorical or had visual referents but through conventional usage have lost their initial power: Someone feels low, or high, or depressed; he has an inflated ego; she is being defensive; he is being slick; that painting is well balanced. The symphony is melancholy. Such words are so pervasive a part of our language that we seldom stop to reflect on the way in which they acquired meaning.[12]

What is ironic is that in the professional socialization of educational researchers, the use of metaphor is regarded as a sign of imprecision; yet, for making public the ineffable, nothing is more precise than the artistic use of language. Metaphoric precision is the central vehicle for revealing the qualitative aspects of life.

The revelation of the qualitative aspects of life, particularly those aspects that deal with what individuals experience in various situations, has been a major focus of artists through the centuries. Let's assume for a moment that we wanted to know something about life in, say, a concentration camp. How would we find out? We could try to locate psychological and socio- logical studies of the inmates and of the organization of such camps, and if we could find such studies we might learn something about how new in- mates were socialized, how they adapted to the conditions of the camp. We might learn something about social mobility, stratification, and class, about the various roles assumed, and about achieved and assigned status. We might learn about the use of sanctions and about the destruction of the ego. Such knowledge is, of course, useful. Based as it would be on concepts and theories within the social sciences, it would describe, through the concepts the theories employ, the various features of camp life and how they function.

But let us say we wanted to know what it was like to be taken to such a camp, to go through the initial screening, to work fourteen hours a day in bitter cold, to have a wretched diet. To know these aspects of life in a con- centration camp, one must go to the forms of expression that convey the qualities of such life to the reader. One could do little better than to read Solzhenitsyn's *A Day in the Life of Ivan Denisovich.*[13] Through literature and through effective criticism we come to know what it feels like to be in prison, to be in ecstacy, to be in a particular classroom in a particular school. Through the arts we have the opportunity to participate vicariously in the lives of others, to acquire an empathetic understanding of situations, and therefore to know them in ways that only the arts can reveal.

If I dwell on these matters, it is because I believe they are crucial for understanding why educational criticism is such an important complement to the existing modes of inquiry in education.

The language of criticism, like the language of the arts, is essentially non- discursive; that is, it informs not by pointing to the facts of the world but rather by intimation, by using forms to *present* rather than to *represent* conception or feeling. Representational symbols, the type used in conven- tional discourse, are like signposts, they point one toward qualities but are not themselves intended to possess expressive qualities. "Listen, listen to the bird" is a literal discursive expression, but "Hark! hark! the lark!" contains an energy absent in the former. The former is representational, it directs our attention so that a certain kind of experience can be had. The latter presents us with a form that itself generates the excitement of the ex- perience. The former is a conventional utterance, the latter is poetic.

Thus far I have tried to identify the functions of qualitative inquiry in education and to distinguish between educational connoisseurship and edu- cational criticism. Before describing in greater detail the major dimensions of educational criticism, it will be useful to examine a brief segment of art criticism written by the distinguished American critic Leo Steinberg. From it, we can get a better sense of what one critic does in the course of one of his criticisms.

PAUL BRACH'S PICTURES

They are very near invisibility.

Invisibility is of various kinds, and to list its varieties while the pictures are up helps to focus attention.

Invisibility by disappearance. An object absent, remote or indistinct leaves a leftover emptiness and a straining to see. This seems relevant to Brach's picures. Their vacant geometry suggests depleted voids, voided containers. Their huge suspended circles can look like extinguished suns. Solar cult emblems snuffed out. Empty icons.

Then, invisibility by extinction of light. This too seems relevant. Not actual darkness—which conveys a specific degree of reduced illumination—but a consistency or opacity that can be neither brightened nor deepened.

And invisibility due to dimmed vision; whether through blindness or the sightlessness of inattention. Brach makes his pictures easy to resist. They court unseeing indifference or disinterest; as if to remain invisible to the averted mind.[14]

Although this constitutes only the first portion of Steinberg's criticism we can use it to try to understand what he does. Consider first the title, "Paul Brach's Pictures." Steinberg does not write a long, complex title but a simple one, one that we shall find is in keeping with the works that he will criticize. Notice also that Steinberg does not refer to "Brach's Paintings" but rather to "Paul Brach's pictures." "Pictures" suggests more of illusion, of image, of icon. "Paintings" suggests a medium, the qualities of the material used, or technique, and as we find as we read on, paint and technique are not essential aspects of Brach's work; his are indeed images of a mysterious kind: *pictures* is more apt than *paintings*.

Steinberg's opening sentence, "They are very near invisibility," hangs there by itself. In some ways, it's an awkward sentence, yet it possesses some of the mysterious magical qualities of the paintings Steinberg is attempting to render. A lesser critic might have written, "Brach's paintings are nearly invisible." But such a sentence does not possess a spell.

Steinberg sets the mood of the work of his opening line and then shifts pace to suggest, in somewhat Aristotelian terms, that the classification of types of invisibility will be helpful to us in seeing Brach's work. And, abruptly, he repeats the fragmented tempo of the opening line, "Invisibility by disappearance." Because the issue is not grammar but mood and insight, the tempo works; it sets up a backdrop for the longer, more expository sentences to follow. Notice the nice contradictory quality of "leftover emptiness." Leftovers usually imply overabundance, not emptiness. Yet this, too, combined with "a straining to see," as Steinberg says, is relevant to Brach's pictures. What Steinberg is doing is depicting by implication and suggestion the pervasive quality of Brach's work. He is preparing the reader psychologically to see the point of the pictures, not only by specific verbal cues (which come later in the criticism), but also by the ambience in his language.

Steinberg then describes the "vacant geometry" of Brach's work, "depleted voids, voided containers," "huge suspended circles" that "look like extinguished suns." He then stops the paragraph as he began it, with a terse nonsentence: "Empty icons."

Again the illusion of Steinberg's language has its parallel in the works to which the language refers, not as an attempt to translate their visual qualities but rather, as Kozloff has suggested in his own writing, "to render" the works. Criticism works by implication, "the most appropriate devices at my disposal have been innuendo, nuance, and hypothesis, because what is peripheral to direct statement in language is often central to a pictorial encounter or its meaning." Steinberg would surely agree.

Steinberg continues in his criticism of Paul Brach's pictures to combine nuance and innuendo with more literal references to the qualities of the work, but always the tempo of the writing epitomizes the suspense and mystery of the work itself. Steinberg ends the criticism as be began, tersely and though it were suspended in space. His last paragraph reads, "They are beautiful pictures, solitary and serious."

THREE ASPECTS OF EDUCATIONAL CRITICISM

Educational criticism is composed of three major aspects or dimensions. One of these is descriptive, another interpretative, and another evaluative. Each of the distinctions that I make I am making for analytical purposes—to illuminate differences in language and intention—but the distinctions are sharper on paper than in fact. All description is in some degree evaluative inasmuch as only a fool would choose to describe the trivial. All evaluation is interpretive to the degree that one seeks to make some sense of what a situation or an experience means. Nevertheless, the distinctions are useful to the extent that they sharpen perception of the foci of criticism and therefore enable us to read or create criticism more intelligently.

The Descriptive Aspect of Educational Criticism

The descriptive aspect of educational criticism is essentially an attempt to identify and characterize, portray, or render in language the relevant qualities of educational life. Such qualities may be the general environment or cultural style of a particular classroom or school. How is life lived in Miss Held's fourth grade? What kind of tempo pervades Mr. Marco's algebra class? Or the descriptive aspects of educational criticism might focus on more limited or molecular characteristics. How does this particular child relate to his peers? What covert messages does the teacher give her students through the tone of her voice? What is the quality of the visual environment of the school, and what does it convey to the student about life in school? Although it is a piece of literature rather than a piece of criticism, the following passage from *Pilgrim at Tinker Creek* illustrates how a perceptive and skillful writer can portray the sensory qualities of a complex environment:

> It was sunny one evening last summer at Tinker Creek; the sun was low in the sky, upstream. I was sitting on the sycamore log bridge with the sunset at my back, watching the shiners the size of minnows who were feeding over the muddy sand in skittery schools. Again and again, one fish, then another, turned for a split second across the current and flash! the sun shot out from its silver side. I couldn't watch for it. It was always just happening somewhere else, and it drew my vision just as it disappeared: flash, like a sudden dazzle of the thinnest blade, a sparking over a dun and olive ground at chance intervals from every direction. Then I noticed white specks, some sort of pale petals, small, floating from under my feet on the creek's surface, very slow and steady. So I blurred my eyes and gazed towards the brim of my hat and saw a new world. I saw the pale white circles roll up, roll up, like the world's turning, mute and perfect, and I saw the linear flashes, gleaming silver, like stars being born at random down a rolling scroll of time. Something broke and something opened. I filled up like a new wineskin. I berathed an air like light; I saw a light like water. I was the lip of a fountain the creek filled forever; I was ether, the leaf in the zephyr; I was fleshlike, feather, bone.[15]

What the author has succeeded in doing is to enable the reader to participate vicariously in the auditory and visual qualities of the layered web of life at the creek. Such writing is in no sense a catalogue of the number of trout, jays, or oak trees that populate the region, it is not a chronicle of happenings, it is the artistic reconstruction of events that may be more vividly experienced through that distillation called a work of art than in direct contact with the creek. This point is an important one, and one that is frequently overlooked. The artist, like the educational critic, does not write about everything that exists in a situation but rather about what he or she brackets, what he or she chooses to attend to. This bracketing of perception and its incisive rendering in an expressive medium allow the percipient of the artist's or critic's work to see, in part, through the bracket what the artist has created. Many have walked through places like Tinker Creek, but few have seen them with the clarity and sensibility of Annie Dillard.

The perception of both the pervasive qualities—those qualities characterizing a situation or object such as the upward thrust of gothic interiors, the scintillation of light in a Monet landscape, the vacuous mechanical regularity of an assembly line—and component qualities—those particular qualities within a whole, such as the tonal passages in the second movement

of Sibelius's First Symphony, the supportive quality of a teacher's smile—
are only two important subject matters for critical description. The nature
of the "game" that is played is also a proper object of critical description.
What are the rules by which educational life in this classroom operates?
What are the regularities, the underlying architecture of social life in this
school? What is the core value within this mode of school organization, or
teaching, or evaluation? The description of these underlying qualities blends
into the process of interpretation as well as description. Nevertheless, such
structures can be conceptualized and described, and in a certain sense the
effort to do so is reminiscent of the structuralist's attempt to locate the basic
architecture underlying language. Again, Erickson makes this point well:

> There are many ways of describing what happens in a social event other than
> in functionally relevant terms. We could, for example, describe the playing of
> chess in terms of movement in millimeters forward, backward and sideways on a
> plane. The behavior of chess pieces on the board could be coded by observers
> this way with high inter-coder reliability, and the resulting data could be manipu-
> lated statistically. Yet such description and analysis would by itself tell us nothing
> about what was going on in terms of the game of chess. The descriptive categories
> would have no relevance to the game being played. For that we need descriptive
> categories with functional relevance for the game—checkmate, defense—terms that
> are meaningful in terms of an understanding (working theory) of the game as a
> whole.[16]

All in all, the descriptive aspects of criticism can be regarded as making
the most artistic demands on the critic. I say this because it is in the
descriptive aspect of criticism that the critic's verbal magic must be most
acute. Recall Steinberg's phrase, "An object absent, remote or indistinct
leaves a leftover emptiness and a straining to see." To be able to express
such an idea, one must not only be in touch with the qualities of a painting
and one's response to it, but also be able to capture such qualities through
the possibilities within words; a poet must speak. Such demands are not
easy to meet, but they are not insurmountable. Indeed, one of the most
striking things that has emerged in working with doctoral students at
Stanford in educational criticism is the sensitive way in which they have
been able to write such criticism. Even students who have had considerable
difficulty writing in the traditional academic mode have produced educational criticism of impressive literary quality. To say this is not to imply that
all will be the Leo Steinbergs, Max Kozloffs, or Susan Sontags of education.
It is to say that the skills of critical writing can be developed and that there
may be a good many students for whom this mode of writing is more compatible than the modes that many of them feel compelled to use in order to
complete their dissertation.

It is of interest to speculate why some students take to this mode of
writing and conceptualization more than others and why some students who

do not do well in one mode do well in the other. It *might* be that the kinds of intellectual processes that nondiscursive forms of conceptions and expression require are possessed to different degrees by different students. Present work in the study of the hemispheric specialization of the brain might be relevant to such an explanation. As mentioned earlier, it has long been known that the left hemisphere is the seat of speech, and in the last fifteen years neurophysiologists have determined that the right hemisphere plays a distinctively important role in dealing with nonlinear, nondigital, nonconventional forms of conception and expression. Gabrielle Rico distinguishes between the functions of the hemispheres this way:

I suggest this fundamental difference lies in the left hemisphere's susceptibility for *order-abiding* capacities and the right hemisphere's susceptibility for *structure-seeking capacities*. The distinction I have in mind which may underlie all the others is clarified by a look at the etymology of "order" and "structure," two words often incorrectly used interchangeably.

Order, from the Latin, *orde, ordini,* literally means "in a straight row, in a regular series." The definition of order encompasses anything from "arrangement," "a regular or customary procedure," "established usage," "settled method," to "a precept or command," or "a regulation." Order, therefore, like discourse defined in Chapter I, suggests receptivity to linear, established, regularly patterned, rule-governed activity. Order is imposed from without. Wrote Wittgenstein: "Following a rule is analogous to obeying an order. We are trained to do so: we react to an order in a particular way....When I obey a rule I do not choose."

Structure, on the other hand, from the Latin *struere,* means "to heap together" to give the quality of wholeness, totality. Structure does not imply seriality or linearity; it does imply coherence, holism. Structure can be discerned even when only a limited number of relevant elements become apparent, as in a motif of a Beethoven sonata or as in a configuration of a Street Figure Completion test item. Moreover, structure can be independent of a linear sequence between what comes before and what comes after because it is simultaneously grasped.[17]

Perhaps those students who are best able to work in a critical mode are those whose strongest aptitudes are located in the right hemisphere. At present, the case cannot be demonstrated, yet it is striking that some students take to educational criticism with a sense of ease and competence that seems to fit almost naturally the way in which they encounter the world. Indeed, one student told me that until he encountered the notion of educational criticism and the possibility of doing it within the School of Education at Stanford, he was living two lives. One was the life he led outside Stanford, which was responsive to the arts, to the poetic and romantic aspects of experience, and the other he encountered at Stanford, which presented a different view of reality and required that he substitute Stanford's reality for his own. He now finds he can draw on his sensibilities and on the modes of thinking with which he is most comfortable for doing his work at Stanford. A cognitively schizophrenic existence is no longer necessary.

The Interpretive Aspect of Educational Criticism

Although there is no sharp and clear line to be drawn between the descriptive and the interpretive, there is a difference in emphasis and focus. The interpretive aspect of criticism asks: What does the situation mean to those involved? How does this classroom operate? What ideas, concepts, or theories can be used to explain its major features?

In the interpretive aspect of criticism, ideas from the social sciences most frequently come into play. These ideas form the conceptual maps that enable the educational critic to account for the events that have occurred and to predict some of their consequences. For example, let's assume that someone functioning as an educational critic observes a classroom in which the use of contracts is pervasive. What we have are children of eight or nine years of age signing written agreements with teachers to plan and monitor their assignments in school. The use of such contracts creates a particular level of involvement in the classroom that the critic characterizes with sensitivity and vividness. But what do these contracts mean to the students and to the teacher? And what are their long-term effects? What kinds of concomitant learning are the children experiencing? What type of social relations do contracts create, and how do contracts, when they are ubiquitous in a classroom, affect a child's conceptions of purpose in school?

To answer these questions, one can refer to a host of theoretical ideas within the social sciences to explain the ancillary consequences of contractual relations in face-to-face groups. One can refer to reinforcement theory to explain why contracts might increase dependency rather autonomy. One can use cognitive field theory to deal with the importance of ambiguity in learning and the effects of contracts on the student's ability to tolerate ambiguity. The point here is not that there is one theory to be used to interpret the meaning of events within classrooms, but that there is a variety of theories. No one is interested in the facts by themselves but rather in the facts interpreted. What theory provides is not single-minded, certain conclusions regarding the meanings secured in school but rather frameworks that one can use to gain alternative explanation for those events. If theories in the social sciences can be regarded as games consisting of rules or structures one lays upon a field of phenomena for purposes of making some sense of the phenomena, the interpretive mode of criticism can be regarded as the application of those games in whatever numbers appear to be useful for getting on with the business of education.

To be able to apply a variety of theories from the social sciences to the events occurring within schools and classroom is no simple task. First, one must know the theories that are to be applied. Second, one must be in a position to determine that this particular instance or situation is one for which a particular theory is appropriate. In legal theory, the process of recognizing that a particular case falls within the province of a law is called casuistry. And casuistry is a complex art that melds both theoretical knowledge and practical wisdom. No less is called for in seeing the connection between, say, Maslow's stages of human development and the kinds of social situations created in classrooms. In the education of teachers and educational researchers, practice in making such applications has been rare. We seldom use films or videotapes of classrooms, for example, in the education of doctoral students, despite all of our talk about the importance of "multimedia." We do not typically use case material as is used in schools of law, social work, and schools of business to which theory in the social sciences could be applied. We operate as if the ability to apply the theoretical ideas one learns in university classrooms is automatic, that no practice is necessary, that such skills take care of themselves. I wonder on what theories such beliefs are based.

The role of interpretation in criticism is related to the concept of "thick description" as used by Clifford Geertz in anthropology:

Ryle's discussion of "thick description" appears in two recent essays of his (now reprinted in the second volume of his Collected Papers) addressed to the general question of what, as he puts it, "Le Penseur" is doing: "Thinking and Reflecting" and "The Thinking of Thoughts." Consider, he says, two boys rapidly contracting the eyelids of their right eyes. In one, this is an involuntary twitch; in the other, a conspiratorial signal to a friend. The two movements are, as movements, identical; from an I-am-a-camera, "phenomenalistic" observation of them alone, one could not tell which was twitch and which was wink, or indeed whether both or either was twitch or wink. Yet the difference, however unphotographable, between a twitch and a wink is vast; as anyone unfortunate enough to have had the first taken for the second knows. The winker is communicating, and indeed communicating in a quite precise and special way: (1) deliberately, (2) to someone in particular, (3) to impart a particular message, (4) according to a socially established code, and (5) without cognizance of the rest of the company. As Ryle points out, the winker has not done two things, contracted his eyelids and winked, while the twitcher has done only one, contracted his eyelids. Contracting your eyelids on purpose when there exists a public code in which so doing counts as a conspiratorial signal is winking. That's all there is to it: a speck of behavior, a fleck of culture—and voila!—a gesture.[18]

The distinction between thick description and thin description is a useful one. Geertz regards it as the anthropologist's work to explicate social phenomena. "It is explication I am after, construing social expressions on the surface enigmatical."[19] Seeking the deep structure of social events, the rules or modes that give them order, is what ethnographers should do, according to Geertz. It is an enterprise that has its place in the interpretive aspects of educational criticism as well.

The Evaluative Aspect of Educational Criticism

It is, perhaps, the evaluative aspects of educational criticism that most clearly distinguish the work of the educational critic from that of the social scientist. Education is, after all, a normative enterprise. Unlike schooling or learning or socialization (all of which are descriptive terms), education is a process that fosters personal development and contributes to social well-being. This is not necessarily the case with respect to learning, schooling, or socialization, to use only three examples. One can learn to become neurotic, be schooled to become a scoundrel, or be socialized to become a bigot. Education implies some personal and social good. But to say this is to raise the knotty question of what kinds of values to apply to phenomena that aspire to be educational. On this matter there is a wide range of different views. The five orientations to curriculum described in Chapter 4 represent some of the values that different groups bring to the development of educational programs and the assessment of educational practice. Yet, even though different individuals and groups hold different conceptions of educational virtue, and even though their judgments of the value of the processes and outcomes of schooling might differ, the need to make these judgments is inevitable. One must inevitably appraise the value of a set of circumstances if only because, in the process of description, selective perception has already been at work. Evaluation, as I have already indicated, pervades the perceptual processes themselves.

But even if this were not the case, the point of educational criticism is to improve the educational processes. This cannot be done unless one has a conception of what counts in that process. Are the children being helped or hindered by the form of teaching they are experiencing? Are they acquiring habits of mind conducive to further development or are these habits likely to hamper further development? What is the relative value of direct learning to ancillary learning within this classroom? Questions such as these require the use of *educational* criteria. The educational critic, unlike the social scientist who has no professional obligation to appraise the educational value of a culture or group, has this obligation part of his or her work.

To make such judgments requires, as I have already indicated, the application of educational criteria. Where can such criteria be found? They can, of course, come from arbitrary, uncriticized preferences. But the truly competent educational critic is aware not only of the educational values to which he or she subscribes, but also of the values that are rejected. The educational critic will be able to provide grounds for the value choices made while recognizing that others might disagree with these choices.

The grounding of such values not only requires knowledge of the history and philosophy of education, it also benefits from practical experience in the schools. Many things the pedagogically uninitiated might be quick to criticize negatively would give an experienced teacher pause. Teaching tactics that might appear inappropriate to someone fresh out of a graduate school of education and untouched by the trials and tribulations of class-room life might be viewed with greater sympathy by one who has taught. One of the first things that the teachers whose classrooms have been the subject of educational criticism want to know is whether the critic has ever taught. Some things can be known only by having acted. Teaching, like swimming, is one of them.

One of the questions that often arises when the evaluative aspects of edu-cational criticism are discussed is whether the critic should make his or her values known in advance. Should one's educational values be laid out—up front, so to speak? To this question I have a mixed response. On the one hand, it might be useful in preparing an educational criticism to describe the kinds of values that the critic holds so that readers can understand where the critic is "coming from." A manifesto of one's educational position insofar as it is describable could, in principle, be provided as a critical prologue to educational criticism. On the other hand, the values one holds permeate the writing one does, just as they permeate the conversations people have about value-saturated issues. After a while those values, even when not explicit, become clear, and after several contacts with a critic's work a prologue might seem redundant. Those who read William F. Buckley, James Kilpatrick, or John Kenneth Galbraith know where these men stand on political and economic matters. I suspect that the same will hold true in reading educational criticism. Indeed, the issue is not whether such values are present but rather whether they should precede the writing of the actual criticism. At this stage in the development of educational criti-cism as a species of educational evaluation, it appears to me reasonable to have it both ways.

The fact that two critics might disagree on the value they assign to a common set of educational events is not necessarily a liability in educational evaluation; it could be a strength. For much too long, educational events have been assessed as though there were only one set of values to be as-signed to such events. The drop in test scores is perceived as a problem, the increase in grade-point average is believed to be a problem, but little or no analysis or few countervailing views are offered. Thus, through a lack of professional leadership, the public takes our lack of analysis and debate on the meaning and significance of such events as tacit assurance that they are indeed indicators of poor-quality schooling. One of the virtues of dif-ferences among educational critics with respect to the meaning and signifi-cance of educational events is that they could open up the kind of discus-sion that educational practice should but does not now receive. Virtually every set of educational events, virtually every educational policy, virtually every mode of school organization or form of teaching has certain virtues and certain liabilities. The more that educational criticism can raise the level of discussion on these matters, the better. What I believe intelligent and professionally responsible deliberation calls for is the application of multiple perspectives on an issue or policy, perspectives that view the phenomena from different angles, weigh the costs and benefits, and lead to the core considerations as well as to the ramifications of alternative policy decisions. The denial of complexity, in educational matters, as in politics, is the beginning of tyranny. Educational criticism could contribute to the appreciation of such complexity and therefore provide a more adequate basis for the making of educational judgments.

What then can we say about the characteristics of educational criticism and how it differs as a mode of qualitative inquiry from the kind of quantitative inquiry that is conventionally used in educational research? First, educational criticism is focused essentially on the events and materials that purport to be educational. Its function is to expand one's awareness of such events and objects so that they are more fully appreciated. Appreciation in this context does not refer to the liking of something, although one might like what one sees, but rather to the achievement of a heightened awareness of the subject matter.

To achieve such ends, an educational critic must possess a high level of connoisseurship within the area that he or she criticizes. Connoisseurship is the art of appreciation, and criticism is the art of disclosure. Criticism can be only as rich as the critic's perceptions. To create such criticism, educational critics prepare material having three major aspects: description, interpretation, and evaluation.

Although there is no sharp line between these aspects of educational criticism, there is a difference in focus and emphasis. The descriptive aspect aims at the vivid rendering of the qualities perceived in the situation. The interpretive attempts to provide an understanding of what has been rendered by using, among other things, ideas, concepts, models, and theories from the social sciences and from history. The evaluative aspect of educational criticism attempts to assess the educational import or significance of the events or objects described or interpreted. The major function of the critic here is to apply educational criteria so that judgments about such events are grounded in some view of what counts within an educational perspective. In the performance of this task, knowledge of the history and philosophy of education is crucial. The former provides the context necessary for purposes of comparison and the latter the theories from which grounded value judgments can be made. An understanding of the variety of orientations to education makes it possible for the educational critic to appreciate what he or she rejects as well as what he or she accepts within educational practice.

Given these characteristics of educational criticism as both a species of educational evaluation and a qualitative inquiry, we can now ask what the distinctive differences are between qualitative and quantitative modes of inquiry in education.

It is patently clear that quantitative- as well as qualitative-oriented inquirers attend to qualities emerging within educational settings. For example, the investigator who is interested in the incidence of teacher approval in the classroom must attend to qualities in order to detect approval and secure data. Furthermore, both quantitative and qualitative inquirers interpret the information they secure from the classroom, and both will, in general, make some value judgments about its educational meaning—although the qualitative inquirer may be more likely to do this than the quantitative inquirer, whose scientific orientation is less likely to *explicitly* emphasize the appraisal or valuative aspect of the inquiry.

I believe the major differences between quantitative and qualitative inquiry to be two. The more important difference resides in the language of disclosure that each uses. The quantitative inquirer is obliged to transform the qualities perceived into quantitative terms so that they can be treated statistically. In this translation the information is altered; differences between qualities are placed on a common scale to make them comparable. This process requires the use of a coding system—number—that is not structurally analogous to the forms that were initially perceived. The number symbol is a representational rather than a presentational symbol.

The qualitative inquirer uses a mode of disclosure that allows the percipient to vicariously participate in the qualities described because the symbols used to describe such qualities are structurally analogous to the event or object. The qualitative description allows the reader to envision and experience what he or she has not experienced directly. Poetry and literature are linguistic paradigms of such description, whereas the other arts—painting, music, dance—provide knowledge in other modes. What most radically distinguishes qualitative from quantitative inquiry is not that the former attends to qualities and the latter does not; they both do. What most sharply differentiates them is how they choose to inform the world about what they have seen.

The second feature that distinguishes quantitative from qualitative inquiry is the tendency of the former to prescribe procedures and to define in advance what shall be attended to. For example, the experiment in education has sought as its ideal procedure one in which all of the variables that might influence an outcome are brought under control. The lack of such controls is considered a confounding factor that makes interpretation difficult. Surprise and uncontrolled variation in educational experimentation are regarded as an epistemological liability.

Take as another example, not the experimental model, but that of systematic observation. Observation schedules are used to predefine what one is to look for; they prescribe to a very high degree what counts and what is to be counted. A qualitative approach to classroom observation is more open ended and flexible; the investigator or critic, rather than the prestructured schedule, is the major instrument through which observations are made.

In distinguishing between qualitative and quantitative approaches to education, I am in no way attempting to argue that one approach is always superior to the other. One approach *is* superior to the other, but only with respect to the nature of the problem one chooses to investigate. Quantitative methods have clear-cut virtues for some types of questions for which qualitative approaches would prove to be weak and inappropriate. And vice versa. It is this judgment—when and for what purposes each mode of inquiry is appropriate—that poses the toughest intellectual task in laying out a strategy for the investigation of educational problems. It is precisely around such judgments that disagreement is the greatest, because the tools investigators are skilled in using also serve to determine the parameters of their perception and thus how they define the problem itself.

RELIABILITY, VALIDITY, GENERALIZATION, AND OTHER MATTERS OF INFERENCE

One of the central reasons given for scientific inquiry is that such inquiry makes it possible not only to secure warrant for belief, but also to establish empirical generalizations. Such generalizations, a product of drawing inferences from a sample, help one anticipate the future. Description, explanation, and prediction are the trinity that scientific inquiry makes possible.

But what of qualitative forms of inquiry that do not employ a scientific model? Can such forms of inquiry yield generalizations? To what extent are the claims they make valid? How is reliability determined? How can we know if educational criticism can be trusted?

The conceptual tools, the statistical procedures, and the research designs available for testing the inferences, reliability, and validity of conclusions in the social sciences are of long standing and highly elaborate. Donald Campbell and Julian Stanley's classic monograph [20] on experimental and quasiexperimental design is an example of existing canons for the conduct of scientific inquiry in education. Distinctions between type I and type II errors, between internal and external validity, between random selection and random assignment, between experimental and quasiexperimental designs, among construct, content, predictive, and concurrent validity, between stability and reliability, these are some of the technical terms that have been created to make scientific inquiry into human affairs more rigorous. Does inquiry in the qualitative arena have similar tools? If so, what are they?

Let's examine first the question that is most frequently raised concerning qualitative inquiry in general and educational criticism in particular: Is it objective? Perhaps the first response that should be raised is another question: What is meant by "objective"? Does objective mean that one has discovered reality in its raw, unadulterated form? If so, this conception of objectivity is naive. All of us construct our conception of reality by interacting with the environment. What we take to be true is a product not only of the so-called objective conditions of the environment, but also of how we construe that environment. And that construction is influenced by our previous experience, including our expectations, our existing beliefs, and the conceptual tools through which the objective conditions are defined. To hold that our conceptions of reality are true or objective to the extent that they are isomorphic with reality is to embrace a hopeless correspondence theory of truth—hopeless because to know that our conceptions correspond or deviate from reality would require that we have two conceptions operating. One is an unmediated view of reality, the other our conception of that reality. Only in this way would we know anything about correspondence. If we knew the former, however, we would not need the latter.

What so-called objectivity means is that we believe in what we believe and that others share our beliefs as well. This process is called consensual validation. It operated as powerfully in once held beliefs in the existence of phlogiston, ether, and a geocentric universe as it does in the religious convictions held by the religiously orthodox. Although a scientifically oriented individual might object and say that scientific beliefs are testable and religious beliefs are not and that the differences therefore are crucial, the religiously orthodox would counter by pointing out that scientific criteria do not exhaust the means through which beliefs can be held to be true. Indeed, they would argue—correctly, I believe—that scientists themselves hold beliefs, even within science, that cannot be warranted by scientific methods. In the social sciences, this most clearly is the case. The differences in basic assumptions among Freudians, Rogerians, Skinnereans, Heiderians, Eriksonians, Piagetians, and the like are not resolvable through science. The fundamental theoretical structures through which each defines psychological reality differ, and there is no critical test that will resolve the truth or falsity of their respective belief systems. Each has a community of believers who reaffirm the beliefs of those working within the system.

My point here is simply this: objectivity is a function of intersubjective agreement among a community of believers. What we can productively ask of a set of ideas is not whether it is *really* true but whether it is useful, whether it allows one to do one's work more effectively, whether it enables one to perceive the phenomenon in more complex and subtle ways, whether it expands one's intelligence in dealing with important problems.

Given this view, what can we say about the means through which educational criticism receives consensual validation? Two processes are important here. One is called structural corroboration and the other referential adequacy.

Structural Corroboration

Structural corroboration is a process of gathering data or information and using it to establish links that eventually create a whole that is supported by the bits of evidence that constitute it. Evidence is structurally corroborative when pieces of evidence validate each other, the story holds up, the pieces fit, it makes sense, the facts are consistent. Take as an example of structural corroboration the work of Inspector Poirot in Agatha Christie's *Murder on the Orient Express*.[21] The inspector finds himself with a dead man, murdered on a train, and the problem of solving the puzzle of who murdered him. Little by little, Poirot succeeds in putting the pieces together so that there are no contradictions, the pieces support one another, and the problem of who killed the man is solved. In the case of the Orient Express, the murdered man once had contact with everyone on the train. The final scene in the book finds Poirot presenting his case to the murderers in the lounge car of the train as it speeds toward Calais. Poirot's brilliant use of evidence works, his conclusions hold up.

The use of structural corroboration is found in jurisprudence as trial lawyers attempt to present to a jury the evidence that will exonerate or convict a defendant. The prosecution tries to create a structurally corroborative set of facts that will persuade a jury to convict, while the defense tries to construct a set that will convince it not to convict. In such circumstances, one has a combination of both *structural corroboration*—the evidence that the respective attorneys try to muster—and *multiplicative corroboration*—the use of a jury of peers to pass judgment on what has or has not been structurally corroborated. The jury in this case provides the consensual validation for the cases that the attorneys have presented.

When we write or read educational criticism we can ask about the extent to which the facts presented or the interpretation of those facts is corroborated by the way in which they support one another. Does the teacher really play favorites in class or was his behavior in that particular circumstance atypical? Is the teacher genuinely supportive of the students or is she merely using a superficial stock response that gives the illusion of caring? These questions and questions like them can be adequately answered only by securing other evidence that would structurally corroborate the conclusions one has drawn from observation.

The process of structural corroboration is not some exotic process that is used in special circumstances in courtrooms and in doing educational criticism, but it is a ubiquitous part of our daily lives. We all use such processes to make judgments about people, to determine whether they are fake or authentic in their relations with us, to understand their limits so that we can effectively relate to them and to cope with the situations in which we find ourselves. We use this process to negotiate the environment. It is a far more characteristic way of dealing with the world than conducting a controlled experiment. In the flux of events and in encountering new situations—a new classroom, for example—we try to read its code, to find evidence for our impressions, to structurally corroborate our initial observations so that our expectations for that situation are appropriate.

Referential Adequacy

Nevertheless, structurally corroborated conclusions can be false. As Geertz points out, nothing is so persuasive as a swindler's story.[22] Something more must be added to validate the observations of the educational critic. That something more is the determination of referential adequacy. The end of criticism, as I have already indicated, is a reeducation of the perception of a work of art. For *educational* criticism the end-in-view is the education of the perception of the educational event or object. We can determine the referential adequacy of criticism by checking the relationship between what the critic has to say and the subject matter of his or her criticism. What the critic does, whether in painting, drama, or schooling, is to write or talk about the object or event he or she has seen. If the talk or writing is useful, we should be able to experience the object or situation in a new, more adequate way. We use the critic's work as a set of cues that enable us to perceive what has been neglected. When the critic's work is referentially adequate we will be able to find in the object, event, or situation what the cues point to. It is in this sense that criticism is a highly empirical undertaking. We look to the phenomena to test the adequacy of critical discourse.

Now it might be objected that the critic might lead us to see certain things in a situation because the criticism biases our perception, that criticism is in a sense something like a self-fulfilling prophecy. I would point out that we all bring to events, situations, and objects certain preconceived ideas; none of us approaches the world with a blank slate. The issue is not whether we come to the world empty minded, because we have no alternative, but whether what we bring to the world is useful for the purposes we consider important. Criticism is a kind of advance organizer, just as theory in general is an advance organizer.

Others might object and say that educational criticism may lead us to neglect aspects of the situation that the critic might not see or write about. This can occur. We never know when we have a comprehensive view of things, because, as in the correspondence theory of truth, we would need to know the thing itself in its comprehensive form to know whether our view of it was comprehensive. Again, if we knew the former, we would not need the latter. Yet, criticism might lead us to neglect certain aspects of the situation, but that is true of any theory, set of cues, or road map. Take as an example the services of a good travel agent.[23] He or she provides the client with information about what can be seen, but that does not foreclose the possibility of seeing other things as well. In the process of providing such guides, the travel agent readies us for sites and sights that we might otherwise overlook if left to our own devices. When the terrain is new or complex, guideposts help. Effective criticism provides such guideposts.

It is frequently pointed out that critics disagree on the characteristics and merits of the events and objects to which they attend. This claim is in some respect exaggerated. Critics in general achieve a high degree of consensus on objects or situations that have a reasonable amount of variation in quality. When critics do disagree, it is usually because the objects or events constituting the group to be judged present to critics a narrow range of unusually high-quality work.

But even when this occurs, the issue of differences among critics with respect to, say, the characteristics of classroom life is not crucial. In standard statistical procedures, interjudge agreement is critical. Low levels of interjudge agreement make a study invalid. What one usually does to ensure such agreement is to simplify the phenomena to be counted and to extensively train the judges. If judges are asked to count the incidence of, say, negative verbal statements given by the teacher, the probability of achieving high interjudge agreement is good. The tendency to focus on what can easily be counted is used as a way of achieving high interjudge agreement, even when what is easily counted might be of marginal educational importance.

The need for unanimity among critics is not characteristic of criticism, because it is recognized that complex phenomena—works of literature, painting, film, and the like—have several layers of meaning and that the greatest works seem inexhaustible in the meanings one can secure from them. What is sought is not the creation of one final definitive criticism of a work; rather, the goal is to have our perception and understanding expanded by the criticism we read. Classrooms and schools are at least as multilayered as works of art, and we should seek, therefore, not a single definitive criticism but rather criticism that is useful. Indeed, we should anticipate that critics with different educational orientations and interests will find in situations as phenomenologically dense as classrooms different things to describe, interpret, and evaluate. The cultivation of such productive diversity is a virtue, not a vice. As in education itself, we do not seek to create an army marching in step to the same tune but individuals who follow their own drummer as long as the beat is interesting.

The specter of having to consider for purposes of educational evaluation a variety of educational criticisms is likely to frighten some people. There is often the temptation to seek simple, clear-cut, unambiguous answers to complex problems. Having to consider alternatives, to deal with dilemmas, to resolve contradictions, to think in a complex way about complex issues may seem to be more of a challenge than some are willing to take. The seductiveness of simplicity is worth resisting. Not everything—whether we like it or not—can be punched on an IBM card.

These two processes, structural corroboration and referential adequacy, are the two major procedures with which to determine the validity of educational criticism. Structural corroboration seeks to determine the extent to which criticism forms a coherent, persuasive whole. It seeks to determine if the pieces of the critical story hold together, make sense, provide a telling interpretation of the events. Referential adequacy is the process of testing the criticism against the phenomena it seeks to describe, interpret, and evaluate. Referential adequacy is the empirical check of critical disclosure.

The task of determining the referential adequacy of a critical description of a piece of sculpture, painting, or work of architecture is to some extent different from determining the referential adequacy of a criticism of a classroom or other social situation. Works of art such as paintings, sculptures, and buildings do not change over time; classrooms do. How can one be sure that what the critic has created actually fits the phenomena a month or two later? How can a piece of criticism be tested against something that has a dynamic, changing quality? This problem is not unique to educational criticism. Ethnographers face similar problems, and even in the arts, such as in music and theater, two performances are never identical. What one assumes in doing educational criticism, as in doing ethnography, is that the salient and significant characteristics of a situation do not radically alter over brief periods of time. Classrooms and schools do have idiosyncratic characteristics that distinguish them from other classrooms and other schools. One of the reasons why it is important for someone functioning as an educational critic to have an extended contact with an educational situation is to be able to recognize events or characteristics that are atypical. One needs sufficient time in a situation to know which qualities characterize it and which do not.

This need for familiarity with the educational situation before a dependable critical account can be rendered is something that virtually all teachers recognize. Teachers do not believe it fair for someone to make a judgment about their teaching on the basis of one fifteen-minute visit or even one full day's visit. Teachers, like everybody else, have good and bad days. One cannot know which is which on the basis of one observation.

To say that competent educational criticism requires familiarity with the classroom or school to which the criticism is directed is to say that criticism as a form of educational evaluation is not a quick and easy procedure. Unlike the administration of standardized tests that are machine scored and computer analyzed, educational criticism requires time. But from my point of view, we have underestimated the amount of time useful educational evaluation requires. Easy test administration and test scoring have been seductively simple tools for evaluating what children learn and experience and what teachers and schools teach. We might very well have to face up to the fact that the kind of evaluation that will be useful to teacher will need to pay attention not only to the outcomes of teaching and learning but also to the processes. Without careful attention to those processes, we will not be in a position to account for the consequences of our activities. Indeed, the sooner educators help the public to understand the need for forms of evaluation that attend to the processes of teaching and learning, the better. The more we legitimize forms of evaluation that we really believe to be inadequate, the more difficult it will be to provide children with the kind of educational programs to which they should have access.

CAN GENERALIZATION BE DRAWN FROM EDUCATIONAL CRITICISM?

Scientific inquiry yields generalizations that help us to anticipate the future. What can be learned from a form of inquiry that is not scientific in its aims and procedures? What lessons can be learned from doing educational criticism? I believe educational criticism yields two types of generalizations. One of these is the generalization of more refined processes of perception. The other is the creation of new forms of anticipation.

The consequence of using educational criticism to perceive educational objects and events is the development of educational connoisseurship. As one learns how to look at educational phenomena, as one ceases using stock responses to educational situations and develops habits of perceptual exploration, the ability to experience qualities and their relationships increases. This phenomenon occurs in virtually every arena in which connoisseurship has developed. The orchid grower learns to look at orchids in a way that expands his or her perception of their qualities. The makers of cabinets pay special attention to finish, to types of wood and grains, to forms of joining, to the treatment of edges. The football fan learns how to look at plays, defense patterns, and game strategies. Once one develops a perceptual foothold in an arena of activity—orchid growing, cabinet making, or football watching—the skills used in that arena build on themselves for other objects and events within that arena. One does not need the continual expertise of the critic to negotiate new works, or games, or situations. One generalizes the skills developed earlier and expands them through further application. Once having learned that there is something to see or to do, one attempts to see and to do. A child does not need to be taught everything. Once a child learns that there is something to be learned in an area, the child not only learns those things but also learns that he or she can learn even more. This process is not unlike what John M. Stephens refers to as "spontaneous schooling." [24] If you teach children half of the names of the state capitals of the United States, it won't be long before they know most of the other half.

The point here is that skills generalize. Their use becomes more flexible and sophisticated. As educational criticism contributes to the development of connoisseurship, the generalization of skills occurs. Indeed, that is what is meant by connoisseurship. It is not the ability to appreciate a single object or event but the ability to appreciate a range of objects or events within a particular class or set of classes. No one is regarded as a connoisseur if only one particular object can be appreciated. What generalizes, therefore, in the case I have just described is a process rather than a proposition. This process we refer to as connoisseurship.

The other type of generalization that is fostered by educational criticism is in the acquisition of new forms of anticipation. Educational criticism illuminates particulars, but it is through particulars that concepts and generalizations are formed that are then applied to new situations. What educational criticism does is to help us appreciate the uniqueness of a set of circumstances; but this uniqueness can be appreciated only if we consider it against a backdrop of other instances and circumstances. For example, to recognize the distinctive or unique quality of mind displayed by a particular student we must be able to recognize the ways in which that distinctiveness manifests itself. To do this, some conception of typicality is required. Once having recognized distinctiveness, we are in a position to look for it in subsequent situations. Thus criticism creates forms of anticipation by functioning as a kind of road map for the future. Once having found that such and such exists in a classroom, we learn to anticipate it in other classrooms that we visit. Through our experience we build up a repertoire of anticipatory images that makes our search patterns more efficient.

The potential liability of such a repertoire is that classification and recognition abort perception. We may overlook what is unique by the precocious application of preconceptions. To avoid this, what we seek is a balance between the inclination toward perceptual exploration and the use of a repertoire of expectations that makes exploration fruitful. Kant put it well when he said, "Concepts without percepts are empty, and percepts without concepts are blind."

The kinds of generalizations that criticism yields are much more like those created during the course of ordinary life than those produced through controlled scientific inquiry. In the first place, no one ordinarily sets up the conditions for producing generalizations by randomly selecting objects or events and then randomly assigning them to some treatment. This is not to say that such procedures are not useful. It is to say that we do not negotiate the world in that way, and yet all of us form generalizations. The central question deals with the dependability of the generalizations we form. As a basis for dealing with complex problems of practical decision making, ordinary experience is far more effective than the attempt to design scientific procedures for creating generalizations from situations whose characteristics might no longer be the same after the scientific work has been completed. The point I wish to argue here, however, is not primarily about the virtues and vices of the practical and the theoretical; rather, I wish to argue that useful generalizations are made from particulars all the time. Criticism is one of the means through which the particular situation can be more effectively experienced and from which useful generalizations can be drawn.

WHO IS THE EDUCATIONAL CRITIC?

Although school districts, universities, and other institutions concerned with the practice of education might eventually employ on their staffs an individual designated as an "educational critic", educational criticism is, as I conceive of it, not so much a role as it is a function. Anyone—student, teacher, supervisor, school administrator, university professor, school board member—might provide educational criticism to enable a colleague or institution to pursue aims more effectively. In fact, to some degree, each of such individuals now provides an incipient type of educational criticism. The teacher provides it when feedback is given to fellow teachers or principals on the character and quality of their work. Supervisors are professionally responsible for such criticism when they consciously attempt to provide pedagogical guidance to teachers. Principals provide it as they appraise the teaching competency of the school staff, and school boards provide it when they attempt to assess the work of the school administrator.

Although the perception and appraisal of such work are not considered forms of educational criticism, the roots of criticism are present. The supervisor, for example, tries to see what goes on in a classroom and attempts to provide useful feedback to teachers. When principals meet their responsibilities as educational leaders, they, too, attempt to perceive, describe, and assess so that the quality of educational practice is increased. What has been lacking is a model with which such practice could be conceptualized, legitimized, and refined.

In making the point that existing forms of professional colleagueship provide incipient forms of educational criticism, I am not suggesting that what is now done is always adequate or useful. It is to say that both professional and lay people responsible for the improvement of educational processes have relied on their own perceptions, sensitivities, and ability to articulate what they see as a way of improving those processes. The refinement of such dispositions is something that should be encouraged. I would prefer this to the formal designation of an "educational critic" within a school or school district. I would prefer the broad utilization of the concept as a tool for educational improvement that all involved in the process could learn to use with skill and sensitivity.

I make this observation because schools are already sufficiently bureaucratized and teachers already too isolated from one another to create the kind of environment that breeds trust and respect. The nonspecialized use of educational criticism within classrooms, schools, and school districts might contribute to the kind of community among staff, students, and parents that would help make schools the kind of supportive and humane places that they can and should become.

Although most of what I have had to say about the subject matter of educational criticism has focused on the activities of teachers and students, educational criticism can be applied to any set of objects and events that one considers relevant to the aims of educational practice. For example, Elizabeth Vallance focused her efforts on the educational criticism of textbooks used in the social studies. The aim of her work was to identify the ways in which textbook writers and publishers conveyed messages to students, messages that were not simply explicit but instead a function of the ways in which books were designed, color was used, words were employed, emphasis was given in the text, and the like. She writes of one textbook:

> Lacking any central focus other than the general subject-matter, the text develops meanings primarily through the images it creates. These general impressions are perhaps the strongest messages conveyed by the materials. There are several of these, some created by the visual qualities of the text and some by the written content itself. The first and strongest is the image of the city as a clean, well-scrubbed, nicely lighted world. It is an image created entirely through the illustrations. The cheerful colors, the comic-book flavor of fantasy in the drawings, the rich photographic tones, and the wholesome scenes which these portray—all contribute to a feeling of good cheer. Most (though not all) of the few pictures of urban grime manage to look clean and tonally rich, and the factory in the drawing of air and water pollution is quite likeable—the gray, thick and bulbous smoke puffing from the smokestack looks friendly as the smoke of *The Little Engine That Could.*[25]

What is curious is that all of us living in the United States in the latter half of the twentieth century know firsthand how design, packaging techniques, forms of advertising, and types of emphasis given to certain products influence our own behavior and attitudes. The advertising industry is built on the fact that the forms used to market a product have an enormous influence on its success. Exposure, although important for a product, is not enough; the way in which that exposure occurs is important and the characteristics of the qualities that constitute the advertisement are critical. Yet these considerations have, until quite recently, never been applied by educators to textbooks, or, as far as I know, to other instructional tools. The recent exceptions, of course, are in the areas of race and sex stereotyping. But there is considerably more that can be attended to in order to discover the covert messages of the materials that children use in schools. These, too, are proper subjects for educational criticism.

Take, as an example, the kinds of images used in illustrations for texts. What sort of men and women are portrayed? What kinds of settings do they work in? What type of emphasis do they receive? How much white space, how much color, what kinds of layouts are used to give emphasis to various aspects of the book? The use of such qualities might seen trivial, but they play on and with the images we hold of people, places, and ideas. The portrait of George Washington on a dollar bill and his heroic image at the bow of a small boat crossing the Delaware amid ice and threatening sky, surrounded by his weary but loyal soldiers, have created an indelible image in the minds of many Americans. Such images influence the ideas we hold, and as such they should warrant our professional attention; yet, educators have given these matters little conscious attention.

Consider as still another example of the objects that ought to receive critical attention the school buildings that we design for students and the furniture we use to fill them.

Buildings represent our ideals about the ways we want to live. State capitols throughout the nation hark back to Greek architecture to express the ideals of government—justice, stability, and historical presence—that citizens believe are conveyed by domes, columns, and white marble. Factories are most often designed with a no-nonsense quality about them. They present an image of work; surfaces are hard, right angles predominate, little is done to refine, embellish, or soften the forms within which people spend a major portion of their waking hours. The factory building expresses what it is, a place of work. Consider bank buildings as another example; although there are exceptions, of course, bank buildings tend to look like the Rock of Gibraltar, having massive shapes and often Greek columns so that they, too, can reap the benefit of association with the past. People who bank their money want a place that looks solid; a fly-by-night image will not do.

And what of schools? What image do schools present to children and parents and the teachers who work there?

School architecture has come a long way since the days when many urban elementary and secondary schools were built, during the 1910s and 1920s. The best of contemporary school architecture is as congenial to the senses as almost anything else that has been built. However, most school buildings, particularly those in cities, are characterized by long vacant halls with nests of well-insulated rooms opening onto them. The rooms are usually identical: strong, rectangular boxes, drab in color and not given to amenities. The rooms speak of functionality but do not address themselves to the aesthetic needs of either students or teachers. They are not places in which one would choose to spend a lot of time.

What do such places say to students? What values do they convey? How do they affect the student's image of the school itself and the experience of schooling? These questions, too, are appropriate ones for educational criticism.

And what of the furniture used in schools? Why the ubiquitous use of formica? Where in the school can one find a soft surface? Where can one encounter a cozy place, somewhere where it is quiet? Where can a student create a place of his or her own? Is a desk large enough for such a purpose?

When in the 1920s the German Bauhaus gave us machine-made furniture that exploited the aesthetic as well as functional possibilities of steel, glass, chrome, and plywood, the concern for proportion, detail, finish, and comfort was critical. The modern furniture of *that* era was so classic in its proportions and style that it is still being sold. What is used in most schoolrooms today is furniture that is neither comfortable nor aesthetically satisfying. What passes for modern furniture is too often so unattractive that we learn how to avoid looking at it. Instead of using the environment of the classroom as a source of psychological nourishment, we try to shut it out of our consciousness. The same environmental qualities exist in most college classrooms. The critic of education who can help us to see what we have learned to shut out may be helping us acquire the kind of critical consciousness that is necessary for bringing about change.

Finally, it is appropriate to direct our attention to the works and performances of the student as proper objects of educational criticism. One of the characteristics of standardized testing is that it describes student performance on a common scale. On norm-referenced tests students are differentiated from one another on a common scale of test items and on criterion-referenced tests in relation to their ability to perform at criterion level. In either case, a set of criteria common to all students taking the test is applied and differentiations are made in relation to those criteria.

But what is the distinctive style of a student's ideas, his or her verbal expression, the quality of his paintings, her analytic abilities, the way in which students respond to new opportunities? Is the student perceptive? Is he sensitive to the implications of new ideas or to the feelings of others? Is her written expression lean, logical, and classical or is it romantic, analogical, and baroque? What qualities of mind differentiate this student from the rest? What is it that uniquely characterizes the student's mode of thinking?

Surely attention to the qualities that uniquely distinguish a student from his or her peers is an appropriate consideration for educators to attend to. Surely what we want to know about students and what we wish to cultivate are not only those qualities that they share with every other student, but also the qualities that give them individuality. Because educational criticism focuses on the particular, because it does not require that the particular be characterized on a common scale, its potential for rendering these qualities in a language that makes them vivid is especially great.

In these pages I have tried to describe what I believe qualitative inquiry is in the context of education. The work needed to demonstrate the promise of such inquiry is under way not only at Stanford but elsewhere in various parts of the world. My hope is that in the near future educational criticism as a species of educational evaluation will become a useful complement to the quantitative procedures that have for so long been our dominant means for evaluating the process and consequences of educational programs.

REFERENCES

1. John Dewey, "Qualitative Thought," in *Philosophy and Civilization*, Minton, Balch and Co., New York, 1931, pp. 93–116.
2. John Dewey, *Experience and Education*, Macmillan Publishing Co., Inc., New York, 1950, passim.
3. John Dewey, *Art As Experience*, Minton, Balch and Co., New York, 1934, p. 324.
4. Jeffreys, H., *Theory of Probability (Third Edition)*, Oxford University Press, London, 1961.
5. Dewey, op. cit., p. 52.
6. Frederick Erickson, "Some Approaches to Inquiry in School/Community Ethnography," in *Workshop Exploring Qualitative/Quantitative Research Methodologies in Education, Far West Laboratory for Educational Research and Development*, in cooperation with the National Institute of Education and Council on Anthropology and Education, Monterey, Calif., July 1967.
7. Clifford Geertz, *The Interpretation of Cultures*, Basic Books, New York, 1973.
8. Morris Weitz, "The Nature of Art," in *Readiness in Art Education* (Elliot W. Eisner and David Ecker, eds.), Blaisdell Publishing Co., Waltham, Mass., 1966, p. 10.
9. Max Kozloff, *Renderings: Critical Essays on a Century of Modern Art*, Simon and Schuster, New York, 1969, p. 10.
10. Ernst Cassirer, *An Essay on Man: An Introduction to a Philosophy of Human Culture*, Doubleday & Co., Garden City, N.Y., 1953.
11. Susanne Langer, *Problems of Art*, Charles Scribner's Sons, New York, 1957.
12. Rudolf Arnheim, *Visual Thinking*, University of California Press, Berkeley, Calif., 1969.
13. Aleksandr Solzhenitsyn, *A Day in the Life of Ivan Denisovich*, transl. by Max Hayward and Ronald Hingl, Praeger, New York, 1964.
14. Leo Steinberg, *Other Criteria: Confrontations with Twentieth Century Art*, Oxford University Press, London, 1972, p. 286.
15. Annie Dillard, *Pilgrim at Tinker Creek*, Harper's Magazine Press, New York, 1974.
16. Erickson, op. cit., p. 23.
17. Gabrielle Rico, *Metaphors and Knowing: Analysis, Synthesis, Rationale*, Doctoral Dissertation, School of Education, Stanford University, 1976.
18. Geertz, op. cit., p. 6.
19. Ibid., p. 5.
20. Donald Campbell and Julian Stanley, *Experimental and Quasi-experimental Designs for Research*, Rand McNally, Chicago, 1966.
21. Agatha Christie, *Murder on the Orient Express*, William Collins Sons and Company, Ltd., London, 1974.

22. Geertz, op. cit.

23. I am indebted to Gail McCutcheon for this example.

24. John Mortimer Stephens, *The Process of Schooling: A Psychological Examination*, Holt, Rinehart and Winston, New York, 1967.

25. Elizabeth Vallance, *Aesthetic Criticism and Curriculum Description*, Doctoral Dissertation, School of Education, Stanford University, July 1975, pp. 174–176.

12

Some Examples of Educational Criticism

Technique is the means to the creation of expressive form, the symbol of sentience; the art process is the application of some human skill to this essential purpose.

The making of this expressive form is the creative process that enlists a man's utmost technical skill in the service of his utmost conceptual power, imagination.

SUSANNE K. LANGER

The preceding chapter was devoted to the theoretical bases of educational connoisseurship and educational evaluation. Its purpose was to provide a ground for their practice by identifying the links that they have with criticism and connoisseurship in general and the epistemological assumptions on which they rest. But theory in education must be translated into courses of action if it is to be useful. Somehow what one believes must be transformed into policy and practice, aim and aspiration. The inability to make such translation is to leave theory in the air when one settles down to the real problems at hand. As far as educational practitioners are concerned, theory that does not guide or suggest, that does not explain or help one anticipate, is a game other people play.

The need to determine the utilities of educational connoisseurship and educational criticism was at once both deeply felt and somewhat intimidating. It is much easier to play with ideas at a level removed from practice than to see if those ideas can actually do what they promise in the classroom. At the same time, it was clear that theory itself becomes corrected and refined as it is applied. Thus, the use of theory in classrooms could help identify the areas that needed to be revised and could make it possible to determine if the idea of educational criticism was viable. Was it in fact possible to create a kind of educational discourse that would significantly complement the approaches to educational evaluation that had for so long been used in the field?

What follows are a series of educational criticisms written by people who were or are, at the time of this writing, my doctoral students in the School of Education at Stanford University. Each one of them has been a part of a research group that has met regularly since September 1975 to discuss, debate, read, and create educational criticism. We have taken it upon ourselves to try to fill out the conceptual issues in doing educational criticism by reading in anthropology, art criticism, philosophy, educational evaluation, and research methods used in sociology and social psychology.

But, perhaps even more importantly, virtually every member of the group has visited schools, school board meetings, and special school events in order to exercise educational connoisseurship and to do educational criticism. We have attempted to practice what we were preaching and through practice to revise and strengthen our understanding of how educational criticism might function.

In doing educational criticism, an individual typically makes contact with a school—usually a classroom teacher but at times the principal—explains what we are doing at Stanford, and tries to find out if there are teachers in the school who might find feedback on their teaching useful. If such a teacher is found, the person functioning as an educational critic will arrange to visit that classroom for an extended period of time, in some cases on a daily basis for two to three weeks. During these visits, the educational critic will discretely observe what goes on. Sometimes what is being looked for will be decided in advance, such as how cooperation or competition is fostered by children and teachers. Sometimes the educational critic will talk to the teacher to try to find out what kind of information the teacher might want, in which case a *part* of what the critic would do is to observe in light of the teacher's needs. Most of the time, however, the educational critic allows the emerging conditions of the classroom to suggest what might be important in this classroom and from such observation constructs a theme or focus for critical description. Each classroom has a pervasive quality—even ones that appear chaotic—and each room (or school) provides an arena for significant events to emerge, events that one might not notice if one's focus is prefigured. What we try to achieve is a readiness to give structure to what is almost always a rich and literally dynamic environment. The educational critic's problem is never not having enough "data," it's just the opposite. The creative task is to confer a telling structure on a field of vision so that sense can be made of it.

This task, of course, is not easy. It requires both a willingness and an ability to perceive subtle particulars and to put them into a coherent configuration. Compared to the use of preordinate observation schedules, educational criticism is an arduous task. The major instrument is the individual doing the observation and the writing. A delicate line must be trod between a mere chronicle of events on the one hand and the unconscious omission of events that do not fit into the story one might want to write on the other. And because the writing of educational criticism has consequences for people, it has a moral dimension as well. One cannot be cavalier about things that affect other's lives; one cannot sacrifice veracity to make a good tale.

Compared to the ease of administering and scoring standardized tests, the use of educational connoisseurship and educational criticism is a time-consuming task. One must find classroom teachers and school administrators willing to have someone observe in their classroom or school on a regular basis. One must be willing to invest hours in a classroom in order to grasp what goes on there. One must appraise what one has seen with a normative conception of education. All of these demands are formidable; educational criticism is not a one-shot, short-term clerical task.

These demands might in the long run be too great to motivate people in the field to use educational criticism as a tool for educational evaluation. "Efficiency" and unambiguous conclusions seem to be preferred to the questions we raise and the problems we encounter. Educational criticism is not efficient—it takes time. And it often leaves its reader with a fuller appreciation of the predicaments teachers and school administrators face. There is no single score carried to the second decimal place that can be added, subtracted, and averaged. What educational criticism has to offer is human judgment—and this might be too cumbersome to deal with in doing educational evaluation.

Yet I know of no other way to know what goes on in classrooms than to be there to see those events occur. I know of no other way to relate facts to consequences than to see both as they unfold in school settings. The observation of those events takes time because those events occur over time. If we accept the notion that the quality of consequences is a function of the character of the events that preceded them, then our knowledge of the latter is a necessary condition for improving the quality of the former. Said more simply, we are unlikely to improve the quality of teaching or of classroom life unless we know what it is. Educational connoisseurship and educational criticism are intended to make that possible.

The three criticisms that follow are examples of the work we have been doing since October 1975. They represent our initial efforts to render vividly classrooms and other educational events. I will make no comment about the content or form of these educational criticism because I believe that they are sufficiently vivid to speak for themselves, except to express my gratitude to their authors for allowing me to include them in this book.

SCHOOL AND SOCIETY REVISITED: AN EDUCATIONAL CRITICISM OF MISS HILL'S FOURTH-GRADE CLASSROOM

Robert Donmoyer

This classroom is almost a caricature of the society.

The curriculum is served up like Big Macs. Reading, math, language, even physical and affective education are all precooked, prepackaged, artificially flavored.

The arts are valued here as they are valued in the larger society. The teacher states simply, "They are not one of my priorities."

Teaching is orderly; learning is ordered. Page 47 always follows page 46. Short-vowel words are spelled before long-vowel words. Discussion of simple feelings precedes discussion of more complex ones.

Each day is remarkably like the day before and the day after. The school year seems to have been made with 174 pieces of carbon paper. The same things are done at the same times in the same ways in the same books. Only the pages change.

As in the larger society, efficiency is both mean and end. If a student needs to use the bathroom, the student must hold up a blue flag and wait for the teacher's nod. If a student needs help with his work, the student must hold up a yellow flag and wait for the teacher's attention. If a student needs to sharpen his pencil, the student must hold up a yellow flag with a green dot and wait for the teacher's permission. There is a flag for getting a drink, and there is a flag for getting one's work checked, and there is a flag for getting permission to step outside the door for one minute to talk to a friend. *Nothing* must interfere with the explaining of the directions, the filling of the blanks, the solving of the problems, the copying of the sentences, the checking of the work.

Here as in the larger society, independent individuals are prized. But, as in the larger society, independence is uniquely defined. Independence here means being able to sit . . . alone . . . unjoined . . . in one's own seat at one's own desk in one's own neatly arranged row doing one's own work which is listed on one's own contracts.

The student must be able to be as disconnected from his work as he is disconnected from other people. The student does not negotiate the contents of his contracts and the contents have little to do with him. But he is expected to do the assignments listed therein. He must answer the problems and fill in the blanks and copy the sentences and, with luck, he remembers to capitalize the Colorados and Massachusettses even though he does not know what a Colorado or a Massachusetts is.

Most students sign on the dotted line. There are exceptions. Kenny, from the very beginning, seemed to have too much individuality to tolerate individualization. By the first recess of the first day of school, even though Kenny had not exhibited any overt misbehavior, the teacher knew he was a deviant and she stated as much. As is the custom in our society, the search for an appropriate label began in earnest. A call was made to his previous school and the appalling news came back: He had not been classified!! Psychological and educational testing was immediately called for. In the meantime he was, on various occasions, called dyslexic, aphasic, educationally handicapped, emotionally disturbed, and finally, in the seventh week, when tests showed that at least some of the labels just didn't apply, he was said to be in need of reality therapy. No thought was given to the possibility that the classroom reality was what was in need of alteration.

But Kenny is the exception. Most of the children compliantly sit at their desks and dutifully complete the terms of their "contracts." This obedience seems to be the result of something more than a desire to avoid missing recesses or staying after school or being late for lunch. Rather there seems to be a conversion to the religion of productivity and the accompanying morality of efficiency. The conversion is not the result of a dramatic rebirth but rather of a more gradual enculturation. This "religious" training takes place continuously through the teacher's words and deeds. The teacher says, "Thank you, Keith, for beginning your work right away," or "I'm glad to see Maritza is not wasting time." Religious instruction is inherent in the teacher's response to classroom incidents. When Sonya is in tears because Patty hit her, the teacher's initial response is to chide Patty for not doing her work. Religious enculturation occurs in private conversations. When Frederick explains that he is sad because his father has left home, the teacher concludes the conversation by asking, "Don't you think your father would want you to do your work if he were here?" The faith that results from all this not an evangelical one involving a passionate commitment. But despite the absence of passion and enthusiasm, a "religious" world view is acquired, and the morality of this classroom, the morality of productivity, efficiency, and independence, is accepted by most the students as their own.

And so it seems that students are being relatively well prepared for life in the larger society, a society with houses . . . unjoined . . . with neighborhoods without neighbors. Students are being well trained for a society of bureaucratic cubicles, assembly lines, and secretarial pools, a society in which even researchers have their questions formulated not by their own curiosities but by the nature of finding, a variety where work provides no intrinsic satisfaction and where intrinsic satisfaction is not anticipated. Students in this classroom receive a superb initiation into modern society, for they learn to efface themselves and instead worship the goddess of productivity and her handmaiden, efficiency. These students, many of whom are the children of poverty and ethnic minorities, should make their way quite nicely in the world of golden arches, Mr. Coffees, foot deodorants, padded bras, and electric toothbrushes.

Yet, a somewhat ancient question comes to mind: Is the function of education merely to initiate the young into the culture that is or is education to be a regenerative force for a society, a means of making a society what it ought to be? The question George Counts asked teachers four and a half decades ago must be asked again: "Dare the school build a new social order?"

Miss Hill, the teacher in this classroom, is hardly in a position to build anything. She is as much a victim as the students she victimizes. She is victimized by the district office run by an evaluation department obsessed with the numbers of standardized achievement tests. She is victimized by a state department of education demanding 1.2 months of growth for every one month students spend in her classroom to indicate that state compensatory funds are well spent. She is victimized by a school which has had four principals in four years and by the new principal who, in seven weeks of school, was too busy to even once visit the teacher's classroom to provide feedback on the quality of life there. She is victimized by the inequities created by financing education with the property tax: there is no money for an art or music or physical education teacher and hence no time during the school day for Miss Hill to catch her breath, much less prepare creative learning experiences; she is given a total of $150 for all supplies (paper, crayons, dittos, etc.) for the entire year. Finally, and probably most importantly, Miss Hill is victimized by her own conscientiousness—her desire to adequately prepare her students for the society in which they will soon have to function.

All these forces combine to produce a profound effect upon the teacher and profoundly influence her behavior in the classroom. She becomes, as she herself has said, an accountant. Most of her day is spent checking and recording what students have and haven't done. Math, spelling, and language assignments must be checked, and if there are mistakes (and there usually are) they must be re-checked and, sometimes, rechecked again. Then checked assignments must be checked off on each student's math, spelling, or language contract. When each contract is completed, each contract must be checked out. After this is done, the student must take home the work included on that contract and bring back a note signed by his parents indicating they saw the work. This note must, of course, be checked in.

This checking and rechecking and checking out and checking in is all performed with mechanized precision. The teacher's face remains immobile, except for an occasional upward turn at the corners of her mouth. The eyes almost never smile.

The teacher exhibits great economy of movement and gesture. It's almost as if Miss Hill were a marionette whose strings are too tight and, hence, her gestures must be tight and close to her body.

There is also economy of voice. Miss Hill parcels out her words sparingly as if inflicted with a chronic case of laryngitis. Instead of speaking, she points. If she wants a student to turn on the lights, she points to the student and then to the lights. She says nothing. If a student is turned around in his seat and talking to the student who sits behind him, the teacher stares, then points, then spins her index finger in a clockwise motion until the student stops talking and turns around. Here, at least, it appears that talk is not cheap.

When the teacher does speak, however, her voice colors all experience within the confines of this classroom, and the color that is vocally applied is shocking beige. Her voice is the perfect accessory for the tan, plastic drapes which cover the windows and hang, straight, without feeling or expression. It's a voice barren of any sort of nuance, as if somehow the hum of the air conditioner were reconstituted into words. During the seven weeks I spent in this classroom, I only rarely heard this voice express anger or joy or emotion of any kind.

Although the resemblance is more spiritual than physical, I could not help but see a pedagogical version of that modern American Everyman, Mary Hartman, hard at work in the classroom I was observing. As with Mrs. Hartman, I could sense something beneath Miss Hill's expressionless face and voice and eyes, something hidden inside the vacuum.

There is, of course, and it wasn't hard to find. It doesn't take long, away from the classroom, talking over coffee, to discover a warm, sensitive, intelligent middle-aged lady interested in music and folk masses and people and people's feelings. In the best Jekyll and Hyde tradition, this proselytizer of the catechism of productivity is completely transformed when she steps beyond the four walls of her classroom, out into the open. True, a certain need for order remains, but there is no evidence of an obsession with acquisition. In fact, she seems to be controlled by an entirely different set of values.

The more I got to know Miss Hill, the more I came to realize how simplistic the view of teachers as villain espoused by the muckracking educational journalists of the 1960s really was. In this regard, I recall an incident that occurred at one lunch hour.

James, a whimsical, somewhat overgrown, overstuffed cherub with an incandescent face, had been kept in because he hadn't finished some work. James couldn't read, spell, or write very well. In fact, it would be more honest to say tha he had virtually *no* written language skills. He was quite verbal; he appeared to be rather intelligent, and he certainly was not unmotivated. His reading problem was said to be the result of a learning disability of some sort. On the basis of what I saw, this seems like a plausible, if somewhat unhelpful explanation. This explanation was certainly accepted by Miss Hill. She arranged for James to spend a large portion of the school day in the room for the educationally handicapped under the supervision of the teacher of the educationally handicapped.

When James was in his regular classroom, he was expected to complete regular assignments. There was no problem with math. Math assignments were made on the basis of individual achievement levels. Besides, James was quite talented in math.

James did have problems, however, with other assignments which usually required some use of language. Miss Hill allowed James to copy other students' work and sometimes she had a "bright" student complete his work for him while James looked on, looking alternately bored and embarrassed.

On the particular day I'm recalling, normally jovial, jocular James apparently had had enough. Tears rolled down his cheeks and after the other students had all gone to lunch, James in a controlled rage, informed the teacher that he hated the teachers who taught at this school.

Miss Hill said nothing for a long while. She just stared emptily at James. Finally, in a voice void of feeling, she asked him why he felt this way.

James blurted out, "Because the teachers here are mean."

Once again, unfilled time. Then, finally, an inquiry, nondescriptly made: "Do you think *I'm* mean?"

The response, immediate, emphatic: "YES!"

Silence. Finally the volley is returned, but in slow motion this time: "Why do you think I'm mean?"

James relates, between sobs, that the teachers at his other school used to let him take his work home if he didn't get it finished in class. Those teachers were nice, he says. Then he adds that he would like to go back to his other school.

The teacher's voice is controlled and calm. As always, empty. Slowly, quietly, she asks, "And did those teachers teach you to read?"

James is a proud boy. He says yes with little more than a moment's hesitation.

The teacher pauses . . . just for a beat this time . . . and then she transforms herself into a divinely underplayed Lady MacBeth. She grabs a book, thrusts it at James and says, "Read this.!"

James tries. Fails. The teacher explains . . . coolly . . . rationally . . . that she does what she does for James's own good, James nods. Leaves. Immediately Miss Hill begins to cry. Her head falls to the table top.

I felt badly for James. I felt even worse for Miss Hill. By now I had begun to sense dissonance between the professional and the person. I knew that teaching was not only psychically but also physically painful for Miss Hill, and I was pretty sure the pain was not being inflicted by her students, most of whom were among the most easygoing, pliable children I had ever seen. (Even the infamous Kenny hardly resembled the problem children I had encountered in other classrooms; only during the last few weeks of my observation did he begin to do some mild, verbal counterpunching, against an increasingly hostile environment. Even then he could not be described as uncontrolled and certainly not uncontrollable.)

No, I was pretty sure that Miss Hill's back pains and nervous complaints were not brought on by Miss Hill's students. More likely they were caused by the district office and its numbers racket, the state department of education's great expectations, lawmakers who rely on the property tax to finance education, an invisible principal under the spell of paper work, and an irrational "rational" society which assumes a priori that more is better. All these forces directly or indirectly make Miss Hill, the teacher, into something quite different from Miss Hill, human being.

After the incident with James, I began to think about what I might be able to write that might make life more bearable in this particular classroom, not only for the students, but also for the teacher. I realized the teacher's liberation was a necessary precondition to changing the students' classroom experience, but I also began to feel that teacher emancipation was a worthwhile goal in and of itself.

I began by considering Mr. Count's challenge of radicalism and I very quickly rejected it. Just as I had come to realize that the analysis of the muckrackers of the 60s was simplistic, I new realized that Mr. Count's question was downright foolish. First, teachers, at least this teacher, don't have any energy to spare with which they could lead a social revolution. Second, and more important, Miss Hill would never consider preparing the children in her charge for a world that doesn't exist. Such an emphasis on a new social order would be viewed by Miss Hill as a cruel hoax on children who must be given the skills to function in the existing social order that they all too quickly enter.

Amitai Etzioni spells out this point somewhat more systematically in his review of Charles Silverman's *Crisis in the Classroom*. Etzioni writes:

> The school is unavoidably a funnel which leads from infancy at home to adult occupational structure in the greater society. . . .
>
> Consideration of the society into which the students will graduate are . . . important; it is unfair and unrealistic to prepare them for the educator's favorite dream world because education does not have the force to transform society. Hence, educating students for life in a society which does not exist, say in Silverman's "humane and just" society or for one in which work is as much fun as play—will *not* yield such a society, but might well serve to prepare a frustrated and disillusioned generation of students. . . .
>
> Silverman correctly stresses that our schools are organized as if everyone will graduate either to work on an assembly line or in a civil service. They are best suited to preparing indifferent cogs for an industrial-bureaucratic machine.
>
> But despite the hip talk about rapid societal change, as far as I can forsee, our society will continue to have major instrumental and technical needs. (Etzioni, 1971, pp. 97,98)

Thus, the idea that Miss Hill's professional life and the lives of her students can be made more tolerable by telling Miss Hill to either ignore the present society or attempt to revolutionize it by using her classroom as her podium seems blatantly ridiculous.

So, is there nothing that can be said to this teacher that might help her to make life in her classroom more satisfying for all who spend time there? Must Miss Hill's classroom continue to reflect some of the most dehumanizing elements of the large society? I think not.

First, Miss Hill can be reminded that, despite all the constraints society attempts to impose on her, she is remarkably autonomous when she closes her classroom door. Certain things that have been labeled constraints, the absence of supervision, for example, actually enhance autonomy. Other constraints, like testing, are really only psychologically limiting since neither the state nor the district can impose any real sanctions on a teacher whose students fail to produce. Even the psychological constraint imposed by the heavy emphasis on test scores could be muted somewhat for Miss Hill by reminding her that she herself has noted that her students don't do well on the tests no matter what she does.

Constraints imposed by budget are real, but not necessarily insurmountable. Gadgetry and gimmicks have been oversold; marvelous things can be accomplished with the most mundane materials. Class size and lack of preparation time are more difficult problems to overcome, yet some compensation is provided by the organization of the school day. As a result of staggered dismissal, three reading lab periods, and the four or five students who spend a large portion of their day with the teacher for the educationally handicapped, the number of students in Miss Hill's room at any given time is frequently only half of the thirty-two member class.

Thus, Miss Hill should be reminded that although society's direct constraints upon her are most certainly real, they need not necessarily be as limiting as Miss Hill now assumes them to be. Still, there is the problem of the indirect constraints imposed by the nature of the larger society and the need to prepare students to function in that society. Here again the constraints may not be as limiting as Miss Hill believes. This can be said for two reasons.

First, it could be argued that Miss Hill's view of the larger society is too limited. True, ours is a market economy that views man as a consumer with insatiable desires and therefore glorifies productivity and its accomplice, efficiency. Yet, as the political philospher C. B. Macpherson (1973) has pointed out, our society has also embraced an altogether different vision of man's essence (partly as an antidote to the somewhat crass self-image outlined above) and this view has provided the basis for the justification of liberal Western democratic societies ever since John Stuart Mill first espoused it. Man, according to this view, is a doer, a creator, a being whose satisfactions come not from consumption but from the exercise and development of his innate capacities. Our society then justifies itself by claiming to provide the most conducive environment for such self-actualization.

The condition of modern society seems to justify having the school foster the creative side of man's nature. Etzioni, for example, while arguing against radical school reform that puts schools out of sync with society, does contend that

> We will be able to work less, and less efficiently, still be affluent, and we can realistically help prepare students for a world with more "work" and less "labor" . . . and a world in which more energy and time are devoted to personal and interpersonal growth, and less productivity. (Etzioni, 1971, p. 98)

There are, in fact, indications that when schools attempt to foster the creativity of their students, they may be aiding societal stability. Increasing automation and unemployment, decreasing natural resources, increasing environmental pollution, and the decreasing desire of third-world nations to be exploited, all would seem to indicate that it may very well be in the best interest of the society to attempt to teach the young to find fulfillment in themselves and their creative powers rather than in consumption.

Thus, our society's self-justification is based on its claim to enhance man's creative powers, and present and future societal conditions seem to allow and possibly even require man to find fulfillment in his own creative abilities. Therefore, it seems logical for schools, in addition to preparing students to take their place in the marketplace, to also provide students with opportunities to have intrinsically rewarding experiences. These experiences would foster the development of individual students' creative potentials and would by their inclusion in the curriculum indicate that such development is of value.

The arts, while not the only source of intrinsically rewarding experience, are clearly some of the most fertile sources of such activity. Miss Hill should be encouraged to alter her view of the place of the arts in the classroom and to make artistic experience an educational priority. She should be encouraged to provide her students with richer, more varied experiences than she now provides. Creativity should mean something more than making paperweights by gluing comic strips on rocks or making Halloween decorations by cutting out black cats previously traced on construction paper. Art should not be made into a prostitute by using it to train students to work independently and to complete assignments, nor should it be merely a reward for completing academic work. Music should be more than an occasional way of filling the time before lunch. And creative dramatics, which Miss Hill does not use at all at the present time, could provide a constructive outlet for students like Kenny, whose expressiveness, as Miss Hill well knows, is sometimes difficult to contain.

Once again, budgetary limitations, as well as the teacher's own limitations, must be recognized. There are no art, music, or drama supervisors, and although

Miss Hill has had experience and considerable training in music education, she lacks an art and drama background. Her lack of training is certainly a constraint. However, teaching in the arts is not based on a scientific formula or a lock-step methodology. Miss Hill must be encouraged to put into use her own creative potential that flowers outside the classroom but that has been made to lie fallow within the confines of the four classroom walls. And probably the the most important thing Miss Hill can do is to value an individual's creative abilities as much as she values the ability to correctly follow directions in the spelling workbook. For this, the teacher needs no particular training.

Three fringe benefits should accrue if the arts are made a classroom priority. First the teacher's role would be expanded. She would no longer simply be an accountant, but in order to provide her students with creative experiences, she would herself become a creator. Hopefully this focus on creativity would not only make classroom life more satisfying for the students, but also for the teacher.

Second, by expanding the activities that are valued in the classroom, more students, students like Kenny and James, would have a greater opportunity to succeed in the classroom. Even in our bureaucratic society, there are more roads to success than presently exist in Miss Hill's classroom.

Third, the granting of the arts a place of importance in the classroom would affect the dynamics of classroom interaction. The teacher would be freed somewhat from her endless checking and rechecking and checking-out and checking-in routine and should have some more time to interact with her students. When "checking" students' artistic work, she would be able to focus on each student's uniqueness rather than measure him by some distant publisher's yardstick of appropriate grade-level performance. There should also be opportunities for individuals to break out of their cells of independence for group singing and drama "performance."

All these benefits indicate the arts deserve a place of prominence in the elementary school curriculum. If Miss Hill continues to doubt this, she should be reminded that ours is a society that sees man as a creative being and justifies its existence on the grounds that it best can foster such creativity. Therefore, it does not seem inappropriate for the schools of our society to cultivate the idea that the ultimate expression of one's humanity is something more than buying a Fonzie T-shirt.

Of course it is important not to limit the development of individuality and creativity to what is thought to be their natural habitat, the arts. Philosopher of science, Paul Feyerabend, speaks to this point. Feyerabend is primarily concerned with the evils of a rule-governed approach to science, arguing that scientific insight has always been the result of methodological proliferation. Occasionally, however, Feyerabend emphasizes the implications of his argument for education:

> Progressive educators have always tried to develop the individuality of their pupils and to bring to fruition the particular and sometimes quite unique talents and beliefs that each child possesses. But such an education very often seemed to be a futile exercise in daydreaming. For is it not necessary to prepare the young for life? Does this not mean that they must learn one particular set of views to the exclusion of everything else? And, if there should still remain a trace of their youthful gift of imagination, will it not find its proper application in the arts, that is, in a thin domain of dreams that has but little to do with the world we live in? Will this procedure not finally lead to a split between a hated reality and welcome fantasies, science and the arts, careful description and unrestrained self-expression? The argument for proliferation shows that this need not be the case. It is possible to retain what one might call the freedom of

artistic creation and to use it to the full, not just as a road of escape, but as a necessary means for discovering and perhaps even changing the properties of the world we live in. (Feyerabend, 1970, p. 27)

There is a second reason why it can be argued that the indirect constraints on Miss Hill imposed by the nature of the larger society may not be as limiting as they may first appear. This argument refers to the concern with basic skills.

It has been conceded that the school should prepare its students for life in the larger society. What will be argued, however, is that a classroom like Miss Hill's that mimics bureaucratic organization is not an appropriate environment for students to learn those skills considered so "basic" to functioning in that society. The point is quite simple: when the school year is made with 174 pieces of carbon paper, it seems logical to assume that the impression left will become increasingly dull.

No radical proposals are being advanced. The teacher's need for a quiet, orderly classroom must be respected. The fact that many students learn best in a relatively orderly environment is conceded, and Miss Hill's belief that most of her students fit into this orderly environment category may, indeed, be correct. It is also conceded that most students can benefit from a careful sequencing of subject matter. Finally the limitation of time and the resultant need for a teacher to, at times, rely on prepackaged workbooks is also acknowledged.

What *is* being argued is that when efficiency and order become ends in themselves, when learning is thought to have *only* a linear dimension, when students do little else but sit by themselves filling in blanks, copying sentences, and doing row upon row of math problems, when the teacher spends virtually all her time checking the blanks and the sentences and the problems, then something is amiss.

Much is made of the fact that because of the socioeconomic status of *"these* children," they require an extra dosage of the 3Rs. It is true that these children are not the children of college professors or corporate vice-presidents or lawyers or doctors; most of these children hold no birthright to the good life, economically defined. Yet this very fact makes Miss Hill's prescription all the more inappropriate. These students have not grown up surrounded by empirical evidence of the social and material advantages that come with playing the school game; most of these students have probably *not* been read to since before they could talk. Because of this it seems highly unlikely that simply increasing the dosage of bland tasting medicine or demanding that more bitter pills be swallowed will cure *these* students' educational maladies.

In the play *The Miracle Worker*, Helen Keller's teacher reflects on the goals she had set for herself. She says,

> I wanted to teach you—oh, everything the earth is full of, Helen, everything on it that's ours for a wink and it's gone, and what we are on it, the—light we bring to it and leave behind in—words, why, you can see five thousand years back in a light of words, everything we feel, think, know—and share, in words, so not a soul is in darkness, or done with even in the grave. (Gibson, 1960, p. 279)

That's not exactly a behavior objective; admittedly, the objective may be a wee bit theatrical. Yet it does seem appropriate for a teacher to try to communicate to her students at least the utility of language. And, more than that, it seems appropriate for a teacher to want to help her students to learn the pleasure to be found in books, to help them look "five thousand years back in the light of words," or possibly help them use books to look into the future. And, too, it seems appropriate for a teacher to want to give her students an opportunity to communicate what they feel, think, know by writing. Finally, it seems appropriate for a teacher to want to provide her students with a sense of the power a knowledge of numbers conveys on the knower and also a sense of the mystery of mathematics.

Unfortunately, these are not Miss Hill's objectives. At least her classroom provides no evidence that she holds these values. Students are never read to, and students are never encouraged nor given time to read on their own own during the school day. In the seven weeks I was there, students were almost never encouraged to write anything beyond spelling tests and language arts exercises. Math, too, never got beyond the calisthenics stage. All this seems unfortunate. If students do not see any value in what they are expected to learn and are never given meaningful opportunities to utilize what they have learned, it seems unlikely that much learning will occur or be retained.

John Dewey spoke to this point over a half a century ago. He was speaking of the exercises of Maria Montessori, but what he said seems equally applicable to the workbook exercises found in Miss Hill's classroom. Dewey writes,

> Exercises which distinguish for the child . . . abstract qualities . . . may give the child great skill in performing the special exercises, but will not necessarily result in making him more successful in dealing with these qualities as they appear in the situation of life. (Dewey, 1915, p. 160)

Dewey at another point says the following:

> The training of the pupil to habits of right thinking and judgment is best accomplished by means of material which present him real problems. (Dewey, 1915, p. 158)

This last statement by Dewey directs attention to another aspect of Miss Hill's academic approach. The "basic skills" needed to function successfully in our modern bureaucratic society extend somewhat beyond the 3Rs. What separates the corporate executive from his secretary is more than just spelling proficiency. The difference between a shop owner and his clerk is not just facility with figures. And the community college student and the Ivy League scholar are likely to be distinguished from each other in many ways, and not just in reading ability. Just what this extra something is is difficult to say, and therefore it seems impossible to provide a simple prescription for fostering it.

A more productive approach to this regard might be found in asking what would *not* foster this extra something.

Salomon and Achenbach define a behavior trait they label associative reasoning (Salomon and Achenbach, 1974). Individuals who rely on associative reasoning might be said to lack what is commonly labeled imagination. Instead of using their reasoning ability to find a solution to problems, they rely on concrete situational clues. Salomon and Achenbach observed associative reasoning in an academic context only and found it to be a severe academic handicap. Presumably, if this way of approaching situations transferred to nonacademic experience, and it seems logical to assume that it would, the individual with an associative reasoning orientation would be equally handicapped under nonacademic circumstances.

No clear cause of associative reasoning has been determined, yet Salomon and Achenbach lean heavily toward environmental explanations. One of their primary hypotheses is "lack of incentives for thinking independently." If Salomon and Achenbach are correct, then the tightly structured, highly routinized environment in Miss Hill's classroom, with its emphasis on following directions and its discouragement of any divergent or independent thinking, is hardly an appropriate training course for the society on the other side of the classroom door.

Miss Hill, despite her intense efforts to program *"these children"* for success in the larger society, may unconsciously be programming them for failure, or, at best, for minimal achievement. Anthropologists indicate that, contrary to the American mythology about upward mobility through education, "education. . . functions in established cultural systems to recruit new members and maintain the existing system" (Spindler, 1974, p. 309). Ethnographies have shown how teachers can be blinded by a "self-sustaining cultural belief system," and have provided numerous examples of self-fulfilling prophesy based on SES status (Spindler, 1963; Spindler, 1974; King, 1967; Rist, 1973).

The teachers' room at Miss Hill's school has many prophets of the self-fulfilling variety. Miss Hill was more discreet than the teachers who lament having to teach the children of welfare recipients because such children are inevitably "behind." Nevertheless, she frequently emphasized the differences between her school and students and middle-class schools and students. For example, she said of Eileen, a new student with excellent academic and study skills, "She must have gone to a middle-class school last year. There, children have a chance to extend themselves."

There *is* a real difference between Miss Hill's room and many middle-class classrooms, but the fundamental difference is the quantitative and qualitative expectations for the students. Eileen is an industrious, capable student; Miss Hill runs an individualized classroom. There is no reason why Eileen should not be able to "extend herself" this year. Yet, if Miss Hill thinks this is impossible, it probably becomes an impossibility.

The problem with Miss Hill's academic curriculum was summed up by John Dewey long ago, when he pointed to the evils of a narrow vocational orientation in education.

A democratic criterion requires us to develop capacity to the point of competency to choose and make its own career. This principle is violated when the attempt is made to fit individuals in advance for definite industrial callings, selected not on the basis of trained original capacities, but on that of the wealth or social status of parents. (Dewey, 1916, p. 119)

It appears, then, that a classroom need not mimic the society in order to provide students with the necessary skills for functioning in the society. Such a mime act may, in fact, be counterproductive. Miss Hill must continue to provide as much structure as her students really need, and she cannot ignore her own need of order. But her excessive emphasis on efficiency and her overreliance on workbooks must be deemphasized.

To begin the transformation of her classroom, Miss Hill might set aside a portion of each day to read to the class. Another period of each day should be set aside for students to read silently to themselves or orally to a partner. A walking trip to the public library near the school should net the necessary books. Also, language assignments that permit students to use language might be presented to the students. Initially these writing assignments might be offered as alternatives to the standard workbook assignments. Pen pal letters, story writing, and journals are some obvious possibilities. Eileen would make an excellent editor-in-chief of a class newspaper. Miss Hill might even consider letting her class run a sale of some sort. A sale would lend itself to all sorts of learning activities: students could become involved with calculating profits, making change, making posters, and writing and acting out sale commercials that could be "toured" to other classrooms.

In this discussion, society has been cast in the role of villain. As always, of course, life is more complicated than melodrama. It could be argued that Miss Hill's personal need for order and her tendency to accept authority unquestioningly should entitle her to equal billing with society. Yet, any flaw that might be embedded deep within Miss Hill's personality need not be a tragic one. And hopefully this discussion has shown that even society does not require that tragedy continue to be acted out in Miss Hill's classroom.

Counts, George S., *Dare the School Build a New Social Order?* New York: John Day, 1932.

Dewey, John, *Democracy and Education,* New York: Macmillan Publishing Co., Inc., 1916.

Dewey, John and Evelyn Dewey, *Schools of Tomorrow,* New York: E. P. Dutton & Co., 1915.

Etzioni, Amitai, "Crisis in the Classroom (A Review)," *Harvard Educational Review,* 1971: 41, 87–98.

Gibson, William, "Miracle Worker," *Dinny and the Witches and The Miracle Worker: Two Plays,* New York, Atheneum, 1960.

Feyerabend, Paul K., "Against Method: Outline of an Anarchistic Theory of Knoweldge, *Analyses of Theories and Methods of Physics and Pcychology* (Michael Rodner and Stephen Winokur, editors), Minneapolis: University of Minnesota Press, 1970, pp. 17–130.

King, Richard A., *The School at Mopass: A Problem of Identify.* New York: Holt, Rinehart and Winston, Inc., 1967.

Macpherson, C. B., "The Maximization of Democracy," *Democratic Theory: Essays in Retrieval.* London: Oxford University Press, 1973, pp. 3–23.

Rist, Ray, *The Urban School: A Factory for Failure,* Cambridge, Mass. MIT Press, 1973.

Salomon, Marion Kerner and Thomas M. Achenbach, "The Effects of Four Kinds of Tutoring Experience on Associative Responding," *American Educational Research Journal,* 1974: 11, 4, pp. 395–405.

Spindler, George D., "Beth Anne—A Case Study of Culturally Defined Adjustment and Teacher Perceptions," *Education and Cultural Process: Toward an Anthropology of Education,* (George Spindler, editor), New York: Holt, Rinehart and Winston, Inc., 1974, pp. 139–153.

Spindler, George D., "The Transmission of American Culture," *Education and Culture,* New York: Holt, Rinehart and Winston, Inc., 1963, pp. 148–172.

OF SCOTT AND LISA AND OTHER FRIENDS
Thomas Barone

The splendid houses perched majestically upon the hills peek out from between the lush growth of trees and well-tended foliage that dress them. Many seem to snicker at the laws of gravity as they balance themselves so casually upon the slanted land. They stare straight ahead, haughtily ignoring the bright green carpet at their feet. The houses maintain a distance from each other; they wrap their fences around their land as if to insist that it is theirs alone.

As I drive past, I wonder about the people in these lavish houses with their redwood paneling and their thoroughbred stallions in the adjacent fields. What are they like? How do they live? Do they balance their lives as effortlessly as they have balanced their houses on these hills? Do they ever stroll through their woods and sniff the honey-colored air and listen to the California mist as it steals softly over the hills? Or do they gaze straight ahead, like their houses? What distances do they maintain from whomever might be their friends? Does each wrap his arms around his life to insist that it is his alone? What is it about them that the world has chosen to reward in a manner such as this? What did they need to learn in order to secure their sumptuous perches on top these hills? And most of all, because I am a teacher, I wonder what kinds of lives they desire for their children.

Past clusters of apricot blossoms that brave the chill of almost-spring, down a hill into a grove of towering fir trees, there the school is nestled. The hills have stolen the breath from the car by the time I reach it. As I step out, the trees protect me from the February breeze until I reach the room.

The room invites me in. It is a large, extended room drawn at the waist: it was once two single rooms that have come together to talk. Surely I could spend a whole childhood here. A wealth of learning materials engulfs me, each piece beckoning me to pick it up. The patchwork rug that hides the floor is soft and fluffy and warm. Some desks have gathered together for serious business. Chairs converse across semicircular tables. At the bookshelf, dozens and dozens of books slouch around, barely in rows, leaning on each others shoulders. Children's drawings line the walls. What are those masses of shiny objects growing from the ceiling like silver stalactites in the secret corners of the room? I focus in on thousands of tiny . . . beer can pull-tabs . . . crunched together, straining to pull the roof in. A massive wooden beehive called The Honeycomb, with geodesic cubicles in which to hide yourself. A towering ten-foot dinosaur made of wire and papier-mâché, splotched with paint. . . blue and red colors crawling up its body. The monster is smiling helplessly—is he not?—because a covey of tiny people have just been tickling him with their paintbrushes.

In another corner, there are several plants growing in small cups. An incubator with eggs. Over there a phonograph and some records. A map on the chalkboard locates the hills I just drove through—the ones presided over by those houses. Next to the map there are frozen smiles on faces captured within tiny squares of paper. Strings connect the smiles with places on the map. This smile lives *there;* that one *here.* But all of the smiles, I have come to learn, live inside this room.

Mostly in this room there are letters and words. Lined up on the walls: Aa Bb Cc Dd Ee Ff. In combinations which have meaning—at least for me: leave, would, said. Blue next to a dab of blue paint. The words appear on the faces of the books and gather together in great multitudes on their insides. On the map. On the material that covers the couch. Soon in my eyes, even when I shut them. And later they pop out of the smiles of the children and hang in the air. Caressing each other in a low murmur, the omnipresent words pervade the room.

Soon I am not alone. The other children are pouring through the door, infusing the room with life, brimming with energy hankering for release. Mostly fair-skinned, light-haired, blue-eyed, and all fresh and ebullient, these are yesterday's Gerber babies. Lots of Erics and Chrises and Heathers and Lisas. Each seems to be drawn to his own corner of the room, his energy pulling him toward a special task. One moves to the bookshelf and snatches up a book. Several take themselves to the math table. Three crawl in the Honeycomb. One tickles the dinosaur with a paint brush. Others string pull-tabs or watch a film.

Several are my special friends. We had become friends on my previous visits to the school. One day I decided that I would become one of them. So I shrank a little in my mind and revisited a world I had left so long ago. I became both-them-and-me, gazing upward at life once more, but from above. A very wondrous process: a grownup seeing through the eyes of children. So it's just two teachers (Mrs. Abramson and Miss Tomlen), and two aides (Miss Carlson and Miss Rogers), me and Eric and Eric and Eric, and Chris and Chris and Chirs, Heather and . . . well, forty-three first- and second-graders in all.

Together we're a town within a room, a real community. Almost a family, I'd say. We scurry about and form amorphous groups that dissolve agains as if by secret signal. Sometimes we bask in the solitude of the Honeycomb, but mainly we clump together in ever-changing twos and threes. And we're always helping each other with our work. Like this one day that Lisa, Bobby, Susan, and I were stringing pull-tabs. Lisa's idea—Lisa and ideas hang around together—was to divvy up the work to get it over faster. "Like when they make cars," she said. "Susan can pick the good tabs out of the box. Bobby can take the tin off the circles. Tom can count and separate them into tens. And I can string them up."

And so we did. We didn't learn much about counting like we'd supposed to. (We all knew how to count to 100, anyway.) But we sure did learn a lot from Lisa, and I learned a lot *about* her too.

We help each other out a lot; the teachers like us to. They don't teach us to compete; so we don't put our arms about our work and guard it with our selves. Not inside *this* classroom. We do not measure our efforts against each other's. You know that from our open gestures and the easy way in which we share our knowledge. The air is perfumed with collaboration. You see no petty bickering. A friend of mine sits reading, and Todd approaches with a hopeful face.

"Eric, wanna help me with my math facts?"

"Sure," comes the quick reply. And off they scramble to an empty corner.

But now I guess it's time to tell you of a sheet of paper that each of us keeps faithfully by his side as we move about the day. It's called a contract, and it is implanted in our lives by the teachers when the day is still an infant. It's our constant companion to the very end. This is how it works: When finished with an activity, we give the contract to a teacher or an aide, who scratches her initials onto the paper. We have to finish six "core" activities that Mrs. Abramson once called "obligatory," and some other things that don't seem to be as important. "Fun things," Mrs. Abramson has called them. Sometimes we can swap three or four of the "fun" activities for a certain "core" activity.

The teachers in this classroom are our friends. I have watched Miss Tomlen a lot and she is always a blur of movement helping everyone to learn. She is a member of our community, she is. A bit like a mother as she comforts and cajoles and watches us as we grow. So you see, I can't help think it a little strange that in a classroom so thick with cooperation and trust that we must attach ourselves to a sort of legal document that certifies our work. That contract, it becomes a part of you. Lose sight of it, and there's an itch in the back of your mind that's hard to scratch until you find it once again.

Most of my friends, I have to say, disagree with me; they assure me that I'll get used to it. Maybe so, but they've never been inside a classroom where you can walk about without a paper stuck in your hand. And if the teacher is your friend, why should she act like a lawyer? Contracts. I don't know. Shouldn't you only need them when you do things with people you don't know so well? Like someone, say, who's going to build your house?

What do we do all day? Well, lots of things, but mainly reading and math. They're very *important*, sitting at the tip-top of our contracts. Why else would the smiles of our teachers become so broad when we have finished them? You can tell it from the omnipresence of the words and numbers that decorate the room. and because when you get to see the teacher, it's almost always to learn reading and math.

Especially the reading. I know the other kids sense its importance because they've told me so many times. Todd told me once, "Well, you can get the other things excused. Like the math. You can do 'four-for-one' (exchange four 'fun' activities for one 'core' activity). But you always have to do the reading assignment."

Reading. It's *basic*, isn't it?

We read every day from programmed texts that a Mr. Sullivan named after himself. We read a line and guess the answer. Then we check to see *what* (not *whether*) the answer's right. I think that knowing that we got it right is supposed to replace Mrs. Abramson's friendly little pat on top your head. My friends and I agree that Mr. Sullivan does not deserve a pat on top his head. He doesn't have the answers that he thinks he has. And yet we faithfully read his books.

Why do we do it, when other sorts of kids might guide their minds to less rigid places? I think we do it because we can't *imagine* that we might *not* do it. We really *need* the teacher's signature on our contract and especially the smile that tags along. Besides, all our friends do it. And their parents read a lot. My friends themselves have told me so. But I would have guessed that anyway. I bet it's very *basic* to their kind of life.

Mr. Sullivan didn't write the books upon the shelf, so they aren't all chopped up. If you know how, and if you let yourself, you can get a very different kind of reward for reading them. A reward from inside the books and inside yourself.

My friend Scott reads a lot of these books. Maybe this would be a good time to introduce you to him. I got to know him when we were holding elections for class officers. Scott knew that I was a true-blue member of the classroom community because Lisa, the classroom's Registrar of Voters, had certified me as such. So right after the assembly at which he was nominated, Scott plopped down at my side and slipped one tiny but sincere hand upon my shoulder.

"Are you gonna vote, Tom?" Scott gets right to the point.

"Hmmm," I said, quickly sensing the question I should ask. "Whom do you think I should vote for?"

"Well," he replied in a sixth-grade tone of voice. "You *could* vote for me."

"O.K. I will," I promised, feeling vaguely like a tool.

By the way, he won the election. I guess he deserved to, because Scott manages his own affairs very, very efficiently. For example, let's get back to those books. One of the very first times I visited the room, when I still appeared to be a "big person" (as the teachers call themselves), Scott asked me to listen to him read. As we sank into the wordy sofa, I noticed that he had already begun. He was skimming across the surface of each word, licking the sentences but not tasting. Soon he had strip-mined the paragraphs of their superficial meaning so rapidly that I wondered how much he really understood. I asked a question about the content of the story, and his answer was so pointed that it stuck me. He had devoured half a book (even if it was a very short one with lots of pictures) and digested it with amazing speed and never once paused to savor it.

Now the clock was urging me to leave, but I was trying not to hear it. For the story had aroused my second-grade curiosity, and I truly wanted the reward of continuing to read it. The clock, however, won, as it is wont to do.

"Scott," I said, "I have to leave."

"Well, will you sign me up?" His outstretched hand thrust the contract forward, as his eyebrows nearly touched the sky.

"But you haven't finished reading the book, Scott."

"Or sure, I've read this book before."

I wasn't reassured, but in one bewildered instant I officially certified his accomplishment for all the townsfolk to see.

Already he had darted to the teacher's side to announce his victory. "Miss Rogers, I've done fourteen things today."

"You did, Scott? Well that's really great!"

Now I think it is truly great that Scott has learned to read and write (and maybe charm his older friends with one disarming smile). But at least *one* of those fourteen things wasn't great, as I'm sure you will agree. Thirteen would have been greater. Even *one* thing—don't you think?—if it really sparkles, can be greater than fourteen that have no luster. For example:

On some enchanted mornings the contracts take a nap and a different kind of feeling fills the air. On one of these mornings Miss Rogers introduced us to her violin. She began to play it as we sat transfixed, floating from the room through our ears. We drifted to a magic land where sounds change into colors, and the colors are fleecy soft. The words still hung around, but now they smelled much sweeter; they were nudged between the songs sung by her magic wand as Miss Rogers taught us how to listen. We listened with our noses, eyes, and ears, and we let them take our minds along.

Then another day Miss Carlson took us to Pakistan, as several of us stirred a dash of imagination into some food. We sprinkled exotic flavors into strange concoctions that so often live a world away. Lord, how we felt when the others inhaled the brown and yellow flavors that we had married together!

But these excursions to an outside world happen all too seldom. For example, we cannot launch ourselves off the art table, for no one teaches us how to see what we paint, like Miss Rogers taught us how to hear her violin. So each of our paintings imitates all the others. The lines to other worlds are never crossed, as far as I can tell.

So usually we remain within the room beside our contracts. Sometimes we sneak out through the books upon the shelf, but usually we race over them, like Scott, using them to erase a portion of our obligations.

We are mainly learning how to read, I tell you . . . and learning how to count. Those words are our tools. When we use them we learn to think a certain way. We line them up, and our world lines up with them. The words are tools for straightening out our world so we can use our number-tools to measure it. With words and numbers we can hammer it and nail it, structure it in accordance with our fond desires. Oh, the kingdom and the power of our words and numbers!

What about the glory of sounds and shapes and colors? Is it not also important for us to learn how they can play upon each other? How we can rearrange them in our dreams? When we imagine other worlds of sounds and shapes and colors, could it not help us to see our own world in a different way? Imagination might even be another tool for conquering the world at hand. (If you really *have* to look at it that way.)

Not so much for the Scotts of the world, perhaps. They'll probably always read because they have to. Maybe they don't really need to dream. They'll always master those important skills. But what about for others who haven't sensed the import of a word-written-down? The "underprivileged" they're called, whose parents never slip a book inside their Christmas stocking. Those who are introduced to reading only very late in life (perhaps by Mr. Sullivan), how will they read about a world they cannot see or smell or hear?

And even you, Scott. How would you feel if you could know that words in books can be savored like spices in a curry? Can hum like the strings of a violin. Can fly you to worlds you've never even dreamed of. That you could hear their purrs and scowls and feel their waves of meaning as they splashed upon your mind. Then wouldn't it be basic and important to you?

As fact would have it, Lisa is the daughter of a psychiatrist. In fiction—sometimes much more truthful—her father might be a business manager or perhaps an engineer. Scott is the son of a lawyer, and that's the *truth*. Scott has been that for over seven years and is likely to remain so.

Scott and Lisa and all my friends are sailing to their houses now, there to act out their lives as sons and daughters, I am sure. And I am thirty-one years old again as I instruct my car to take me to my other home. But on my way I still hear the words of babes as they echo through these hills. I glance again at those houses and now I think I understand their smugness. For I have befriended their future, and know that they can well afford their airs of nonchalance. Their well-groomed heirs are returning in a little yellow school bus. They carry with them their well-honed skills and each a piece of the warmth in which they passed the day. (There are much, much worse ways to live a life in school!)

But I sigh softly to myself, for I still don't know if anyone within these houses ever sees these fluffy hills, with their fur now changing to a tawny brown. Who catches the scent of eucalyptus trees as it mingles with the sunlight? Or who can understand those distant lives—in much, much darker places—lives crunched upon each other like jagged, rusty tin cans in a garbage heap? Who feels the excitement that throbs inside majestic works of art? For whom are books the tunnels to imaginary worlds that never were before and yet have always been?

As I whiz on my way, I notice that many of the apricot blossoms have fallen now, lying shriveled on the road. Just before they are pressed beneath the insistent wheels of my automobile machine, in a flash I wonder if my good pals Scott and Lisa will forever gaze past them—straight ahead. Or will they learn to see their colors?

That would be really great.

A CONFLICT OF INTERESTS: AN EDUCATIONAL CRITICISM OF MR. WILLIAMS'S FOURTH GRADE[*]

Gail McCutcheon

Introduction

Mr. William's fourth-grade room is a room of contrasts. Students' richly colored crayon designs and poetry are pinned up on a bulletin board, proclaiming their creative individuality by their differences in topic, form, and sophistication. From atop a cabinet, a blue parakeet scrutinizes the class, chirpingly lecturing the twenty-six students from time to time. Dried weeds, plants, ship models, and ceramics line the shelves in front of windows that serve no apparent instrumental function.

Yet below these decorative, expressive articles sit an SRA reading kit, a row of spelling and phonics workbooks, several sets of mathematics texts and workbooks, and a pile of math contracts. Somehow, they seem out of place among the expressive articles.

The contrast between materials bears silent testimony to the temporary compromise Mr. Williams has reached between teaching according to his beliefs and teaching according to parents' desires, two major sources of influence on his curriculum. The compromise over this conflict of interests is only temporary, though, for Mr. Williams knows he will have to reach another solution next year for his own peace of mind.

Children in Mr. William's room engage in both independent activities and intellectual discussions held in a large-group setting. Independent activities range along a continuum between those Mr. Williams assigns and plans to a great extent and those over which each child has greater control. In the first section of this study, we will examine the independent activities and then we will turn to the class's intellectual discussions, which occur in groups. Along the way, we will also

[*] An earlier version of this study appeared as Chapter IV in my dissertation, *The Disclosure of Classroom Life* (unpublished doctoral dissertation, Stanford University, 1976). Appreciation is extended to several who commented on that chapter, including Elliot Eisner, Bernard Siegel, Lawrence Thomas, and Elizabeth Vallance, and also to "Mr. Williams," who graciously permitted six weeks of my observations and questions.

consider the relative effects of Mr. Williams's beliefs and parents' desires on the curriculum of this classroom.

Independent Activities

CHILD CONTROLLED ACTIVITIES

When children have a great deal of control over their activities in Mr. Williams's room, the control is generally over the content of those activities. Children are free to choose within a broad range of topics—an incident from the exploration of California, a feeling, a science subject. But all children are to express themselves in the same way—through pictures, a poem, a report or whatever; the content, not the form, is up to individual choice. All projects are due on the same date, although children spend varying amounts of time working on them.

For example, one day in a social studies lesson, each child portrays a different scene from the early exploration of California through large, colorful chalk drawings. Mr. Williams's comments while they work call attention to his interest in their concern with technique, style, and expressive qualities as well as the picture's content and reporting ability. Later, the children cooperatively arrange the pictures chronologically. Their deliberations demonstrate that they know a lot about this history, and the activity provides an opportunity for them to apply their knowledge.

On another day students write poetry. First, Mr. Williams reads poetry about personal feelings; then he asks students to try to think of a personal feeling to convey. "Try to make everything in the poem lead up to that feeling," he says. Students work intensely, occasionally reading a line to a neighbor softly or to Mr. Williams for help or just to hear it out loud.

I WISH / *by Andrea*

I wish my mom would let me
do more things like
        go more places
        cook more things
        and be more Independent
for the first time yesterday I got to cook—
I made soup.

Somehow we know what kind of soup Andrea got to cook.

WHEN I FEEL GOOD / *by Jim*

I wish I could take a plane
and parachute onto a beach
with sandstone hills and slopes,
or go off to a nice little brook who
whispers softly to my wading feet
and up my body on a hot day,
or climb a mountain called Mozeltop
and daydream a funny dream.
but all I can do is fly a paper
airplane and imagine
or take a bath and slosh
or climb my tree. I

can scale a castle, swim a
channel or climb the Empire
State Building.
    All you need is
imagination.

The students work with a quiet intensity, and while they work Mr. Williams visits among them with an occasional question or statement, a section pointed to, or a suggestion. Mr. Williams does not comment on the feeling children chose to communicate, but occasionally he suggests making it more vivid by recounting specific instances or using more graphic words. The content, rhythm, and rhyme scheme (or lack thereof) are designed by each student.

In this lesson, Mr. Williams reveals one of his own interests, that of writing poetry. Mr. Williams is popular among his students, who like to play soccer with him at recess. His enthusiasm about poetry along with his popularity may explain the intensity with which these children write.

His interest in language arts is also revealed in a science lesson. On another day, children begin to plan and write reports. Twenty-six children are using the ordinary, middling, standard commodities found in every fourth-grade classroom across the country—books, papers, crayons, scissors, pencils, pictures, and curiosity. But these children seem excited; a quiet, busy hum of purposeful self-direction permeates the classroom as they leaf through books and pause a while to read, jot down questions on 4 × 6 note cards, draw a diagram, discuss a difficulty with Mr. Williams or each other, and share information with a "Wow, look at this!" or "Oh, neato!" to a friend. Although they are using everyday equipment and are doing things children do every day in classrooms, their excitement and involvement are unmistakable.

Earlier in the lesson, Mr. Williams asked each to choose a science topic from a comprehensive list. Although he was not concerned when several chose the same topic, it did matter whether students were interested in the topic and whether they could obtain relevant information. After listing their questions about the topic, they were to group the questions into related categories of their own design to facilitate the structuring of their reports.

Teachers who allow children to pose their own questions often find that children's questions are more interesting than the questions we adults answer for them when we write their textbooks or teach their classes. James is not unique in this classroom in the quality of his questions as he wonders about clouds:

How do they float?
How do they get up ther?
What are they made out of?
How can planes fly throw them whith out making howls?
How does rain get to them?
How do they let out the rain?
Are the clouds the fog?
Do all coulds maake it around the world?
Can ther be two clouds be the same shape? [sic]

Obviously, James's work is cut out for him if he plans to answer these questions, and he is busy looking at books, drawing pictures, and noting facts. Mr. Williams circulates, helping children use the index to locate their topics in various books, discussing difficulties with them, and accepting their questions rather than correcting spelling or grammar, although he occasionally asks children to generate more questions. He treats the questions seriously.

Children in a classroom undoubtedly learn many different things from the same activity. In this case, since the topic of the activity varies among children, outcomes related to information about science will vary among them. James will learn about clouds, Sarah about salmon, Claire and Joey about sharks.

Outcomes related to the medium of expression (in this case, writing reports) may also vary. James struggled with topic sentences and spelling, Sarah with punctuation, and Joey with transitions among paragraphs. In this lesson, then, children were able to learn about an interest of their own, but they also were able to develop skills in writing reports. They had the opportunity to improve their reporting skills in different ways, without the need for a test diagnosing a weakness and the teacher prescribing exercises to treat those weaknesses. That is, in many classrooms, diagnostic tests are administered to ascertain what particular individuals need to learn in language arts, then dittoes or worksheets are provided to remediate the problems uncovered by the test. But in this classroom, the problems became evident while children worked; the problems emerged in context and were worked on in context. Mr. Williams circulated to help spot the difficulties and give aid where necessary. A diagnostic test was not given, yet children worked on particular skills they needed to develop in the process of writing the report.

Since most of these children will go to college, skills in writing reports and the inclination to wonder about their own interests are important. More importantly, though, for the present, this experience may empower children with knowledge and tools for answering their own questions. Activities like this may encourage them to be active seekers of information about their own interests rather than passive recipients of what someone else deems important.

Mr. Williams facilitates this type of inquiry in several ways. Several times a day, he himself wonders out loud and plays with ideas inventively, acting as a model. In a reading lesson, he says,

"For a penny you can buy a whole lot of alum but not so many jujubes." Why does Oswald say *this?* Maybe he just likes jujubes—alum isn't nearly as good— its really bitter. So he's saying, maybe, that the *amount* isn't always what's important.

Did you ever think of *your* house as a jewel? I suppose you could. Jewels are precious, and some people think their homes are, too.

Wondering aloud, he allows children to develop on his stream of consciousness— his questions and thoughts.

In addition to modeling, he also facilitates this sort of independent activity by circulating to spot difficulties and by being available for consultation. For the most part, he circulates at the beginning of a work period. As the year progresses, he is less available, for he hopes to foster a sense of independence. He looks over students' shoulders, occasionally remarking about the work, asking for a clarification, teaching a necessary bit of information or skill to a student, or helping like a capable librarian aids one to find a reference. He may occasionally remind certain students to get to work—"Jack, get down to it!"—in no-nonsense, unangry terms. More often, Mr. Williams is at the back table doing some of his own work: writing math contracts, making a bulletin board, or assembling materials for the next lesson. Students do not perceive him as inaccessible, for they approach and ask him questions. He often replies by quietly reassuring the students of their competence in finding answers or recalling particularly expedient ways to approach the problem.

Joey: Is this book about sharks' habitats?
Mr. Williams: You have to really look in a book to see if it has what you need. Remember to look in the table of contents and index, not just at its cover.

By not circulating throughout a work period and telling students what to do, but being available for help, Mrs. Williams may be building the sense of independence he hopes to foster. If he continually directed students, they would not have an opportunity to practice independence. If he goes around to help all period, he believes students who know an answer may rely on him, just because he happens to be close at hand. So he maintains a little distance, hoping children will try to think about an answer themselves first.

Another way in which Mr. Williams facilitates this type of independent activity in addition to modeling an inquiry approach and consulting when needed is to provide a variety of activities for children. All are assigned, but the assignments appear to be within the capabilities of the youngsters in the classroom. And the modes of expression differ, which may permit children who have different abilities to excel at different times; the limelight is shared. In many classrooms, a verbal mode of expression predominates to the exclusion of all others. Mr. Williams, though, arranges activities in various modes. James's cloud report may be very good, but Andrea's soup poem and Holly's pastel drawing may also be excellent. Their reports may not be as well done as James's, though. Arranging for different modes of expression not only permits a wider range of children to excel, but it also guarantees that all children will at least be exposed to varied modes of expression—verbal and pictorial, linear and metaphorical, partist and holist, synthetic and analytic.

In these independent activities, then, in which children have a role in planning the content, structure and occasionally the form of their work, they seem highly motivated, persevering in their tasks, and involved in them. Mr. Williams's role is one of modeling, consulting, and arranging the environment and activities. These activities are most likely to occur in language arts, social studies, and science.

TEACHER-CONTROLLED ACTIVITIES
Other independent activities are less structured by the children and are more formally assigned by Mr. Williams. In these lessons, children work with the SRA reading kit and do math problems or workbooks, assigned through contracts as well as en masse. These activities are assigned and structured for the most part by the teacher or a publisher. That is, a child working on one of these lessons cannot select the content, format, or media in which to work; they are pre-ordained by the publisher of the materials being used and were assigned by Mr. Williams. So in math, for instance, everyone does a common set of problems in the book, and some students also work on contracts. Group lessons focus on a common problem set—lines and rays, addition with regrouping, diameter and radius, or whatever—and on correcting yesterday's problems by having students put answers to different problems on the board. This group lesson ensures the exposure of all students to the same information, which concerns Mr. Williams. He is afraid that if all students work only in contracts, the group's knowledge is likely to be fragmented and highly varied. Additionally, Mr. Williams realizes he cannot deal with concepts on an individual basis because of time constraints. And he believes concepts cannot be gleaned from a book by many individuals. He hopes that presenting the same information to all will provide everyone with a common base of mathematics knowledge, conveyed in an unpressured way by students checking their own work. Additionally, the lesson provides a group task. When a great deal of work in a classroom is individualized, it may produce a

sense of loneliness, of disunity, a lack of group feeling. But in this classroom, each student is not always at a desk working on different material as alone as if separated by glass boxes, and the sense of isolation does not seem to be present. During math, many children help each other discover answers to problems but do not give answers to one another outright. Teacherlike Lauren helps Cathy learn how many times longer the diameter of a circle is than its radius by having her trace a radius and a diameter, then compare the two to see how many radii are needed to equal a diameter. Learning is a shared task for these two. Other children work alone, finishing the assigned group work quickly, then they work on math contracts.

Writing math contracts is a time-consuming task for Mr. Williams, for to a limited extent he attempts to provide materials more suited to or interesting for particular students instead of merely pacing all through the same book at different rates. He does this by consulting the index of a few math books and enrichment workbooks as he writes contracts and frequently catches up on a contract or two while the children are doing their math. But one book forms the basis for the math curriculum. This results from the citywide adoption of a series of math tests teachers are obliged to administer throughout the year; the tests were constructed to accompany one particular mathematics text, so Mr. Williams is constrained to use that text.

Mr. Williams does not believe writing math contracts is very helpful, for it does not provide an involving enough sort of activity, in his view. He does it to assuage parents who are interested in individualization and have pressured him into the contract system. While parents cannot defend their faith in individualization, Mr. Williams has yielded to their pressure because he knows of several instances in which a few vocal parents have gotten teachers fired or transferred or have made teaching so unbearable that the teacher resigned.

Some of Mr. Williams's activities are also assigned by contract. Children work in the inevitable SRA kit and in reading workbooks. But they also read works of children's literature, as we shall see in a later section of this study.

When we examine these different sorts of independent activities, we can deduce that Mr. Williams considers activities according to several criteria before choosing them. Until these criteria were presented to him, he seemed unaware of them, but he recognized that he was indeed utilizing them in his planning. These criteria are not ranked in any order, for they play different parts in different lessons he provides. One of these criteria is providing for the varied interests and abilities of children in his room. He permits their interests to be part of the curriculum as a vehicle for learning more about the interest, for learning how to inquire about it, and for learning how to use a particular mode of expression. In a way, a second criterion opposes the first. This is his concern for the class to have a common body of knowledge rather than everyone having different skills and knowledge. While he takes into account individuals' needs and interests, Mr. Williams does not want to increase the differences too greatly, for he recognizes this would make teaching more difficult. Many of these activities done in common revolve around Mr. Williams's own interests. They also revolve around his belief that certain skills are needed by all children, such as research and communication skills. A third criterion is whether Mr. Williams knows about a topic well enough to lead it or teach it. In some cases, such as writing reports, it is not necessary for him to know all of the content of various reports, but merely how to teach children to write. In other cases, he needs to know more about the content to lead a lesson. A fourth criterion is that of providing assignments necessitating the use of varied modes of expression so more children can excel at different times. His concern for fostering independence is also apparent in planning activities and forms a fifth criterion. Others are (6) appeasing the parents, (7) covering the traditional subject matter areas (science, social studies, art, music, physical education, language arts, and math) at some time during each month, and (8) conforming to local guidelines established by testing practices. Mr. Williams believes he must cover each subject matter at some time so he will "have something to put down on the report card," although he is not concerned if he spends two weeks on a science project early in the month, excluding several other subjects, later spending two weeks with social studies. Math and language arts have times reserved for them every day, though. As stated earlier, the city testing program dictates certain skills in mathematics to be covered, and Mr. Williams uses a series that accompanies the city-adopted test. In this case, it can be seen that both the structure of the report card and the testing practices of a school system can directly influence the curriculum of a classroom.

These eight criteria are not utilized in each of Mr. Williams's curriculum decisions, for some contradict each other (such as the first and second). While he plans series of activities for different subjects, Mr. Williams appears to do little long-range planning other than that necessitated by film and book ordering schedules. His planning is primarily done, then, on a short-range basis, and the selection of activities involves several criteria that are applied with different emphases according to the activity being considered.

In providing this differentiated student activity, Mr. Williams seems to emphasize independence, originality, self-direction, and competence in dealing with various media. Students' inventive use of language is evidenced in their poems; their willingness to ask difficult but original questions is apparent in their science reports. Additionally, student interest in learning does not appear to have been stifled. After doing assigned work, they engage in many activities. They draw the tree outside, write poetry, read magazines, paperbacks, or each other's poetry. During the activity itself, most seem excited and involved. If Mr. Williams goes to the school kitchen to bring back a cup of tea or to the office about one of the many persistent interruptions, students continue with their activities. He does not appear to be perceived as a watchdog, an enforcer who ensures that work gets done; children seem self-directed and interested in the work or they believe it is important enough to do it even if he is not in the room. These students appear to be achieving one of Mr. Williams's major goals for them—independence and self-direction when working.

A friendly, busy hum generally pervades the room during these work sessions. Friends sit together, coloring, writing, chatting quietly, speculating, helping one another, or criticizing each other's work.

But students are differentially involved in these two types of experiences—teacher-fashioned and partially student-fashioned ones. That is, during certain experiences most students appear to be deeply involved, but in others the involvement seems more superficial. When students write poetry or science reports or make pictures portraying an aspect of California exploration, they are deeply involved. Work-noise buzzes through the room, students write, read, or draw intensely; conversations generally concern the work, and most behavior is related to the activity. Little could draw them away from their work, it seems. But during time for SRA kit or math work, students are more likely to talk about other things—last night's unexpected rain or an exciting National Geographic special about the great apes. Bill opens his math book to the page indicated on the contract. "Ooh! Lookit all of that!" Walking across the room, he says, "I'm gonna get a drink," very near Mr. Williams, perhaps hoping to lure Mr. Williams into telling him to get busy and remove the responsibility for getting to work from himself. But Mr. Williams does not go for the bait or does not hear Bill. Bill stands, pokes his loose tooth, then ambles into the coatroom before returning to his desk. James bores holes through the dirt on his desktop with an eraser that has become a drill. Many types of behavior that is not task-oriented are in evidence.

Several differences between these sorts of activities may account for the varying student attention. Students report they prefer doing science reports, poetry, and California history pictures over SRA kit and math at a ratio exceeding four to one (twenty-one students to five). Most say the former activities are more interesting, and they may prefer them for several reasons. I suspect a major difference between the two regards the setting of the task. The materials themselves extensively structure the content and dictate the approach to the task in SRA kits and math books, so they may connect less with children's personal interests and desires than the other activities. However, the content of the science report, poetry, and California history pictures were determined substantially by students. Mr. Williams set a general task, but children filled in particulars themselves, permitting them to choose personally interesting topics, and perhaps as a result they are more willing to devote sustained, intense attention to them.

Another reason for their preference may pertain to the apparent relative routinization of the activities. Mr. Williams emphasizes certain activities such as work in spelling, SRA kit, and math by providing time for them every day. Other activities (poetry writing, science reports, and social studies pictures) are engaged in less frequently and may seem less routine, more novel and unique, and may capture students' attention as a result.

Additionally, they may perceive Mr. Williams's preferences. He enjoys poetry writing, science, and social studies, but he inserts work in spelling, the SRA kit, and math contracts into the day because of obligations—obligations to parents, to the report card, and to the testing program. In all likelihood, he is more enthusiastic about his own interests and less so about the obligations; in fact, those obligations may make him resent them or regard those subjects as drudgery—tasks to complete, but no more.

Oddly mixed, hidden messages may be transmitted to children about these independent activities. On one hand, certain activities—SRA kit, math, and spelling—are provided every day and must be finished before other activities can be pursued, so they must be important. But on the other hand, Mr. Williams does not seem particularly interested in them—he just puts page numbers on the board or on contracts and doesn't discuss them much; they seem very routine.

Social studies, art, music, science, and poetry writing are not assured a daily place, so they may be perceived as less important. Yet Mr. Williams seems enthusiastic about them. He holds discussions about them, elaborating on ideas, provides challenging activities related to them, and spends a lot of time talking about them. So they must be important. Children, in fact, may believe they are more valuable than the daily activities for reasons already cited. It there any evidence of this?

Since all finish their daily assignments, everyone has the opportunity for both types of experience. But the SRA kit and math contracts are not engaged in as fervently, intensively, or as wholly as the other activities. In my experience, they were never selected as activities when children finished assignments or projects. Complaints were voiced about math and SRA kit work, but not many were raised about science reports, poetry writing and social studies. About the SRA kit and math, children said.

Do I hafta do all *this*?
Oh, no, this is like the last page!
These [SRA] stories are dumb.

These [SRA] answers are too obvious. Really!
Anyone could do them.

James tried to have his math contract scaled down.

On balance, Mr. Williams might reconsider the emphasis placed on math contracts and SRA materials, for they do not connect as greatly with children's interests, are not worked on as earnestly, and may not be as instrumental for achieving his goals of creativity, independence, and information seeking as other activities he provides that are more intensively attended to and seem to be more relevant and interesting to these children. To be sure, if he changed his plans this year, he would have to contend with parents and with the testing program. Perhaps it is easier for him to live with the compromise of including these less interesting activities in his program. These activities may also serve as a break from intensity. Not everything can be engaged in with equal passion; perhaps these activities serve as a sort of rest period for all involved.

Intellectual Discussions

The other major activity in Mr. Williams's classroom consists of intellectual discussions among students and teacher held at least once a day. These are most likely to occur when Mr. Williams reads the class a story, when a reading group discusses a chapter or book, when students share current events or their recent experiences and ideas, or in a science or social studies lesson. For example, Mr. Williams reads a story to children in which a character takes a patent medicine.

Mr. Williams: What is a "patent medicine?"
Lauren: It's like . . . it's a public medicine.
Mr. Williams: I'm not sure I understand. Someone else?
Kevin: It's a drug sold without subscriptions in a drug store.
Jim: Like aspirins, that Contac stuff, cold syrup, Phillips Milk of Magnesia, rash ointment, or vitamins.
Mr. Williams: I don't know. Is a vitamin a medicine?
Aaron: Well, vitamins keep you healthy and medicine does.
Sarah: Medicines cure sickness; vitamins just keep you healthy, so it isn't a medicine.
Jim: It would be a medicine to make sure you don't get a cold.
Mr. Williams: If you take vitamins, does that mean you won't get a cold?
Jim: You'll be more resistant.
Mr. Williams: Ah! More resistant!

As evidenced by the discussion, interchanges do not always return to the teacher and Mr. Williams raises issues out of students' contributions, lending to it the quality of a discussion instead of a predetermined list of questions to answer. His responses to students may provide a model of an adult who listens to conversations. Students also listen and raise questions out of the content of a lesson. According to Mr. Williams, many of the best discussions—the most penetrating, lively, and involved ones—arise on the spur of the moment as he realizes a particular idea needs to be addressed or a student raises a question. This indicates his lessons can never be totally preplanned and exemplifies the willingness of many teachers to set aside a planned agenda in favor of something that seems more valuable at the time. When teachers are held to schedules or lesson plans or rigidly and precisely preplan their activities, this flexible, responsive teaching is unlikely to occur, teaching that responds to a situation, event, topic, or question arising in the course of the day. Mr. Williams reports that he does not plan specific questions or particular information to provide, although he has a few key questions in case they need help in starting the discussion. He also knows several ideas he wants to help the group develop, but most of the questions flow out of the discussion he has with the students, he says.

Another quality of these discussions is a lack of closure on some issues, perhaps permitting children to continue to consider them. Mr. Williams wonders aloud during a discussion about a book the students are reading:

Mr. Williams: I wonder why the ocean never fills up if all these rivers keep pouring into it.

Jim: The ocean goes on and on—it never fills up. It's very big.

Sue: People take water out of it to drink, in reservoirs.

Mr. Williams (surprised): To drink?

Jack: It evaporates and lotsa people use it to drink.

Mr. Williams: Water from the ocean?

Jack (flustered, correcting himself): Oh, no. It's salty. But it evaporates and then it rains.

In this discussion, Mr. Williams does not fully resolve the question by answering it precisely, making it possible for children to continue to wonder about it. Additionally, he does not restate Jack's final point, perhaps forcing children to listen to one another if they are to enter the discussion rather than only to him. Some children may wonder about the question Mr. Williams raised the next time they go to the ocean; others may completely forget about it. Leaving some questions unresolved may also demonstrate that not every time one wonders about something should one expect to find an answer; some questions need extensive thought, others require more facts, and one may move on to consider another question. Children may learn to tolerate ambiguity, indefiniteness, and uncertainty as a result of being exposed to this type of experience. It may also reveal to children the fun of wondering, imagining, and asking for its own sake instead of merely wondering for the instrumental purpose of obtaining a definite answer. But it may also model question asking, an important part of inquiry.

In another example of Mr. Williams's intellectual discussion mode, a reading group considers a chapter in Kenneth Grahame's *Wind in the Willows*, while other children read stories they will discuss tomorrow, work in the SRA kit, and choose magazines or paperbacks to read. For an hour the group pays close attention to this chapter, ferreting out its meaning, concentrating on interpretation rather than on how to decode the words.

Mr. Williams reads about winter when "nature is deep in her annual slumber," pointing out nice phrases along the way ("riot in rich masquerade"), providing his own interpretation to the students, and moving his hands to virtually enact particular phrases:

What is happening is in winter everything is bare, the leaves fall, everything is nice and clear, snow comes down, everything is white and all of these things seem kind of exposed and kind of sad [as his hands and he become the tree] because it's like the tree is saying, "Don't look at me now" [his hands move defensively], you know. "Wait until summer comes and I'll have leaves all over me and I'll have shadow and shade [his hands are leaves unfurling], and . . . places to hide and everything will be a lot different."

While he thinks aloud and provides an interpretation at this point, he asks students for theirs elsewhere. "Why do the animals carry plants in their pockets when they go into the wild wood?" he asks. Children conjecture: to get food. Mr. Williams disagrees. Medicinal value? Perhaps, but John, Aaron, and Jim conspire to point out the magic value of certain plants such as garlic worn around the neck to prevent vampires from biting one. They relate stories about Dracula they've read and seen in movies.

Children in third and fourth grade seem particularly curious about the diaphanous boundary between magic and real and possess all sorts of facts about Dracula and black widow spiders, monsters and dinosaurs, Star Trek and the Apollo missions, spell-casting witches and Houdini. Mr. Williams seems aware of this as he fishes for the information needed to interpret the part of the story about plants. He accepts the boys' interpretation regarding plants' ability to cast spells and ward off evil. While none may have been able to interpret this aspect of the story alone, as a group they are able to reach and support an interesting interpretation. Later, he asks:

What do you think the author had in mind when he wrote this scene?
What was the difference between the world Mole lived in and the one Water Rat lived in? Do people live in different worlds?

Reading a phrase, he points out that the author of *Wind in the Willows* makes the river have life, describing it as an animal playing with leaves, chuckling:

Mr. Williams: Did you ever sit by a river?
Jim: It gurgles. Others murmur assent.
Mr. Williams: You can have a conversation with it.

Moving the questions among students skilfully so all have a chance to answer in front of the class, Mr. Williams is not willing to accept just any answer. He may tell a student to reread a section, to find evidence, to clarify the meaning of what was said, to amplify an interpretation, or to rethink a position. And he may sum up previous explanations before asking for more plausible alternatives. While this could conceivably deflate some children and prevent them from being able to respond to another question, in Mr. Williams's class, children do not seem to be particularly bruised by making mistakes in front of their peers and being told their answers are wrong. Their hands go back up, they answer again. It is a supportive group, they do not ridicule one another's mistakes, and Mr. Williams generally lets students know their answers are wrong in a matter-of-fact tone, not accusingly or sending messages that the child is stupid. Another group reads a story and is trying to interpret a passage.

Mr. Williams: Why did Oswald say that his legs are younger than Grandpa's?
Holly: Because he's younger than Grandpa?
Mr. Williams: I think there's more to it than that.

He communicates clearly, but without recrimination that the answer is incomplete. There are, after all, right and wrong answers, complete and incomplete ones, central and peripheral contributions to discussions. It seems more honest and responsible to let children know their answers are wrong in a supportive setting than to go along willy-nilly and accept any and all answers. These children may have more poise speaking before a group, have better conversation skills, and be able to spot worthwhile, valid contributions to discussions than children in classrooms in which discussions do not occur or are not as skillfully handled. Since we engage in discussions in our personal, working, and student lives, it seems reasonable for a teacher to attempt to improve students' conversation skills.

Through these discussions, children in Mr. Williams's reading groups usually deal with complex stories of children's literature rather than simpler ones contained in basal readers. They try to reconstruct and make sense out of the story and critique it, frequently disagreeing with each other in an effort to understand it. Additionally, they examine the author's use of language and literary devices. After Mr. Williams reads a poem, "The Pheasant," to the class (because he had seen a pheasant on the way to school and liked the poem), they discuss why "shining like a jewel" is particularly appropriate. "Like a hymn from beak to tail," says Mr. Williams. "Wow! That's beautiful!" They listen as he reads.

> The geese flying south
> in a long V shape
> pulling winter.

Discussing the economy of the words, they examine the suitability and contribution of most words and the entire image of the geese pulling winter. They seem excited, eager, and involved as they think about and discuss geese, winter, the economy of words, and the image in the poem.

Reading is caressed; the words, language, and fun of reading are communicated to children. Moreover, Mr. Williams demonstrates that we have to dig the meaning out of stories, not always the easiest thing to do. They practice interpreting, criticizing, and analyzing stories and consider the author's use of literary devices and language. Less attention is paid to decoding skills—phonics or linguistics—as Mr. Williams believes these children already know how to decode words, a belief supported by listening to children read. Even very difficult words (by fourth-grade standards) such as "imperiously," "contemptuous," "insatiable," and "boisterously" are read with ease. Perhaps certain decoding skills are being learned in context rather than separately on worksheets. By providing opportunities for this type of discussion, Mr. Williams appears to desire for children to learn how to deal with the printed work on a relatively sophisticated level for fourth grade, a level at which students demonstrate they are able to function in groups. Lauren admits she does not "usually understand everything before a discussion, but afterward it's a lot better." Perhaps a discussion format is really the only way to learn how to analyze, interpret, and critique such complex stories effectively, particularly at the beginning of the process. The group's strength in interpretation may be greater than an individual's. In many reading programs, a better job may have been done of teaching children *how* to read than of teaching them *to* read. We may be winning the decoding battle but losing the reading war by neglecting to transmit the fun of reading. In this case, though, Mr. Williams believes his children have functional reading skills, so he tries to develop interpretive and critical skills and an appreciation for reading and literature.

Mr. Williams also conveys the feeling that it is okay to talk to a river, to wonder why the ocean doesn't fill up, or to enjoy the beauty of a poem about geese or pheasants for their own sakes, not for any particular goal or for the purpose of answering a particular question. An activity can have intrinsic merit as well as an extrinsic merit; we can engage in an activity because it's joyful or pleasant to do, not only because we can get an answer or a product out of the activity.

Another time in which intellectual discussions occur in Mr. Williams's room is when he introduces science or social studies material such as a lesson about the contents of the galaxy.

Drawing galaxies, stars, planets, and comets on the board as they talk, Mr.

Williams lectures students and converses with them, providing conceptually complicated but clear information about different bodies in the solar system. His hands dance athletically through the air, helping him express his ideas to the children who are perched, draped, and sprawled on the table, chairs, desks, and floor near the board in the front of the room.

Interweaving particular facts, personal attitudes, and general concepts, they discuss the bodies in the solar system and galaxy. Through a visual presentation (the chalk pictures) and a spoken one, they consider the galaxy and solar system. "What is the name of our galaxy?" he asks. "It has a kind of a neat name." After several guesses, one child tells the others: "The Milky Way." And Mr. Williams speculates about the name aloud: "I suppose from a distance it looks kind of whitish and maybe one of the rays looks kind of like a milky way." He draws the galaxy with large, chunky colored chalk on the board—a side view, then a top view. His performance is greeted with "oh wows!" "gees," and "ooos" as children watch and listen with rapt attention, perhaps a little enviously. While he is the main actor, telling them about the movement of the galaxy accompanied by his expressive hands and chunky chalk, and about the galaxy's shape and our position on one "spirally arm," the students seem to be listening. Many can probably relate other information to this talk because of their reports about bodies of the solar system; others are astronomy buffs. They ask him questions, answer his, make sounds of awe at appropriate times, do not impatiently wiggle and squirm or play with nearby objects.

Mr. Williams tells them about one little statistic he knows. He doesn't go in much for statistics, he confesses, but he does know that 109 worlds—earths—would fit across the sun, illustrating its immensity. While it seems doubtful that fourth graders could envision precisely how immense the sun actually is from this fact, they may appreciate its hugeness, as they ooh and wow, and the immensity seems to be what Mr. Williams was trying to convey.

Instead of telling students all of his information first, he asks them for facts they know about the sun, perhaps providing for a break in the one-way flow of information. Several volunteer: "it's super duper hot," "it's our closest star," "it gives us light," "in the middle it's 40,000 degrees," but they disagree about its actual dimensions.

Then Mr. Williams goes on to provide his information about the sun, and students interject questions once in a while. Andrea wants to know how scientists can tell what temperature the sun is. Many teachers would be reluctant to deal with such an obviously difficult question, particularly in front of an outside observer (no matter how good the relationship between the teacher and that observer may be), provided they even know the answer. But Mr. Williams explains simply how astronomers measure the temperature through a special sort of photography and use the light spectrum and special instruments to determine the temperature. He later confides a belief that "teaching is a two-pronged venture. First you have to figure out what to tell the kids. Then you have to communicate it to them on their own level. It's the last one that was the bear about this question Andrea asked," he said.

On other occasions when he does not know the answer, he acknowledges his lack, asks if anyone else knows or asks someone to find the answer, although he may not always remember to follow up by asking the student to share the information.

Ah, there's some disagreement about how hot it really is in the center of the sun. How about some of you experts finding out? [Jim volunteers.]

Reinforcing the notion that everything in space moves in many directions, he discusses the idea that the mass of almost the entire solar system is comprised of the sun. He realizes at this juncture that he must define "mass" meaningfully before students can understand his point. He did not preplan this part of the lesson, but realized this necessity while he was talking, he later confides. The notion of mass is difficult, but he relates it to children through an example.

> If we'd put all of us together, we'd be a mass [giggle], and if we put all the desks and books into a blob, they'd be a mass. If we put all the comets, planets, moons, and sun together all into one blob, the biggest part would be the sun.

He moves on to discuss comets and asks about their composition. Having recently written reports about comets and being astronomy buffs, many students want to answer. Eagerly, they stretch their hands up and say "Oh!" to attract attention in hopes of being called upon, and perhaps indicating their willingness to answer and belief that they have information worth sharing. But it is an orderly, unboisterous thing. Rocks and gases? Gases? Icy particles? Mr. Williams agrees that it's a combination.

Near the sun, comets go faster, but he asks what else happens to a comet near the sun.

Jim: It gets a bigger tail.
Mr. Williams: What's happening? Why does it get a tail? The sun gives off what?
Students: Heat.
Mr. Williams: If you put ice near the heater, what's going to happen to the ice? It's going to what?
Students: Melt.
Mr. Williams: That's what's going to happen to the comet.

His hands and body acting to help catch and elicit the point and drawing on the board, he says, "The sun gives off heat. That heat is powerful. It radiates and pushes away. So it pushes away the vapors and then you get the tail." Weaving several tactics in this exchange, Mr. Williams conveys information by eliciting some from students, and he tells certain parts of it himself, vividly describing it through movement and drawing. He is like an actor, using the stage and his movements and playing the audience to convey his lines. But a good actor also knows how to pace the scene. Mr. Williams paces the lesson by setting up a rhythm in which he presents a great deal of information and then they discuss a question or children's knowledge about the topic for a while before he presents information again. This rhythm may provide a breather for him and for students.

Clearly, the presentation is rich with information, and Mr. Williams knows a great deal about astronomy. If he knew enough to teach every science and social studies unit this extensively, he'd be a Renaissance man! Not all students could deal with the quantity or quality of information he presents. Children who are not as verbal as these nor as intellectually advanced could find the presentation troublesome or boring. But most of these students seem able to deal with it, as evidenced by their entering into the discussion, giggling at appropriate times, oohing and ahing, asking relevant (and conceptually difficult) questions, and remaining attentive for 45 minutes despite two recess bells for younger children and a noisy playground directly outside. Mr. Williams's playing with the ideas he presents and his apparent interest in learning about topics like the solar system provide a model to students of an intelligent person who is creative and playful with ideas, one who seeks knowledge. Since he is an important person to them (their teacher), and they like him, his modeling influence may be particularly strong.

Providing an opportunity to deal with a great deal of clearly and graphically presented complex information exposes these children to a situation that could nurture certain abilities. For one thing, they may learn to deal with many facts in a short period of time without short-circuiting and reaching information overload. Their attention is quite amazing; this lesson lasted more than 45 minutes, yet almost all students seemed attentive and involved, even though they were dealing with ideas rather than being involved in more active physical activities.

In this lesson, the richness of information, Mr. Williams's graphic portrayal, his eliciting questions and answers from students, his provision for background experiences to provide a fund of knowledge to which students can relate this lesson and from which they can draw to answer questions and construct meaning, his enthusiasm and potentially strong modeling influence, and students' middle-class backgrounds combine to make this lesson what it is. No single element of the configuration probably accounts for the students' rapt attention, but together they help us understand why children attend for so long and so keenly.

Learning how to deal with complex ideas by sitting and listening or reading and discussing will be helpful for their educational careers, for most of these children hope to attend college, and will probably do so, given their middle-class backgrounds. But they are also important skills of social discourse. Because of practice in dealing with complex information, children in this classroom may have a positive attitude toward learning, thinking, dealing creatively with intellectual problems and with knowledge in general.

Intellectual discussions in Mr. Williams's room, then, have several salient qualities. (1) They are *discussions,* in that they flow among participants in an easy give-and-take and do not appear to be extensively preplanned. (2) They do not always resolve the questions or issues raised. (3) The group is supportive of its members. And (4), as a group, they deal with more complex information and reach more incisive answers than individuals could alone.

In general, what do we have here? In Mr. Williams's room, children deal with ideas. They obtain and express the ideas through discussions, reading, drawing, and writing. But they deal with ideas at a relatively sophisticated level for fourth graders, apparently an appropriate level, for these children are able to function on it. The ambience is unpressured and informal, but intellectual, and the class is a group, not a set of twenty-six individuals.

Mr. Williams seems to respect students, encouraging them to think, organize information, ask creative questions, and express themselves effectively in a variety of ways. He does not talk down to them or coddle them but deals with their ideas seriously. He seems to emphasize quality—well-organized reports, expressive poems and artwork, insightful contributions to conversations, and creative questions of personal importance in structuring reports. He is not afraid to tell students matter-of-factly to generate more questions, to create a more vivid image, or to rethink an answer, which does not seem to threaten them, for they bounce back and answer, write, question, or whatever. Perhaps children are stronger than many think who write that we must be careful to accept what children say so we don't discourage them or thwart their creativity and interest.

This seems to be an environment that could nurture both creative problem solving and finding particular answers. These children seem to enjoy inquiry processes of problem solving and finding answers and may learn to enjoy reading, wondering, and thinking for their intrinsic merit as well as for instrumental purposes of solving problems or finding answers for an extrinsic reward. Many answers are highly creative and original, as evidenced in poems and reports, and children also demonstrate their ability to locate specific answers for math contracts, SRA kit work, and spelling.

However, conflicting messages may be communicated to children by guaranteeing a place in the curriculum for spelling, math, and SRA materials. This is in conflict with Mr. Williams's apparent valuing of poetry and report writing and story interpretation. The conflict may cast certain activities into an unfavorable light, for they may be perceived as onerous tasks and other activties as treats. This may interfere with learning the tasklike activities because of children's attitudes toward them. A reason for the conflict may lie in the fact that Mr. Williams does not particularly like the tasklike activities; he enjoys the report writing and intellectual discussions more. The math contracts, SRA kit, and spelling have been forced upon him by parents and by the adopted testing program.

The actvities he enjoys seem to be richer than the tasks, for they provide opportunities for more varied outcomes and for worthwhile ones, and the children enjoy them. There is a sense of unity about the activities he provides that he enjoys, of enthusiasm and commitment on virtually everyone's part, but the harmony is shattered by the inclusion of activities not in keeping with his beliefs, style, and his modes of teaching. The tasklike activities clash with the intellectual discussions and the independent activities fashioned by the children as surely as the SRA kit, workbooks, and contracts clash with the expressive articles on the shelves by the windows.

On the whole, Mr. Williams's classroom appears to be a good place for children to be if they are bright, conversational, independent, and inquisitive, or if they need to learn and practice skills in conversation, problem solving, creative use of language, dealing with complex information, writing reports, and interpreting stories or poems. In this classroom, children may learn grammar, reading, and language skills in context rather than in isolated drill. It is an intellectually intense, stimulating, and supportive environment.

As we have seen, Mr. Williams has forged an uneasy truce with parents and with the administration's testing program by including things he does not fully support. Parents of these children criticize Mr. Williams for not teaching the basics more extensively (math, number facts, phonics, and grammar), although Mr. Williams believes the children have mastered most of these skills and that children can learn them contextually better than through isolated drill. Mr. Williams feels parental pressure to such an extent, even though he has tenure and is therefore largely beyond parents' reach in terms of job security, that he has decided to leave teaching at the end of this year.

This case is an example of a situation in which parental involvement in schools met with unfortunate results. I do not mean to imply here that parents should not be involved in schools or that all their involvement is deleterious. However, parental involvement is not always beneficial, either. Clearly, Mr. Williams is leaving teaching because he feels their pressure. Yet many features of his classroom were worthwhile for these children.

In addition to illustrating a negative instance of parental involvement, this case also demonstrates the need for parents to understand what happens in their children's classrooms. With that understanding, I believe they might have supported Mr. Williams, and the conflict of interests between him and the parents might have been resolved in a more satisfactory manner.

13

A "Final" Word

I'd rather learn from one bird how to sing than teach ten thousand stars how not to dance

E. E. CUMMINGS

On the preceding pages I have tried to adumbrate views of education and to identify some of the problems and issues that pervade educational planning and evaluation. In many respects, the ideas I have expressed fly in the face of those that have guided our thinking about education and evaluation. For this I make no apology. So many of the assumptions that we have used have, in my view, been inappropriate for the problems with which teachers and others concerned with planning school programs must deal. Rather than to continue to pursue, virtually exclusively, goals and to use methods that have borne so little in relation to the effort, it has seemed to me useful to try to broaden the base from which educational inquiry can be undertaken. One aim of this book is to help establish that base and to contribute to its legitimation by indicating how qualitative forms of educational inquiry might be undertaken. In this final chapter, I would like to identify and discuss some of the major ideas found in the pages of this book that have given direction to my thinking.

The metaphors and images of schooling and teaching that we acquire have profound consequences for our educational values and for our views of how schooling should occur.

All of us through the process of acculturation and professional socialization acquire a language and a set of images that define our views of education and schooling. These images do not enter our cortex announcing their priorities. They do not herald a position or proclaim a set of virtues. Rather, they are a part of the atmosphere. When we talk about learners rather than children, competencies rather than understanding, behavior rather than experience, entry skills rather than development, instruction rather than teaching, responses rather than action, we make salient certain images: our language promotes a view, a way of looking at things, as well as a content to be observed. This language, I am arguing, derives from a set of images,

261

often visual images, of what schools should be, of how children should be taught, and of how the consequences of schooling should be identified. Language serves to reinforce and legitimize those images. Because differences between, say, terms such as *instruction* and *teaching* are subtle, we often use a new word without recognizing that the new word is capable of creating a new world.

The process of professional socialization is particularly influential in this regard. When prospective teachers and graduate students are trained (educated?), they are in a vulnerable position. Their careers are at stake. The selection of reading lists used in courses, the student's dependency on his or her professor's positive regard, the language that pervades the culture of the professional school or department, the need to use the right jargon on essays and exams, all of these factors create a powerful culture for socialization into the profession. The images are easily instilled: it is an overstatement to say that the student's professional life depends on it, but not much of an overstatement. Doing well means at least in part being able to use—indeed, to believe in—the images, concepts, and language of the culture within which one works as a student.

In arguing the importance of images and metaphors in shaping our conception of schooling and teaching, I am not suggesting that we would be better off imageless. All of us need some conception of education, schooling, teaching, and the student's role in order to deal with the professional world, just as we need some conception of honesty, truth, virtue, and affection to deal with our world in general. Fundamental conceptions are the bedrock upon which we build our theoretical palaces. They are indispensable. What I do argue is that the critical analysis of these images is seldom undertaken, and because they enter our minds unannounced we are in a poor position to treat them with the kind of scrutiny they deserve. What so often happens is that when our views are challenged by those holding different ones, instead of examining our own we tend to attack theirs, thereby avoiding the critical examination of what we believe by investing our energies in demolishing other views. The moral here is not to rid ourselves of the conceptual structures that allow us to make sense of the world but rather to recognize what these structures are. This will help us guard against the unwitting internalization of subtle but powerful concepts that pervade the pages of professional journals in education, public debate about schooling, and other forms of persuasion and socialization.

The dominant image of schooling in America has been the factory and the dominant image of teaching and learning the assembly line. These images underestimate the complexities of teaching and neglect the differences between education and training.

Tolerance for ambiguity is not a national characteristic. We are a nation of happy endings. In the preceding pages, I have argued that both image and language play a crucial role in shaping our conception of schooling and that the images and the language that they yield are necessary for con-ceptualization to occur. Imageless thought is empty.

At the same time, the images we hold—whether of education, society, democracy, or the good life—deserve analysis and critical appraisal. All images are not created equal. The images of schooling, teaching, and learning often reflect a factory view of schooling and an assembly-line con-ception of teaching and learning. Consider, for example, our interest in control, in the productivity of schooling, in the creation of measurable products, in the specification of criteria against which products can be judged, in the supervision of the teaching force, in the growing breach be-tween labor (teachers) and management (administrator), in the talk about quality assurance and quality control, in contract learning, in payment by results, in performance contracting, in the hiring of probationary teachers on the one hand and superintendents on the other. What happens is that such terms become ubiquitous, their conceptual implications are taken for granted, they become a part of our way of educational life without the benefit of critical analysis. The consequences of such concepts and the images they imply are, in my view, devastating. They breed the illusion of a level of precision in practice that is likely to be achieved only by re-ducing education to training. The assembly-line mentality that was so per-suasively described by Callahan in his study of the scientific management movement in education between 1913 and 1930 has been reborn in the 1960s and is still with us. Such an image of education requires that schools be organized to prescribe, control, and predict the consequences of their actions, that those consequences be immediate and empirically manifest, and that they be measurable. In such a school, the exploitation of the adven-titious, the cultivation of surprise, and the use of ingenuity are regarded as "noise." They disturb routine and require that formula be replaced with judgment. For, as everybody "knows," judgment is not to be trusted.

There are several motives for the use of industrial metaphors in educa-tional discourse. First, the use of such metaphors implies technical acumen on the part of the user. It affords educationists with a technical language that suggests systematization and rationality. When one is working in com-plex organizations that do not lend themselves well to systematic control and long-range planning or prediction, the illusion of control and prediction can be secured by using language from domains where control and predic-tion are possible. Eventually, the use of such language changes the aims of the enterprise. Aims that do not lend themselves to the precision or criteria that the users of such language value are deemphasized. If none of the old aims will do, new ones are created. The curriculum specialist's position gets converted to that of a program manager. The education of school adminis-trators increasingly takes place in the business school. Education becomes converted from a process into a commodity, something one gets and then sells.

For the lay public, the use of industrial metaphors is reassuring. Schooling is, after all, serious business. It is not surprising that business procedures should be regarded as more effective than discussions about mind, culture, wisdom, imagination, sensibility, and the like. Such terms and the images they convey have no business in an enterprise concerned with the really serious business of getting ahead in the world.

Rationality has been conceived of as scientific in nature, and cognition has been reduced to knowing in words; as a result, alternative views of knowledge and mind have been omitted in the preparation of teachers, administrators, and educational researchers.

The use of industrial metaphors in educational discourse is itself reflected in the ways that both lay people and professional educators conceive of human rationality. This conception is one that is scientific in nature. By *scientific* here I mean scientific in the context of verification rather than scientific in the context of discovery. *To know* has come to mean to be able to state some form of proposition and to be able to verify the truth of that proposition through scientific criteria.

Consider, for example, the term *cognition*. Cognition to a great many educators is contrasted with affect: cognition refers to thinking and thinking means linguistically mediated thought. Hence, unless one can utter in discursive terms what one believes one knows, one does not know. Given such a view of thought and rationality, human performance and experience that take form in nondiscursive modes of conception and expression are regarded as arational, somehow less a function of human intelligence and clearly having little to do with knowing or understanding.

This is perhaps nowhere better exemplified than in the use of the Scholastic Aptitude Test and the Graduate Record Examination, both of which focus on the use of discursive language and mathematical reasoning. Each of these areas depends on the student's ability to apply rules to the tasks that constitute the tests. The student's intellectual ability is operationally defined as his or her ability to deal with such tasks, regardless of his or her ability to deal with tasks that are not rule governed or that lie outside of those areas of human performance or ability that the tests test. The intelligence needed to create poetry, music, or visual art simply does not count.

This view of human rationality is not only reflected on those widely used tests, it is also reflected in elementary and secondary curricula. At the elementary and secondary levels, the primacy of scientific rationality is evidenced in the subject areas that are given priority, in the forms of human performance regarded as most important, in the amount of time devoted to particular fields of study, and in the requirements for graduation from secondary schools. Approximately 90 per cent of all high school districts require some work in the sciences as a condition for graduation. Only about 10 per cent require any work in the arts in order to graduate.

This view of human rationality permeates programs in teacher education, school administration, and educational research as well. Part of the impact results from an overt emphasis on the importance of systematic planning, on the use of operationally defined goals, and on the need for scientifically valid methods and criteria for determining educational effectiveness. The tacit ideal is that of the hard sciences, the methods used in the laboratory, and criteria that can be quantified and hence made "objective." The other part is due to the absence of other views of mind, knowledge, and intelligence, views that have a long and distinguished intellectual history but virtually are never considered in the curricular conversation.

I speak here of the views that argue the importance of tacit forms of knowing, of nondiscursive knowledge, of the expressive power of qualitative symbols, and those of Dewey as expressed in *Art As Experience*, one of his books that goes unread by American educators. When one view of mind, knowledge, and intelligence dominates, a self-fulfilling prophecy emerges. School programs emphasize certain modes of expression and certain subject matter fields. Educational evaluation uses modes of assessment consistent with the assumptions in fields that are emphasized, and "the most able" students are then rewarded by criteria that do not afford equal opportunity to students whose aptitudes reside in areas that are neither attended to in school programs nor adequately assessed. We legitimize our own view of what counts without serious consideration of alternative or complementary views.

The model of natural science on which much educational research is based is probably inappropriate for most of the problems and aims of teaching, learning, and curriculum development.

One might be more sanguine about the promise of conventional forms of educational research if past efforts had been more productive in guiding practice. The fact of the matter is that there is precious little practice in education that is data based. When research does guide practice it is often because the values embedded in the research are consistent with the values of the practitioner. In such cases, the practitioner uses the research to legitimize what he or she already believes.

Some argue, of course, that the reason practitioners do not base their practices on research is because they do not read it. Although it is true that most teachers and school administrators do not read educational research, one can only wonder about the relationship between the effort and the return. There is little in research that can be used to guide practice; for example, the descriptions of the methods used in experimental research are minimal, dependent measures almost always underestimate the range of outcomes with which teachers are concerned, and one is almost always forced to violate the limits of scientific generalization in applying research findings to one's own teaching circumstance. Even those who do experimental educational research in teaching seldom use the results of such research to influence their own teaching.

If research conclusions as they are now presented in the pages of educational research journals do little more than advance the careers of educational researchers, what function do they have in guiding practice at the elementary and secondary levels? Educational research provides not so much conclusions or recipes for practice as it does analytical models for thinking about practice. I believe the models that are most readily used are those that are consistent with the educational views one already holds. Rogerians are seldom converted to a Skinnereian world on the basis of data.

In emphasizing the impracticality of conventional forms of educational research, I many have risked overstating the case. There are *some* educational practices that are based on research findings—computer-assisted instruction, behavior modification techniques, the Distar Reading Program, are examples—but compared to the world of educational practice, research-guided practices are rare. When they do occur, it is because they are highly focused and control oriented. When it comes to educational aims that focus on the cultivation of productive idiosyncrasy, the development of imaginative thought, the acquisition of the skills of critical thinking, the invention of new modes of expression, educational research has not been notably productive. The character of the context has imposed itself too prominently. The contingencies are too salient when people are allowed to exercise free will. In such contexts, rules cannot replace judgment; procedures cannot be substituted for intelligence. The natural science model may not after all prove to be the most helpful means for improving the quality of educational practice or for understanding what occurs in human affairs. Our most difficult task might reside in determining when in our concerns and aspirations such a model of inquiry is appropriate and when other forms of inquiry are more felicitous.

The canons of behavioral science have too often determined what shall be studied and what shall be regarded as important in education.

The point here is straightforward. When an enterprise tacitly or explicitly establishes certain criteria for respectable intellectual work, problems are defined that can be treated by the methods that can meet those criteria. In educational research, this has meant that problems that do not lend themselves to methods regarded as empirically rigorous are neglected or, even worse, dismissed as pseudoproblems or inherently meaningless ones. The paradigm case of such occurrences is in doctoral programs, in which students are expected to do some types of inquiry but not others, with the true experiment being the most rigorous ideal. Students who see other lights, who wish to march to other drummers, are often subtly persuaded that they will be seriously out of step, that nonscientific modes of inquiry (with the exception of analytic philosophy and history) are not really acceptable ways to do a doctoral dissertation. Furthermore, there is precious little offered in the way of courses on nonscientific research methods that would prepare students for such inquiry. In professional schools of education, research is defined by methods taught in courses on statistics and research design—which almost always means quantitatively oriented inquiry.

When one adds to this the fact that research journals—access to which determines many young assistant professors' chances for promotion—define research in the ways that research methods courses conceive of research, the significance of method in circumscribing the problems into which one can inquire is magnified even further.

The influence of canonized research methods does not stop here. Not only do such methods define what is amenable to study, they also often result in naive and misleading conclusions about teaching and learning in school. That this should occur is ironic, because scientific research procedures are intended to yield objective, unbiased, factual conclusions. Consider, for example, research on class size. According to a great many research studies, class size has no bearing on what students learn. But when one looks to the indices of learning that were used in such studies, it turns out that learning is defined as achievement measured on standardized achievement tests. No attention is devoted to what children learn that tests don't measure.

What happens is that our view of learning is shaped by what we can measure, because what we can measure defines what we regard as learning. Because what is not measured is not considered, the conclusion we draw from what we do measure may seriously bias our perception and understanding. The bias in this respect is not a function of the logic of the inquiry but rather a function of what the criteria used in the inquiry exclude. We come to regard the ear of the elephant, if not as the whole, as its most critical feature.

The procedures and criteria used to evaluate students, teachers, and school administrators have profound effects on the content and form of schooling.

By and large, tests and testing procedures are not developed to influence the content and form of schooling. The major commonly held reason for their use is to determine how well students and teachers are doing in their respective roles. One uses tests to find out if students are learning, if teachers are effective, if school administrators are providing adequate leadership and guidance. Tests are used for these purposes, but their ancillary consequences are even more important. Because test performance is used as an index of educational quality, being able to do well on tests becomes a critical concern for students and teachers alike. As this concern grows, educational programs become increasingly focused on those content areas and forms of teaching that are related to test performance. The curricula of the school and the priorities that both students and teachers come to hold are influenced by what they think will influence test performance.

Because tests test what psychometricians can measure, the canons of measurement indirectly influence what is taught in schools and what priorities will be established among those fields that are taught. Consider again the Scholastic Aptitude Test. This test is given to approximately two million students each year. It has two major parts: one verbal and the other mathematical. Scoring well on this test is important for admission to many colleges and universities. Students who want to score well believe—whether true or not—that the more courses they take in mathematics the more likely they will receive high scores on the mathematical section of the SAT. Thus, students often feel compelled to forego courses in which they may have a genuine interest in favor of courses in mathematics that may improve their chances for admission to the college of their choice.

The influence of testing on school curricula is also felt at the lower levels of schooling, at the kindergarten and primary levels, where the quality of education is judged in terms of student reading scores and at the intermediate level where tests in mathematics and language arts become the public criteria of educational quality as test scores find their way onto the pages of local newspapers. Few teachers can withstand the almost certain public pressure for high scores on district- and state-mandated tests, even if the teachers wanted to pursue educational values that those tests did not assess. The social significance of the means used to measure student performance through testing is profound. I do not believe that major changes can be made in the content and aims of educational practice in schools without significantly broadening the criteria and methods used to assess educational effectiveness. The formalized rites of passage provided by tests are likely to constrain any effort to put into practice a really broad view of human development, despite our aspirations to the contrary.

Operationalism and Measurement have focused so heavily on behavior that the quality of the student's experience has been generally ignored or seriously neglected.

The employment of empirical procedures that lend themselves to operational definitions, definitions that can be measured, has been one of the tenets of the social sciences. In education this has meant that overt behavior is to be the primary referent for determining the success or failure of a new teaching method, curriculum, or form of school organization. The measured variable referenced in what students do is critical for achieving objective description. The quantified variable can provide a score to the third or the fourth decimal place. Scores have attractive features; they can be added, subtracted, averaged, multiplied, and divided. They can be subjected to sophisticated forms of statistical analysis on the most up to date modern computers. Statistical conclusions can be derived that provide a compelling illusion of precision and objectivity, a value-free image of pristine description, untouched by personal judgment, bias, or human failing. Furthermore, the tests that often yield such data are prepackaged, almost hermetically sealed, before the students open them, and they are identical for all students taking the test. It is almost as if we did not want to touch or get to know the student; the aim is to remain distant, dispassionate, aloof, unbiased.

This attitude, often erroneously regarded as a mark of scientific objectivity, leads us away from understanding the quality of life the student is experiencing. Because our focus is on behavior, our aim is to shape that behavior and our success is achieved when that behavior is displayed. But what of the student's experience? How does he feel about what he is doing? Is what she is learning becoming a part of her world view? Are the major lessons he is learning those that are being taught? To answer these questions, we must of course look beyond behavior. We must make inferences from behavior about experience. We must seek an empathetic understanding of the kind of lives children lead in school. But this means that we must make judgments, that we must attend to what is not easily standardized, and that we must get to know students as people. These are not relationships to which operationalism and quantification lend themselves. And when we add to this our penchant for efficient forms of standardization, all in the name of impartiality, we risk seriously misreading what students are learning in school. Beethoven's Fourth Symphony is not, after all, the incidence of d minor occurring in its four movements. It is not even the notes taken in their entirety on the score. Beethoven's Fourth Symphony is first and last music, sound, and experience. Rank forms of reductionism miss the point, and I fear that in our efforts to be "objective" and operational we too often miss the most telling points of school experience. Our penchant for standardization hampers our ability to perceive what is truly unique about students, and our preoccupation with measured behavior distracts us from appreciating and understanding what students experience in school and what they genuinely learn after all the test taking has been completed.

In urging that attention be devoted to the quality of life students experience in school, I am not suggesting that attention to performance be neglected. There has been in some schools at some periods in our educational history so much romantic attention to the students' feelings that the development of various forms of competence was seriously neglected. The neglect of competence and the failure to foster it appropriately can be a major source of emotional difficulty for children. Yet, our focus today is not in that direction. Our infatuation with performance objectives, criterion-referenced testing, competency-based education, and the so-called basics lends itself to standardization, operationalism, and behaviorism as the virtually exclusive concern of schooling. Such a focus is, I believe, far too narrow and not in the best interests of students, teachers, or the society within which students live. Empathy, playfulness, surprise, ingenuity, curiosity, individuality must count for something in schools that aim to contribute to a social democracy.

The history of the curriculum field has been dominated by the aspiration to technologize schooling and to reduce the need for artistry in teaching.

Except for notable exceptions during the progressive era and during the free school period of the 1960s, the pervasive orientation among curriculum theorists and school administrators has been an effort to develop a scientifically based technology of curriculum and teaching. This aspiration was first articulated during the scientific management movement I have already alluded to. But it also was central in the writing of those who attempted to ground educational practice in scientifically based knowledge derived from educational research. The optimum aim of such inquiry was to yield laws that would do for educational practitioners what the work of Boyle, Einstein, and Bohr did for physical scientists. It was aimed at eliminating the chancy and undependable, and replacing them with rule, procedure, and method. What is the best method for teaching reading? What is the best method for instruction in mathematics? What is the optimal ratio of students to teacher in the classroom? How can we formulate aims that are so clear that anyone who can see can determine whether they have been achieved? How can we study the community to discover what our educational needs really are?

In the curriculum field, per se, this orientation culminated in the aspiration to develop teacherproof curriculum materials. Nothing was to be left to chance. The intelligence of the teacher was not something one trusted. Ideally, the teacher was to serve as a handmaiden to the materials that were produced by a set of methods that approximated those used in the manufacture of cars, washing machines, and television sets. If such procedures worked so well in these industries, why would they not work in schools, particularly in the design of curriculum and in the process of teaching. Examine our metaphors: they are right out of the computer sciences and the assembly line. Somehow, if curriculum planning could be systematized and teaching appropriately monitored, the complexities of large schools and school systems might be managed more efficiently. The whole affair would be simplified, everyone concerned would know just where we want to go and how to get there: nothing would be left to chance.

For teaching, the tack has been the same: what we need is precision teaching; we must diagnose and prescribe; we must above all individualize instruction. Never mind that these concepts have seldom been analyzed, they possess an aura of conceptual rigor. Particularly when the pressure is on, the vicissitudes of art and artistry can hardly be tolerated.

What is ironic is that most administrators, I believe, would regard most of what they do as resting on judgment rather than rule, as more a matter of art than a matter of science. Getting a feel for an organization, developing a sense of where your support rests, looking for openings in which you can move, bringing coherence and spirit to the central staff, keeping your finger on the pulse of the community, enjoying the playing of school politics;

generalizations must always be interpreted and that judgments that exceed the information provided by the generalizations must always be made if they are to be used in classrooms. Yet, despite practitioner's recognition of the arts of the eclectic, to use Schwab's phrase, those arts seldom get examined in the research literature. Indeed, they are often regarded with derision, something to be excised rather than cultivated, appreciated, or emulated. If scientific research on teaching provided more to practitioners than it does at present, its potential might appear more promising and the assumptions on which it is based more robust. This is not the case. Perhaps it is time that other assumptions about teaching and curriculum planning be entertained, not as a substitute perhaps, but surely as a complement to what we have been doing over the last seventy-five years.

Knowing, like teaching, requires the organism to be active and to construct meaningful patterns out of experience. At base, such patterns are artistic constructions, a means through which the human creates a conception of reality.

Man, Aristotle once observed, by nature seeks to know. To construct a meaningful world requires that we conceptualize patterns of the environment, recognize the rules that are both tacit and explicit in our social life, feel sufficiently free to play and to take risks so that conceptual invention can occur. The creation of these patterns means in part the construction of structures that hang together, that are coherent, that express both order and interest and enable us to make sense of the world. This sense making is, I believe, an artistic act. We function as the architects of our own enlightenment; we build our own conceptual edifices and we want them to be beautiful as well as serviceable.

How telling that in our vernacular we talk about a *sense* of justice, making *sense* of things, having a *sense* for what is fitting and proper. Pattern is an inescapable quality of the organization of thought. Logic in action preceded logic as rule. The former made the latter possible, not vice versa. But patterning is not limited to propositions, it is a part of practical action and of activities aimed at the creation of art, per se. For schooling, or more properly for a theory of education, the notion that the human organism is stimulus seeking and pattern forming is crucial. What it implies is that all forms of learning, and some more than others, are at best creative acts. The organism must always act, even to make simple distinctions among sensory qualities. For the more complex forms of conception, more complex distinctions and patterns are necesary. But to make such patterns well requires an environment supportive of exploratory thought that encourages children to entertain ideas in a spirit of tentativeness. It is an environment that recognizes the desirability for children to have opportunities to create and play with patterns that enable them to appreciate the structure of ideas and to enjoy the process through which those structures are formed. In short, the aesthetic of both process and form must become a consciously sought virtue in schooling if schooling is to be converted from an academic experience into an intellectual one.

Teaching that is not hamstrung by rule-governed routine also requires the creation of patterns of thought by a teacher orchestrating an educational environment. Such a mode of thought is of course not required when teaching is like working on an assembly line. But to move teaching in such a direction is to deny students the opportunities to see creative intelligence at work. The classroom should be what it is trying to foster.

Practical judgment based on ineffable forms of understanding should not be regarded as irrational. It might reflect the highest forms of human rationality.

Universities have a tendency to make those who have high degrees of practical knowledge feel uncomfortable if they cannot provide reasons for action. In the academy, knowing how is nowhere near as honorable as knowing why. To know means, whether one can act appropriately or not, to be able to state in words what one knows.

Yet the tasks of teaching are far more demanding than discursive knowledge can explain. Indeed, if our activities as teachers and school administrators needed to be justified in relation to data-based, scientifically validated knowledge, most of educational practice would come to a standstill. We know, as Polanyi has pointed out, more than we can say.

The foregoing remarks should not be taken as a prolegomenon for mindless teaching or for curriculum development unenlightened by theory. In any case, neither is possible: mind requires conception to operate just as conception requires mind to exist. What the foregoing remarks do emphasize is that the process of knowing often uses qualities that are ineffable, that these qualities exist in both profusion and interaction, and that they must be "read" quickly and acted on swiftly if the information they yield is to be educationally useful. One example of how such knowledge is used is found in the activities of the standup comedian. To be sure, a comedian is not necessarily a teacher and a teacher is not necessarily a comedian, but an examination of the overlap between the two will be instructive.

For the standup comedian to function effectively, he must be able to "read" the qualities emanating from an audience. These qualities change as he proceeds with this act. The tone of the laughter, the tempo of his own words, the timing from line to line; all of these must be grasped immediately. Indeed, it is almost as though acting becomes second nature; no time to formulate hypotheses, no time to consult and compare theory, no time to seek substantiating evidence or data, and certainly no time to administer tests to determine the level of interest. Out of the flux of interacting the comedian must blend his own; a line one second late falls flat. And the configurations change. Automaticity and reflectivity must go hand in hand. The act must reach a crescendo and finally, when the audience has nearly had enough, be brought to closure.

The exercise of intelligence involved in such action is apparent in a Jack Benny, Bob Hope, Danny Thomas, or Milton Berle, yet no comedian could give a theoretical account of why what he does "works." We appreciate the comedians' skill, we recognize their artistry, but we do not expect from them psychological explanations that account for their effectiveness.

Because such explanations are not forthcoming, should we regard such activity as irrational or arational? Should we regard it as outside the realm of intelligence? I think not. What we are seeing when we see artists work— on the stage, in the studio, in the concert hall, and in a classroom—is not the absence of rationality and intelligence but the ultimate manifestations of its realization. Such individuals work with the creation and organization of qualities, the act with the qualities of speech and gesture, the musician with those of sound, the painter with color, line, and form, and the teacher with words, timing, and the creation of educational environments. What all of these artists have in common is the aspiration to confer a unique, personal order on the materials with which they work. And most work in contexts that are in a state of continual flux. No recipe will do. No routine will be adequate, even if routines must be acquired as a *part* of one's repertoire. The point here is that much of what we know and the basis for much of our action rest on inexpressible forms of consciousness that recognize the feel of things and sense the qualities that lead to closure and consummation. When we see such abilities displayed in public, whether on the stage or in the classroom, we should give them their due. The achievement of art is not, after all, a menial accomplishment.

The process of curriculum development, like the process of doing quantitative empirical educational research, appears much neater and much more predictable in textbook versions of curriculum development and research than it is in practice.

Philosophers of science characteristically distinguish in their writing between the context of discovery and the context of verification. In the context of verification, the rules of inference and logic are applied to determine the veracity and consistency of statements about the world. The context of discovery, however, is another matter. How ideas are generated, how insights are formed, and how fresh conceptions emerge into consciousness are not now adequately understood. And so, too, in writing about curriculum development and in reporting the results of empirical quantitative research, the illusion is created that the "rational" procedures outlined for describing curricula are the ways, in fact, that curricula are, can be, or ought to be created. It is not that the vicissitudes of curriculum development are denied, it is simply that they go unmentioned. As a result, the novice may get the impression that curriculum development typically proceeds or ought to proceed with the neatness with which it is described in textbooks. This is misleading on several counts. First, it gives the inexperienced reader an oversimplified image of a process. Second, such descriptions tacitly imply that if one does not proceed along the lines suggested in the textbook, something is wrong. One isn't doing one's job well. Third, such presentations make curriculum development seem essentially like a technical task. Once the objectives are formulated, the task is simply to follow a set of steps to achieve them. Such an image fails to help students of education know how messy program planning really is and how much flexibility, ingenuity, and tolerance for ambiguity are needed to do it well. But perhaps most importantly, such a rendering of what is a complex, fluid process serves to sustain a limited conception of rationality and tends to underestimate the qualities of playfulness, humor, and artistry needed to do really excellent work in the curriculum field. It is important for students of education to understand that what is finally published is a sanitized version of the reality that preceded it, a reality that in many ways is often far more interesting than its written description.

The aspiration to create teacherproof materials rests on a mistake. Teachers need materials that stimulate their ingenuity rather than materials to which they are to be subservient.

There is a temptation in the development of curriculum materials to try to create materials that will replace the need for teachers to exercise judgment. The aim is to design materials that are so robust that they can withstand even the most incompetent teaching. The reason for this aspiration is clear: if such materials can be created, then one can control the educational process from a distance; one can build an error-free program. Having done this, one need not rely on the frailties of human judgment; decisions on the part of the teacher can be minimized. Routine can replace reason.

Such an aspiration operates, of course, in the creation of the assembly line. The ultimate manifestation of such an orientation to development is to have the worker become an extension of the machine he or she uses. Personal identity and idiosyncratic thought are replaced by something more impersonal and more predictable.

Because some curriculum developers want the materials they develop to be effective, they seek to make them as errorless as possible. All one needs to do is to follow the directions right on the package. The aspiration to construct such teacherproof materials is, in Illich's terms, the aspiration to create anticonvivial tools, tools that eventually define and determine what a person should do. Although the assembly line is a paradigm case of an anticonvivial tool, such tools abound in cultures with high technology. In the long run, such tools restrict rather than expand choice.

Convivial tools—the telephone, for example—expand one's options, can be used without extensive training, do not restrict what messages one can convey, and do not impose time constraints on their use. Convivial curriculum materials can have similar characteristics. They can provide a structure within which a teacher can operate, but they still can provide options; indeed, they can stimulate ingenuity.

Although different teachers may require different amounts of detail in the curriculum materials they use, the ultimate aim of such materials is to minimize the teacher's dependency on them, to offer to the teacher materials that will foster a sense of competence both in pedagogical matters and in the content to which pedagogy is directed. In short, one function of well-designed curriculum materials is to free the teacher to teach, with ingenuity, flexibility, and confidence.

Now such an aspiration, such a conception of teaching and the materials that teachers use, seems to some to be a utopian dream. Teachers, some say, do not as a group have the intelligence to use such materials, most do not want to change or learn, and the creation of such materials requires a level of sophistication that teachers do not possess. And on and on.

I believe that most people want to make their lives more interesting and that we seek events, ideas, and materials that help us achieve a more interesting life. The view that teachers are largely dullards is, in my opinion, false. It is simplistic and leads to a control-oriented conception of curriculum and an assembly-line view of the tasks of teaching. And even on the assembly line the results fall far short of their goals.

The creation of curriculum materials cannot be separated from our conceptions of what teaching is and what the teacher's role is to be. If the teacher is to be a functionary in a system that is standardized, a system that is intended to yield common outcomes for all students, then the aim of standardized materials in form, content, and use is consistent. Although there may be some educational services that lend themselves to such a view, its pervasive use diminishes the very qualities that educational programs, as distinct from training programs, can foster.

Differences among both educators and lay people regarding particular educational issues and practices are often based on more fundamental, deep-seated differences regarding the functions and aims of schooling.

Differences of opinion about the virtues of particular educational practices are often the hubs of intense educational controversy. Should students be placed in tracks according to achievement? Should children be given letter grades in elementary school? Should curriculum content include controversial issues? Should common minimum standards exist for students at each grade level? Should elementary schools assign homework to students regularly? Should teachers be encouraged to take children on field trips? These are some of the questions for which a great deal of disagreement exists. Yet the difference among lay people and educators alike with respect to these questions are not limited to the particular questions posed. If one digs a bit deeper, one finds far more fundamental differences in the ways in which the contesting parties conceive of the school's function—indeed, in how they conceive of education itself.

The existence of disagreement about educational practices should not be conceived of as a liability. It would be a serious liability indeed if a subject so important as education were not a matter of concern and dispute. The resolution of these views, even a temporary one, can be treated on two levels: through accommodation and compromise and through encouraging the contending parties to penetrate more deeply into the values that animate the controversy. It is here that the school administrator has a truly educational function to perform. That function is one of helping community members understand the implications of their educational values, to appreciate the alternatives, and to anticipate the second- and third-order consequences of the practices they are considering. Clearly, at some point in the debate, a state of readiness exists; the community or a portion of it is interested in an educational issue. Before positions get crystallized, before the prospect of a public reversal of a position makes it impossible for positions to be altered, the school administrator can help initiate the kind of dialogue that might educationally enlighten a community about an educational policy.

The major orientations to education that underlie disputed policies in schooling have been identified in Chapter 4. Although these views do not exhaust the possible positions groups might take, the five views described provide a framework through which the value base underlying the symptomatic issues might be identified and discussed.

The factors that influence schooling may have their source far from the school or school district.

Because schools are social institutions—that is, institutions created by the society for the achievement of socially defined purposes—they are influenced by the forces that pervade that society. Some of these forces operate in close proximity to the school: the availability of excellent teachers; the support, both moral and financial, that the professional staff enjoys from the community the school serves; and the quality of the physical resources with which teachers and students work are a few examples. But other factors also shape the direction and priority of the school, and some of these are subtle. The development of a pill to control conception, for example, has had an enormous influence on what schools will offer students in the way of school programs. The influence is not direct, but it is extremely potent nevertheless, because with fewer children in school, there is less money made available to schools by the state. With less money, school boards must cut back on expenditures. Because most of the money a school district expends goes into salaries, when funds are cut salaries must be cut, and this means the loss of programs.

I use the birth control pill as one example of an important source of influence on schooling, an influence that is several times removed from schooling itself, yet has had significant consequences.

Other influences such as national testing programs, college admission criteria, and federal funding made available for some fields but not others also have important effects on the climate within which schools operate.

This climate makes it possible for certain priorities to emerge and for certain groups to exercise influence. Sputniks I and II put the capstone on a growing sentiment during the first half of the 1950s that American public schools were too soft. With Sputnik, those holding this view had the leverage they needed to drive home the message and to have it supported by increasing amounts of federal funding for curriculum development and teacher training in mathematics and the sciences. Thus, what occurred halfway around the globe influenced what happened in our educational backyard in the United States.

What such examples illustrate is that educational practices and educational priorities are not the sole consequence of the aspirations of either educators or those in the communities that educators serve. Schools are a part of a large cultural ecosystem. They respond to that system in ways that are not always obvious. If those interested in educational change are to be successful, aspects of that system—though they be far removed from the school—may need to be altered. In sum, the alteration of constraints and other forms of influence at several levels removed from the school may be the most effective way to change what goes on in schools. A direct attack on an immediate school problem might not be the most effective way of dealing with the problem.

To identify these distant constraints calls for a holistic, ecological view of schooling. One must be in a position to see the system as one whose boundaries extend well beyond the contours of the school district. Furthermore, one must have the conceptual ability to identify and analyze the relevant forces. Politics, the so-called architectonic science, is one potentially useful frame of reference for such an analysis. But whether the framework is that of political science, sociology, social psychology, economics, or cultural anthropology, analytic skills are not sufficient. One must know what is educationally significant in order to give direction to analysis, and one must be able to exercise the arts of political action if analysis is to lead to more than an academic understanding of a state of affairs; the point of analysis is to lead to the creation of the conditions that will allow the educational process to thrive.

The arena of school practice and the arena of education in institutions of higher education are so far removed from each other as to function in almost total independence.

The study of education in institutions of higher education and the world of educational practice as it occurs in the public schools exist in a state of benign neglect. Aside from teacher training, it is rare that schools and school districts look to universities as resources for improving the quality of what they do. Similarly, it is relatively rare that scholars and researchers in education regard the operations of the school as a primary concern. For those doing educational research as it is typically conceived, schools are places where one can secure the data one needs. As often as not, the results of such research are not fed back to the schools that provided the place where the data were collected. Schools, in short, tend to be used (in both senses of that word) by researchers largely to further their careers in the field of education. Whether the research that is done has any utility to practitioners is a secondary or tertiary consideration. What matters most is that what is published impresses the reference group that the scholar or researcher believes important.

Now it might be argued that in doing research or other forms of scholarship that impress other scholars or researchers the interests of the school are being served. I don't believe that such an argument holds. The central issue in gaining a reputation, whether for an individual professor or for a school or department of education, is to have material published that increasingly approximates the publications in the mother disciplines. The more educational philosophy is indistinguishable from philosophy in general, the more educational psychology cannot be distinguished from "pure" psychology, the more educational sociology reads like the articles published by sociologists, the more respectable they become. Indeed, in some institutions of higher education this orientation is pushed so far that when new faculty appointments are being considered in philosophy of education, educational psychology, or educational sociology, only those trained in the "pure" branches of those fields are considered. (It makes one wonder why, if those most competent to teach philosophy of education, educational sociology, and educational psycholgy are trained in the pure departments, there should be a need for doctoral programs in these fields in schools of education.)

The reasons for the breach between the public schools and the departments and schools of education in universities are several. First, the reward structure for university professors is seldom, at least in prestigious universities, found in providing services to the public schools. One does not consult elementary or secondary school teachers to find out about the usefulness of a professor's work when it comes time to consider the professor for promotion. What does count is published material, more often than not in journals that educational practitioners do not read.

Second, engagement with problems of educational practice in the schools is time consuming and theoretically messy. To spend one's time in the field is to have less time to spend doing work that is methodologically neat. There are few nontenured professors who are willing to risk the chance of promotion by too heavy an involvement with problems significant to teachers and school administrators.

Third, the aptitudes, attitudes, interests, and skills of professors of education are often unsuited to problems of school practice. Many professors teaching in schools and departments of education have had no experience as practitioners in the public schools, have little interest in the problems practitioners face, and regard their work in universities as theoretical or basic, that is, without immediate application. They often express a hope and some an expectation that what they do will ultimately have practical utility but recognize that for the present this is not the case. Their skills and expertise are, in fact, in an area independent of schooling. For some, too close an association with the public schools and public school practices is a professional liability, because it may imply to others that they are more practical than theoretical in their work.

Educational slogans serve to replace educational thought and enable school practitioners to avoid dealing with the persistent problems of practice.

The problems that beset schooling are not due to the behavior of any single group. I have already argued that, by and large, those working in universities tend to have marginal interest in the improvement of educational practice, per se. Similarly, educational practitioners, particularly those serving in administrative positions, have a tendency to avoid the tough educational problems by grasping the slogans that parade through the field of education year after year. Consider, for example, the back-to-basics movement. Throughout the United States, communities (or vocal segments thereof) are urging a return to "basics." School leaders are all too willing to oblige. Because the mass media proclaim that schools are slipping in their effectiveness, that test scores are dropping, that bonehead English is oversubscribed in colleges and universities, the time appears ripe to return to the basic. But what are the basics anyway? Are they the same for all students? If they are the skills of reading, writing, and arithmetic—the three Rs—does it matter at all *what* is read and *what* is written? Does imagination count in writing? Does any book or magazine article count equally in demonstrating the ability to read? At what level does competency in mathematics exceed what is basic? Alas, such questions seldom get asked. Instead, slogans replace analyses, and school practitioners too often lead the race toward an ideal that has not had the barest form of analysis or critical scrutiny.

This example is not an isolated case; *individualization* is another one. What counts as a form of individualization? Does individualization refer to the rate at which students move toward the achievement of common objectives? Does it require that goals be differentiated, as well? Does individualization refer to the differentiation of teaching methods for different students, to the differentiation of the response modes that students can use to demonstrate what they have learned, to the forms of presentation by which they encounter new concepts? If one looks at the field, one finds hardly a soul who is against individualization, but when one presses for a clarification of what the term means, too often a superficial understanding of the term's possibilities is revealed.

Similar conditions exist with respect to terms such as *open education, flexible scheduling, peer tutoring, learning by discovery, the inquiry method,* and the like. The virtues of such slogans for the practitioner—particularly for those in administrative positions—is that they provide a public image of up-to-date educational practice. In addition, they confer on the educational practitioner who uses them in the presence of lay people an aura of technical sophistication. Such a consequence of technical language is not unusual: medicine is another prime example of an area where language is so used. And technical language has, of course, its virtues; properly used, it increases precision in discourse. But in education, such language is all too often pseudotechnical; it covers up or substitutes for the kind of rigorous thought that educational problems require.

The school is the basic unit of educational excellence.

By and large the most "natural" unit in schooling is the school. The school both physically and psychologically defines the environment of teachers and students. It is the school that establishes the structure within which teachers and students must function and that establishes a territory distinct from the rest of life. The school possesses a physical character that no other aspect of education can achieve: a school district is too large and a classroom is an integrated part of the physical structure of the school. The school stands out as an entity; it is something that secures allegiance and provides students with an identity.

But beyond the physical characteristics of the school and their impact on our perception, the school defines a set of social parameters, as well. The structure of classrooms, the rules, time schedules, and the psychological climate create the milieu within which the purposes of schooling are realized.

For the school to function as an organization, some modus vivendi must be established, some balance must be secured among the forces that animate it. As in a living organism, the parts exist in a transactional state, and changes in one part must be compatible with the rest of the structure or the changes must be so potent as to change the rest of the organizational structure. If the structure of the school as a whole is resistant to change, as is true of many schools, then it is likely that the change agent will itself be changed rather than the school.

Consider, for example, the life-style of beginning teachers. Beginning teachers often enter the school with strong aspirations acquired during their professional training or on their own. Most new teachers soon realize that their aspirations must be significantly changed to fit the school. For some teachers, the compromise is such a difficult ethical problem that they choose to leave teaching rather than alter their core educational values. After a few years of teaching, those who choose to remain adapt to the institutional press and eliminate the sharp corners of professional idiosyncrasy. They become a well-rounded lot, a more homogeneous and adaptive group that does what it needs to survive.

Because the press of the institution is so significant, the problem of bringing about change within classrooms cannot be isolated from the school's constraints on and incentives for change. In this regard, the principal of the school is of central importance. In general, the principal sets the tone for the school and provides the formal positive and negative sanctions, even when a well-regulated evaluation system is not in force. His or her expectations for punctuality, record keeping, student performance levels, educational priorities, and the like are communicated in both formal and informal ways. Other factors, including timetables, the allocation of fiscal resources, and the allocation of space, further define both what counts in school and what is possible. Given these conditions, attention to the macrostructure of the school becomes crucial for those interested in raising the quality of the educational experience for students. It is difficult for a teacher to sustain a mode of teaching or to achieve educational aims that are contradicted daily by the culture in which he or she works. Such a teacher must almost always adapt to or leave the school; only in rare cases can a teacher alter the macrostructure. So what I am arguing is that the professional lifestyle of the teacher is significantly shaped by the characteristics and structure of the living organism we call a school. In a rational model of schooling, the form of the school organizationally as well as physically follows the function it is intended to perform. In the real world, it is more often the case that the function of the school is defined by the forms we create to manage it.

The current emphasis in schools on verbal and mathematical reasoning seriously biases our conception of human intelligence and significantly impedes the development of socially valuable interests and aptitudes.

The coin of the realm in schooling is words and numbers, so much so as to constitute a form of educational inequity for students whose aptitudes are in realms other than verbal or mathematical. Consider the impact of testing on the educational mobility of students. Virtually all achievement tests given to students in elementary and secondary schools by school districts or state education agencies assess verbal or mathematical performance. Students whose aptitudes are verbal or mathematical or who have opportunities out of school to learn in these areas of human performance are advantaged. The game being played, as it were, is consistent with their backgrounds or capacities.

But what of those students whose aptitudes lie outside of these realms: the dancer, the poet, the painter, the filmmaker, the composer? As things now stand, their aptitudes never enter the equation for calculating intellectual ability. To clarify this problem, consider what would happen if current practice were reversed. Instead of verbal and mathematical criteria, suppose that a student were admitted to college on the basis of the quality of his or her drawings, musical performance, dance, or films. Suppose that written skills did not count, nor did mathematical skills. How equitable would that be?

This is not a plea to substitute nonverbal and nonmathematical forms of performance for the forms now used but rather to broaden both the curricular options and the criteria that affect students' lives.

A part of the reason such skills are now emphasized, I believe, is that they lend themselves to forms of testing that appear objective. For example, Educational Testing Service, which once tested the writing skills of students by having them write compositions and having readers judge their quality, has now devised a "writing test" in which students respond to multiple-choice questions that can be machine scored. Because the multiple-choice test correlates highly with the scores assigned by judges to written compositions, the latter is an efficient way to learn about the former. Yet one cannot help but wonder what readers were attending to when they were judging compositions that were actually written: insight, imagination, sensitive use of language, ability to use metaphor, inventiveness, significance of the substance of the topic?

We see once again that our technique defines our ends; rather than servant, it becomes master. What we can efficiently do that meets one model of objectivity sets the ceiling on what we believe we ought to do. This goes so far as to determine who is gifted. In California, for example, students who have a measured IQ of 130 or more are classified as "mentally gifted minors" and the school is entitled to additional state funds. What about the artistically gifted minor?

The cost of such a parochial view of the human mind is borne not only by the students who must experience the inequity of denied opportunity but also by the society that may never reap the benefits that such children could provide to the culture at large. The time for changing this situation is long past.

What often goes unnoticed by both secondary school faculty and those working in colleges and universities is the impact of testing on the curriculum of both institutions. This impact is essentially a conservative one. Because universities use high school test scores to predict success in college and because those scores are derived primarily from performances on written and mathematical tasks, the predictive ability of the scores increases as the tasks in college increasingly approximate the skills tested. The same holds true for high school grades. If one seeks to make good predictions, one can do this by designing programs and using criteria that share common assumptions and require similar skills. Either the secondary school program must approximate that of the university, or the university program that of the secondary school. Given the aspiration to predict, a conservative circle emerges. The greater the competition for admission to universities, the more conservative the secondary school program becomes for those who seek such admission.

When one adds to this the fact that many university admission committees discount grades in art, music, theater, and other creative forms in calculating grade-point average, the liability to the student who wants to take secondary school courses related to his or her interests—if those interests are in the arts—is quite clear.

The school must be a growth environment for the teacher if it is to be an optimal growth environment for the student.

Very little attention has been devoted in educational planning to the impact the school has on the professional staff who work there year after year. Somehow we expect the central problem in planning educational programs to be that of designing an environment or a set of learning opportunities that will foster the growth of the student, almost independent of the effects those conditions may have on teachers and school administrators. I want to suggest that neglecting the needs of the professional staff of schools is one of the surest ways to decrease the quality of the educational service provided to students. Teachers, like everybody else, somehow adapt to or change the environment in which they function. When change is not possible, adaptation occurs. For many teachers and school administrators, such adaptation has resulted in the development of routine repertoires, stock responses that they have learned to use to cope with the demands made on them. Rather than having an environment that stimulates, they function in an environment that affords them few new challenges. They want to do well in the eyes of their students, and many have developed the kinds of routines that will enable this to occur. But life in the fullest sense is that lived outside of school; it is reserved for weekends, vacation periods, and sabbaticals. Growth occurs outside rather than inside the place where teachers spend most of their waking hours.

For many teachers, especially midcareer teachers, this has begun to pose a problem of the first order. Opportunities for professional advancement are not as plentiful as they used to be, because of the decline in school enrollment. Because of budget cuts, sabbatical leaves are more difficult to secure. The public's desire to judge the school's quality by the measured performance of students exacerbates these pressures. For many teachers unionization has been one way of coping with these problems, but increases in pay will never adequately compensate for an inadequate professional life space. What will it require of school programs to provide the conditions for teachers and school administrators to have time for reflection, for experimentation, for adequate planning, for consultation with new colleagues? Would the achievement level of students decrease if teachers were given three or four hours each week to meet for purposes of educational planning or individualized work?

The specific forms that such planning might take may differ from school to school, but the need to work in an environment that allows—indeed puts a premium on—the teachers' and administrators' professional growth will not.

One of the things I have learned in talking to school administrators is that a great many of them moved into school administration to escape the constraints and the routine of the classroom. What they were seeking was not so much power or money but a more interesting professional life, a wider field in which to play. The creation of an expanded professional life space, the development of an environment that is educational for teachers and administrators as well as students, is, I believe, one of the most seriously neglected needs in education.

Incrementalism is a useful way to change schools if one has a sense of the place of the increment in a larger pattern or strategy for change.

Virtually every student of education has the aspiration to change schools, that is, to bring about improvement in the ways in which schools function. Yet it has been observed by students of change and by those who are old enough or interested enough to have a long view that, although change in schooling occurs, it often occurs in spite of our efforts to bring it about. Schools change—and they have changed significantly in structure and form over the last fifty years—because of developments in the society more than because of the efforts of educators to bring them about. This should not be surprising. The form and function of schooling are closely related to the values and expectations of the society. People expect the schools to support the values they hold. Significant deviation from those values is seldom tolerated.

For some students of education, the situation called for a radical or revolutionary approach to schooling. They believed that, somehow, enlightened pupils and the enlightened adults in the community could radically alter the character of American schooling. If this could not be done within the existing system, then new schools—free schools—would be established to serve as an alternative.

The animation of the late 1960s has all but dissipated, and free schools are largely dead. Even in their prime they touched less than 1 per cent of the students in American schools. If revolution within the schools is not a viable means of bringing about improved forms of schooling, then what is? Two answers seem to me to be possible. One is that educators can have no significant impact on the character of schooling and therefore must always follow rather than lead the aims of the polity. The other is that schools can change on a guided, incremental basis through the efforts of those in the field of education. The former view severely constrains the aspirations of those who attempt to conceptualize and develop better educational programs. If one regards change in the schools as a result of the forces of history, the prospects for professional educational leadership are dim. To be sure, those forces occur and are potent, yet history also indicates that there have been schools that have had the kind of leadership and community support to rise above these so-called irresistible forces. Furthermore, in an incremental process educators can develop the kind of coalition with other educators and lay groups to support the forms of educational practice that they value. This process is at base a political one, but it can, and I would argue should, be based on an educationally enlightened constituency. This means, of course, that the leadership of the school or school district must regard its clients to be not only the pupils who attend the schools, but also the community that supports them. This kind of leadership must tread a narrow line between the desire to impose a perspective—which is likely to fail—and the desire simply to serve the prevailing perspective. School administrators and teachers, theoretically at least, are by virtue of their training better prepared to contribute to the dialogue about both the means and ends of schooling.

I realize that many—perhaps even most—teachers and school administrators do not have such skills and understandings at present, but it is the principle I am arguing for, not the status quo. I would like schools to be better than they are. I believe that educators should lead the dialogue about schooling, and I believe that enlightened dialogue can contribute to the creation of improved educational practice. Such an aim need not require a revolution. It can be achieved through a gradual process that incrementally seeks the approximation of an educational ideal.

Schools teach both more and less than educators realize.

In Chapter 5 I pointed out that each school offers children three curricula: the explicit curriculum that is public and advertised, the implicit curriculum that teaches because of the kind of culture that a school is, and the null curriculum, those voids in educational programs that withhold from students ideas and skills that they might otherwise use. The utilities of distinguishing among these types of curricula are several. First, it allows one to raise questions about what children are learning that would never be identified if one were to focus only on the intended goals of the explicit curriculum. We tend in the planning of school programs to act as though what schools explicitly teach constitutes the whole of what students learn. Yet what schools teach by virtue of their structure, their expectations, their timetables, and their rules might in fact have a much greater impact on what students learn.

Second, by distinguishing among these three types of curricula we are in a position to evaluate the consequences of each. A school might offer an exhilarating course on critical thought about social problems and yet might, in its general culture, be promulgating a type of intellectual dependency that contradicts the values and skills the course attempts to foster. Consider, for example, the use of student hall guards in secondary schools. In some schools, such guards are on duty at every intersection in the building. Monitoring these halls guards are teachers, one assigned to each floor or section of the school. Monitoring these teachers is a vice-principal who from time to time makes rounds to be sure that the teachers are on duty; the teachers in turn monitor the hall guards, who in turn ask each student who walks through the halls after classes have begun to see his or her hall pass.

What we have is a hierarchical system, all in the service of control. One might wonder what such a system teaches students who are enrolled in courses dealing with critical thought about social problems.

Third, these distinctions remind curriculum planners to look beyond what is now traditionally offered in school programs in order to identify areas of human understanding that have been neglected. A great deal is offered to students in school that is not a function of choice but rather a function of tradition. Much of what we teach, we teach because it has always been taught. The concept of the null curriculum reminds curriculum planners to ask about what has been neglected. For example, which forms of knowing have been omitted and what is their significance? What are the potential consequences of curricular neglect? I am not suggesting that the program of the school can teach everything or that it can be all things to all people. I am suggesting that content inclusion–content exclusion decisions are among the most important decisions curriculum planners can make. These decisions, as far as possible, should be made with appropriate consideration to what one rejects as well as to what one accepts for inclusion in school programs. What we don't teach might be just as important as what we do.

The complexities and significant qualities of educational life can be made vivid through a method used to describe, interpret, and evaluate other cultural forms. This method is one of criticism; in education it can be regarded as educational criticism.

One of the central focuses of this book concerns the influence that testing has on the ways in which we conceive of the effectiveness of schooling, curricular content, and educational aims. Since the turn of the century, testing has rested on fundamental beliefs about how we come to know; our use of testing as means of educational evaluation is itself rooted in the epistemology of science. Knowledge about educational practice and its consequences is to be derived by applying methods of social science to the study of education. The more closely those methods approximate those used in the laboratory, the more positive we can be about their conclusions.

Although I do not advocate abandoning scientific methods to study educational phenomena, I have argued in this book that those methods in no way exhaust the means through which educational phenomena can be studied. This book has attempted to provide not an alternative but rather an invitation to the pursuit of a complementary approach. The approach that my students and I have been using at Stanford University is called educational criticism. It depends on the observation and appreciation of the events or materials that constitute educational life. The object of such attention is to perceive those qualities that are educationally significant.

The appreciation of such phenomena requires, I have argued, the application of educational connoisseurship. But connoisseurship is a private event, and, to be made public, some externalization of what one appreciates must occur. It is here that criticism operates. The aim of criticism is to reeducate one's perception of the phenomena to which one attends. Criticism is a written or spoken statement about something. Educational criticism is about educationally important matters. Because criticism is in large measure—although not exclusively—an artistic creation (the critic must render the qualities he has perceived in a form capable of eliciting, in part, an empathetic understanding), the skills the critic needs are significantly artistic in character. The critic needs to perceive what is subtle and complex, must appreciate the connotative meaning as well as the denotative meaning of events, and must be able to make those meanings vivid through the language he or she uses to communicate. The major aim of such activity is not primarily to discover laws but rather to illuminate, to provide those concerned with education with the kind of understanding that will enhance their own teaching or professional deliberations. In this sense, educational criticism leads to a more complex and particularistic view of an educational situation. It aims not at the reduction of complexities but at their illumination in order that the factors and qualities that make situations unique as well as general can be understood. With such understanding I believe that both educators and lay people are more likely to be able to exercise intelligence about the matters of concern to them.

That such an approach to educational evaluation has not been salient in the literature is obvious to anyone familiar with it. Our conception of research, our conception of knowledge, and our conception of evidence have derived from other premises. The time has come, I believe, to look to other views, not as a rejection of the old ones, but for the promise that a fresh perspective can provide. Educational criticism represents one place on which to stand.

Index